HYPNOTISM

An Objective Study in Suggestibility

WILEY PUBLICATIONS IN THE
MENTAL HEALTH SCIENCES

THE ORGANIZATION OF BEHAVIOR:
A Neuropsychological Theory
by DONALD O. HEBB

HYPNOTISM:
An Objective Study in Suggestibility
by ANDRÉ M. WEITZENHOFFER

FUNDAMENTALS OF PSYCHOANALYTIC TECHNIQUE
by the late TRYGVE BRAATØY (in press)

HYPNOTISM

An Objective Study in Suggestibility

ANDRÉ M. WEITZENHOFFER

14527

JOHN WILEY & SONS, INC., NEW YORK

CHAPMAN & HALL, LIMITED, LONDON

COPYRIGHT, 1953
BY
JOHN WILEY & SONS, INC.

———

All Rights Reserved

*This book or any part thereof must not
be reproduced in any form without
the written permission of the publisher.*

Library of Congress Catalog Card Number: 53–11388

PRINTED IN THE UNITED STATES OF AMERICA

TS4
w43h

14527

To my wife

GENEVA

Preface

To students and workers in the field of suggestibility in general, and of hypnotism in particular, the year 1933 represents an important landmark. In that year, C. L. Hull published his now classical study *Hypnosis and Suggestibility: an Experimental Approach.* This work may be said to have been the first large-scale authoritative integration of scientific data obtained from careful investigations of hypnotic and allied phenomena.

This is not to say that before the publication of the above-mentioned work no scientific reports were available. It is rather that well-organized or well-designed experiments were rare and scattered. The spirit of investigation nevertheless can be found as far back as Mesmer who attempted to formulate a scientific theory of animal magnetism. The majority of individuals whose names have come down to us in the field of hypnotism appear to have been genuinely interested in finding out what it was they were working with. Furthermore, among these men were unquestionably professional individuals of high integrity, as well as trained observers and thinkers. Yet, extensive as may have been the reports and investigations of such individuals as J. Milne Bramwell, or H. Bernheim, and great as may have been their reputations, it is nevertheless true that what they have handed down to us is most unsatisfactory insofar as establishing empirical proofs and constructing theories are concerned. At best we can get from their records only an over-all picture of the various aspects that suggestibility phenomena may assume, but we cannot tell how much is real and how much is mere appearance or artifact.

Of course, we should realize that many of the tools available to the modern psychologist were not known in the early days of hypnotism. Indeed, most of the methodology of psychology was as yet undeveloped. Furthermore, the majority of the early investigators were physicians who, for the most part, were far more concerned with hypnotism as a therapeutic agent than as a subject of academic interest. Those who did have the inclination and found the time to do research were often inadequately prepared for such work. In consequence, much of the early material that is available * is in the form of hearsay, personal anecdotes, case histories, and inconclusive experiments.

Still, it cannot be denied that much can be garnered from even this kind of material, provided a sufficient number of conclusive experiments are also available. Furthermore, although many of the reports considered singly have little statistical validity, considered as a large group showing general agreement they gain some statistical weight in the final appraisal. Reports like those of Bernheim are not only enjoyable reading but also even today are well worth the time spent on them.

Historically then Hull was probably the first to set forth a really definite program of investigation for the study of suggestibility phenomena in which particular attention would be paid to approved methods of inquiry. This meant primarily the use of statistical design and of controls. Since that time, investigational work in hypnosis has pretty well followed the way outlined by Hull, although in more recent times there seems to have been a tendency for some investigators to be satisfied with less stringent requirements than those set forth by Hull. He was also the first to attempt seriously to integrate acceptable data into a whole and to examine the results in the light of contemporary psychology. It is clear to us, however, when we read the results of his efforts that a number of topics were never taken up, and that others were far from being settled in any definite manner at the time he wrote his book. Considering the limitations of the framework within which Hull must have had to work, it is remarkable that he accomplished as much as he did.

Since the appearance of *Hypnosis and Suggestibility,* twenty years have elapsed during which more than five hundred reports and books have been published, representing the efforts of hundreds of investigators. Many of these works deal with topics mentioned only briefly by Hull, and quite a few are concerned with subject matters that never found their way into the latter's work. In other reports, newer techniques of investigations or refinements of older ones have made their appearance in the interim and have shed new light on old topics, demanding a certain amount of revision. There are also available

* Meaning by this before 1925. It is difficult, if not impossible, to establish a date for the beginning of scientific hypnotism. One could indeed argue that it began with the experiments of Braid. Furthermore it is true that nearly all the known phenomena of hypnosis were discovered long before 1925. I have chosen this date rather arbitrarily because it seems to mark the beginning of the use of modern methods of investigation in this area.

additional data on old problems. In some instances these data support previous conclusions but in others contradict them. Finally, the field of application has seen some important changes. Before World War II, the use of hypnosis and of suggestion techniques in psychotherapy had lost most of its adherents to psychoanalytical methods. However, somewhere along the time the second world conflict came into being, new interest arose once more in the therapeutic value of suggestion techniques largely because of the need for more rapid methods of therapy. Hypnosis received a tremendous boost and as a result today shares an increasingly important place alongside of psychoanalysis, the two being combined into a new powerful analytical method of therapy. There has also been a recurrence of interest in the use of hypnosis in such areas as dentistry and obstetrics. Thus, what hypnotism was in 1933, as seen from an empirical, theoretical, and applied standpoint, is not what it is today in 1953. There have been considerable changes in several directions, and the time seems to have come for a new presentation of the facts, as well as for a re-examination of what these may mean.

This book attempts to fulfill this need by presenting a critical and integrated compilation and appraisal of the scientific work done to date in this field. It also attempts to construct a new theory of suggestibility and hypnosis that will account for both the general and the specific results of investigations. The necessity of keeping the size of the work within reasonable bounds has led to a highly condensed presentation of much of the material. Because of this feature, some readers may consider that I have been rather dogmatic in treating the subject matter. This is an unfortunate aspect that cannot be remedied short of expanding the text beyond a desirable length. However, in an attempt to obviate this undesirable characteristic, each chapter has been written in such a way as to present first a summary of the results and conclusions as reported by the various investigators mentioned in the text. † This is followed by a brief appraisal of the validity, reliability, and general significance of these results and conclusions as I see them. For the most part, because of the great amount of material that is covered and the necessity of restricting the length of the book, few of the arguments on which my opinions are based have been given in detail. The exception to this will be found in the last part of the

† Even in doing this it is almost impossible for a reviewer not to bias his account since his understanding of an investigator's thoughts cannot help but reflect a certain amount of interpreting on the part of the reviewer.

book, where I have presented my own theory of suggestibility phenomena.

On the other hand, it may be well to emphasize that this book is not directly concerned with the applications of hypnosis to therapy. Nor is it intended to teach how to hypnotize. Either one of these topics would require a volume in itself.

The book is divided into four parts. In the first, a number of basic notions and facts necessary for a clear understanding of the remainder of the text have been presented. Many readers will find the reading of this material unnecessary. The second part takes up the subject matter of suggestibility in all its major aspects, with special emphasis on hypnosis. The third part then proceeds to consider the various phenomena that may be produced by means of hypnotic suggestions. Parts 2 and 3 can be read pretty much independently of each other. In the fourth and final portion of the book various theories of hypnosis and suggestibility are considered. This is followed by an attempt to formulate a new theoretical approach to the entire subject matter.

Every effort has been made to present as complete and as up-to-date a bibliography of modern investigations as possible. Many of the older and classical studies which are more of historical than of scientific interest have not been listed in the bibliography, although many have been mentioned within the text.

In spite of my efforts to cover the field of suggestibility thoroughly and to give credit wherever it is due, it is a near certainty that in a survey of this magnitude some relevant material may have been omitted and/or that credit may have been incorrectly given. I hope that the reader will feel free to call my attention to such errors. In addition, during the process of publication of the book a certain amount of new material has appeared in the scientific literature. Unfortunately it could not, for the most part, be incorporated into the text.

It should also be mentioned that certain omissions have been intentional. I have tried as much as possible to remain within the experimental setting. Consequently, most of the considerable work reported in the field of therapy has been left out. This is, however, not meant to imply that much valuable information cannot be derived from the therapeutic setting. Indeed, I would be one of the first to urge a closer collaboration between therapists and nontherapists. Unsatisfactory data have also led me to ignore certain topics, although I readily admit that I may have drawn a rather fine line of demarcation in my choice of what to include and what to exclude. Thus, for example, I would not insist that I was fully justified in ignoring the factor of monotony in trance induction while giving the factor of attention a central role. The data are admittedly about equally poor on either of the two. To a large extent theoretical considerations, and probably some personal biases, were responsible for this choice and others.

I would also like to emphasize at this time that I do not consider the ideas, views, or interpretations, and particularly the theory offered in this book as final in any way. These represent what seemed derivable in terms of the data available at the time the bulk of the book was written late in 1952. That future investigations and considerations may cast doubts, invalidate, or at least place limitations on the generality of some of the basic data examined in the pages that follow is more than likely. Should this be the case, the theory and concepts that I am presenting may have to be radically revised—even discarded. How eminently true this can be is well demonstrated by the fact that a recent issue of the *Journal of Abnormal and Social Psychology* (July 1953) carries an article that appears to challenge seriously the generality of H. J. Eysenck's notions of primary and secondary suggestibility. Should this new contribution withstand critical examination, and, especially, be confirmed, it probably will mean that my own position on suggestibility will have to suffer a certain amount of revision in the future. In the meantime, I do not believe that these new results seriously affect the major aspects of the theoretical structure presented in Part 4.

This book was primarily written with the aim of serving as a useful source of information. But it is also my hope that it will serve to stimulate further research in the area of suggestibility phenomena. Suggestibility is, to my way of thinking, a rich field for experimentation—one that will prove rewarding to those who venture into it. I am particularly convinced that out of the study of hypnosis and allied phenomena, material of basic importance for the fundamental problems of psychology can and will arise. It is also my belief that hypnosis may be a very important tool for the study of psychosomatic phenomena. In the domain of applications to human management, we have witnessed in recent times the increasing success of a rational application of hypnosis to therapy. I suspect that this is only the beginning and that the future will see further valuable developments in this area as well as extensions of the use of hypnosis to nontherapeutic situations in everyday life.

In conclusion, I wish to express my appreciation for the friendly and constructive criticisms of the original manuscript by Dr. Bernard E. Gorton. I also desire to record my indebtedness to my wife, not only for the very substantial help she supplied in the form of helpful criticisms and in the preparation of the manuscript, but also for her continual encouragement in this venture.

ANDRÉ M. WEITZENHOFFER

Department of Psychology
University of Michigan, September 1953

Acknowledgments

I would like to make the following acknowledgments of courtesies extended to me in the form of permission to use quotations.

To the American Psychological Society for a quotation from H. J. Eysenck and W. D. Furneaux, Primary and Secondary Suggestibility: An Experimental and Statistical Study, *J. exp. Psychol.*, 1945.

To The Journal Press for quotations from M. V. Kline, Hypnotic Age Regression and Intelligence, *J. genet. Psychol.*, 1950; and from M. H. Erickson and E. M. Erickson, Concerning the Nature and Character of Post-hypnotic Behavior, *J. gen. Psychol.*, 1941.

To Paul B. Hoeber, Inc., for a quotation from M. H. Erickson, Hypnotic Investigation of Psychosomatic Phenomena: I. Psychosomatic Interrelationships Studied by Experimental Hypnosis, *Psychosom. Med.*, 1943.

To the Houghton Mifflin Company for several quotations from H. C. Warren's *Dictionary of Psychology*.

To the Oxford University Press for a number of quotations from Hinsie and Shatzky's *Psychiatric Dictionary* (first edition).

To *The Psychoanalytic Quarterly* for the use of a number of headings from M. H. Erickson, Experimental Demonstrations of the Psychopathology of Everyday Life, *Psychoanal. Quart.*, 1939.

To *The Journal of Projective Techniques* for a quotation from K. N. Levine, J. R. Grassi, and J. M. Gerson, Hypnotically Induced Mood Changes in the Verbal and Graphic Rorschach, Part I, *Rorschach Research Exch.*, 1943.

To Dr. Lauretta Bender for the lengthy quotation from P. Schilder and O. Kauder's book, *Hypnosis* (1927 edition).

To Dr. Lewis R. Wolberg and to Grune and Stratton, Inc., for a quotation from the book, *Medical Hypnosis*.

To the William Alanson White Psychiatric Foundation and to Dr. James A. Christenson for quotations from his paper, Dynamics in Hypnotic Induction, *Psychiatry*, 1949.

To the American Medical Association and to Dr. Wayne Barker for a quotation from his paper, Brain Wave Patterns during Hypnosis, Hypnotic Sleep, and Normal Sleep, A.M.A.: *Arch. of Neurol. and Psychiat.*, 1949.

To the Cambridge University Press and to Drs. O. L. Zangwill and H. Banister for a quotation from their paper, Experimentally Induced Visual Paramnesia, *Brit. j. Psychol.*, 1941.

Contents

Contents

PART

· *1* ·

ORIENTATION

Preliminary Considerations

Since the material that follows in the remainder of this book presupposes some knowledge on the part of the reader of what suggestibility, hypnosis, and suggestion consist of, the next few pages will be devoted to certain basic aspects of this topic. This material will serve as framework for future discussions. It should, however, be kept in mind that what is being presented now is not necessarily the final formulation to be derived from the considerations of this book. It is merely a guide. We shall have to talk from the outset of such notions as "hypnosis," "suggestion," "suggestibility," and so on. By defining these from the start, many misconceptions which might arise in later portions of the volume may be forestalled.

Some Definitions

Let us then first define some useful terms:

1. SUGGESTION. (i) Process, especially indirect, by which mental processes in, or the behavior of, an individual are altered by influence from without, in the absence of conscious volition on the part of the individual thus influenced. (ii) Verbal material used to produce such an influence.

2. SUGGESTIBILITY. The capacity of an individual to be affected by such influences as may be called suggestions.

3. SUSCEPTIBILITY. Synonymous with suggestibility.

4. HYPNOSIS. "An artificially induced state, usually (though not always) resembling sleep, but physiologically distinct from it, which is characterized by *heightened suggestibility*, and as a result of which certain sensory, motor, and memory abnormalities may be induced more readily than in the normal state" (455).

5. TRANCE. Synonymous with hypnosis.

6. HYPNOIDAL. A state resembling to a certain extent the milder hypnotic conditions, but usually brought about by different means.

7. AUTOSUGGESTION. Suggestion given by an individual to himself.

8. HETEROSUGGESTION. Suggestion given by an individual to *another* person.

9. RAPPORT. (i) Special heightening of susceptibility to suggestions emanating from the hypnotist that is transferable to others by simple suggestion of this. (ii) Also refers to an apparent pseudoinsensibility to all

3

stimuli that emanate from persons other than the hypnotist or persons designated by the latter.

10. POSTHYPNOTIC PHENOMENA. Phenomena taking place subsequent to "waking," that is, after coming out of the hypnotic state. These are usually the result of suggestions called *posthypnotic suggestions.*

11. POSTHYPNOTIC AMNESIA. A state of amnesia, following hypnosis upon waking, for events having taken place during the hypnotic state, and for even the fact of having been in this state. It is usually the result of a posthypnotic suggestion but may also occur spontaneously.

12. NORMALITY. This rather difficult concept to define is used in this book in at least three senses. The context will usually make clear which of these senses is meant:

(i) An individual is said to be *normal* if he shows no extensive variations in his psychological and physical characteristics from those that are typical of the majority of individuals belonging to the same cultural or subcultural group as he.

(ii) An individual is said to be in the *normal state,* irrespective of whether or not he is a normal individual (sense i), if the characteristics he exhibits are typically those shown by him most of the time.

(iii) Finally, an individual will be said to be in the *normal state* or simply *normal* when he is not under the influence of suggestions. The term *waking* state will be reserved to designate such situations as may occur when the individual may be affected by suggestions but is not hypnotized.

13. STATE. Mode of existence.

14. STRENGTH (of suggestion). Denotes the effectiveness of a suggestion. It is measured by the completeness with which the subject's response follows a suggestion. In many instances where the response can be assigned a numerical value, such as in the motion of the subject's arm, this value is often used as a measure of strength of response and of suggestion too.

15. TASK. Used synonymously with "suggestion" and "test." The context will always indicate which is meant.

16. TEST. (i) A situation so constructed as to elicit a specific type of behavior, response pattern, or performance from an individual, and such as to allow one to assign a score or rank to his performance, usually in respect to some arbitrary or standard reference. (ii) Synonymous with "investigation," "experiment," etc.

Waking Suggestion versus Hypnotic Suggestion

The history of hypnotism is too well known to require more than a passing note here. Scientific hypnotism may be traced back to Anton Mesmer in the 18th century. He ascribed the observed phenomenon to a rather mysterious "magnetic fluid" emanating from the hypnotist, then called a "magnetizer." He formulated a rather interesting theory of "animal magnetism" which was investigated by a special commission appointed by the French government. This commission brought a verdict against Mesmer and his theory, thus ending any further investigation by the scientific bodies of that time. Interestingly enough, this commission in its final report unknowingly hit upon a very important fact which was not to be brought to light again until the close of the 19th century. This was the role of psychic * factors in hypnotic phenomena. These factors were then summed up under the word "imagination." Although interest died within scientific circles, a number of individuals persisted in working along the lines outlined by Mesmer. There has been some question whether the latter really ever hypnotized his subjects in the sense of bringing about the so-called "sleeping trance." In the light of present-day knowledge it would appear that a good many of his subjects merely developed spontaneous hysterical convulsions and possibly hysterical trance states. In any event, the first report of a genuine "sleeping trance" seems to have been made by the Marquis de Puységur in 1784. Much of the investigational work performed in those days fails to meet the criteria of the scientific method. Yet, in view of the fact that science was then still in its infancy and that the scientific method had not been yet clearly formulated, much of this work has earned the right to be called scientific. By 1825 the supporters of animal magnetism had uncovered all the well-known major hypnotic phenomena, such as negative and positive hallucinations, hypnotic analgesia and anesthesia, catalepsy, lethargy, and posthypnotic phenomena, which will be described a little further on. The culmination of this viewpoint can probably be best seen in two little volumes of Hector Durville (103) entitled *Traité expérimental de magnétisme* which leave little to be desired as a manual for experimenters and students of his time.

The turning point from the physical to the neuropsychological aspect of hypnotism, as well as the recurrence of interest in it, dates back to 1843 when James Braid demonstrated that the "sleeping trance" and some of its associated phenomena could be induced by mere visual fixation of a bright object. To him we owe the term "hypnotism." It is also to his credit that he recognized that hypnosis was distinct from natural sleep. At first Braid theorized that it was a purely neurophysiological phenomenon. Later he became more inclined toward looking at it as a psychological phenomenon. Unfortunately he was rather vague on this point. Charcot about 1880, following in Braid's earlier footsteps, fought bitterly against any psychological interpreta-

---

* By "psychic" is meant purely mental, that is, entirely a product or function of the mind, completely independent of the soma and of the physical world.

tion; he probably more than any other person is responsible for the establishment of the three well-known stages and artifacts of hypnosis referred to as lethargy, catalepsy, and somnambulism. The culmination of the dispute and the shift toward an entirely psychological theory came about under the tutelage of Liébeault and Bernheim during the period 1866 to 1886. With these men it was conclusively demonstrated that hypnotic phenomena could be entirely brought into being through the sole medium of verbal suggestion, and thus the psychological nature of hypnosis was definitely established. The acceptance of this point of view was not easily obtained, however, for, with Charcot's justly acquired prestige as a scientific investigator, his appearance upon the scene aroused a heated controversy which was not resolved for many years after. The reader interested in this historical aspect will find interesting details (and further references of historical interest) in Hull's (213) account.

That hypnosis results from suggestion is not in question anymore. Whether it can be induced by other means will be considered later, as well as the question of whether there are one or several kinds of hypnoses according to the method of induction used. On the other hand, if we are willing to accept, for the time being, that hypnosis represents a psychophysiological state of the individual that is different from his normal state, it appears that suggestions can be given to him in either state. Accordingly one distinguishes between *waking* and *hypnotic* or *trance suggestions.* Considerable space will be devoted later to investigating the nature of these two types of suggestion. For the present and for the purpose of these introductory pages it may be pointed out that this dichotomy is rather artificial. The point that must be clearly kept in mind at present is that, quite independently of, and in addition to, the fact that suggestions can be used to induce hypnosis, once such a state has been induced through some means or other, one may give suggestions to the hypnotized subject in the same way one would if he were not hypnotized. This is the true basis of the above distinction. Actually, most, if not all, of the phenomena one can obtain with suggestions given to a hypnotized subject can also be obtained without going through the preliminary process of hypnotizing him. This has led some investigators to question whether after all a subject may not be said to be hypnotized from the time he first responds to suggestions, regardless of what may have been done with him before the suggestions were given. This is no easy question to answer—if it can be answered at all.

The Hypnotic State and Its Induction

One of the clearest descriptions of the induction of hypnosis and its characteristics has been given by Schilder and Kauder (392). No better can be done than to quote these authors here. They have the following to say:

I hold a key before the eyes of a person lying in a recumbent position, and command him to fix his gaze on the key continuously. Simultaneously, I repeatedly and gently stroke his brow, pronouncing again and again in a rather monotonous manner sentences to the effect that he is getting tired, drowsy, sleepy, that he feels a heaviness in his limbs, that he has the sensation of being about to go to sleep, that it is only with difficulty that he succeeds in keeping his eyes open, that he cannot help closing them. In the case of some persons, the eyes will close as a result. In the case of others, it will be necessary to pronounce a definite instruction to close the eyes. The person experimented on is now recumbent like one sleeping. He barely moves, perhaps does not move at all. I now raise the person's arm gently and release it. The arm does not drop back flaccidly, nor remain in its position, but descends in slow degrees until it reaches the original position. I stroke the arm of the person experimented on and repeat in a convincing manner: "You feel that the arm that I am stroking has become warm." I stroke the other arm, simultaneously assuring the subject that the arm has lost all sensation. I prick the hand with a needle; the subject winces slightly. I again stroke the brow and say: "You can see a beautiful flower with perfect clearness." I now "wake" the person experimented on, by pronouncing the following formula: "When I have counted three, you will open your eyes and will feel perfectly sound, fresh, and bright; you will feel no dizziness, no headaches." I count three; the subject opens his eyes promptly, and makes the following report: He has not been asleep, and has heard all my words. He has felt fatigue and a heaviness in the limbs, but might have opened his eyes and moved about, had he wished. He has felt the sensation of warmth, also the prick. He has not seen anything. He says he now feels a slight dizziness and a slight headache. This is the type of a very superficial hypnosis.

In other cases the outcome is the same, with the exception that the patient declares, after waking, that she cannot remember what was said to her. On hearing the signal to wake up, she may take time in opening her eyes, may glance about in surprise and rub her eyes. To be sure, although this is by no means a rule without its exceptions, such cases very frequently allow the hand that has been raised to drop back in a relaxed and inert manner, or to maintain the hand in a state of cataleptic stiffness in the position to which it has been raised. But has the subject executed the commands issued during hypnosis or not? It is impossible to resort to questioning in this connection after the waking; questions are asked during the hypnotic procedure. We are given information as to the result of the suggestion by means of nods of the head or more or less subdued speech. We are here pointing out that type of hypnosis in which—in spite of a low degree of suggestibility and perhaps a paucity of muscular phenomena—amnesia is nevertheless present as to the experiences during the hypnotic state.

In other cases serious muscular phenomena occupy the foreground. Those hypnotized present an extreme laxness of the muscles, or a stiffening of the whole body, catalepsy, although no verbal suggestion has been made to this effect. Sometimes catalepsy and muscular tension can be attained only by the use of suggestion. In spite of the presence of extensive muscular phenomena, suggestibility is not necessarily encountered in other fields; amnesia may be present or absent. During such hypnoses, there may also be inability to speak; not a word is pronounced, and this may in some cases result in a keen sense of fear.

Motor phenomena in the form of twitches, hysteriform tremors, even in the form of more or less pronounced hysterical attacks, may also constitute the content or preliminary stage of hypnoses producing the impression of a profound sleep.

Hypnotized persons in a "deep sleep" must in many cases be addressed in a summary manner before it is possible to communicate with them again; one has the impression that it will be necessary to waken them at least partially. The voices of persons thus hypnotized at first sound hoarse, low, barely articulate, and do not become cleared until the conversation in hypnosis has continued for some time, gradually approaching the voice while awake. Complete relaxation of muscles is observable in such cases; it may as a rule—but not always—be easily turned into catalepsy by the use of suggestion. Motionlessness is not always recorded. Those hypnotized may make disturbing movements with the entire body and with the extremities. Suggestions of warmth, anaesthesia, suggestions of smell and taste are frequently accepted, but not always optical suggestions. The degree of optical suggestibility varies considerably in these cases. Spots, mists, clouds, colors, are more readily accepted than definite outlined or personified optical images. Persons producing form outlines frequently will produce only those that are agreeable to them, let us say, images of intimate friends, and refuse to accept hallucinations of indifferent objects, such as flowers, landscapes, etc. If the hallucination involves definitely outlined optical images, such as the flower, for instance, it is usually easy to induce the hypnotized person to reach out for the suggested object as he might reach out for the real object. Hypnosis of the kind described above may, but need not necessarily, be followed by amnesia. The persons experimented on who do not have amnesia with regard to their experiences during the hypnosis, will communicate varying data on the reality of what was "seen, felt, experienced." Some will describe their experiences in such a way that they may hardly be called more than a vivid perception, others describe them as seen images, others again give rise to hardly any doubts as to the reality of the objects beheld. In many cases, we are told by the subjects that the hallucinations were quite clear, in other words, actually present in consciousness, but were vague in outline and color, or seemed covered with a veil. The judgment of reality in these cases is to a great extent independent of the degree of corporeal concreteness. . . . In the case of some hypnotized persons it is possible to obtain hallucinations in the field of all the senses, even when the eyes are open, while real bodies actually present may be rendered non-existent to the hypnotized subject. . . . The subject's behavior is then determined entirely by the objects suggested.

As clearly seen in this description, *there is considerable variability in the manifestations of hypnosis,* a fact that all hypnotists will subscribe to readily.

The method of trance induction described above will be referred to hereafter as the *standard method* of induction. Essentially, it consists of the combination of two methods, the fixation of a bright object, and the use of sleep suggestions. There are a great many other ways of producing a hypnotic state, and these have been extensively reviewed by Milne Bramwell (45). But, in general, most techniques are variations of the above one. This statement should not be misconstrued, however, to mean that all methods are alike. On the contrary, success as a professional hypnotist is largely dependent on using the method most suited to a given individual in a particular situation.

Criteria and Stages of Hypnosis

The account quoted from Schilder and Kauder in the last section lists fairly well the various symptoms of hypnosis. In general these include contractures, paralyses, positive hallucinations (seeing things not present), negative hallucinations (inability to see things present), delusions (false judgments and false beliefs), analgesia (insensibility to pain), anesthesia (partial or complete loss of sensation), amnesia (inability to recall), and posthypnotic suggestions. When all of these are obtained in a trance, one may speak of the subject as being in a deep state of hypnosis. In terms of the number and kind of symptoms that appear in other trances, one may grade the *depth* of hypnosis. The exact procedure for doing this and its basis will be discussed in a later chapter.

Some readers may object at this point that these symptoms could easily be simulated by individuals pretending to be hypnotized for reasons of their own. This is unquestionably true and does happen in fact. But for the experienced hypnotist there are certain clear differences between simulated and true symptoms which are not at all obvious to the uninitiated. Also there are other symptoms that may be sought; to a large extent this is a matter of personal proficiency. In general, the experienced hypnotist is not easily fooled. In any event, the test of suggested analgesia usually uncovers any simulator.

As already implied, the hypnotic state appears in various degrees or depths, in a manner reminiscent of sleep, narcosis, and gas anesthesia. There exists a near-perfect correlation between hypnotic depth and suggestibility.

In the older literature, and still to some extent today, hypnosis was said to occur in three distinct stages. This notion was first introduced by Charcot. According to him, these stages were *lethargy, catalepsy,* and *somnambulism.* Lethargy could be induced by simply closing the eyes of the subject and applying light pressure upon the eyeballs. In this stage, the subject could neither speak nor hear, but, if certain nerves were pressed, interesting states of contracture could be obtained. Once lethargy was produced, one needed only to open the subject's eyes to obtain catalepsy; the subject would pass immediately into this new stage. In the cataleptic stage, the subject was still unable to speak or hear, but now his limbs could be placed in any position, however uncomfortable it might seem, and they would remain thus. This is the so-called waxy flexibility. Finally, if a friction were applied to the top of the head of a cataleptic subject, he would pass into the final stage, somnambulism. Here the subject could hear, speak, see, feel, and in general all of the phenomena of the trance state which have been described could be elicited.

We shall not attempt to explain here how this particular theory came into acceptance. Let it be said merely that it is now definitely obsolete. Today hypnosis is considered to lie upon a continuum, and no special manipulations of the subject's body are required to cover the phenomenological range of hypnosis. Various scales have been devised. At present we shall limit ourselves to one proposed by Davis and Husband (91) which describes hypnosis in five stages as follows:

Depth	*Symptoms*
Insusceptible	
Hypnoidal	Relaxation, fluttering of the eyelids, closing of the eyes, complete physical relaxation
Light trance	Catalepsy of the eyes, limb catalepsies, rigid catalepsy, glove anesthesia
Medium trance	Partial amnesia, posthypnotic anesthesia, personality changes, simple posthypnotic suggestions, kinesthetic delusions, complete amnesia

Depth	*Symptoms*
Somnambulistic trance	Ability to open the eyes without affecting the trance, bizarre posthypnotic suggestions, complete somnambulism, positive visual hallucinations, posthypnotic; positive auditory hallucinations, posthypnotic; systematized posthypnotic amnesias, negative auditory hallucinations, negative visual hallucinations; hyperesthesia

The use of the term somnambulistic trance in the above is a throwback to the Charcot classification which is rather unfortunate insofar as, medically speaking, there exists a somnambulistic state. Because of this it is customary to speak here of "artificial" in contrast to "natural" or "spontaneous" somnambulism. Somnambulism hence refers to three different phenomena: (a) a form of hysteria, (b) a disturbance of natural sleep, and (c) the deepest stage of hypnosis. Hereafter, unless otherwise specified, the last meaning will be the only one used in this book. It may be pointed out, however, that these three meanings of somnambulism may not be entirely unrelated.

Tests of Suggestibility

Since certain specific test situations recur time and time again in the sort of investigations with which we shall be concerned, it seems advisable at this time to examine some of these situations. The tests that will be surveyed are employed with various alterations by different investigators, but they remain sufficiently unaltered that we can refer to them by name. In general, wherever significant variations have been introduced they will be taken up as part of the discussion of the experiment in which they have occurred. The following twenty tests are the most frequently used.

1. *Arm or Hand Levitation.* The subject is told emphatically, over and over, that one of his hands is becoming light and is tending to rise. For purposes of scoring, it is usual to limit suggestions to a standard period of time. Scoring can be based on the amount of movement induced in the hand, which can be rather easily recorded by means of a stylus connected to a string attached to the subject's hand and maintained taut. The stylus is so arranged as to record hand motions on a revolving drum.

2. *Body or Postural Sway.* The subject is made to stand still, relaxed, with his eyes closed, and suggestions are made to him that he is either falling forward or backward. Scoring is based upon the amount of sway obtained during a given period of time. A stylus can

again be used to record sway, which is usually measured in inches. Complete fall is given an arbitrary score of 12 inches (or some other figure).

3. *Hand Clasping.* The subject is asked to interlock his fingers in front of him and to clench his hands tight. Suggestions are then given that he will be unable to unclasp his hands. The difficulty he has in doing this when told to try to unclasp is used as basis for scoring.

4. *Eye Closure.* The subject is told that his eyes are heavy and are going to close. This is emphatically and repeatedly suggested. Time required for closure is usually recorded. In very exact experiments a stylus can be connected to the eyelid and their actual motion recorded.

5. *Catalepsy of the Eyelids* (or *Eye Catalepsy*). The subject is told to close his eyes. The suggestion is then given that he will not be able to open them. His difficulty in doing this when challenged is used as basis for scoring.

6. *Hand Rigidity.* The subject is told that his extended hand is becoming stiff and rigid, that he cannot move his fingers or close his hand. Scores are based on the time taken to get any response and also on the extent of response.

7. *Picture Report* (or *Fidelity of Report*). The subject is shown a picture for a short period of time. A series of leading questions are then asked, a number of which have suggestions of fictitious details. For instance, if the picture shown is of a crowd, one such question might be "In the picture of the crowd, where is the little dog?", when actually there is no dog in the picture at all. The score is the number of such suggestions that are accepted.

8. *Chevreul Pendulum.* The subject is shown a small bob hanging on a thread. He is told that, if he holds the pendulum thus formed over a ruler and looks fixedly at the bob, he will soon notice the bob starting to swing along the ruler, even though he himself remains passive and refrains from making any deliberate movements. The experimenter demonstrates how it starts swinging and then gives it to the subject and repeats the instructions. Continuous strong suggestions are given to the effect that the bob is beginning to swing, is swinging, etc. . . . The score is the actual swing in inches.

9. *Ink Blot.* A Rorschach or similar ink blot is shown to the subject who is told that it appears to different people to resemble various things. Two of the common responses are described, and four other inapplicable ones are added. The subject is then asked if he can see anything resembling these. The score is the number of suggestions accepted.

10. *Odor Suggestion.* The subject is told that his sense of smell is to be tested. Six bottles are placed before him; they are labeled in order: pineapple, banana, vanilla, rose, jasmine, and coffee. He is told that the bottles will be uncorked at a distance one at a time and brought slowly toward his nose. He is to report as soon as he detects an odor. A starting distance of about 2 feet is good. In each case the subject is told as the cork is removed what odor to expect. All but the last three bottles contain the specified essence. These three have only water. The score is one point for each suggestion accepted. It should be noted that the first three odors are chosen in the order of their decreasing strength. This should be kept in mind if a different series is substituted.

11. *Progressive Weights, Impersonal.* Twelve boxes, identical in appearance, are placed before the subject. He is told that they all differ in weight and that he is to compare 1 with 2, 2 with 3, 3 with 4, and so on, saying each time which is the heavier of the two. Of the first five, each successive box weighs actually more, by equal amounts, than its predecessor. The last seven are all equal in weight to box 5. The score is the number of boxes called "heavier" minus the number called "lighter."

12. *Progressive Weight, Personal.* The same setup as in test 11 is used here, and only the method of scoring is changed. Now the score is obtained by adding together the number of times the boxes are called "lighter" and the number of times they are called "heavier." The reason for this is rather interesting and will help to throw some light on testing techniques. In test 11, one is interested only in the effect of suggestion caused by the particular arrangement, that in every case the next box picked up will be heavier than the preceding one. The scoring used takes only this effect into account. On the other hand, in test 12, the scoring takes into account the effect of the verbal suggestion that the weights are all different.

13. *Heat Illusion.* A small heating element is applied to the forehead of the subject. The latter is shown beforehand how the element becomes hot as he turns a calibrated knob connected with a variable resistance. He is asked to turn the knob slowly until he just detects the first sign of heat in the element; then he is to remove the element from his forehead immediately and call out the reading on the dial. He is then asked to repeat the procedure, and on this occasion a secret switch is silently opened, preventing current from flowing. As the dial reading approaches the previous reading, the subject's attention is called to this fact: "Be on the alert now, you should soon feel

the heat." A score of one is given to those who report feeling the heat when the switch is open.

There are several variations of this test. In one, the subject places his finger within a heating coil. In another, a mild electric shock is substituted for heat.

14. *Press and Release.* This is a variation of the hand-clasping test. A rubber ball is connected through a rubber tubing to a particularly large tambour which in turn activates a lever which writes on a kymograph. Thus a record of pressure on the ball is made continuously. The ball is given to the subject to hold. In the press test, he begins holding it so as to exert a slight amount of pressure (this allows one to record any negative reaction). Suggestions are then given that the subject is grasping the ball more firmly. In the release test, he starts by squeezing the ball hard, although not maximally. Suggestions are then given that he is releasing his grip. Of course he is made to understand that he is expected to keep his pressure steady. The score is the maximum motion of the lever.

15. *Trap Line.* A series of 12 lines are drawn on white paper and shown one at a time, each for 7 seconds. The lengths of the lines are as follows: The first is 12 millimeters long. Each of the next four lines is 12 millimeters longer than the one preceding it, and the same is true of lines 7, 9, and 11. But lines 6, 8, 10, and 12, the so-called trap lines, are each the same length as the line immediately preceding. The subject, upon being shown each line, is asked to make one of exactly the same length on a paper furnished him, placing the first under the second, and so on. Scores are obtained by assigning 1 point to each trap line that he increases.

16. *Progressive Line.* Ten parallel lines starting at varying distances from the margin are presented, one by one, to the subject. As in test 15, the first is 12 millimeters long. The next four increase progressively by 12 millimeters each. The last five are equal in length. The procedure of administration and scoring is identical with that for test 15. Each of the last five lines that the subject increases rates 1 point.

17. *Line Test with Suggestion.* Eleven lines 60 millimeters long are shown one at a time. The subject is asked to reproduce these. The first one is presented without comment. The second line is shown with the comment: "Here is one that is longer." On the third the statement is "Here is one that is shorter." And so on alternately through the series. Scoring consists of 1 point for every suggestion accepted.

18. *Illusion of Smell*. This is a variation of test 10. A small bottle of water is shown to the subject with the following explanation: "In this bottle there is something that I think you have never smelled before. I am going to pour some on a piece of cotton, hold it in the air, and begin counting one count a second. When you smell it, you are to put the number you hear me say on your paper. Remember, all you need is one number, the number you hear me say when you first smell this." The examiner then pours some of the water on a piece of cotton, holds his head away as if the odor were disagreeable, and begins counting to 100. Scoring is made by the all-or-none method. A score of +10 is given if any number is recorded, 0 if none is given (or a statement of not smelling anything is made), and −10, if the test is challenged (that is, if the subject pronounces the test a fake).

19. *Contradictory Suggestion of Line Length*. A series of 24 numbered lines is shown to the subject. The length of the shortest is 12 millimeters, and each succeeding line is 4 millimeters longer than the preceding one. The subject's task is to determine which of the lines in the series is comparable in length to three other lines exposed one at a time. The first of these is 32 millimeters (equal to number 6 in the series), the second is 56 millimeters (equal to number 12), and the third is 80 millimeters (equal to number 18). A line of this second series is exposed for 5 seconds, after which the subject makes his choice from the first series. Irrespective of the choice, the experimenter points to the line immediately below and asks: "Is it not rather line ——?" If the subject agrees, the experimenter points to the next one below and repeats the same question. Scoring is as follows: 0 for complete resistance, 10 for acceptance of the six suggestions, 8 for 5, 6 for 4, 5 for 3, 3 for 2, 1 for 1.

20. *Directive Suggestion of Color*. Six colors are used: red, orange, yellow, green, blue, and violet. These colors are on 1-inch squares, and there are 15 of each (90 squares in all). The subject is first asked to hand the experimenter 3 red, 1 green, and 2 blue squares. This is followed by asking him how many of each of the three colors he picked up. This procedure is repeated next with 1 yellow, 3 violet, and 2 green. Finally the subject is required to hand 1 red, 1 violet, and 2 yellow. This done, the subject is asked how many violet, red, and *orange* squares were used. If the subject states no orange was used, he is then asked how many yellow. The score is either 10, indicating the number of orange squares, or 0.

Phenomena Elicited in Hypnosis

We have already seen briefly some of the phenomena that can be obtained in the state of hypnosis. We propose to take these up a little more in detail in the present section. From what has been said concerning the depth of hypnosis, it should be clear that the eliciting of any particular phenomenon depends upon first obtaining a specific depth of trance, all other things being equal of course. It shall therefore be assumed in the present discussion that a somnambulistic state has been obtained, and that there are no interfering factors, in which case all of the various phenomena to be considered are theoretically possible. We say theoretically, because in many instances, all phenomena are not always obtainable, at least on first trial. Subjects have sometimes to be "trained," so to speak. The significance of this point will be left to a later section for discussion.

When considering suggestibility phenomena, we need first to distinguish between *spontaneous* and *induced* (or *suggested*) phenomena. The former just seem to appear of their own accord when a certain state of suggestibility is brought about, or are found to be associated with other responses that have been suggested. Rapport and posthypnotic amnesia, for instance, are often present, without any suggestions having been given to that effect. In other situations, suggestions have to be given to obtain these same effects. Another division of the observed phenomena is in terms of *physiological* and *psychological* effects. These may in turn be spontaneous or induced. Thus, muscular relaxation is a physiological correlate of hypnosis in some cases, while mental passivity appears to be a psychological correlate. Induced color blindness appears to be functional, and hence primarily psychological, while a suggested increase in heart rate would be considered to be physiological. In many instances it is difficult to decide which of the two is involved, and in many others there is little question that one is dealing with a combination of the two, that is, with a psychophysiological phenomenon, where no clear separation is possible. Typical of this last is increased salivation upon the suggestion being made to the subject that he is very hungry and is chewing a delicious piece of steak. In any event pure somatic effects are never the result of suggestions, but only psychosomatic ones are possible. This is a natural consequence of the nature of suggestion itself.

The distinction between spontaneous and suggested effects is also sometimes difficult to establish, for there is always a question in the former of the subject having responded to a suggestion of which the hypnotist is not aware. This has been particularly true of posthypnotic amnesia. For a long time it was considered to be an inherent characteristic accompanying deep trance states in an invariable manner. In recent times, however, as we shall presently see, serious doubts have been cast upon amnesia as a criterion of hypnosis. The subject often comes to the hypnotist with preconceived ideas of what will happen, and these may well act as autosuggestions. Often, quite unconsciously the hypnotist himself gives the subject cues which the latter interprets as instructions. For instance, to consider a purely fictitious situation at this time, suppose changes in respiratory rate are being investigated in connection with the induction of hypnosis. Suppose, furthermore, that a decrease in rate is observed. Does this mean necessarily that the two go together? A little reflection on this matter will show that the decrease in rate may be merely an artifact which results from the suggestions given to the subject to relax. Furthermore, in inducing hypnosis, it is not uncommon practice to give the subject such suggestions as ". . . take deep breaths . . . breathe rhythmically . . ." After hypnosis has been induced, any decrease in rate might be the result of these pretrance instructions. There will be numerous opportunities in later portions of this book to examine actual instances of this sort of situation.

In general, the changes involved in hypnosis can be classified under the headings of hyperfunction, hypofunction, afunction, and parafunction. The first of these denotes a rise in level of functioning above the normal level. The second in contrast denotes a decrease in this level. The third refers to the absence of a function normally present, while the last refers to distortion of functions. For instance, in hyperaudition the individual's sensitivity to auditory stimuli is very much increased. On the contrary, in hypoaudition he loses his sensitivity to certain stimuli normally heard. Auditory afunction is deafness, while para-audition involves such things as hearing sounds when none are produced, or again hearing sounds in a different manner than they are normally heard.

Since each of these four categories of changes represent, for any given individual, deviations from the norm, one may consider these under the general term of abnormal functions, and as such, the classification given by J. F. Brown (56) appears to fit the present situation perfectly. Following him, we shall therefore speak of:

A. Changes (abnormalities) of the cognitive processes:
  1. Sensation.
  2. Perception.
  3. Attention.
  4. Association.
  5. Memory.
  6. Thought.
B. Changes (abnormalities) of the motor processes:
  1. Muscular activity.
  2. Reflex acts.
  3. Habit.
  4. Voluntary acts.
  5. Total behavior.
C. Changes (abnormalities) of the emotional processes.

Under the topic of sensation one may place the following subject matters:

(a) Vision.	(e) Pain.	(i) Kinesthesis.
(b) Hearing.	(f) Pressure.	(j) Static sensitivity.
(c) Smell.	(g) Cold.	(k) Organic sensitivity.
(d) Taste.	(h) Hot.	

Under drives and motivation one may place

1. Physiological drives.
2. Special motives.
3. Personal motives.

In closing this section the following partial list due to Milne Bramwell (45), giving actual topics investigated, may be instructive:

A. Changes in the voluntary muscular system:
  Echolalia.
  Paralysis.
  Special muscular states as found in: Lethargy.
                                        Catalepsy.
                                        Somnambulism.
B. Changes in the involuntary muscles and vasomotor system:
  Pulse.
  Respiration.
  Bleeding.
  Local redness of the skin.
  Blistering and prevention of blisters.
  Changes in temperature.
  Menstruation.
  Bowel movements.
  Urination.
  Lachrymation.
  Perspiration.
  Lactation.

C. Changes in the special senses, muscular senses, common sensations and appetites:
   1. Increased action:
     Sight.
     Hearing.
     Smell.
     Muscular sense.
     Common cutaneous sensibility.
     Thermosensibility.
     Appetite, hunger, and thirst.
   2. Decreased, arrested, and distorted action of the senses.
   3. Sensory delusions, hallucinations, and illusions:
     Positive.
     Negative.
     Retroactive.
     Deferred.
     Of memory.
D. Other distortions:
   Changes of personality.
   Motor.

The above material should give the reader an idea of the range of phenomena that may be expected and that can serve as topics for investigation. This list is far from exhaustive, and certainly does not represent the only way in which hypnotic phenomena may be classified. It should also be kept in mind that, although Milne Bramwell declared that all of the above have been obtained, and although there is no question but that he was writing in good faith, he was doing this in a period when the exactitude of modern science was at best to be found only in the physical sciences. It will be the aim of a considerable portion of this book to examine the validity of these claims.

On the Art of Hypnotizing

Of the readers perusing this book, some may have had more or less successful experience in hypnotizing. Others may have it in mind to try their hand at it. Let it be repeated once more that this particular volume is not aimed at teaching how to hypnotize, but rather it is aimed at giving the reader a basic understanding of what hypnotism is and what it can do.

If one pays no attention to depth of hypnosis, one may accept Milne Bramwell's estimate that 78 to 97 per cent of the population can be hypnotized. Among young adults, his report would indicate that 10 to 20 per cent attain a somnambulistic trance. With a highly susceptible subject almost anyone possessing a modicum of intelligence can have success by following the steps described earlier in the quotation from Schilder and Kauder. With a little more training in the various methods that can be employed, the average individual can expect fair success without extensive experience, meaning by this that he might expect around 20 per cent success. On the other hand, it should be pointed out that the material from Schilder and Kauder is not intended as instruction. Furthermore, merely reading books on methods is only a small portion of the work necessary to become a skillful hypnotist. As Jenness (225) has pointed out, hypnotizing is an art for which a thorough understanding of human psychology and considerable practice are essential. Such practice is best obtained under the guidance of a competent hypnotist. There is little question but that just about anyone can bring about some degree of hypnosis in some individuals, with a minimum of instruction. But, as it is hoped this book will demonstrate, hypnotic phenomena are very complex indeed and often involve deep psychosomatic alterations with which only the professionally trained individual can cope adequately. We cannot overemphasize the undesirability of the use of hypnosis by poorly trained individuals. Properly handled, hypnotism is a very useful tool for both therapy and research. But in the hands of the dilettante, particularly when employed for the sake of curiosity or amusement, it can lead to disastrous results not only for the subject, but equally for the hypnotist.

PART

· 2 ·

EXPERIMENTAL
FOUNDATIONS
Intrinsic Characteristics
of Suggestibility and Hypnosis

Suggestion

If any single topic in the field of suggestibility can be said to hold a central position, *suggestion* has this honor. Not only are suggestions the basic tool of investigation, but they are also the means by which the phenomena of suggestibility are brought about.

The reality of suggestions is a well-established fact. The postural sway test which is generally accepted to be a typical suggestion leaves little doubt of this. Furneaux (152), testing 100 subjects, found that 42 per cent fell completely, 55 per cent showed a sway of more than 6 inches over basal sway,* and the remaining 3 per cent exhibited sway ranging from none to slightly less than 6 inches. These figures are in agreement with similar data obtained by other investigators. On the basis of existing data it can be estimated that probably better than 90 per cent of the normal population will give some definite response to postural sway suggestions.

Suggestions have been classified in various ways. It is with this topic that the present chapter will be mainly concerned.† As was indicated in the first chapter, we distinguish between *autosuggestions,* or suggestions given by an individual to himself, and *heterosuggestions,* or suggestions given by one individual to another individual.

An obvious but important distinction can also be made between *verbal* and *nonverbal* suggestions. In practice, nearly all suggestions are of a verbal type.

Another classification groups suggestions as *direct* and *indirect*. The former are direct statements of the expected responses, the subject being aware of the suggestion and presumably being able to accept or reject it. In their most extreme form, such suggestions reduce to mere commands, at least in appearance. Hull (213), however, has presented arguments against the identification of suggestions with

---

* By *basal sway* or *normal postural level* is meant the mean amount and direction of body movement that takes place before the giving of the suggestions.

† A discussion of the nature of suggestions will be left to the last chapters of the book.

commands. According to him the main point of difference between the two lies in the postulation that, in commands, symbolic activity is involved in the determination of the response, whereas, in direct suggestions, the subject withdraws to various degrees the influence of his symbolic processes upon the elaboration of his response. To what extent this point of view may be correct will be examined later on. An indirect suggestion on the other hand never states, but implies the desired responses in such a way that the subject is not aware of being directed to behave in a certain manner.

Results reported by Furneaux (152), Eysenck (131), and Reymert and Kohn (363) show that from 22 to 90 per cent of tested individuals respond to indirect suggestion. This percentage is found to be a function of both the type of indirect suggestion used and of the kind of individual acting as subject. The figures given earlier for postural sway suggestion can be regarded as typical for direct suggestions in general.

McDougall is said to have been the first to introduce the notions of *prestige* and *nonprestige* suggestions. Among older investigators who have made use of these terms one may list Binet, Henri, Vaschide, and Giroud. More recent investigators who have done the same include Otis (329), Aveling and Hargreaves (8), Estabrook (126), Messerschmidt (307), and Hull (213). Prestige suggestions are a type whose effectiveness is very much dependent on the prestige the suggestor holds in the eyes of the subject. This is not true of nonprestige suggestions. In support of this classification, the last four mentioned investigators have offered the fact that suggestions appear to fall into two distinct groups, on the basis of the type of statistical distribution that the scored responses give rise to. According to them, prestige suggestions are associated with J- and U-shaped distributions, whereas nonprestige suggestions are associated with Gaussian curves.‡ In discussing prestige suggestions, Coffin (71) has pointed out that one should really subdivide such suggestions into two further categories on the basis of the degree of complexity that characterizes the prestige employed. Thus he speaks of "prestige by personal influence" in which there is a strict subject-experimenter relationship; and "prestige in a broader 'social context'" where the personal relationship just referred to gives way to what Coffin describes as a "broader 'social' setting,"

‡ It is to be noted that Aveling and Hargreaves, as well as Eysenck and Furneaux, have presented arguments in support of the thesis that the J and U shapes were artifacts. This point will be considered later on.

in which the influence of majority (group) and/or expert opinion (authority) holds sway.

The entire classification of suggestions in terms of the presence or absence of prestige is rather unsatisfactory for a number of reasons. First, it does not give a unique characterization of suggestions. Obviously, for a given suggestion, the amount of prestige present will vary with the character of both the suggestor and the suggestee, and will even be influenced by the general situation in which it is given. Then too, whether there can ever be a situation in which two individuals interact in which prestige plays no part is a question. Finally, there is also some question as to whether the prestige factor does not really reduce to a matter of attitude formation and/or expectation. In any event, in regard to prestige in the limited sense of personal influence, we shall see later that we can approach the results just cited in a manner that does not necessitate the mention of prestige.

The subject of prestige considered in the broader sense is at present rather ambiguous, mainly because the notion is poorly defined. An appreciable number of investigations have been made in this area, but the resulting data do not seem to lead to any clear-cut conclusions. It would seem that there is probably some sort of relationship between this sort of prestige and suggestions. However, it is not at all clear what the relation is. In my opinion, it is a moot question whether one should consider at all the broader sort of prestige as taking a part in giving suggestions their potency. It may be that the relation is only in the form of common factors, or, better still, that suggestion is one of the factors that makes up the complex called "prestige," rather than the assumed converse.

For the above reasons prestige suggestions, with a few minor exceptions, will not be given any further consideration in this book. However, in view of their fairly frequent mention in the past literature, it was considered that something should be said about them.

Still another way of describing suggestions has been the use of the terms *personal* and *impersonal*. A large number of investigators have employed these expressions in the past to designate prestige and non-prestige suggestions, respectively. Another group, headed by Hull (213), appears also to designate as "personal" those suggestions delivered in person by the suggestor, in contrast to "impersonal" suggestions delivered through some medium other than an individual, such as a tape recorder for instance. Both Hull (213) and Estabrook (125) have shown that recorded suggestions are just as effective as the same suggestions delivered in person. This particular distinction, however, seems rather trivial and is mentioned here only for the sake of completeness.

Sidis (412) has also distinguished between *immediate* and *mediate* suggestion. According to him, a suggestion is immediate if the suggested idea is carried out, while it is mediate if an idea associated with the suggested idea is the one carried out. These are not to be confused with direct and indirect suggestions. As a matter of fact, direct and indirect suggestions can themselves be mediate or immediate.§

Possibly related to these last two types are two other forms of suggestion that have been largely ignored in the literature although they account for a number of important effects observed in connection with hypnotic phenomena. One of these I call a *marginal* suggestion. It is an element or set of elements not intended to be part of a suggestion that is being given, but is nevertheless associated with it, either as a separate suggestion or as an integral part of the given suggestion, thereby altering the latter. For instance, a facial expression on the part of the suggestor often acts as a marginal suggestion. The same is true of voice inflections. There is a special instance of marginal suggestion which I like to call a *contextual* suggestion. This is a marginal suggestion inherent in the context of the suggestion that is being given. Many discrepancies and peculiar results which have been obtained in various investigations have their source in the fact that different subjects will interpret one and the same suggestion differently because of marginal suggestions.

As will be seen later, there are reasons for questioning whether we should speak of "suggestion" in respect to the results that led Sidis to make his distinction. To some extent this remark may also apply to the concepts of marginal and contextual suggestion. In any event none of these four types are fundamental. They need, however, to be kept in mind, particularly the last two, in designing experiments or analyzing results in the area of suggestibility. This last remains true, regardless of the validity of speaking of suggestions here, inasmuch as the effects that have led to making the distinctions have independent existence.

As was remarked earlier, we speak of heterosuggestion and of autosuggestion. Hull (213), Eysenck and Furneaux (129), Berreman and Hilgard (29), Baernstein (9), and Baumgartner (21) have shown the reality of autosuggestion. They have also demonstrated that heterosuggestion and autosuggestion are equally effective, at least insofar as

§ Sidis has presented empirical evidence for this categorization.

suggestions of postural sway are concerned. Hull (213) and Berreman and Hilgard (29) have shown that nonverbal suggestions are also quite effective, by having subjects imagine that they were falling backward. These last two investigators found a high correlation among the results obtained for imagined, autosuggested, and heterosuggested postural sway, showing thereby that there is a common factor to the response in all three types of suggestion.

Finally, we commonly speak of *waking, hypnotic* (or *trance*), and *posthypnotic* suggestions. The last is a suggestion given while the subject is in a trance and in such a way as to be effective at some time after the trance is terminated.|| A hypnotic suggestion is one given during hypnosis, in contrast to a waking suggestion, which is any suggestion given in the absence of a hypnotic state. These statements presuppose, of course, that there is a basis for the existence of these types of suggestion. This matter will be taken up later. For the time being it will be taken for granted.

|| It is a particular case of a more general phenomenon which may be called a *delayed suggestion,* that is, one becoming effective some time after its termination.

·3·

Suggestibility.
Its Universality

From what has been said in the last chapter, it is clear that all individuals will not respond alike to suggestion, all other things being equal. Again, the same individual will show variations in his responses to a given suggestion as the general conditions under which the suggestion is made are varied. There is then a certain capacity for response to suggestion. This we shall call the *suggestibility* of the individual. It is usually measured in terms of the speed with which the response takes place, its intensity (magnitude), or the degree to which the observed response agrees with the suggested one (completeness or fidelity). According to some investigators, suggestibility also denotes the state of the individual that is responsible for this capacity. There is no question that certain psychophysiological states can be brought into being in individuals whereby their suggestibility appears to increase much beyond its normal value. We shall have more to say about this later. On the other hand, the normal average individual appears to possess a certain capacity for responding to suggestion, which can hardly be spoken of as a "state," and he shows no evidence of any feature or group of features that could be distinguished by this term. Other investigators consider suggestibility as a personality trait. In some respects it does take on the aspects of such a trait. On the other hand, suggestibility in any given individual possesses a variability that makes it poorly suited for this role. Furthermore it appears to be a function of so many factors, some of which are themselves closely connected with personality traits, that it appears doubtful whether we can indeed speak of suggestibility itself as a personality trait. Possibly we could speak in these terms of an individual's mean suggestibility. This unfortunately presents the difficult problem of obtaining a representative sampling of his suggestibility over a sufficiently long period of time.

We have already seen in the last chapter that the reality of suggestions is beyond question. By this same token, the reality of suggestibility is established. As a matter of fact, most of the investigations mentioned in the last chapter were aimed primarily at establishing the existence and properties of suggestibility, and not of suggestion. In general, the method of investigating suggestibility in an individual is quite simple. It consists of giving the subject any one of the test suggestions described earlier, or some other one similar to these. The score the subject makes on such a test is then used directly or as a basis for his suggestibility rating.

As will be seen presently, suggestibility in normal and abnormal persons appears to differ only in degree, but is otherwise essentially the same. It is therefore permissible to speak of suggestibility in a very general way, as will be done in the next few pages.

Types and Varieties of Suggestibility

Quite early in the study of suggestibility a fundamental question arose that was responsible for much research, namely: Is suggestibility a unitary phenomenon or not? That is, is there a single kind of suggestibility, or are there many specific suggestibilities? Or, as a further alternative, is there a general capacity for responding to suggestion which is supplemented by a number of specific capacities for the same?

Sidis (412) was one of the first to propound the existence of more than one kind of suggestibility. Thus he speaks of direct, indirect, mediate, and immediate suggestibility. His experiments unfortunately do not demonstrate the actual existence of these four types.

Prideaux (352), another early investigator, also believed in four types of suggestibility which he called individual, conditional, specific, and personal. But it turns out he was speaking only of general characteristics of suggestibility and in any case offers no empirical evidence for his thesis.

In more recent times, Bird (33) has maintained that there is a direct and an indirect suggestibility. Hull (213) spoke instead of prestige and nonprestige suggestibility, and of waking suggestibility as contrasted to hypnotic suggestibility. However, there is considerable overlapping between situations that presumably evoke direct and prestige suggestibility on the one hand and those responsible for eliciting indirect and nonprestige suggestibility on the other, and it is doubtful whether one could speak of these four as distinct suggestibilities. Furthermore, there seems to be some confusion in the minds of these investigators in regard to the distinction between suggestion and suggestibility. It does not follow from the fact that suggestions can be classified in the above manner that the corresponding classification exists for suggestibility.

As a matter of fact, Aveling and Hargreaves (8) who presented an empirical basis for classifying suggestions as prestige and nonprestige also went further. On the basis of the rank order correlations which they obtained between the test items they had employed in their study, they arrived at the conclusion that there is a general factor of suggestibility over which are superimposed group and specific factors. Other studies of a similar nature have been made. Otis (329) reported evidence supporting the results of Aveling and Hargreaves. On the other hand, Brown (58) and Estabrook (126) found no evidence supporting this conclusion. The same is true of Allport (3) and Britt (54). Both conclude that no unitary trait of suggestibility exists. Thus far then, opinion on this matter is about equally divided.

Now a possible reason for this lack of agreement, and in any event a reason for not leaning too heavily on either group of results, is that the above-mentioned workers left uncontrolled a number of factors which might, and in fact have been shown, to influence the suggestibility of the subjects. This is particularly true of intelligence. Eysenck, first alone (130–132) and then later with Furneaux (129), showed in a series of well-controlled studies of a large number of subjects that a factor-analytical examination of scores obtained with a test battery leads to two types of suggestibility, and possibly to a third. These they have named *primary, secondary,* and *tertiary* suggestibility. The last named appears to be an intermediate form, partaking of the nature of both primary and secondary suggestibility. In general, direct and prestige suggestions tend to evoke primary suggestibility, while indirect and nonprestige suggestions tend to elicit secondary and tertiary suggestibility. Thus, the postural sway test, the progressive weight test, and the heat illusion test are associated with primary, secondary, and tertiary suggestibility types, respectively.

In addition to these results, the above two investigators found that tests of primary suggestibility give rise to scores that follow a J- or U-shaped distribution whereas tests of secondary suggestibility give rise to a bell-shaped distribution. They furnish no information in this respect for tertiary suggestibility tests. However, Aveling and Hargreaves (8) did obtain such data which show that the heat illusion test has a U-shaped distribution. An analysis of variance led Eysenck and Furneaux to conclude that primary suggestibility is probably a unitary factor, but that secondary suggestibility probably is not.

A clear understanding of the position held by the heat illusion test is rather important as a background to later material. This test was found to have some correlation with secondary suggestibility tests and none with primary suggestibility tests. Because of this, this test was initially classified as being of secondary suggestibility. However, later studies showed it to have a much weaker correlation with secondary suggestibility than was at first believed. At the same time, it was also established that it was highly correlated with hypnosis, which itself was strongly correlated with primary suggestibility tests. Consequently, the heat illusion test holds a unique position which has led to postulating a tertiary suggestibility. More will be said about this later.

Although Eysenck and Furneaux speak of primary, secondary, and tertiary suggestibility, it is important to realize that these are really names for three *factors*. According to them there is no general trait of suggestibility. Suggestibility as it is ordinarily measured by the tests described earlier is an expression of these factors. The importance of this is that it helps to tie together the various classifications of suggestibility which have already been mentioned. Thus direct and indirect suggestibility are identified with primary and secondary suggestibility, respectively. The same is true of prestige and nonprestige suggestions as defined by Aveling and Hargreaves. However here we must be on guard, for reference to prestige suggestibility is found in the literature in relation to a different sort of situation, where the influence of opinions of individuals with prestige value upon the attitudes of subjects is what is referred to. Eysenck (131) has pointed out that at present there is some doubt whether this form of prestige suggestibility is independent of either primary or secondary suggestibility, although he believes that the main correlation will probably turn out to be with secondary suggestibility.

Again, Eysenck and Furneaux (129) have reported evidence that primary and secondary suggestibility can be subdivided into *active* and *passive* suggestibility.* This is a rather unfortunate designation be-

* Eysenck and Furneaux (129) divide their subjects into two groups as follows: "(1) the alert, active type, who executed every suggestion rapidly, and (2) the passive, inactive type, who tried to achieve a state of complete restfulness, and who was much keener on carrying out suggestions which led to such a state (e.g., lowering of his arm), than on carrying out suggestions which had the opposite effect (e.g., raising his arm)." Eysenck and Furneaux report that primary suggestibility correlates highest with a tendency toward passive types of responses. However, examination of their basis for this statement places some doubts upon the generality of the conclusion.

cause analysis of their evidence shows that they are really talking of the types of responses that are obtained. These and not the suggestibility itself have a general character of passivity or activity, as the case may be. It may be added that this is not a new observation. Binet, Féré, Charcot, Bernheim, and Moll, among older investigators, had observed this too. More recently White (479) has discussed this to some length.

On the whole, the concept of primary, secondary, and possibly tertiary suggestibility as developed by Eysenck and Furneaux appears at present to be the most satisfactory and will be used in this book as basis for further discussions.

Suggestibility in the Normal and Abnormal Individual

When we think of suggestibility phenomena, this is usually in regard to normal individuals. It is however of some importance to consider the abnormal group also, particularly since it was once held that high suggestibility was symptomatic of abnormal mental conditions. The investigation of the relationship of suggestibility to normal and abnormal personalities has thus constituted another important area of study.

Cushing and Rush (85), using a personality inventory type of test to measure suggestibility, reported that delinquent girls are more suggestible than normal ones. Landis (250) using the postural sway test found that about 50 per cent of delinquent girls are negatively suggestible,† the remainder being positively suggestible.

Davis and Husband (91), using the Thurstone Personality Schedule to measure neuroticism, found little relation between suggestibility and neurosis. In this instance, suggestibility was measured by means of a scale devised by these investigators. Bartlett (15) tested with the postural sway test the suggestibility of hospitalized individuals diagnosed as psychoneurotics. She concluded that normal and neurotic individuals are about equally suggestible. Messer, Hinckley, and Mosier (306) agreed with Bartlett. Their data were obtained through the use of the Bernreuter Personality Inventory and the postural sway test.

† There are occasions when some subjects react in a way exactly opposite to the suggested response. They are said to possess *negative suggestibility*. This should not be confused with *negativism* in which the individual does not respond at all. This last is usually found to be true not only for suggested responses, but also in an indiscriminate manner for all responses. In the former instance the subject is usually very co-operative and may show negative suggestibility only for certain suggestions.

Bartlett (18) has also investigated the relationship of neurotic tendencies, as measured by the Bernreuter and the Maller personality tests, to suggestibility, as measured by the postural sway test. The resulting correlation was very small. This same investigator repeated (16) a study initially made by Travis (442) in which variations in auditory threshold, psychoneurosis, and suggestibility had been shown to be connected in such a way as to relate high suggestibility with psychoneurosis. Bartlett could not substantiate this. Dahm and Jenness (87) also repeated this experiment and arrived at the conclusion that the method employed was not valid. Barry, Mackinnon, and Murray (14) also declared that they could not find any relation between variations in auditory threshold and suggestibility. Hull (213) in summing up the available data concluded that there is no relation between neuroticism and high suggestibility.

However, since the publication of Hull's book, a number of careful studies of this question have been reported which throw a new light upon the entire problem. Eysenck (130–132), making use of over 1000 subjects diagnosed as psychoneurotics, studied their responses to the postural sway test. He was able to demonstrate that both psychoneurotics and normal individuals show the presence of primary and secondary suggestibility (as well as tertiary suggestibility). Furthermore, in the case of primary suggestibility, neurotics were found to be the more suggestible of the two groups. Arcieri (5) reported indirect confirmation of this by means of a picture test in which certain details are suggested to the subject. Since it is probable that this sort of test is not entirely one of primary suggestibility (in spite of the investigator's belief that it is), it may be better to say that he partly confirmed Eysenck's report. More direct confirmation has been offered more recently by Furneaux (153) who reported the results of giving mass suggestions of body sway to a normal group of men and women totaling 127. He found that less than 3 per cent of the subjects actually fell, as compared to the figure of 42 per cent reported for neurotics in an earlier study of his (152). However, as he remarked, the two investigations are not fully comparable since in the earlier one the subjects were tested individually. In particular, the effect of the group situation is an unknown quantity here. In spite of this, the results are suggestive. Ingwarson and Lindberg (220) tested individuals diagnosed as psychoneurotics by means of the odor illusion test. Although they themselves did not arrive at any definite conclusions, their results suggest that psychoneurotics (including hysterics) are more suggestible than normal persons are. This confirms and complements the conclusions of Eysenck. Gill (161) also concluded on the basis of his clinical experience in using hypnosis on war neuroses cases that neurotics are the more suggestible.

In a later report (131) Eysenck found that the degree of suggestibility of neurotic individuals is a direct function of their degree of neuroticism. His data were secured by means of a seven-point scale of neuroticism which he derived from a factor-analytical study of personality using mental patients. These last results, however, need further substantiation before they can be definitely accepted. Finally Himmelweit, Desai, and Petrie (197) found a correlation of 0.51 between response to body sway test and psychiatric diagnosis of neuroticism and deduced that this test had a factor saturation of 0.69 for a general factor of neuroticism isolated by means of the same technique as the one used by Eysenck (131). The main weakness of this study is the fact that no attempt was made to equate subject intelligence.

At this point a question arises. Which of these two groups of investigations are we to accept, or, to put it another way, how are we to account for the contradictory results that have been reported? A careful examination of the various investigations belonging to the first group shows that some of these cannot be given too much weight because of lack of adequate controls and/or the small number of subjects used. Second, Guilford and Guilford (174) and Mosier (318) have shown by means of factor-analytical methods that, for the Thurstone Personality Schedule and for a test very similar to the Bernreuter Personality Inventory, the individual tests for introversion–extraversion actually measure a large number of different traits. It is therefore a debatable point whether one is really measuring neurotic tendencies with such tests. Since this was the very basis for classifying individuals as neurotic and normal in the group under discussion, the validity of the results becomes questionable. Finally, those instances where suggestibility was measured by an inventory-type test cannot be said to be comparable to those in which actual suggestions were employed as test.‡ In spite of this it must be remarked that the relatively large number of reports in this group somewhat offsets its weaknesses.

On the other hand, the second group of investigations unquestionably represents a much superior group of studies from the standpoint

‡ This applies equally well to comparisons made between the results of studies like those of Eysenck and of Arcieri. The tests of suggestibility are not entirely comparable, but they do tend to be similar in character. Furthermore, when we say that they substantiate each other, we mean in regard to suggestibility in general and not in respect to any specific kind of suggestibility.

of number of subjects used, controls involved, and general procedures and techniques employed. Also greater attention is paid to details. We should then be led to give more weight to this particular group of studies, were it not for the fact already mentioned that the large number of investigations belonging to the first group gives it a certain amount of statistical reliability. It does not appear possible at this date to discard this group entirely in favor of the one headed by Eysenck. A better solution to the problem might be reached through a study of comparability.

The most outstanding difference between the two sets of investigations is that in one neuroticism was established by means of a *psychiatric diagnosis,* whereas in the other the same result was achieved on the basis of *inventory-type tests.* One apparent exception to this is the later report of Eysenck (131) in which the degree of neuroticism was measured. However, an examination of the questionnaire-type test he used shows that this last has some definite comparability with other forms of psychiatric examinations in its general character. It does appear then that we can decide the following from these various investigations: *If we define neuroticism in terms of the results of a standard psychiatric examination,* then the evidence strongly favors the conclusion that *neurotics are more suggestible than normal individuals.* On the other hand, *if we define neuroticism in terms of the results obtained from personality inventory-type tests,* particularly on the basis of introversion-extraversion scales, *neurotics would appear to be no more nor less suggestible than normal individuals.*

In other words, the contradictions between the two groups of results can be resolved by realizing that some of the tests used measure different things. There are indeed good reasons to believe that this is so. In the first place, a psychiatric examination aims at formulating a diagnosis on an over-all picture of the subject's total behavior. Personality inventory tests and other similar tests tend to lead to a judgment arrived at on the basis of a study of a small number of elements which either characterize certain aspects of behavior or presumably cause these aspects. Second, personality inventories and their like really measure *tendencies* toward neuroticism rather than *neuroticism itself.* It is not even certain that individuals with such tendencies necessarily become neurotic. On the other hand, a psychiatric diagnosis of neuroticism usually means that a definite neurotic state is present and not just a tendency toward one.

Although hysteria belongs to the psychoneuroses, it was singled out historically when it became the focus of a rather remarkable controversy. Without going into detail, it may be said to have centered about Janet's (223) assertion that the most important symptom of hysteria was increased suggestibility. Although a great many investigators have reaffirmed this statement, there is actually little empirical evidence for it. Travis (443), Bartlett (15), and Ingwarson and Lindberg (220) among others investigated it to some extent, but their results are inconclusive. Eysenck (132) was able to show, making use of psychiatric diagnoses of hysteria and of other psychoneuroses, on the one hand, and of a battery of suggestibility tests, on the other, that *hysterics are no more suggestible than other psychoneurotics,* although primary suggestibility appears to be slightly higher for the former. Arcieri (5) has confirmed these results.

Eysenck (131) has brought up the question of what type of suggestibility is invoked when psychiatrists state that there is a relation between neurosis (or hysteria) and suggestibility. In attempting to answer this question he points to a description by Janet (223) of what a suggestion is. This, he remarks, appears to best designate primary suggestibility. Furthermore, as Eysenck also remarks, Janet and nearly all if not all of those who accepted his views took hypnotic suggestibility as the prototype of all forms of suggestibility. But, as has been mentioned and as will be seen more in detail later, primary suggestibility is highly correlated with hypnosis, in contrast to secondary suggestibility. It would appear then, for the time being, that primary suggestibility is what Janet and others were referring to.

The suggestibility of one more category of individuals, the psychotics, remains to be examined. According to Kraepelin and Bleuler, manic depressives are suggestible, in contrast to schizophrenics who are not. Naumov (320) has stated without further qualification that insane individuals are four times more suggestible than sane persons.

Williams (487) tested psychotic individuals by means of the postural sway test. He reported that catatonics are negatively suggestible but that there is no difference between the suggestibility of schizophrenic paranoids and that of normal persons. Manic depressives were found by him to be a little more negative and somewhat less responsive than normal individuals. Barry et al. (14), using their own scale of suggestibility, also found that catatonic subjects tend to be negatively suggestible, compared to other schizophrenic types. Bartlett (15, 17) has repeated Williams' investigation and has substantiated his results in part, but not entirely. Inasmuch as Webb (459) has shown that the validity of Bartlett's investigation is in serious doubt, we should not place too much reliance on it. Ingwarson and Lindberg (220) have reported results that show no essential differences between normal and psychotic suggestibility, though on the average schizophrenics seem to tend somewhat toward lesser suggestibility, whereas manic depressives are not different from normal individuals. Arcieri (5) found that suggestibility increases in this order: schizophrenic, normal, psychoneurotic. Within the schizophrenic group, he found hebephrenics to have the least suggestibility, then catatonics, and finally paranoids. Whether schizophrenics as a group are just merely less suggestible than normal persons, or really negatively suggestible, is not shown by his results. On the whole his findings are in agreement with those obtained by Williams.

Regarding the induction of hypnosis as a measure of suggestibility, there is further indication that psychotics are suggestible to even a high degree. Wilson, Cormen, and Cole (491) have found that in general one can hypnotize individuals suffering from organic and functional psychoses (this statement applies to schizophrenics of the functional type only), contrary to popular opinion. However, changes in induction technique have to be made, and they point out that their results indicate that new criteria for the various stages of hypnosis will probably have to be developed to cover these situations.

It is generally agreed that feebleminded individuals are not suggestible. Whether this is an inherent trait or is merely the result of an inability to communicate properly with such individuals is not known. Both reasons are probably true. In line with the work of Wilson et al., it definitely appears that the question of accessibility to the subject at the communication level is a powerful limiting factor in any attempt to test suggestibility. It is most probable that earlier negative reports and others showing a depressed suggestibility may have arisen out of this limitation rather than out of a true innate lack in suggestibility.

On the whole, it can be said that, when standard suggestions and standard methods of giving suggestions are used, *psychotics are less suggestible than normal and psychoneurotic individuals.*

Summary and Conclusions

In conclusion and review it would appear that suggestibility is universal, and to be found in normal as well as abnormal individuals. Although the criterion chosen of what constitutes acceptable evidence of suggestibility is rather arbitrary and will of necessity increase or decrease the percentage of individuals who may be said to be suggestible, it would appear safe to state that nearly everybody is suggestible to some degree insofar as primary suggestibility is concerned. As was already mentioned, Furneaux found that 97 per cent of the population will sway more than 6 inches when given the postural sway test. Although, as will be seen subsequently, age, sex, and other factors affect suggestibility to some extent, the universality of this phenomenon persists. On the other hand, even after such factors have been equated, it is found that suggestibility varies with different individuals.   In respect to normal and abnormal personalities, suggestibility has been found to decrease in the order psychoneurotics, normals, psychotics, as follows:

Mixed psychoneurotics ⎱ Psychoneurotic group
Hysterics   ⎰

College students ⎱ So-called "normals"
Nonstudents   ⎰

Paranoid schizophrenics ⎱ Psychotic group
Catatonic schizophrenics ⎰

This has been most satisfactorily demonstrated for the case of primary suggestibility and less so for secondary suggestibility. It should not be inferred from the above that highly suggestible individuals must necessarily be neurotic, nor that nonsuggestible subjects must be schizophrenic. Even if it were not an observed fact, we would expect some normal individuals to show high suggestibility and some to have low suggestibility, purely because of natural variations between individuals. If neurotics are more suggestible *on the average* than normal persons and psychotics are less suggestible, this, we must assume for the present, is the result of alterations superimposed upon natural tendencies.

States of Heightened Suggestibility

Thus far we have spoken of suggestibility as if it were a constant characteristic of individuals, that is, as if, for a given individual, and with respect to a specific test, we always found the same degree of suggestibility. It will be seen later that actually there are a number of factors capable of influencing the degree of suggestibility of any individual. In fact, from the discussion of the last chapter it has already been seen that the presence of neurosis appears to be associated with an increase in suggestibility, while psychosis seems to be connected with a decrease. But in most such instances the change in suggestibility with respect to the normal mean value is not very large. Furthermore these conditions are relatively static and appear primarily in the form of a slow shift of equilibrium; that is, they are of the nature of quasisteady states. There is, however, a set of circumstances that does usually produce a spectacular heightening of such a magnitude that we often speak of "hypersuggestibility" being present. In addition, the change involved usually takes place over a relatively short period of time and is more in the nature of a kinetic, if not a dynamic, process. There is also another reason for distinguishing this sort of increase in suggestibility from others that will be taken up presently. It is with the production of "hypersuggestibility" that the present chapter will be primarily concerned.

The Problem of Hypersuggestibility

The nature of the problem considered here may possibly be better understood if a few of its aspects are considered first. Heightening of suggestibility is most apparent, of course, in the use of hypnotic suggestions. Normally, in such instances, the experimenter is dealing with a subject who shows some suggestibility to waking suggestions, but to no particularly large degree. The experimenter then proceeds to induce hypnosis by means of a standard technique such as visual fixation combined with suggestions. This may take but a few minutes. After this treatment, it may be observed in most instances that the subject has become extremely suggestible—so much so that many investigators have been led to consider "hypersuggestibility" a characteristic and criterion of the hypnotic state. Whereas, before being hypnotized the subject could carry out only simple suggestions, it is now found that he will execute extremely complex ones. As a matter of fact he now appears able to perform tasks that are beyond his voluntary capacities. Apparently then, the subject's capacity for accepting and executing suggestions has been increased.

A closer examination of this situation appears to indicate, however, that there is more to it than the above. Schilder and Kauder (392), for instance, have pointed out that a number of earlier investigators as well as they themselves had found it efficacious to give their subjects some waking suggestions easy of execution before attempting to hypnotize them. This appeared to facilitate the process. Bernheim (28), as well as the majority of hypnotists who have succeeded him, have also noted that, once an individual has been hypnotized, he appears to be more receptive to subsequent suggestions in the *waking* state. I myself have observed numerous instances that support the above and have been able to make effective use of these facts in my practice. Finally, to all this we must add the fact that a subject's waking suggestibility can be very much improved by means of post-hypnotic suggestions directed at this objective. Here then we have situations of heightened suggestibility other than the hypnotic state itself.

It is to Hull (213) and his co-workers that we owe the empirical demonstration of the actual existence of heightened states of suggestibility and of some of the properties these states possess. However, before considering their findings, a little more needs to be said concerning the notion of "hypersuggestibility." Hull (213) has employed this term primarily in connection with suggestibility as observed in the hypnotic state. At the same time we get the impression from reading his book that he also meant by it *any* heightening of suggestibility resulting from an individual's response to a prior suggestion.

The fact of the matter is that "hypersuggestibility" is not at all well defined in the literature. To what degree an individual's suggestibility must increase and what standard it is to be measured against before it may be qualified as "hyper-" have never been stated. While it is true that neurotics are more suggestible than normals, they also show considerable heightening of suggestibility when hypnotized. It is a significant fact that no neurotic has yet been shown to have a degree of suggestibility higher than the highest degree attained by any normal individual. Clearly, heightened suggestibility, as observed in neurotics, is not apparently what we call a case of hypersuggestibility.

If we examine some of the characteristics of hypnosis, it soon becomes evident that one of these is that a whole group of suggestions exists to which an individual who has never been hypnotized before usually will not respond. Obviously the capacity to respond to such a group of suggestions is what, for the majority of hypnotists, constitutes hypersuggestibility. It is therefore tempting to use as reference point either the average normal suggestibility or the average maximal suggestibility attained by normal individuals. Then any individual showing suggestibility greater than the point of reference would be said to be hypersuggestible.

Unfortunately, this does not work satisfactorily. In the first place, the tests that are available have shown, by the distribution curves associated with them, that the normal individual exhibits all degrees of suggestibility as measured by these tests. As will be seen later, many individuals showing maximal suggestibility (i.e., the average maximal value for the population under consideration) may reach a still higher value when hypnotized. Furthermore, the mean value cannot be used, for this would force us to classify as hypersuggestible all individuals grouped on the half of the distribution curve that includes all values greater than the mean. Yet many of these when hypnotized will show a considerable rise in suggestibility. Obviously what is needed is a definition of "hypersuggestibility" that will enable us to make the demarkation line between hyper- and normal suggestibility *specific for each individual.* Something of this sort was implied by Hull (213) when he remarked that hypnotic hypersuggestibility had only a relative significance, since what constituted hypersuggestibility for one might not for another. These observations lead us to define "hypersuggestibility" as follows:

*Given a set of suggestions, graded in terms of the difficulty met in obtaining responses to them, we shall say that an individual is in a hypersuggestible state when he is able to respond to the least difficult suggestion that he had failed to respond to previously while in the waking state.**

* This definition is quite general, and the use of "waking suggestion" in it should not be taken to imply that hypersuggestibility is defined for hypnosis only. It might be added here that the least difficult suggestion that the subject fails to respond to under any set of conditions establishes his *limiting suggestibility,* LS, for the particular set of conditions. If this LS is used as reference value for further tests, it becomes what may best be called the subject's *basal suggestibility level,* or BSL.

In this manner we can set up a scale of suggestibility which is on a continuum extending through the region of hypersuggestibility. In the sense of this definition, and only in this sense can we speak unambiguously of hypnosis as a state of hypersuggestibility.

From what has already been said, it appears that it has generally been held that the act of carrying out a suggestion predisposes the subject more favorably toward carrying out future suggestions, that is, creates a state of heightened suggestibility. Again, it is generally agreed that hypnosis is associated with a similar state. Finally, there exists a widespread belief that certain drugs can bring about a state of hypersuggestibility. The remainder of this chapter will deal with these situations.

Homoaction, Heteroaction, and Allied Phenomena

In order to test for hypersuggestibility it is necessary to give the subject a minimum of two test suggestions: one at the start of the experiment and one at the end. Two experimental situations then arise: (a) The two suggestions are similar, that is, call forth the same response, or (b) they are dissimilar, that is, call forth different responses. Hull (213) has proposed that, if hypersuggestibility is observed, it be designated as *homoactive* in the first instance, and it be called *heteroactive* in the second.

Now presumably either kind could arise through the influence of any number of factors. In particular we may consider the situation consisting of nothing more than giving the subject suggestions of various kinds with varying intervals of time between suggestions. Here one studies the influence of responding to a suggestion upon the response to a subsequent suggestion. This can be done with all the suggestions being given in the waking state, all of them given in the hypnotic state, or some given in the waking state and the others given in the hypnotic state. Of special interest in this connection are the suggestions employed to produce hypnosis, which will henceforth be referred to as *trance-inducing suggestions*. These hold a rather special position, inasmuch as they are neither entirely of the waking type nor entirely of the hypnotic type, but partake of both types. For, obviously, at the start of the trance induction the suggestions are being given while the subject is in the waking state, whereas at the termination of these suggestions the subject is hypnotized. Somewhere along the way the suggestions pass from the waking type into the hypnotic type. Just how the suggestibility of the subject changes as the induction of hypnosis progresses is an important question. Of equal importance are the changes in suggestibility that follow a return to the waking state.

Assuming that some heightening of suggestibility is observed following the administration of one or more suggestions, Hull (213) has pointed out that this might be the result of at least two phenomena taking place singly or together. One of these he assumes is a true property of suggestibility and is what he appears to refer to when he speaks of homoactive or heteroactive hypersuggestibility. The other is a property of responses in general whereby repeated trials produce a facilitation of succeeding responses. This is usually called the *practice effect*. In general, then, observed hypersuggestibility would result from the addition of two increments of different origins. Conceivably some instances of heightened suggestibility might arise entirely through practice effect. These would not be considered true cases of hypersuggestibility. Another effect which Hull and his associates have been concerned with is as follows: When two suggestions are given in succession and each while the subject is in a different state, if the two states themselves have an effect upon suggestibility independently of any possible effect the suggestions may have, it is possible that the influence of the first state might carry over into the second state. Consequently, any change observed in the second state in regard to suggestibility would be partly spurious insofar as resulting from the influence of the first suggestion. Thus the investigation of hypersuggestibility becomes a somewhat more complex problem than might at first have appeared. Fortunately, for the purpose of this book the general situation can be greatly simplified.† It may be said quite generally that there is a *homoactive effect*, or *homoaction*, whenever the response to a suggestion alters the response to a subsequent *repetition* ‡ of this suggestion. On the other hand we may say that there is a *heteroactive effect*, or *heteroaction*, whenever the response to a suggestion alters the response to a subsequent but *different* suggestion. If the effect is a true increase in suggestibility, the homoaction or heteroaction will be said to be *positive*, whereas, if a decrease in suggestibility ensues, these two actions will be said *negative*.§ We shall also say in the first instance, and only then, that there is a *cumulative*

† The reader interested in the more complex aspects of this problem will find an excellent treatment of it in Williams' paper (488).

‡ Or a similar suggestion, that is, one evoking the same response.

§ Most work done in this area has been concerned with positive influences; hence, unless otherwise stated, we shall use "homoaction" and "heteroaction" in the next pages to designate only the positive form.

effect (or *cumulation*) if two and only two suggestions are involved. If a series of suggestions is given, each giving rise to positive homoaction, we shall speak of *multiple cumulation* being present. Whenever the effects on suggestibility of a given state (usually hypnosis), or of responses given to suggestion in a given state, persist, that is, are carried over into a different and subsequent state, we shall say that there is a *perseverative effect* (or *perseveration*). Whether or not all of these effects are truly distinct from each other will be considered shortly. Let us however now consider the available data.

Evidence for Homoaction and Heteroaction

Hull and Huse (214) have shown beyond question that repetition of postural sway suggestions increases the subject's suggestibility up to a certain point. This homoactive effect, they found, follows rather closely the trend shown by standard habituation curves. Williams (488) repeated this investigation, making use of additional tests of suggestibility. His results substantiate those of Hull and Huse in respect to postural sway. On the other hand, his data also showed that all tests are not equal insofar as homoaction is concerned. Thus, while the progressive weight test showed homoaction of the same order of magnitude as the postural sway test, the heat illusion test did not appear to be able to bring about homoaction, and the progressive line test gave a slight negative homoactive effect. Caster and Baker (67) found appreciable homoaction when suggestions of horizontal arm swaying were given. Hull, Patten, and Switzer (215) have confirmed the results for postural sway. This was also done by Berreman and Hilgard (29). On the average, it appears that the maximum increase in suggestibility that may be obtained by homoaction is of the order of 20 per cent for simple cumulation, and as much as 60 per cent for multiple cumulation.||

Hull, Patten, and Switzer (215); Patten, Switzer, and Hull (333); and Patten (336) later have been unable to find any evidence of heteroaction in connection with postural sway suggestions. On the other hand, Corn-Becker, Welch, and Fisichelli (81) have found evidence of a heteroactive-like effect in the form of "abstract condition-

|| It needs to be emphasized that "homoaction" and "heteroaction," as employed in this discussion, are more general than Hull's notions of heteroactive and homoactive hypersuggestibility, and in particular include any habituation phenomenon that might be present. One of the problems the investigator is faced with here is the determination of how much of observed homoaction or heteroaction is contributed by, say, practice.

ing," which will be taken up at greater length in a later chapter. Inasmuch as the evidence indicates that two distinct processes are probably active in these two sets of studies, there is no real contradiction between the reported results.

The results of Hull and Huse (214) and of Williams (488) have shown that homoaction takes place to about the same extent in hypnosis and in waking, insofar as primary suggestibility is concerned. In the case of secondary suggestibility, hypnosis appears to favor homoaction to some extent. No data are available in regard to heteroaction.

Effects of Hypnosis on Suggestibility. Perseverative Effect

Suggestibility to specific suggestions in hypnosis and in waking have been considered by Hull and Huse (214) and by Williams (488). These investigators found in general that there was greater suggestibility in hypnosis. Postural sway suggestion showed the greatest advantage, this being of the order of 30 to 40 per cent. Other tests showed a smaller increase. The progressive weight test was observed by Williams to be associated with greater suggestibility in the waking state. However, there is reason to believe that this resulted from an artifact created by the technique used. Caster and Baker (67), using suggestions of horizontal arm motion, have confirmed the conclusion that primary suggestibility is higher in hypnosis. Jenness (226) has substantiated this last study.

Hull and Huse (214) concluded from their data that perseveration is a reality. Williams (488) substantiated this for postural sway. On the other hand, he could not find any evidence that perseveration was present in connection with the other tests he studied except for the heat illusion test which showed a slight trend in this direction. Caster and Baker (67), on the other hand, did not find any evidence of perseveration. It may be that this was caused by their placing a different interpretation on their results. We shall come back to this in a moment. In general, perseveration of homoaction from one state to another has been the only effect investigated in the above, although, since the investigators did not attempt to eliminate the possible perseveration of trance hypersuggestibility itself, the reported figures may be somewhat higher than they should be. Perseveration under the above conditions appears to be of the order of 20 per cent. The effect is observed to be present both when the subject is passing from trance to waking state and conversely, although it is definitely less in the second instance, thus supporting the view that there is also a perseveration of hypnotic hypersuggestibility. That there is was shown by Krueger (244).

A phenomenon closely related to perseveration is the influence of the response to waking suggestions upon actual trance induction. It is generally agreed that there is a facilitating effect. Caster and Baker (67) have observed that suggestions of arm movement facilitate trance induction when they precede it. This was substantiated by Jenness (226). The heightening in suggestibility amounts to 20 or 30 per cent. Because of the intermediate position that trance-inducing suggestions hold, we cannot exactly speak here of perseveration. On the other hand, since the influence was of arm movement suggestions upon lid closure and other associated responses, it is of a heteroactive type. This is a rather significant fact, for, as was brought out a few pages back, it has not been possible to demonstrate heteroaction between suggested head movement and suggested arm movement, although both showed the presence of homoaction. Since, as was just mentioned, trance-inducing suggestions hold a somewhat special place, this apparent contradiction was not brought up earlier. It should be clear now, however, that a complete treatment of heteroaction must take this aspect into consideration.

The Fate of Suggestibility During and Following Trance Induction. The Decay Effect

Krueger (244) has made a very interesting investigation of the fate of suggestibility during trance induction, after the appearance of the trance, and after waking has been reinstated. His results showed that homoactive hypersuggestibility is present. It is found to rise rather rapidly during the induction phase, reach a maximum shortly after the appearance of the trance state,¶ and then, following a small dip which may or may not be significant, level off for an indeterminate amount of time (at least 10 minutes). The maximum rise in suggestibility which Krueger reported was 70 per cent, whereas, after leveling off, the trance suggestibility showed a heightening of about 60 per cent. After the waking from the trance, the suggestibility showed a rapid drop at first and tended to level off after a few minutes, slowly reaching a level corresponding to a 20 per cent hypersuggestibility at the end of about 60 minutes. Krueger did not obtain data beyond this length of time. There is a general belief, however, that trance hypersuggestibility tends to persist to some extent for a longer period than this.

¶ This is assumed to have taken place when lid closure is obtained.

The above decay of hypersuggestibility is not characteristic only of trance hypersuggestibility. A study of the data which have been reported by the various investigators cited in previous pages of this chapter shows that the increase in suggestibility associated with the cumulative effect decays in time after the cessation of the suggestions. The demonstration of this effect from the data just referred to is rather involved and will not be given here.* There are also indications that the decay curve in this case is a negatively accelerated trend. Furthermore, the initial rate of decay appears to vary inversely with the initial height of the suggestibility. In this instance the rate of decay is relatively slow. For homoaction it can be shown to cause a drop of about 9 per cent in 24 hours, the decay being greatest in the first few hours. This phenomenon can in a fashion be directly inferred from the observation by Hull and Huse (214), Williams (488), and others that repeated suggestions lead to a progressive rise in homoactive hypersuggestibility which follows a negatively accelerated trend. It is clear that there must be a decay of such hypersuggestibility since it is well established that under these conditions the hypersuggestibility reached at any given state does not last forever. On the other hand, if the drop in hypersuggestibility following cessation of the suggestion, or rather the response to it, was instantaneous, or nearly so, it would not be possible to observe the above progressive rise in suggestibility. The very existence of a summation effect leads to the prediction of a relatively slow decay.† As will be shown presently, other properties of the curve of heightening of suggestibility are explained by the existence of such a decay effect.

As pointed out above in connection with the decay of the cumulative effect, there appears to be a relationship between rate of decay and initial height of the suggestibility at the time the decay starts. A somewhat analogous situation also appears in relation to the increment in suggestibility resulting from homoaction. This increment would seem to be inversely related to the initial height of the subject's suggestibility, or rather to vary directly with the distance (on the suggestibility continuum) which separates his present suggestibility from the

---

* Though the data of Patten et al. (333), Hull et al. (215), and Berreman and Hilgard (29) form the basis for this, it should be noted that none of these investigators has derived such an effect from their results. At least they have made no explicit statements to this effect.

† To anticipate a little, it may be added that this applies equally well to the interpretation that hypersuggestibility is merely the result of facilitation inherently associated with performance of *any* response.

maximum suggestibility he may have reached under the existing conditions. The existence of this property can be derived from the same analysis which demonstrates the existence, properties, and magnitude of the decay effect.

Hypersuggestibility and Habituation

It was remarked earlier that Hull and his associates believed that heightened suggestibility could be the result of two distinct and separate phenomena. One would be an intrinsic property of suggestibility whereas the other would be a similar property of all responses. This last is what is usually called the practice effect. Two other alternatives obviously exist: (1) Heightening of suggestibility is entirely the result of practice, and, conversely, (2) it is entirely the result of the said intrinsic property of suggestibility.

Hull (213) has offered some very strong arguments in favor of the hypothesis that hypersuggestibility in general is a habituation phenomenon arising through practice effect and hence is essentially a learning process. The basis for his contention lies in the results that have been reported by him and his associates. Hull and Huse (214) found for postural sway suggestions given in hypnosis and waking a progressive facilitation of responses which obeyed a negatively accelerated trend. Williams (488) has reported similar trends.‡ Krueger's (244) results are also in agreement with this. Patten, Switzer, and Hull (333) have also substantiated the results for postural sway. Krueger (245) studied the question for hypnosis. He investigated the effect on trance susceptibility § of inducing hypnosis in quick succession, and of repeatedly hypnotizing with longer time intervals between. He also investigated the effect of allowing a relatively long period of time to pass between two such series of trance induction (periods of disuse). His results show effects similar to those that are observed under similar conditions in habituation phenomena. On the other hand, Eysenck and Furneaux (129) stated that they could not find evidence of any practice effect for postural sway. Actually, what these investigators call practice appears to be simply the cumulative effect. Their results are puzzling, however, because they are careful investigators and the reported study appears to be entirely satisfactory from an experimental point of view. Furthermore, with 100 subjects

‡ Williams has reported figures on the extent of day-by-day and test-by-test practice effect. It is clear, however, that his figures do not show whether or not they were the result of a habituation phenomenon, or even only in part.

§ That is, the suggestibility of the subject to trance-inducing suggestions.

the statistical validity of the results appears assured. On the other hand, there is little question but that the evidence for the existence of cumulation is overwhelming at present. Possibly the answer for this discrepancy is to be found in the measures used in the two groups of studies. Eysenck and Furneaux made use of maximal sway in inches for a specific duration of suggestion. In the other studies that have been discussed, the duration of suggestion required to bring about a specified amount of sway was employed for measure. It is my opinion that this last type of measure is much more sensitive than the first and could well lead to detecting differences not shown by the former. Also, Eysenck and Furneaux made use of mental patients for subjects, whereas normal individuals were employed by the other investigators. Though it has been shown that suggestibility is universally found among normal and aberrant individuals, it is still possible that some of the aspects of suggestibility might not be the same in the two groups. In any event, the reality of heightening of suggestibility appears established.

It is not possible to deny the strong resemblance between homoactive phenomena, and the properties of trance suggestibility as seen thus far, on the one hand, and habituation phenomena, on the other. However, to go so far as to say that they are identical is not prudent. In the final analysis, there is little evidence that heightening of suggestibility results from a combination of an intrinsic property of suggestibility and practice effect. Hull and his associates have taken the position that suggestibility phenomena are entirely habituation phenomena. It is my opinion, on the contrary, that suggestibility may not be identified with habituation, unless the concept of habituation be revised and expanded, for there are a large number of facts typical of suggestibility that are not accounted for by present-day theories of habit formation. For instance, habituation does not explain the existence of two and possibly three types of suggestibility. Habituation would lead us to expect heteroactive effects similar to those observed for homoaction. But that has not been the case thus far. As will be seen shortly, the effects of certain drugs on suggestibility do not hold for habituation. The same may be said of other factors which appear to be associated with high and low degrees of suggestibility. Finally, the comparative ease and rapidity with which *certain* phenomena can be induced through suggestibility has no equivalent among habituation phenomena. As a matter of fact there may be some question whether certain suggestibility phenomena can be produced through habit formation. Further arguments against Hull's viewpoint will be given in more appropriate places. In any event, a great many more aspects of both suggestibility and habituation will have to be investigated with possible identification in mind before more definite conclusions can be reached. It may be remarked, however, in addition to the above, that the existence of similar characteristic trends is by no means proof of identity. There are a great many phenomena in nature that give rise to similar trends and mathematical expressions because they possess similar (isomorphic) structures and yet are not at all the same in other respects. That habituation and suggestibility should give rise to similar phenomena may arise in another way, namely, from the fact that both express themselves through the neuromuscular system. In fact they are properties of this system and may be expected to exhibit common characteristics, although this is not necessarily so. Until more definite evidence is made available that the two phenomena are identical, it seems best to speak of homoaction and heteroaction as phenomena characteristic of suggestibility, and to say that, though in many respects they resemble habituation, and like it are expressions of neuromuscular properties, they are to be considered as distinct from habituation.

Other Issues

Before we pass on to the last topic of this chapter, a few words should be said concerning three questions connected with the heightening of suggestibility by suggestions.|| Patten (336) has considered the possibility of raising the suggestibility of an individual, with respect to a given suggestion, through the heteroactive influence of another suggestion directly aimed at this effect, this being done in the waking state. He reports finding no evidence of such an action. However, Patten's experiment leaves something to be desired, since the suggestion that there would be increased suggestibility was given in a very indirect manner and one can hardly draw general conclusions from it. Certainly, if we are to believe Wells (473), who unfortunately does not furnish much evidence in support of his claims, waking suggestions specially aimed at producing hypersuggestibility for other waking

---

|| One might also point out that Hull and his co-workers employed as a criterion of hypnosis the closure of the subject's eyes. No particular attempts seem to have been made to determine the actual trance depth, or to deepen the trance state following this event. Since, as will be seen later, the degree of hypnosis attained by a subject at the time of eyelid closure is variable, and since his trance may be deepened after this event has taken place, one must use Hull's data with some qualifications.

suggestions should be effective. Of course, it is a well-accepted fact that posthypnotic suggestions may be employed to raise suggestibility to waking suggestions. For instance, the author has measured the time required to obtain lid closure the first time with three medium and three very suggestible subjects. They were given the same code word during the first session, with the suggestion that any time the author said it they would immediately go into a very deep trance state. Measurements made when the code word was employed showed an average thirty-fold increase in rate of induction. On the other hand, when trance-inducing suggestions were used a second time to induce hypnosis, the rate of induction was found to be on the average only one and a half times faster.

In view of the existence of homoaction, it might be suspected that the effectiveness of a suggestion may depend upon its length, that is, duration. For in one respect repetition of the desired effect is equivalent to giving repeatedly a shorter suggestion, and, if the subject gives any amount of response whatsoever to such a suggestion at any stage, homoaction effective for the next repetition should appear. From this point on, multiple cumulation should be the consequence. Not too much information is available on this matter. Eysenck and Furneaux (129) have studied the effect of giving a large group of subjects the postural sway test for 30 seconds and 2½ minutes. On the average they observed an increase in maximum sway of 4 to 5 inches when the longer suggestions were given. Since they could not find evidence of practice effect in this case, they concluded that the increased length was the effective factor. Further substantiation for this comes from Krueger's (244) study on the rise of suggestibility during trance induction. His results show that trance-inducing suggestions of duration less than that required for lid closure bring about a more or less proportionally smaller increase in suggestibility. Although the question of just where the waking suggestions in trance induction become hypnotic suggestions has not been answered, the fact that we know that homoaction is not appreciably affected by hypnosis permits us to accept the above as evidence that increased length of suggestions favors heightening of suggestibility within limits.

Finally, we should mention an interesting and significant observation reported by Williams (488). He found, somewhat by accident, that, when nonsuggestible subjects *simulated* the characteristics of both the trance behavior and a positive response to suggestions of postural sway, they exhibited an actual *facilitation* in their simulated response to postural sway (they showed a more rapid response). The improvement was of 11.5 per cent and definitely less than that shown by hypnotized subjects. Other effects, such as perseveration and cumulation, were also found to be present, but to a lesser degree than is observed in the case of true responses to suggestions. This rather interesting observation is in itself evidence against the habituation hypothesis, since, if the latter were correct, we should expect simulation to give rise to effects of the same magnitude as nonsimulated responses. On the other hand, these results appear to indicate that *it is probably the response to a suggestion* more than the suggestion itself that is responsible for heightening of suggestibility.

Suggestibility and Drugs

The effect of drugs upon suggestibility remains to be considered. Earlier investigators like Milne Bramwell, and Schilder and Kauder have advocated the use of ether, chloroform, and various narcotics as adjuvants to hypnosis.

Hull (213) has reported testing the effect of alcohol on suggestibility. Unfortunately he never concluded this investigation. He believed, however, that, although definite physiological effects were obtained, there was little if any influence on postural sway.

Starkey (422) has reported that light ether "hypnosis" increases suggestibility. Schilder and Kauder (392) agree with this, but prefer evipan and paraldehyde to ether and chloroform as less variable and more certain. Haupman (185) shows a preference for intravenous evipan. Stungo (433) also found that a 10 per cent solution of evipan administered intravenously in subanesthetic doses increases suggestibility. He goes further and asserts that it can also induce a sort of artificial hypnosis. Dick (96) agrees that evipan increases suggestibility, and also lists pentothal as doing the same. Horsley (209) reported that nembutal, sodium amytal, and sodium pentothal increase suggestibility and can be used to bring about a state of narcosis in which all of the phenomena of suggestibility can be produced. Brotteaux (55) has compounded scopolamine and chloral into what he calls scopochloralose. He maintains that with it he can obtain reliable hypnosis in the most refractory subjects, even in those with whom other drugs have failed. Rogerson (373) reported observing an increase in suggestibility following intravenous injections of various barbiturates and also after the inhalation of nitrous oxide. Wilson (494) has reported that caffeine increases suggestibility and also that breathing a mixture of nitrous oxide and air (or oxygen) will produce a state of perfect suggestibility with persistence of consciousness. The actual proportions for the mixtures are found to be variable and a function of the subject. Kubie (246) has reviewed the various drugs that are employed in practice to induce so-called "hypnagogic states." Though such states are not to be identified by any means with hypnosis, it is usually considered by those making use of these states that the induction of hypnosis is facilitated either by the hypnagogic states themselves or by the drugs. Hadfield (175) and Wolberg (497) are of this opinion. Ravitz (359) also reported that amobarbital reduces resistance to hypnosis.

Unfortunately not much is available on this topic along experimental lines. An incomplete study by Hull on the influence of alcohol has already been mentioned. Baernstein (9) studied the effect of sco-polamine upon suggestibility to postural sway and found that the drug caused an increase in suggestibility, but only if the subjects were initially suggestible. Those that were nonsuggestible (resistant) re-mained so. Eysenck and Rees (133) have pointed out quite justly that in Baernstein's experiment it may be questioned whether the drug actually increased the suggestibility, and may not have simply in-creased the subject's static ataxia. They declare that Eysenck has found a correlation of 0.60 between static ataxia and body sway sug-gestibility. In order to circumvent this possible weakness, Eysenck and Rees made a similar study using the press and release test and studied the comparative effects of sodium amytal and of nitrous oxide on the responses to these tests. Their investigation is probably the best of its kind made thus far. Their results agree with those of Baernstein and show that subanesthetic doses of either drug increase primary suggestibility, but only if the subjects are normally suggestible to begin with. The increased suggestibility was found to be on the average 1.3 to 2.3 times the suggestibility before narcotization.

As will be seen in a later chapter, the use of the term "drug hypnosis" has been an unfortunate choice and is rather misleading, since it implies something it does not do, for all evidence points to the fact that narcosis, even when light, is not the same as hypnosis. Drugs create neither hypnosis nor suggestibility. As Horsley (210) has re-marked, if hypnosis is present when certain narcotic drugs are used, it is *superimposed* upon the state of narcosis and is brought about through interaction between the experimenter (or practitioner) and the patient, and not by the drug itself.

There are various possible explanations for this facilitation. One is that such drugs induce relaxation in the subject, a state that has been generally believed to favor suggestibility. There is little experimental evidence for or against this belief. Barry et al. (14) have made a study of suggestibility to postural sway suggestions in the "normal state," the "relaxed state," and in the "daydream state." They found evidence that these three states have some influence on suggestibility, the daydream and relaxed states being most alike in this respect and the waking and relaxed states the least alike. Unfortunately they do not report in what direction these influences were, so that the above belief remains unsubstantiated.

To terminate this discussion, we might mention a number of reports concerning the influence of hyperventilation on suggestibility. Cohen and Cobb (72) found some indication that hyperventilation increases susceptibility to hypnosis. This had been suggested at an earlier date by Stockert (430). Sargant and Fraser (389) reported the same for neurotic individuals. This was confirmed by Talbot et al. (438) and by Seeligmuller (408). Since hyperventilation leads to alkalosis, it can be considered in this respect as a pharmacodynamical agent. How this influence comes about is still to be determined. It should be noted that the above holds primarily for hypnosis, or rather its induction, and can be said to apply to waking suggestibility only indirectly through the latter.

Summary and Conclusions

It may be well to summarize briefly the main results examined in this chapter, inasmuch as the numerous facets of the problem of heightened suggestibility tend to be confusing. In general, it has been seen that primary suggestibility can be increased through homoaction, that is, through the repetition of the same suggestion, provided the subject responds to some extent, however small, to the first statement of the suggestion. This appears to be a consequence of the fact that response to a suggestion tends to facilitate response to a repetition of this suggestion. This facilitation persists over a period of time, although it gradually decays. When repeated similar suggestions are given with sufficient rapidity, the suggestibility for the same progressively increases, eventually attaining a limiting value. The trend that this increase follows is similar to that followed by habituation. This homoaction is found to be the same in properties and magnitude in both waking and hypnosis. Furthermore, homoaction produced in one state tends to persevere into the other. Although homoaction is also found in secondary and tertiary suggestibility, its properties are less well defined, and its magnitude is definitely smaller. Except in connection with trance induction, no evidence of heteroaction has been found for primary, secondary, or tertiary suggestibility.

Trance-inducing suggestions hold a place that is unique, inasmuch as they are employed to produce hypnosis and are only partly of a

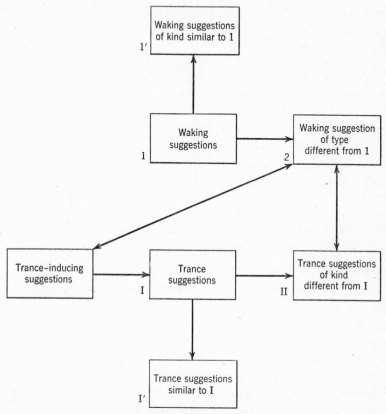

FIG. 1. Interactions between Suggestions

Arrows indicate direction of interaction. Thus, for instance, trance suggestions I affect suggestibility to trance suggestions I′ or II in a unidirectional manner. But waking suggestions 2 and trance suggestions II have a bidirectional effect on their respective suggestibility.

waking character. They are also unique in that they have a very strong heteroactive influence on other suggestions, besides showing a similar homoactive effect. In respect to this last, trance-inducing suggestions do not appear to differ essentially from other suggestions capable of eliciting primary suggestibility. They *appear*, however, to

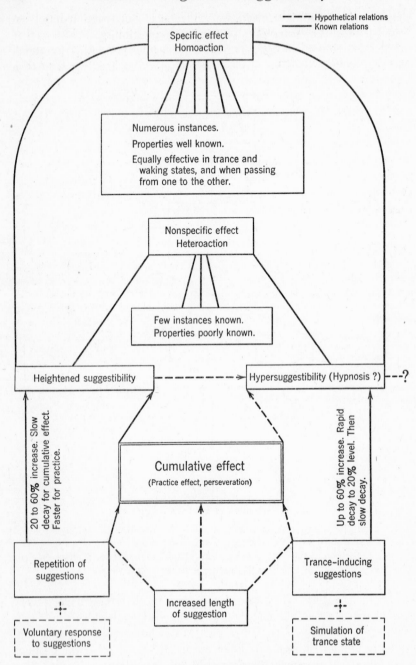

Fɪɢ. 2. The Heightening of Suggestibility

lead to a much higher hypersuggestibility through multiple cumulation than has been obtained with other suggestions. Since the latter have never been studied entirely under the same conditions, there is no reason to believe that this characteristic is peculiar to trance-inducing suggestions. In any event, hypnotic hypersuggestibility is found to last for some time after the trance-inducing suggestions have ceased, and to persist into the waking state, although there is a progressive decay.

Investigation has also shown that subanesthetic doses of various anesthetics as well as hypnotics ¶ cause an increase in *primary suggestibility*, provided the subject possesses *initially* a modicum of suggestibility. In other words, these agents cannot and do not create suggestibility where there is none to start with.

A diagrammatic summary of this chapter will be found in Figures 1 and 2.

¶ There does not appear to be any general agreement on the distinction between anesthetics and hypnotics. According to one schema of classification, hypnotics include anesthetics as a special case. Another way to look at it is in terms of the degree of loss of consciousness that is brought about by the various agents being considered, the term hypnotic being reserved for those that are habitually used to cause only a partial loss of consciousness (sleep-like state). General anesthetics on the other hand are usually employed to bring about complete loss of consciousness. Since actually most hypnotics can be employed to produce anesthesia, it is proper and even necessary to distinguish between anesthetic and subanesthetic dosages in their case too. The second mode of classification is the one that has been primarily used in this book.

· 5 ·

Suggestibility in Hypnosis

The Depth of Hypnosis and Its Measurement

Just as waking suggestibility is found present in various degrees in different individuals, and can be increased progressively within limits, one also observes that hypnotic suggestibility behaves in a similar manner. As mentioned earlier, the *depth of hypnosis* (or trance depth) of a subject is, by convention, the degree of suggestibility attained by this individual during hypnosis at the time the measurement is made and as determined on an accepted scale. A variety of scales have been proposed for this purpose. All are based on the same principle, that all suggestions do not require the same suggestibility in order to elicit a response, and hence that some suggestions can differentiate between individuals of different suggestibility.

The four main scales that have been developed are those of Barry, Mackinnon, and Murray (14); of Davis and Husband (91); of Lecron and Bordeaux (255); and of Friedlander and Sarbin (148). In general, a scale for the measurement of depth of hypnosis consists of a set of graded * waking and hypnotic suggestions and a *standardized method* of inducing the hypnotic state. Some system for assigning scores is usually arranged in such a way that (*a*) the higher an individual's suggestibility, and hence the greater his trance depth, the higher his final net score will be, and (*b*) the score will be unambiguous. Davis and Husband (91) have formulated an important principle in relation to the design and construction of such scales. This principle, which is really in the form of a criterion, states that, if any item in the series is failed, all items following it should also be failed, and, conversely, if any item is passed, all items preceding it must also be passed.

In general, it may be stated that, from the standpoint of validity, reliability, and standardization, the scale developed by Friedlander

* Graded in terms of the degree of difficulty encountered in having the suggestion carried out.

and Sarbin (148) is the most satisfactory.† The most practical, however, is the one devised by Davis and Husband. In terms of this
scale, subjects can be assigned a net score ranging from 0 to 30 and
placed in five main categories in respect to depth of hypnosis as
follows:

Depth	Net Score Range
Insusceptible	0
Hypnoidal	1–5
Light hypnosis	6–11
Medium trance	13–20
Deep trance	21–30

The phenomena that characterize these categories are as follows:

1. *Insusceptible.* Total lack of response to suggestion.
2. *Hypnoidal.* Relaxation, fluttering of the eyelids, closing of the eyes,
complete physical relaxation.‡
3. *Light Trance.* Catalepsy of the eyes, limb catalepsies, rigid catalepsies,
glove anesthesia.
4. *Medium Trance.* Partial amnesia, posthypnotic anesthesia, personality
changes, simple posthypnotic suggestions, kinesthetic delusions, complete
amnesia.
5. *Deep Trance.* Ability to open the eyes without affecting the trance,
bizarre posthypnotic suggestions, complete somnambulism, positive visual
hallucinations (posthypnotic), positive auditory hallucinations (posthypnotic), systematized posthypnotic amnesias, negative auditory hallucinations,
negative visual hallucinations, hyperesthesias.

It is of interest to consider the percentage of individuals that come
under each of these classifications when hypnotized. Below will be
found values reported by various investigators. The last column
(mean %) contains the mean calculated for each row. The values
reported by Hull are mean values computed by him from a large
number of earlier reports (213). The values given here for Barry
et al. are as reported by Friedlander and Sarbin (148).

Classification	Hull	Davis and Husband	Barry et al.	Friedlander and Sarbin	Van Pelt (448)	Mean %
Insusceptible	10.5%	9%	16%	33%	5%	14.70
Hypnoidal light trance	32.7	47	37	50	35	40.34
Medium trance	34.6	15	28	12	35	24.92
Deep trance	22.2	29	19	5	25	20.04

† The reader who is interested in more details concerning the relative merits
of these various scales as well as the differences existing between them should
consult the very extensive study of Friedlander and Sarbin (148).

‡ To some extent the order in which these various characteristics are given in
each category is also the order of increasing depth within each stage.

In looking over the figures in the above table, we should keep in mind that, since each scale makes use of different units, we should not expect to find too much in common between the percentages reported by the different writers. For this reason the final computed mean has only a relative meaning. If we examine each column of percentages, we will note that the fourth alone (Friedlander and Sarbin) shows any semblance of order within itself (a trend). This means that the distribution is not normal. Hull (213) is rather emphatic in his belief that suggestibility should be distributed according to a Gaussian curve. Presumably then, the depth of hypnosis should be distributed in a like manner. Friedlander and Sarbin (148) have pointed out that one can assume normality, but then it becomes necessary to increase the discrimination of the test (and scale) at its lower end. This can be done by either introducing more items at this end or retaining the same number of items and stretching their raw score values. This last, however, was what Davis and Husband (91) essentially tried to do in designing their scale. Normalization of the scores did not result. On the other hand, to increase the discrimination in the manner just indicated would probably tend to introduce subjective criteria, a feature that is rather objectionable. There remains one possibility, to extend the scale at the upper extremity as Friedlander and Sarbin (148) did. It is permissible to do this as long as we can find items in which clear-cut behavior differences are exhibited.

It is the conclusion of Friedlander and Sarbin (148) that the observed skewness in the distribution appears to be due to more than artifacts. In any event, as they remark, there is to date no basis for assuming that normality is a necessary characteristic of hypnosis.

The reliability of the various tests of suggestibility which are employed in practice is a rather important question. There have been very few actual studies of the reliability of the various item suggestions employed in making up the various scales mentioned in this chapter, although there seems to be a general feeling that they are satisfactorily reliable. Saltzman (383) has made a brief report on an attempt to remedy this. With this in mind, he examined a number of semiprestige and prestige tests including the electric shock illusion (analogous to the heat illusion), pendulum test, hand steadiness test, and arm sway test. With the exception of the hand steadiness test (test-retest reliability of 0.485) he found reliabilities above 0.88 for all other tests. He concluded that suggestibility as measured by such tests is a comparatively stable aspect of human behavior. In regard to the scales which have been discussed, Friedlander and Sarbin (148), and Barry et al.

(14) report test-retest reliabilities of the order of 0.80 (Pearson r). Although certainly not the best possible value, this is nevertheless satisfactory.

Closely related to the question of reliability is that of validity. First of all, we may ask whether the available scales cover the entire range of possible depths of hypnosis. As will be seen later on, a number of investigators, among whom Milton H. Erickson is foremost, have been maintaining, or at least implying in their writings, that there might be further levels of hypnosis beyond the highest one measured by the available scales. That is to say these scales do not extend far enough. Thus far no specific effort has been made to investigate this matter further. If this is true, however, we would have to answer the first question negatively. A second question that may be asked is to what extent do the available scales really measure hypnotic depth. If we examine the various proposed scales, we notice that many of the suggestions used in the lower half or third of these scales are of a kind that can be expected to give rise to excellent responses in the waking state. Such scales are therefore not capable of differentiating between waking and hypnosis. They measure depth of hypnosis *only if it is first established that the subject is hypnotized.* There are two ways in which this can be done. One may agree that hypnosis is present when suggestibility is increased by various techniques beyond a certain more or less arbitrary critical value; or one may agree that, if a subject gives certain responses to certain suggestions of the trance-inducing variety, then he is in a state of hypnosis. In practice both criteria have been used alternatively and concurrently. All the scales of hypnotic depth either include eyelid closure suggestions at the start or involve a testing procedure working up to these. Actually, however, we may question whether lid closure is a sufficient criterion. The reason for this will be made clear in Chapter 19. In the meantime this leads us to question the validity of using these scales at all without a better criterion of what constitutes hypnosis.

A possible way out of this dilemma may be in the use of various existing psychological tests, or at least of parts of these. Lane (251) found indications in Rorschach responses that hypnotized individuals may be more introversive § than waking ones. Her results suffer

§ It should be kept in mind here and in the remainder of this book, particularly in connection with Chapter 14, that the use of interpretative terminology in describing results obtained with the Rorschach and the Thematic Apperception Tests is not to be taken as necessarily indicating our acceptance of the correctness of the interpretations usually given for the responses in question. In the light of

unfortunately from the fact that only one subject was involved, and also from a defect in the controls that were employed (the waking responses may have been affected by suggestions given at an earlier date in spite of their subsequent removal). In spite of these defects, Lane's claims may be correct, for an examination of Rorschach records reported for other purposes by Bergman et al. (26) and by Levine et al. (262) appears to show some substantiation of her results. In general, all three studies show in hypnosis an increase in the M responses, with either no change or a decrease in the C responses, as compared to the same responses in the waking state. Such an increase in the M:C ratio is presumably indicative of increased intro-version. On the other hand, it must be remarked that other responses which would have been expected also to change in definite directions showed no consistent shifts. In addition, Rorschach scores reported by Sarbin (386) in still another study show changes in hypnosis that are exactly in the opposite direction for most of the relevant responses. If anything, his subject became less introversive. But since only one subject was used in this investigation, we cannot give too much weight to this study in this connection. On the whole the results are only suggestive.

We will come back very shortly to the problem of the differentiation of hypnosis from the waking state, but, before we do so, let us examine another aspect of the nature of hypnotic susceptibility.

Hypnotic Susceptibility and Hypnotizability

Although the investigations of Krueger (245) tend to show that waking and trance suggestibility lie on a single continuum, this does not necessarily prove the identity of the two. Actually, there exists no conclusive proof, but there are available data that suggest that the two forms of suggestibility have at least a partial identity, so to speak, in the sense that they appear to have something in common. Eysenck and Furneaux (129) and Furneaux (152) have been able to obtain very good evidence to show that an individual's responsiveness to

the existing poor validation of the above tests, it is by no means certain that the standardly accepted interpretations are anywhere near correct. But because they are widely accepted and employed it is convenient to use these here in describing data of the kind under consideration. In addition, it should also be remarked that, even if we could state with certainty that, for instance, a high M:C ratio is related to introversive tendencies, we still could only say in the case of Lane's experiment that the subject showed introversive-*like* responses to a greater extent in hypnosis than in the waking state.

trance-inducing suggestions involves primary suggestibility, and that responses to the latter are of the passive kind. In addition to the fact that the distribution of responses to trance-inducing suggestions is of the same kind as that for responses to postural sway suggestions, in itself additional evidence for the above, correlational and factorial analyses have also confirmed this. The results of the above investi- gators have shown that, whatever the factor or factors underlying responses to postural sway suggestions, they constitute better than 50 per cent (55 per cent to be exact) of the factors responsible for susceptibility to trance-inducing suggestions.|| Similar information was also obtained in regard to the heat illusion test, although the analysis shows that probably a third or intermediate type of suggestibility is involved in the responses obtained on this test. More recently, Fur- neaux (153) obtained data that tend to support the above conclusions for normal subjects. He gave to 125 individuals mass suggestions aimed at producing postural sway and hypnosis. Sixty-five subjects reported having been affected by the suggestions of sway. Of these, 43 also reported having felt some effects of the trance-inducing sug- gestions. Furneaux reported a tetrachoric correlation of 0.68 between the two groups (compared to one of 0.72 obtained in earlier studies (152, 129) with psychoneurotics). As he remarks, in making in- ferences from this we should remember that we are dealing with reports and not direct observations (because of the group testing situa- tion) of responses to suggestions; that we have here a group situation instead of an individual testing situation as in the studies with psycho- neurotic subjects; and, finally, that there may be a difference between actually swaying and feeling a tendency to sway. In spite of all this, the results are suggestive.

The basis for stating that response to trance-inducing suggestion is of the passive type consists in the observation that hypnosis correlates rather highly with the release test, whereas the correlation with the press test is rather small. It may be well to say a little more at this point in regard to this aspect. Eysenck (132) has observed that the arm levitation test can be given in two forms, one with the arm rising, and one with the arm dropping. Outwardly these two tests appear similar and equivalent. However, when both tests were used on the

|| Actually these results were obtained only from psychoneurotic subjects. Both Eysenck and Furneaux believe they can be generalized to extend to normal indi- viduals, on the basis that earlier studies, with samples from the same population of subjects, had given, on the same tests, results qualitatively comparable to those given by normal individuals.

same subject he found that they showed an intercorrelation of only 0.35. On the other hand, postural sway can also be tested in two ways, falling forward and falling backward. These two forms again appear to be equivalent and are indeed found to correlate to the extent of 0.91. Finally, the press and release test, which can be considered to be two forms of a test, like the arm levitation test also gives a relatively low intercorrelation of 0.47. An examination of the dynamics of the tests shows that in both the press and the arm rising tests the subject must expend energy, that is, must play an *active* role. On the other hand, in the release and arm dropping tests, work is done on the subject who therefore plays essentially a *passive* role. The dynamics involved in the falling tests are not so easily analyzed. Both appear to require a definitely passive role, except possibly in the first few moments. The induction of hypnosis is obviously a test requiring an essential passivity on the part of the subject. This, of course, is in agreement with the results reported by Eysenck (132) which show that primary suggestibility correlates highest with responses of a passive type. As remarked earlier, although Eysenck and Furneaux (129) have been led by this to speak of "passive" and "active" suggestibility, I cannot concede that this is a correct designation if we agree to define suggestibility as the capacity to respond to suggestions.

As has been seen in the last section, not every individual attains the same trance depth when hypnotized. As a matter of fact, individuals differ in a great many ways in the manner in which they respond to trance-inducing suggestions. Some respond rapidly, others slowly. Some develop a passive type of hypnosis, whereas others tend to be active. Certain subjects appear to develop the maximum depth they are capable of the first time they are hypnotized. Other individuals do not do this, but can apparently be trained or conditioned to reach an increasingly greater depth, so to speak, over a period of time involving many successive trance inductions, until they too reach a maximum depth. Finally, some subjects are more responsive to a given technique of induction than to other ones. If thus we were asked to describe accurately an individual's capacity to be hypnotized, we would have to take all of these aspects or variables into consideration, and possibly others too. In other words, the description of how an individual responds to trance-inducing suggestions is a *multidimensional* affair. Essentially, it constitutes what the expression *hypnotic susceptibility* taken in its most general sense denotes. In practice, however, for reasons that need not be considered here, investigators have made use of this expression to refer nearly exclusively to the *maximum depth of hypnosis* an individual is capable of attaining under specified conditions. In keeping with this conventional use of the terms, this is also what we shall mean by hypnotic susceptibility in this book.¶ It should be emphasized, however, that it does not necessarily give a complete description of the individual's capacity for hypnosis,* being only one of the dimensions we have listed. On the other hand, it is essentially a very practical mode of description, because it is one of the few, possibly the only one, that can be predicted from an individual's waking behavior. This is, of course, a very important consideration, since in practice one often needs to know what sort of a hypnotic subject a person would make without actually hypnotizing him to find out.

One of the bases for inferring hypnotic susceptibility from waking state behavior has already been indicated, although in a different context. As was pointed out at the beginning of this section, Eysenck and Furneaux (129) have shown that there is a definite correlation between susceptibility to hypnosis and response to various waking suggestions. Those responses for which high correlation exists can be and are taken as waking tests of an individual's capacity to develop a hypnotic state. An interesting feature of the above-mentioned investigation is that certain pair combinations of tests have greater predictive power for foretelling the subject's response to trance-inducing suggestions when given together than when either component test is given singly. The postural sway test was found to have the highest predictive value of all single tests (tetrachoric correlation of 0.73 with hypnosis and highly significant). The heat illusion test was also found to be a fairly good index of hypnotic susceptibility (correlation of 0.51). However, the two combined as a test battery have the highest discriminatory power of all tests and test pairs (correlation of 0.96). A later study of Furneaux based upon several hundred subjects confirmed these results. It appears, on the basis of these results, that the factors underlying the two tests, when combined, can account for over 90 per cent of the subject's susceptibility.

¶ Some investigators also call it "hypnotizability." This term will be reserved here, however, to denote a different although related aspect of hypnosis.

* Whether it does or does not depends on its relationship to the other dimensions. It may be that they are all highly intercorrelated. Although no investigation of this matter has been made, there is evidence, for instance that rate of induction is probably, at least in part, related to susceptibility. On the other hand, the maximum attainable trance depth appears to be the more fundamental of the measures in the fact that the other ones have meaning *only* as long as the subject can be hypnotized to some degree, however small it is.

The fact that combined tests have shown themselves to have greater predictive power than the component tests taken singly can best be interpreted at present as indicating that hypnotic susceptibility, if not hypnosis itself, depends upon more than one factor † and that each of the component tests measures the influence of a given factor more than it does the influence of other factors. Eysenck (131) has followed this approach in trying to interpret the fact that, although the heat illusion test does not correlate with the postural sway test, yet they increase each other's predictive power in respect to hypnotic suscepti- bility. He proposes that possibly the postural sway test measures the motor effect of suggestions whereas the heat illusion test measures the sensory effect. If we assume that both effects are a part of hyp- nosis, then the score of the subject on hypnosis would be a combination of two relatively independent partial scores. The correctness of this supposition remains to be demonstrated.

Leaving this question, in general it appears safe to state, on the basis of the above results, that *any test that measures primary suggestibility also measures susceptibility to hypnosis.*

Attempts have also been made to find a relation between hypnotic susceptibility and various aspects (or traits) of the personality. Wells (468) who is responsible for some of the earlier work on this question does not appear to have found anything particularly significant. How- ever, his investigation cannot be considered overly reliable for a num- ber of reasons too long to discuss in these pages. Possibly we may best sum up the matter in this respect by stating that his study does not stand up to a critical analysis. A word of warning should be given, however, in the event that the reader might wish to look up Wells's report. This is that he appears to attach a different meaning to suggestibility from the one we have used. Whether he means exactly the same thing by "hypnotizability" as has been designated here by "susceptibility" is not clear from his paper, although presumably this is what he does mean by it.

A far superior investigation was made by White (481) who showed that it is possible to predict success in hypnotizing an individual on the basis of his social attitude and his attitude toward hypnosis,‡ particularly in terms of his response to card 12M on the Thematic

† Or, again, we may speak here of various "aspects" of hypnosis.

‡ Some readers may question whether one can speak of attitudes in the sense of traits. Inasmuch as the entire nomenclature in the field of personality is very confused, there seems to be little basis for any argument. Since attitudes are probably partly determined by traits in any event, the above has some justification.

Apperception Test. The most significant finding here was that the subjects showing a positive attitude toward hypnosis when responding to this card were the more susceptible to hypnosis. This has been confirmed by Rosenzweig and Sarason (380).

In another study involving the Rorschach test, Sarbin and Madow (384) reported that the W/D ratio increases with trance susceptibility. However, Brenman and Reichard (48) repeated this study and were unable to find this difference. They conclude, on the other hand, that some significant differences exist in the over-all scores on the Rorschach made by good and poor hypnotic subjects, respectively.

Related to this group of studies is the very careful investigation of Steisel (427). His work will be considered in greater detail in Chapter 6. We may state here, however, that he was unable to find any consistent relationship between nine different Rorschach measures of suggestibility and the responses to postural sway suggestions, as well as to certain suggestions given in an autokinetic situation. Since the factors underlying suggestibility to postural sway suggestions do not appear to account for all of an individual's susceptibility to hypnosis, these results do not necessarily invalidate those reported by Sarbin and Madow, or by Brenman and Reichard. In addition, as will be seen later, Steisel's study is not fully comparable to these two in other respects.

There is also some evidence that intelligence, as measured on a Binet type of test, is positively correlated with hypnotic susceptibility.

Rosenzweig and Sarason (380) have investigated the relation of hypnotizability § to repression on the one hand and to three types of reactions to frustration on the other, which they call impunitiveness, intropunitiveness, and extrapunitiveness. They conclude from their results that hypnotizability has a positive relationship to repression and impunitiveness, whereas nonhypnotizability is associated with displacement and projection, and with intropunitiveness and extrapunitiveness. On the other hand, Petrie (345) has reported data that do not entirely agree with the above and that also cast some doubt upon the validity of the hypothesis. As both Petrie (345) and Eysenck (131) have pointed out, the validity of any demonstration of the triadic hypothesis depends on the reliability of "repression"-type tests such as were employed by Rosenzweig and Sarason (380) and by Petrie (345). Petrie made an investigation of her own test of repres-

§ Hypnotizability is employed by these investigators in the sense of susceptibility as defined in this chapter.

sion and found it possessed no reliability to speak of. It may be argued, however, that this does not necessarily invalidate the test used by Rosenzweig et al. These two tests cannot be said to be entirely comparable. Petrie could not find any confirmation for that portion of the triadic hypothesis that links "repression" and "hysteria." On the other hand, she obtained definite correlations between repression and suggestibility, thus confirming this part of the investigation of Rosenzweig et al. Eysenck (131) also pointed out that, if one substitutes the word "neurotic" for the term "hysteric" in the triadic hypothesis, the results obtained by Petrie give additional support to the triadic hypothesis. This may be so because Petrie's method of classification, based upon factor-analytical methods, includes under "neurotic" numerous cases that Freud and many others would have classified as "conversion hysterics" and "anxiety hysterics." Thus there is no essential disagreement between Eysenck and Petrie on the one hand, and Rosenzweig and Sarason on the other. It is certain that Eysenck's (131) factor-analytical classification of abnormal personalities into five categories is not comparable to the more usual systems, such as that used by Rosenzweig et al. Until the exact relations between the two modes of classification are better established, no further conclusions can be drawn on this issue.

This then is the extent to which one can infer from waking behavior an individual's responsiveness to trance-inducing suggestions, or more precisely what we have chosen to define as the subject's hypnotic susceptibility. It should be quite clear that the methods available are rather limited. Their greatest weakness is possibly that they do not allow us to scale susceptibility. For, although it is true that we know from correlational studies that, the higher the rating on a certain variable, the higher is the susceptibility, the actual regression equations are unknown. That is, we cannot predict with any exactness the numerical value which, for instance, on the Davis-Husband scale will correspond to the maximum trance depth developed by a subject.

Although as pointed out, in practice susceptibility has been largely the sole variable employed to characterize hypnotic subjects, it may be far from giving a complete description. Particular attention should now be called to at least two other variables which may be of some importance. As stated earlier, one finds that subjects of identical susceptibility vary considerably in regard to rate of induction and passivity–activity. Possibly part of the reason little attention has been given to these two additional variables is that, in regard to the first, it seems to have been generally assumed in the past, at least implicitly, that suggestibility and rate of response to suggestions are positively correlated; and, in regard to the second, no one had been particularly aware of its existence and has been even less aware of its possible significance. The time appears to be at hand, however, when both of these must be given some recognition.

Let us then first look at the temporal aspect a little more closely. No specific studies of the relation of the rate of hypnotic induction to susceptibility have been reported. However, on the basis of general experience, it appears to be generally true that, the more susceptible an individual is, the more easily, that is, the faster, he responds to trance-inducing suggestions and reaches a given depth of hypnosis. However it does not follow that two individuals of equal susceptibility have the same rate of induction. There is evidence to the contrary. Furthermore, there exist situations in which a relatively rapid rate is associated with a relatively low susceptibility, and conversely those in which a relatively slow rate is associated with a relatively high susceptibility. A particularly extreme instance of the first situation is seen in situations where shallow hypnosis is induced by means of a posthypnotic signal. There appears indeed to be no direct positive relation in all cases between rate of induction and maximum depth attained, particularly when one is not referring to the first trance induction in an individual. Thus there appears to be a basis for speaking separately of induction rate and susceptibility. It is proposed here that we refer to the time required for the induction of an individual's maximum hypnotic depth under specified conditions as his *hypnotizability*.

Actually, the above is an oversimplified approach to the temporal aspect of trance induction. What we should really inquire into is not the over-all rate involved in attaining maximum depth, as was done in the above, but the actual step-by-step variation in rate as the individual progresses from waking to the maximum depth. What the precise shape of the curve describing variation in rate with depth would be is of course not known. It certainly would not show proportionality or constancy through the entire depth range, since when maximum depth is attained the rate must drop to zero. As a matter of fact we can safely guess that in general the curve would probably show no over-all linearity. One exception to this might be predicted for the curve describing hypnosis by means of a posthypnotic signal. It would be expected to show a near constant rate until the neighborhood of maximum depth was reached. In general, we might expect the shape of the time curve for induction to be particularly influenced by the factors known to influence suggestibility. Further elucidation must be left to future research.

As was just remarked there are no data available on the relation of rate of induction to susceptibility. In fact, this paucity of data extends even to the range of time taken for the induction of hypnosis in practice. If we may judge by various reports and claims, it would appear that the induction of hypnosis can require anywhere from a few seconds to several hours and even days! One of the difficulties in trying to get a clear picture here is that many of those who have given such estimates have failed to specify the depth of hypnosis induced and whether this was the first attempt at hypnosis for the subject. I am personally tempted to agree with Wells (474) that it is a rare subject indeed who can be hypnotized *for the first time* to the deepest state (or somnambulistic stage) in a matter of seconds, although it is possible and probably does happen. Under *normal circumstances,* the chances for this are probably less than one in 100. As Wells points out, whenever one comes across reports or claims of so-called instantaneous hypnosis, one may strongly suspect not only that the subject had been hypnotized on a number of previous occasions, but also that he has been given special posthypnotic instructions to speed up the process.

This healthy skepticism should not, however, be carried too far. It will be noticed that the last few statements were made with the provision that one was dealing with normal circumstances. In view of the fact that various factors (other than prior hypnosis and posthypnotic suggestions) appear capable of altering an individual's suggestibility, it is necessary to keep in mind that some circumstances may exist that can appreciably facilitate hypnotic induction.

I have particularly in mind here the surprisingly high percentage of success ‖ in hypnotizing that has been claimed by or for various stage hypnotists. As we have seen, one would expect on the average that only two out of every ten individuals selected by the hypnotist from the audience would go into a deep trance (five out of ten would go into a medium trance). If we want to be even more conservative, we can use the data of Friedlander and Sarbin which reduces the above odds to five in 100 (and 12 in 100). Many stage hypnotists claim to be able to do much better than that, and there seems to be, at face value, some truth to this contention. Wells (474) accounts

‖ By success we mean here both percentage of subjects going into a relatively deep trance and high speed of trance induction.

for this in terms of deception, declaring that the hypnotist uses trained subjects (or "stooges"). There is little doubt that some hypnotists do this. On the other hand, it is not proved to be true in all cases, and in addition there appears to be a possibility of explaining the particular high incidence of suggestible subjects on a different basis: namely, that the conditions under which subjects are obtained from the audience may well be conducive to a selective sampling that favors the procurement of a spuriously high percentage of highly susceptible individuals. For it is entirely possible that most people who volunteer as subjects do so because they are highly suggestible in the first place and the request of the hypnotist for volunteers acts selectively as a suggestion upon these very individuals. This alone would tend to insure the hypnotist of much greater chance of success than one would otherwise expect. In addition to this, it is my observation that many volunteers appear to come to the hypnotist with a very strong positive attitude which not only facilitates hypnosis but in itself may also have been partly responsible for the individual's volunteering.¶ Thus, biasing of the sampling by the method used to gather the subjects may well increase the hypnotist's chances of success.

After this short digression let us return to the question of the time required for induction under normal circumstances on the first trial. Wells (474) contends that one cannot bring even the upper 25 per cent of the potentially somnambulistic subjects to the somnambulistic stage in less than two hours. Leaving out the possibility that Wells is using a different scale of hypnotic depth differing considerably from the conventional ones, I cannot go along with this statement. In my own experience, using the Davis-Husband scale,* I have found it possible to induce a deep trance in many subjects in 30 minutes, and often in less time. As for the statement Wells makes that several days may be needed in some cases, its relevance to the present discussion may be questioned on the basis that we are talking here of induction rate on the first trial, and the situations Wells referred to involve successive rehypnotization. This of course does not make these situations less relevant to the problem of hypnosis in general. In fact, it

¶ Although nearly every audience has some hecklers determined to show up the hypnotist, these constitute usually a very small percentage of the volunteers. Some of these sometimes even turn out much to their own surprise to be very good subjects in spite of their negative attitude. In any event a good hypnotist can usually pick out troublesome individuals and eliminate them.

* There is actually some evidence that Wells may have in mind trance depth going beyond the Davis-Husband scale.

strengthens the statement made earlier that there is really more to susceptibility than the maximum trance depth that can be reached. There is no question that many subjects can be trained or conditioned, so to speak, to develop very deep trances, in spite of the fact that the first induction can only bring about a relatively light trance. Furthermore the technique of induction itself may have a definite effect in this regard. From a practical standpoint, say, that of the psychotherapist, the subject's ability to develop a deep trance in the long run following proper training or use of the proper technique may be of far greater importance than his ability to develop such a trance depth on the first attempt. Ability to predict such an outcome should be of great value. Unfortunately, not only is the extent to which the above is true largely unknown, but also we have no way of predicting it from the subject's waking behavior. This is one of the reasons we have chosen to retain the restricted meaning of susceptibility and to differentiate it from hypnotizability.

At the other extreme of reported induction rates we have induction by means of a posthypnotic signal. Everyone agrees that it is very fast. Wells estimates it as a few seconds. Actually this may be an understatement. As reported elsewhere in this book, I have occasionally measured the latencies of response to such signals and have found these to be as small as $\frac{1}{5}$ second, the resulting depth being in some instances very intense. It does not, however, appear to be universally true that trance induction at a signal leads automatically to the subject's maximum depth, as Wells appears to believe. In many instances further deepening seems to be possible. Furthermore it is a noteworthy fact that rapid hypnosis by means of a signal can be associated with a relatively shallow maximal depth.

So much then for the question of the time variable in trance induction. The other variable we have mentioned as being possibly important enough to warrant some further consideration is passivity–activity, or what might be called the *degree of inertness* of the subject. At present its empirical significance is far from clear. All we really know is that there is evidence that some subjects tend to respond very passively and others very actively to suggestions, quite independent of their trance depth. From a practical point of view this is of some importance in determining the outcome of hypnotic suggestions. At present it is possible to ascertain to some extent in the waking state whether the subject will be passive or active when hypnotized by means of the arm levitation test and the press-release test, as shown by Eysenck. This is far from a satisfactory approach since we cannot assign scale values to the subject's inertness by these means. (At best we can construct a two-point scale for this.)

The Suggestibility Continuum

As remarked earlier, trance-inducing suggestions must of necessity act at first at the waking level, and hence as waking suggestions. This alone would suggest that hypnotic suggestibility is not essentially different from waking suggestibility, or at least that the one can and does merge into the other. Again, as was seen in the last chapter in respect to homoaction, waking and hypnotic suggestibility behave alike. We also saw that it is possible to raise waking primary suggestibility to a level comparable with that of the heteroactive aspect of trance suggestibility by means of multiple cumulation. This is rather significant for an understanding of the nature of hypnotic suggestibility when it is remembered that hypnotic suggestibility is of the primary type. Finally, it is a well-known fact that it is possible to obtain a great many, if not all, of the so-called hypnotic phenomena in the waking state, that is, without preliminary use of trance-inducing suggestions. Wells (468) has been very emphatic about this. He claims to have been able to produce all hypnotic phenomena in the waking state. Unfortunately, his report is lacking in essential details and therefore cannot be considered overly conclusive. It is not even possible to determine from it how inclusive his study was. However, there is little doubt that the above is a fact.

All this leads us to conceive of waking and hypnotic suggestibility as lying on a single continuum, more or less at opposite ends, and merging at some point somewhere between the two extremities. This at least would be true for primary suggestibility. It would partly account for the observation that some individuals possess a waking suggestibility that is higher than the hypnotic suggestibility of others. It would also explain in part why certain individuals show a remarkable increase in suggestibility when they are hypnotized whereas others do not. Finally, on this basis it is seen that, *to the extent that the same degrees of suggestibility can be attained in the waking state as are obtained in the hypnotic state, "hypnotic phenomena" will be possible in the "waking state."*

I have observed on occasions another phenomenon that lends support to the continuum hypothesis, namely, that, when progressively more difficult waking suggestions are given in rapid succession to some subjects, they appear to pass into a state that may best be described as one of light hypnosis. This suggests *that subjects will pass at some stage or other into the hypnotic state, notwithstanding the fact that no trance-inducing suggestions have been given and that lid closure has not taken place.* This observation needs further substantiation before a more definite conclusion can be drawn, but it may be remarked that it integrates rather well into the present hypothesis.

All of this leads to a somewhat disturbing thought: Is there, after all, a hypnotic state? In answering this question we must be very careful to interpret the data correctly, particularly in relation to the limits within which they are valid. As we have seen, hypnotic hypersuggestibility possesses a heteroactive component which does not appear to be characteristic of waking suggestibility. On the other hand, the homoactive component does not appear to be essentially different from homoactive hypersuggestibility as produced by repetition of waking primary suggestions. Thus, even if we should agree in the present chapter that hypnotic and waking suggestibility cannot be distinguished from each other, *this statement must be restricted to primary suggestibility and to the homoactive aspect of hypnosis.* Within the boundaries of this restriction, it does appear, however, that hypnotic hypersuggestibility is primarily and simply an expression of multiple cumulation created by repeated waking suggestions. That is, trance induction appears simply as a method of stepping up primary suggestibility from the lower end to the upper end of the suggestibility continuum by means of the homoactive effect of a rapid and sustained repetition of the elements that form the content of the suggestions used for this purpose. But, as already intimated, the same end result presumably can be reached in other ways. Trance-inducing suggestions are mainly singled out by the fact that experience has shown them to be capable of bringing about a rapid and marked rise in general suggestibility in individuals known to be susceptible to hypnosis (as determined by tests). If we wish for convenience to speak of "hypnosis" here, we should say that *a hypnotic state exists whenever an individual reaches a state of hypersuggestibility † measured by a standard scale of trance depth and equal to the degree of hypersuggestibility he is known to attain under the influence of trance-inducing suggestions.*

Summary and Conclusions

In looking back over the data available on suggestibility in hypnosis, it appears at first glance that there is no essential difference between waking and hypnotic suggestibility. Both appear to lie on a single

† Brought about by other means than trance-inducing suggestions.

continuum of suggestibility. From this viewpoint, trance induction is merely a way of stepping up suggestibility, that is, shifting it from the lower end of the continuum to the upper end. This shift would appear to result primarily through cumulated homoaction produced by rapid repetition of the elements in the trance-inducing suggestions. A closer examination of the facts shows, however, that the above picture is probably correct only insofar as primary suggestibility is concerned. As pointed out in the previous chapter, a marked heteroaction is present in hypnosis which is not usually found to be characteristic of primary suggestibility. It appears therefore that, at least for the time being, it may be better to say that primary suggestibility constitutes a continuum extending from the waking state into the hypnotic state, and that the homoactive aspect of hypnotic hypersuggestibility seems to be a property of this continuum. Another reason why we cannot state at present that waking and hypnotic suggestibility in general are the same and lie on the same continuum is that studies comparable to those made for primary suggestibility have not been made for secondary and tertiary suggestibility. On the other hand, practical experience seems to indicate that waking tests of suggestibility have a predictive power in regard to hypnotic susceptibility, and that scales developed for measuring depth of hypnosis have a certain validity. This may be taken as an indication that there is a relationship between waking suggestibility and hypnotic hypersuggestibility. This relationship appears, however, to be somewhat more complex than we might have suspected.

· 6 ·

Factors Influencing Suggestibility and Hypnotic Susceptibility

It is the general consensus of opinion that suggestibility is related to various characteristics of individuals in such a way that, given one of these characteristics, it is possible to predict whether the individual will have, on the average, a higher or lower suggestibility than the population norm. As mentioned in an earlier chapter, neurotic individuals appear to be more suggestible whereas psychotics appear to be less so than normal individuals. It remains to be seen now whether a similar relationship can be found between suggestibility and other factors or traits, particularly those that are specific to normal persons.

The Influence of Age

It is generally agreed that children are more suggestible than adults. Bramwell (45) among early writers concurred in this. More recent investigations have shown that suggestibility is a variable quantity in relation to age, with a maximum around the age of eight. Reymert and Kohn (363) have demonstrated this, using the heat illusion test. Messerschmidt (307) confirmed it on the basis of results obtained with a wide battery of tests of both primary and secondary suggestibility. Other investigators who have held the opinion that suggestibility is highest in childhood include Small (416), Gilbert (160), Rose (374), Giroud (164), Papov (331), Sherman (411), Binet (31), and Guidi (173). The only dissenting vote is Hurlock (217), who arrived at a negative conclusion on the basis of results obtained with the Otis Group Test of Suggestibility. However, a study of Otis' own report (329) on this test shows rather clearly that it probably does not measure primary or secondary suggestibility, and that in any event it certainly would not do it in a manner comparable with tests employed by other investigators. There is therefore no real conflict between the reported results. Both Hull (213) and Coffin (71), on reviewing the available data, concluded that the ages of seven to eight show a peak in suggestibility. After the age of twenty suggestibility appears to

76

level off. What the actual trend is beyond twenty has not been investigated.

Influence of the Sex of the Subject

It has been a common belief among hypnotists that women are more suggestible than men. Otis (329), using the test she developed for suggestibility, found that this is true of children, although the difference between the sexes is small. As has just been pointed out, we cannot attach too much weight to this investigation. Fortunately Messerschmidt (307) was able to demonstrate the same results in a manner beyond question. Hull (213), using postural sway suggestions, found that women are somewhat more suggestible than men. Further evidence in support of this comes from the investigations of Ingwarson and Lindberg (220), Brown (58), Cason (65), Wegrocki (461), and Roach (369). Aveling and Hargreaves (8) concluded that sex did not make any difference in the suggestibility of children. Actually their data, obtained from a well-designed experiment, show a small difference in favor of girls. Two possible explanations were available for this, one of which did not involve the sex of the subjects, and this one was chosen by the investigators. It must be remarked that the data give no indication as to which explanation is more valid. In the light of information now available, however, it appears that the alternative would have been the more correct choice. Eysenck (132) also reported not being able to find a difference between the two sexes in the suggestibility of adults. Analysis of his data appears to indicate that there probably was a small difference favoring the women, but that this small superiority was masked by the greater suggestibility of the male subjects who were more neurotic than the women (all subjects were psychoneurotic in this case). Davis and Husband (91) have reported that the hypnotizability (meaning susceptibility) * of women is greater than that of men. This has been confirmed by Friedlander and Sarbin (148), Brown (58), McGeogh (298), Lodge (272), and Seashore (407). Papov (331) and Manzer (284) do not find any difference.

In general, the data point toward the conclusion that women and girls are slightly more suggestible than men and boys, respectively. This is true for both waking suggestibility and hypnotic susceptibility.

---

* In this instance more than susceptibility was really meant, these investigators having found that more women can be hypnotized and also that on the average they attain a greater depth of trance than men do.

Influence of Intelligence

There is little question that a subject must be of sufficient intelligence to understand what is desired of him if suggestions are to be effective. Such states as would hinder intelligent communication between the subject and the suggestor can be expected to affect the manifestations of suggestibility. It is definitely important to distinguish clearly between the subject's innate capacity to respond to suggestion and factors blocking the manifestation and activation of this capacity. In many instances, an irresponsive individual may well be highly suggestible, but for some reason his response is blocked, or communication is hindered. For this reason it is not possible to say truly that feebleminded individuals are not suggestible, even though their behavior would incline us to arrive at such a conclusion. The danger in jumping to conclusions has been demonstrated by Wilson, Cormen, · and Cole (491), who have shown that, contrary to the general opinion of long standing, psychotics including catatonics and senile individuals can be hypnotized, provided the suggestions used are properly designed and the general technique employed is custom-made for the subject.

Leaving such special situations, we may now ask whether there is a relation between suggestibility and intelligence in normal individuals. In general, the trend seems to be in the direction of a small positive correlation between the two, at least insofar as Binet-type tests are concerned. Aveling and Hargreaves (8), making use of a pool of suggestion tests for both primary and secondary suggestibility have shown that this held true for children. Barry et al. (14) have shown that the same relationship existed in college students when hypnotic susceptibility was employed as a measure of suggestibility. White (477) measured intelligence by means of a scholastic aptitude test and confirmed this. Hull and Life (216) reported a small positive correlation between high university grades and suggestibility to postural sway suggestion. Finally Friedlander and Sarbin (148), using an aptitude test, observed a small positive correlation between good scores on this test and suggestibility as measured by a battery of tests, but only in women. In contrast to these positive results, Reymert and Kohn (363) reported finding no relation between IQ and suggestibility to the heat illusion test, and obtaining an inverse relation between this last and the MA of children. Roach (369) found a small negative correlation between primary suggestibility and college ability. He obtained a similar result when measuring suggestibility by means of another test of rather questionable validity. More recently he has reported (370) a low positive correlation between suggestibility measured by autosuggested body sway and intelligence measured on the OCA Test. Curtis (84) has made a careful study of the relationship of intelligence to hypnotic susceptibility, using the Stanford-Binet test for the former and a scale very much like that of Husband and Davis for the latter. He found a positive correlation between suggestibility and intelligence which is by no means small. This particular study, though of high caliber, is not free from criticism. One of the stronger objections is that the data obtained by Curtis appear to show a curvilinear correlation rather than the positive linear correlation he assumed. This might account for the somewhat large value he obtained. Eysenck (132) also reported a curvilinear relation between primary suggestibility and intelligence, with a maximum occurring at the point of average intelligence. In this case, intelligence was measured by means of the Progressive Matrices. Eysenck also found that secondary suggestibility and intelligence were related linearly and negatively. Arcieri (5) obtained results that he believes tend to agree with those of Eysenck for primary suggestibility. More recently Eysenck (131) concluded that the curvilinearity he had reported earlier as existing for the relation between primary suggestibility and intelligence was an artifact, inasmuch as a study made with a greater number of subjects argued against such a relationship. In addition, he pointed out that the test for curvilinearity that he had employed previously was not without weaknesses. His new estimates lead him to conclude that the correlation is negligible, being very small and negative for men and very small and positive for women. In any event since the Matrix Test was used by Eysenck, his results are not entirely comparable with those obtained by other means. We might remark, however, that a mathematical analysis shows that the existence of a curvilinear relation between suggestibility and IQ is a strong possibility.

This last remark leads us to question to a certain degree any linear correlations that have been reported between IQ scores and suggestibility. It should also be noted, in respect to the results of Reymert and Kohn, that they tested only tertiary suggestibility. Roach also restricted his tests to secondary suggestibility. In the light of this, their results cannot be taken as entirely contradictory to those obtained by other investigators. In general, it appears safe to conclude that a small positive correlation exists between primary suggestibility and intelligence. Whether the relationship is slightly curvilinear or fully linear remains to be ascertained more conclusively. It may depend on the type of measures that are employed for studying the two variables. The data regarding secondary suggestibility are inconclusive.

The Influence of Personality Traits

This is unquestionably one of the most ambiguous areas. A great many assertions have been made about the relation of personality traits to suggestibility, few of which have been substantiated in any satisfactory manner. Among earlier investigators, Kretschmer associated hypnotic susceptibility with pyknics and cyclothymia; Wertheimer and Hesketh found that a high chest volume to height ratio and synthropism are correlated with hypnotic susceptibility. Jung affirmed a direct relationship between susceptibility and extraversion. Gross believed that a short secondary function was to be associated with hypnotic susceptibility. Stern connected objectivity with susceptibility while Janet believed the relation was with hysteria. Finally, Kraepelin and Bleuler thought manic-depressive individuals were particularly susceptible to suggestion. Conversely, these various investigators related the opposite of these traits with nonsuggestibility.

In more recent times Baumgartner (21) has reported evidence of a slight relation between suggestibility and a complex of traits including "sympathy," "sweet temper," and "tactfulness." Postural sway suggestions were used in this instance. Aveling and Hargreaves (8) found a rather low correlation between secondary and primary suggestibility as measured by a variety of tests on the one hand and "perseveration," "tendency to give up" (in the face of obstacles), and "originality of ideas" on the other. White (477) and Barry et al. (14) have considered such traits as height, weight, "extraversion," "dissociability," "assertiveness," and response to group suggestions. According to them, "extraversion" is about the only trait showing any amount of correlation with suggestibility. Bartlett (18) reported a slight correlation between suggestibility as measured by the postural sway test on the one hand and "habit patterns," "readiness to confide," "lack of dominance," "social adjustment," "lack of mental health," and "introversion" on the other. Davis and Husband (91) observed some signs of a relation between "introversion" and hypnotic susceptibility, but only for women. Using the Thurstone Personality Schedule, they found only a very small correlation between hypnotic susceptibility and neurosis. Similarly, Messer, Hinckley, and Mosier (306) could not find any correlation between scores on the Bernreuter neurotic inventory and suggestibility as measured by postural sway. These investigators, however, believe that postural sway may be related to "social maladjustment" and to "dominance." Wells (468) has reported a correlation between hypnotizability and "noncompliance," and also between the former and "ascendance." Eysenck (132) has observed evidence of a negative correlation between "personal tempo" and suggestibility. On the other hand, he reports that "perseveration" does not show any evidence of being related to suggestibility. This is true for both primary and secondary suggestibility. Friedlander and Sarbin (148) declare some relation exists between hypnotic susceptibility and "sociability" as well as with "extroversion" and with "dominance." Dahm and Jenness (87) report a negative correlation between "introversion" and suggestibility in men. According to Roach (369) suggestibility (measured by a variety of tests, none of primary suggestibility) correlates with scores on the Bernreuter Personality Inventory. He also reported that "introverted" women are more suggestible than "extraverted" ones. This relation, however, is not true of men. In a later study, Roach (370) used two groups of subjects. For one of these, made up of 19 students, he had the individuals rated as "extrovert" and "introvert" by three judges. In the other, the subjects, 36 in number, were rated in a similar manner by means of a scale (not described) of introversion–extraversion. The suggestibility of both groups was measured by means of autosuggested postural sway. Roach's results, as reported by him, are somewhat contradictory. In one part of his paper he stated that there was a significant difference in the distance swayed in favor of the introverts; but a little further on he summarized the results by concluding that the sway method of measuring suggestibility is unsatisfactory for certain statistical reasons. In a similar manner in his later paper he contradicted his earlier results (369) by stating that no differences had been found.

R. W. White (480) has reported that, in general, active hypnotic subjects score high on "deference" and "affiliation," but that the passive type scores low on these items. In contrast, the passive group scores high on "counteraction," "infravoidance," "abasement," and "anxiety."

Rorschach believed that color responses, or form and color responses, were indicative of affective suggestibility. Beck and Bell, among modern authorities on the Rorschach test, appear to also hold this opinion. None of these men has attempted to validate this belief through the use of external criteria, or even to find what possible empirical relation might exist between Rorschach scores and suggestibility. The first attempt in this direction seems to have been made by Sarbin and Madow (384) who gave Rorschach tests to subjects that had been classified as susceptible and insusceptible to hypnosis. Their results showed that one could not differentiate between the two groups of subjects on the basis of their individual Rorschach psychograms. Nor was this possible by using the various Rorschach factors in combination. They did find that a W/D ratio greater than 0.40 was characteristic of susceptible individuals and one less than 0.40 was associated with insusceptible subjects. This was a difference of high statistical significance. They concluded from this that hypnotic susceptibility is a function of Rorschach's *Erfassungstypus,* and that susceptibility is also correlated with abstract attitudes.

Brenman and Reichard (48) attempted to repeat this study and reported that free-floating anxiety is associated with susceptible subjects. Labile affectivity (as defined by Rorschach) may also be positively correlated with hypnotic susceptibility. Again, extratensiveness is related to the susceptibility. On the other hand, they could not find any evidence that the W/D ratio was related to hypnotic susceptibility.

Of the two studies, the second might be considered somewhat superior in that a larger number of subjects was employed (38 against 24). On the other hand, this is possibly compensated for by the use of analysis of variance in the first investigation. On the basis of an observation reported by Steisel (427), it is very likely that the above two groups of investigators were working with skewed distributions of scores. In this case, unless the skewness was slight, their statistical analyses of the results are probably none too meaningful. In any event, the two studies are far from being comparable for two reasons. First, Sarbin et al. scored the Rorschach responses using Beck's system whereas Brenman et al. employed the scoring system of Klopfer.† Second and more important, Brenman and Reichard made use of a mixed group of psychiatric patients and normal individuals, in contrast to Sarbin and Madow who presumably employed only normal subjects.

In spite of certain weaknesses, the best study of this problem to date is probably the one reported by Steisel (427). He derived nine probable measures of suggestibility from the Rorschach test ‡ and studied their relationship to suggestibility as measured by (*a*) postural sway suggestion, (*b*) the subject's responses in an autokinetic situation, and (*c*) a variation of the ink blot test of suggestibility (see Chapter 1). His results led him to conclude that there is no consistent relationship among the various scores he obtained.

† Although it is said that interscorer reliabilities are high.

‡ These were arrived at on the basis of the interpretation of Rorschach scores by various authorities, and on the basis of a number of views concerning the nature of suggestibility. To this last we will come back shortly.

Unfortunately it is not possible to make use of Steisel's results to confirm or disprove the conclusions of either Sarbin and Madow or Brenman and Reichard, because again there is a lack of comparability. As remarked earlier, these two groups of investigators measured hypnotic susceptibility. On the other hand, Steisel measured suggestibility in three specific waking situations. Of these, only one, the postural sway test, is known to have a definite relation to hypnotic susceptibility, and, as mentioned earlier, suggestibility to this test accounts at most for about 55 per cent of hypnotic susceptibility. The ink blot test has been shown by Eysenck and Furneaux (129) to be a test of secondary suggestibility. In fact, they found that suggestibility to it accounts for only about 4 per cent of trance susceptibility. As for the autokinetic test used by Steisel, it may well be questioned, on the basis of the data available,§ whether it would bear any relation to hypnotic susceptibility.

In connection with the lack of comparability, it should also be observed that the statistical treatment of the data of these experiments was not entirely the same. Steisel based his conclusions on the correlations between normalized scores, whereas Sarbin et al. and Brenman et al. used differences between the means of unnormalized data.||

Steisel himself suggested a number of possible reasons for his negative findings. The design of the investigation might be the cause. Or possibly the suggestibility measures cited by other users of the Rorschach test are true only for deviant populations. Or perhaps after all there is really no correlation between the particular Rorschach measures used in his study and his criterion measures of suggestibility. In this last supposition Steisel possibly seems to have come closest to the truth of the matter. One may indeed question rather strongly the validity of at least five of the nine premises on which his measures were based, namely, that there is a negative relationship between suggestibility and (a) degree of intellectual control in affective situations,

§ More correctly stated, there is no evidence one way or the other. Studies thus far have been concerned with the effect of prestige situations on autokinetic streaming, the main ones being those of Sherif (410), Bray (46), Kelman (231), and Bovard (43). This is the reason why the autokinetic phenomenon has not been taken up in this book. It is unfortunate that Steisel has not reported the correlation between his scores on the autokinetic and the postural sway tests, since this might throw much light on this question.

|| Other points of noncomparability were the use of the Beck system and of normal subjects by Steisel and also the fact that, except for one Rorschach measure, the others were different from those employed by Sarbin et al. and by Brenman et al.

(b) conscious control, (c) critical ability; and a positive relation between it and (d) conformity of thinking, and (e) number of responses to the Rorschach test.¶

Looking over this material, we cannot help but feel somewhat confused. Data are not lacking, but they show no definite pattern; ambiguity appears to be the keynote. Analysis of the situation seems to indicate two main reasons for this: First of all there is little basis for comparison of data. Not only have investigators used nonequivalent scales for measuring suggestibility and hypnotic susceptibility, but also they have employed a large variety of noncomparable tests to study various personality traits. This leads to a second and even more fundamental weakness of this area of investigation, namely: "Personality" itself is a very poorly defined topic, and on the whole the instruments that are available for the investigation of so-called personality traits are rather crude. It is doubtful that the situation will clear up until investigators in the field of personality standardize their tests and scales better. Until then little can be concluded from the reported results.

Influence of Attitudes, Expectancy, and Motivation

The majority of hypnotists contend that a co-operative attitude on the part of the subject is a help in inducing hypnosis. Eysenck and Furneaux (129) maintain that attitude is a factor in waking suggestibility, the latter being the resultant of an innate capacity for response to suggestions and of negative or positive attitudes. R. W. White (481) holds the same view. He has reported data showing a correlation between hypnotizability * and general social attitudes, and again between hypnotizability and the subject's attitude toward hypnosis itself.† Brenman and Reichard (48) found from Rorschach scores that some subjects able to resist any attempts to induce hypnosis show also a definite negativism.

Furneaux (152) has not been able to find any evidence that expectation affects susceptibility to hypnosis. Wells (469) is also of this opinion, reporting also that Braid, Bramwell, Moll, and Brenman and Knight (52) agree with this. Wells attempted one of the few experi-

¶ The reasons for questioning these premises must be left to the theoretical portion of the book. However, it may be stated here that each premise is a belief of old standing which has no specific empirical validation.

* Used in the sense of susceptibility.

† This last was determined by the subject's response to Card 12M of the Thematic Apperception Test.

mental investigations of this question, repeating an older investigation made by Crane.   Unfortunately, the entire investigation suffers from serious weaknesses which make the results, and particularly the conclusions, of dubious validity.

R. W. White (480) has made an extensive study of the role of motivation in suggestibility. He found some indication that motivation does play a role in determining hypnotic susceptibility. He concludes that a pattern of needs disposing the subject toward being hypnotized favors trance induction. McDougall (295) has proposed that subjects were satisfying an "instinct" of submission when passing into the hypnotic state. Rivers (368) considers hypnosis as resulting from a "herd instinct." Finally, Sarbin (385), developing White's hypothesis further, adds that hypnosis is a form of a general sociopsychological behavior which he calls "role-taking." We might also add to this list the names of various investigators who support the psychoanalytical interpretation of hypnosis. Certainly the attainment of pleasure goals, for instance, could be considered under the present heading. However, this material might be better suited to another heading.‡

In looking over the above material, we find a certain amount of ambiguity existing among the various investigations. It results from the fact that attitude, belief, expectation, and to some extent motivation are not always clearly separated from one another. There appear to be situations in which such a separation seems to be rather difficult, if at all possible, to achieve. It might be pointed out that the results White obtained using Card 12M can be interpreted in a different manner from the one he employed. Namely, one may consider the card as constituting nothing more than a test suggestion, no different from those that have been discussed in previous pages. It is obvious that, if the card is so structured as to have the capacity of a direct suggestion and to act as one, response to it should bear a relation to hypnotic susceptibility. It is my belief that this is the true character of this test.

White's study of motivation in its relation to suggestibility constitutes a very thorough and comprehensive investigation and is the only one upon which any reliance can be placed. However, whether or not one will agree with him regarding the influence of motivation on suggestibility depends largely on whether or not one understands and accepts his definition of need and motivation, a definition which is a little out of the ordinary. According to White, and assuming that I understand

‡ It might be remarked that it was included by White in his study, largely under the topic of "latent needs."

him correctly, needs are aroused by specific situations and do not exist apart from them. This is in contrast to the point of view that the need exists prior to any given situation and causes the individual to seek out such situations as will satisfy his need. That is, a need is a particular over-all reaction of the organism to a given situation. This reaction becomes antecedent to the individual's subsequent behavior as long as the said situation remains unaltered. In terms of this, the hypnotic situation appears to be nothing more than another situation that tends to reorganize the subject's neuromuscular apparatus into a complex pattern which exhibits the characteristics of the various needs found related to hypnotic susceptibility. This is a viewpoint that merits further attention.

On the whole, there is some evidence that a positive attitude favors suggestibility, and conversely. Expectation appears to be a negligible factor. Needs and motivation appear to be related in various ways to suggestibility. But whether they are to be considered as determinants of suggestibility is a debatable point. These results as well as those of later sections are probably well summarized by Ehrenreich's (107) conclusions that various unconscious factors influence hypnotizability,§ and that it may be best thought of as a selective and individualistic acceptance of various suggestions. It does not appear either necessary or correct to deduce from this, as Ehrenreich does, that we should therefore assume the existence of various kinds of suggestibilities or hypnotizabilities, except possibly in one sense to be considered later.

The Influence of Dynamic Factors

In accordance with Hinsie and Shatzky (198), by dynamism we shall mean "the action of psychic structures and . . . the forces behind the action. A dynamism 'is a specific force operating in a specific manner or direction.'" If we think of a psychic structure as the total system of interactions existing among the various elements that make up an individual mentally speaking, a question arises as to what possible influence preferred structures may have on suggestibility.

Rosenzweig and Sarason (380) have investigated one aspect of this question. As mentioned earlier, they report having found that hypnotizability has a positive relationship with "repression" and "impunitiveness," whereas nonhypnotizability is associated with "displacement" and "projection," and with "intropunitiveness" and "extrapunitiveness."

§ Meaning susceptibility.

Petrie (345) does not fully agree with this, although, if one substitutes, as Eysenck (131) has suggested, the term "neurotic" for "hysteric" in the triadic hypothesis, Petrie's results are found to be more in agreement with those of Rosenzweig and Sarason.

The Influence of Transference

Ferenczi (138) believed that susceptibility to hypnosis depended on the extent of transference formed between subject and hypnotist. According to him a parent-child relation is involved. To a certain extent the results of White and of Rosenzweig and Sarason would seem to indicate that there may be considerably more to the role of a submission-dominance relationship in hypnosis than at first appears. It does not follow, however, from the results that a transference effect must of necessity evolve. This relationship can manifest itself in other ways. Wolberg (497) conceives hypnosis as resulting from the subject's desire to obtain pleasure goals in the form of security and avoidance of pain. Kubie and Margolin (247) also agree that transference phenomena are part of the trance induction and carry over into the hypnotic state; however, they do not make it the basis of hypnosis as others have done. Jones (228), Freud (146), Schilder and Kauder (392), Speyer and Stokvis (418), and Lorand (276) all postulated or reported having found erotic components in hypnosis. Hull (213) could not find evidence for this. Friedlander and Sarbin (148) and Eysenck (132) have been unable to find any effect caused by the sex of the suggestor. White (480) after reviewing all available data concludes that there is no evidence that the sex of the hypnotist is a factor. On the other hand, Rosenzweig and Sarason (380), in analyzing their results, remark that they believe there is evidence of an erotic component connecting hypnotizability with impunitiveness. This evidence does not appear to be particularly strong.

That transference phenomena unquestionably do occur in connection with the induction of hypnosis and even during hypnosis appears to be a fact. But there is no evidence that such phenomena are invariably present at such times, nor that they are necessary for the production of a trance state. Some inductions of hypnosis are probably favored by transference phenomena, but only because they act in such instances in the same manner as attitudes and motivation. On the whole, it appears more logical to accept transference as a *concurrent* phenomenon which may well be facilitated by hypnosis but which in itself is not instrumental in bringing this state about. Evidence in support of this point of view comes from the observation that manifestations with erotic components are not uncommonly seen during the early stages of gas anesthesia, particularly with nitrous oxide. One would hardly maintain because of this that transference is responsible for the production of narcosis and anesthesia. Instead, if present, it can only be as a side effect. It is more likely that the same holds true for hypnosis. In support of the point of view held here, evidence reported by Mazer (294) shows that the interpersonal relation involved in hypnosis varies considerably with subjects and that it can express itself in many ways other than through eroticism or dominance–submission.

Thus the entire question of transference appears to reduce to a statement that hypnotic phenomena occur within a framework of interpersonal relations, and that classical transference is merely one manifestation of this.

Influence of Miscellaneous Factors

Drug Addiction. Although smoking can hardly be considered a drug addiction, it does constitute a good introduction to this section. Valance (446) has studied the comparative suggestibility of smokers and nonsmokers, using the postural sway test. He found the first group less suggestible than the second one. Whether smoking brings about a decrease in suggestibility or those who are smokers are already negatively suggestible is not shown by this investigation.

Vogel (451) has made an extensive investigation of the suggestibility of opium, morphine, and heroine addicts. Postural sway suggestions were employed. He reports that addicts tend to be hypersuggestible, and that this hypersuggestibility tends to decrease with withdrawal. Vogel concludes that addicts are probably normally suggestible before coming under the influence of the drugs. Whether the rise in suggestibility when the subject is under the influence of drugs is caused by a positive action of the drugs upon suggestibility or is only the result of an inhibition of natural tendencies toward negative responses is not known. In the light of the results obtained on the effects of subanesthetic doses of various hypnotics, and considering that addicts normally take comparable doses, the first alternative appears highly probable.||

Abnormal Personalities. This topic has been considered in detail in Chapter 3 and will not be taken up any further here.

|| This does not necessarily exclude the second alternative which may represent another effect.

Summary and Conclusions

In summary, it appears that we may say that suggestibility is highest at the ages of seven to eight, and that it is somewhat greater for women and girls than for men and boys, and greater for individuals of higher than of lower intelligence (these being measured on a Binet-type test). In regard to personality traits no general conclusions can be drawn.

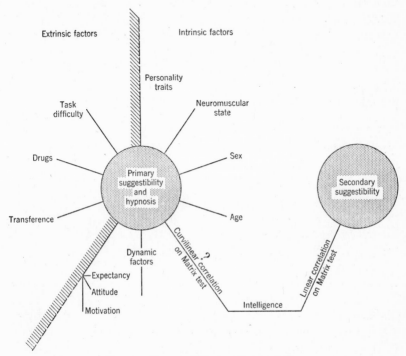

Fig. 3.   Factors Affecting Suggestibility

Attitudes and motivation appear to have some influence upon suggestibility, a facilitation resulting when they are positive. Data on the role of expectancy are inconclusive. There is also some evidence that a definite relation exists between repression (or its lack), the type of reaction to frustration employed by the subject, and susceptibility. Although transference may enter as a factor in determining suggestibility in some instances, there is no evidence that this is universally true, but rather the contrary. Addicts to certain narcotics are found to be hypersuggestible. This is probably a direct effect of the drugs and not an innate trait of addicts.   An attempt has been made to diagram some of these interactions in Figure 3.

If any one conclusion can be derived from the material thus far covered, it is that, in general, *the effectiveness of a suggestion is a function of the subject, its own content, and the total situation in which it is given.*

The Hypnotic State in Relation to Wakefulness and Sleep

The classical picture of hypnosis has many outward points of resemblance to natural sleep, so much so, that one often speaks of
"hypnotic sleep." It is standard terminology to speak of "waking up"
the hypnotized subject and to refer to his being in the "waking state"
when not hypnotized. Again it is customary to induce hypnosis by
means of suggestions of "sleep," in which various symptoms antecedent
to sleep as well as the notion of sleep are suggested. Nevertheless,
hypnosis has also at times characteristics atypical of natural sleep.*
Generally, in the absence of further suggestions, the outward appearance of the subject after the onset of hypnosis is one of a person asleep.
Every so often relaxation becomes so complete that the subject col-
lapses to the ground and appears as if he had fainted. However, when
suggestions are given that are aimed at bringing about various activities on the part of the subject, he may appear outwardly as if he were
awake.

Inasmuch as a great many, if not all, of the phenomena obtained
under hypnosis can be brought about, at least in some subjects, in the
waking state (without the help of any prior hypnotization), and,
furthermore, since one observes the occurrence in psychopathological
individuals of phenomena such as paramnesia, paralysis, and glove
anesthesia in no way different from similar phenomena produced
through hypnotic suggestion, it becomes a moot question whether
hypnosis has any relation at all to sleep. Furthermore, individuals in
natural sleep normally do not respond to suggestions.† Yet it is also

---

* The reader will find an excellent account of the outward appearance of hypnotized individuals in Schilder and Kauder's monograph (392).

† It is said by various authors that one can transform natural sleep into hypnosis
by giving trance-inducing suggestions to the sleeping person. To this extent then
a sleeping individual may respond to suggestion. It should be noted, however,
that this in itself does not necessarily mean that sleep has anything to do with it.
If, as is usually interpreted, the sleeping person is partially conscious, it should

clear that the observed heightening of suggestibility which follows the induction of a hypnotic state, particularly its heteroactive aspect, is not normally present in the waking state. We may therefore also question the identification of the hypnotic state with wakefulness.

Physiological Changes in Sleep and Hypnosis

An objective approach to this question is accessible in the guise of a study of the physiological correlates of sleep, wakefulness, and hypnosis. Since narcosis appears to bear some relationship to both sleep and hypnosis, it will also be included in this group. The existing literature on the physiology of sleep is voluminous. Fortunately, this material has been conveniently compiled and critically examined by Kleitman (234), and it is to this single but excellent source of information that the reader will be referred in regard to data on sleep and wakefulness.

Generally speaking, the state of the skeletal musculature and the position of the body in sleep and in hypnosis have only a superficial resemblance to each other. In particular, the postural reflexes are for the most part inoperative during sleep but are fully active in hypnosis. Relative immobility and a dorsal or lateral position of the body are usually characteristic of sleep but not of hypnosis. There are also less obvious differences. On the whole, hypnosis bears little resemblance to sleep in these respects and is much more like wakefulness.

Sleep appears to diminish the strength of reflexes and to increase reflex time. This is particularly true for the tendon reflexes which may vanish altogether. On the other hand, the galvanic skin reflex is increased. In contrast, during hypnosis, it has been reported by Bass (19) and by Brown (59) that there is no alteration of tendon reflexes. True and Stephenson (445) have substantiated this. Peiper (343) and Levine (264) could not find any evidence of changes in skin resistance during hypnosis. However, both Brown (59) and Estabrook (127) observed a rise in skin resistance. It is entirely possible that in these two last cases the subjects actually passed from hypnosis into a state of natural sleep, thus invalidating the observations. Or perhaps both investigators were dealing with a state of "passive" hypnosis as defined by Davis and Kantor (92). These two investigators speak of "passive" hypnosis in reference to situations in which suggestions of deep sleep only are given and of "active" hypnosis in instances where suggestions

indeed follow that, if he also has any suggestibility, he should respond to suggestions whether asleep or waking. In fact, sleep might favor suggestibility for reasons similar to those given for narcosis.

other than of sleep are given (such as paralysis of the arm). They report that skin resistance in active hypnosis is the same as in waking but resembles that for sleep during passive hypnosis. Ravitz (359–360) has reported that, when standing potentials (measured between the forehead and the palm of the hand) are studied in subjects, it is found that the potentials in hypnosis are smoother than in the waking state. In addition there is an increase or decrease of the mean potential in a manner that appears to parallel the depth of hypnosis. On the other hand, when hypnosis is compared to sleep, it is reported by Ravitz that the two can be distinguished only when hypnosis causes a rise in potential difference. That is, sleep and drowsy states cause a drop in voltage in no way different from that which is produced at times by hypnosis.

During sleep, various changes are observed in the composition of the blood. Observations made by Goldwyn (166) and by Wittkower (495) during hypnosis show no comparable changes. Kleitman (234) is of the opinion, however, that blood changes in sleep are not physiologically significant, being simply the direct result of postural changes. Most investigators appear to agree that heart rate and pulse rate decrease in sleep. Kleitman (234) believes that this merely results directly from the associated relaxation. Electrocardiographic changes which are also observed in sleep are probably directly caused by the change in rate. A fall in blood pressure is usually reported by investigators, as well as a decrease in fluctuation. Recent evidence seems to indicate that a rise in intracranial pressure and in cerebral blood volume (whenever possible) accompanies sleep. The evidence for comparable circulatory changes in hypnosis is rather ambiguous. Jenness and Wible (227) report finding no differences in electrocardiograms obtained during hypnosis and waking. Whitehorn et al. (484) report a slight decrease in heart rate during hypnosis. This has been substantiated by other investigators. Relaxation, however, may account for this. On the other hand, True and Stephenson (445) did not find any difference in pulse rate between hypnosis and waking, but they observed various degrees of increase in pulse rate during the induction of hypnosis itself. Walden (453) found by means of a plethysmograph that hypnosis produces vasoconstriction of the arm. On the other hand, Doupe, Miller, and Keller (101) were unable to find any such change. Nygard (326) reported observing no alteration in the cerebral circulation during hypnosis.

In general, during sleep changes in respiration are observed. These can best be accounted for, at least in greater part, as resulting from a depression of the respiratory centers. Although the situation in regard to hypnosis is not without ambiguity, the best data thus far obtained and as reported by Jenness and Wible (227) show no obvious changes in respiration during hypnosis.

Most investigators agree that the basal metabolic rate is decreased in sleep, the reduction being on the average about 10 per cent. This may be partly or wholly the result of the accompanying relaxation. Whitehorn, Lundholm, Fox, and Benedict (484) have not been able to find any changes in BMR during hypnosis, even when the subjects were trained to relax. Grassheim and Wittkower (170) and Fulde (150) confirm this fact. Goldwyn (166) did observe, however, an average reduction in BMR during hypnosis, but amounting to only 3.88 per cent. His results are therefore essentially in agreement with those of Whitehorn et al. and others.

It is generally agreed that sleep brings about fundamental changes in encephalograms. Loomis, Harvey, and Hobart (274, 275) have been able to distinguish five stages of sleep by means of brain potentials. In a similar manner Blake and Gerard (36) found six stages. It is generally said that the alpha wave disappears during sleep and is replaced by random delta waves and sometimes by spindles.

It has been the consensus of opinion in the past that encephalograms observed in hypnosis show no appreciable difference from those seen in the waking state. Thus Loomis et al. (273) report never having observed random delta waves or spindles during hypnosis. Blake and Gerard (36) and Sirna (415) have confirmed this. Dynes (104), Ford and Yeager (143), and True and Stephenson (445) arrived at similar results. More recently, however, Franck (144) declared he had observed random deltas during hypnosis. Unfortunately, he does not make any details of his investigation available, so that no comparison with other works is possible, nor can we obtain an estimate of the validity of his findings. Darrow, Henry, Gill, and Brenman (88, 89) have made a study of relationships existing between encephalograms obtained from different cerebral areas (primarily in terms of phase relationships). They reported definite evidence that, in respect to such relationships, hypnosis differs from wakefulness and that hypnosis cannot be distinguished from drowsiness and the early stages of sleep (hypnoidal states). With increase in depth of sleep a difference appears, similar to that observed for waking and hypnosis. Here, too, there is a lack of detail concerning the investigation which renders it difficult to evaluate the correct significance of the results. The high level of confidence at which the observed differences were found to hold compensates somewhat for the above. It would seem, therefore, that, although outwardly electroencephalograms show hypnosis to be more like wakefulness and less like sleep, a more refined study of the records shows hypnosis to be more like *light* sleep, and like neither waking nor deep sleep.

In summary, thus far with a few minor exceptions it would appear that hypnosis is not at all like sleep, but resembles wakefulness in regard to a large variety of physiological phenomena. A possible exception to this would be so-called "passive" hypnosis. For a validation of this, we must turn to further data obtained from electroencephalographic studies.

"Hypnotic Sleep" and Hypnotic Hypersuggestibility

Even on the general character of observed encephalograms there is more to be said than has been reported earlier. This was demonstrated by Barker and Burgwin (12, 13), whose work has thrown a completely new light on the entire matter. They observed that, if hypnosis is induced by means of visual fixation combined with eye closure suggestion,‡ no changes are observed in the encephalograms of the subjects. However, if after the induction of hypnosis by this method one tries to bring about a state resembling sleep by means of suggestions specifically directed at producing the symptoms of sleep,§ then the brain wave patterns take on the same aspects as those seen in natural sleep. The similarity is so complete that the two investigators conclude: "Sleep indistinguishable electroencephalographically from normal sleep in various stages may be produced by hypnosis."

On the basis of these results, Barker and Burgwin maintain that it is essential to distinguish between what they call "hypnotic sleep" and "hypnotic suggestibility." They point out, for instance, that what Dynes (104) refers to as a "trance" is nothing else but what they have called "hypnotic suggestibility." Partial and indirect confirmation of the above distinction can be found in an earlier investigation of Lundholm and Lowenbach (280). The results of Davis and Kantor (92) on skin resistance show that "active" hypnosis as defined by them is most probably the equivalent of "hypnotic suggestibility," whereas "passive" hypnosis appears to be nothing more than "hypnotic sleep."

‡ It is not entirely clear from their report whether suggestions such as those of relaxation were given besides those of heaviness and closing of the eyes.

§ Suggestions of relaxation and of loss of sensory contact with the environment were primarily used for this. In addition, the subjects were told that ordinary sleep was now desired.

In terms of these findings it also appears now that earlier investigations of brain potentials in hypnosis were dealing primarily with active hypnosis (or hypnotic suggestibility). Inasmuch as Darrow et al. (89) speak of "alert" states, particularly of "alert" hypnosis, it may be that their results are nothing more than a confirmation of the above. Unfortunately they have not explained what they meant by this expression.

True and Stephenson (445) have questioned the findings of Barker and Burgwin, stating that they were unable to obtain sleep EEG's, in spite of the fact that they had instructed the subjects to sleep. It is my impression, however, that the otherwise excellent investigation of True et al. was in no way comparable to that of Barker et al., particularly in relation to the suggestions used to bring about "sleep." It is quite clear from the report of Barker and Burgwin that more than instructions to "sleep" are required. Any attempt to disprove their results will first have to duplicate their procedures point for point.

Hypnosis and Narcosis

So much for the question of whether hypnosis is similar or not similar to natural sleep. The next matter we must consider is the possible relation of hypnosis to sleep-like states induced by various means, and more precisely by drugs. Numerous attempts have been made to bring about by artificial means states comparable to natural sleep. There is no need to go into detail here: the reader is referred instead to the excellent account by Kleitman (234). In general, it has been found that functional and surgical deafferation will bring about such a state. Furthermore, the same sort of phenomenon can be obtained by mechanical, electrical, and chemical stimulation of various parts of the brain. The resulting states appear to be *unrelated* to either hypnosis or narcosis.

Bechterew (23) has maintained that sleep, narcosis, and hypnosis are of the same nature. As was just seen, this is far from correct insofar as hypnosis and sleep are concerned. It might be thought, however, that narcosis and hypnosis are related, in the light of the facilitating effect light narcosis seems to have on suggestibility and on the induction of hypnosis. There is actually no evidence for this. The changes in physiological functions, particularly in brain potentials, which are brought about by various degrees of narcosis induced with the barbiturates have been investigated in both human and animal subjects. We may cite in this connection the reports of Brazier and Finesinger (47), Swank and Foley (436), and of Cohn and Katzenelbogen (73). Comparison of these data with those obtained for hypnosis shows that *the two types of states are basically different*. Marinesco, Sager, and Kreindler (291) have compared electroencephalograms obtained in sleep, hypnosis, and barbiturate narcosis, and they arrive at the same conclusion in regard to light narcosis. It may also be noted that light narcosis was not found to bear any resemblance to sleep either, whereas deep narcosis is reported as showing some points of similarity. Ravitz (359) in his study of standing potentials found that amytal narcosis differed from hypnosis and sleep. Here then we have proof of a statement made earlier (Chapter 4) to the effect that, *though light narcosis does facilitate the induction of hypnosis, it does not in itself produce hypnosis*.

A possible meeting ground for sleep, hypnosis, and light narcosis lies in a peculiar state which Kleitman (234) describes as being neither sleep nor wakefulness, and which may be considered as a mixture of both in various proportions. It is found present just before the onset of definite sleep or definite wakefulness. This state appears to be intermediate between sleep and wakefulness and might well be called a *borderline state*. It may be significant that it is accompanied by characteristic subjective phenomena which bear a strong resemblance to similar phenomena observed in hypnosis and particularly during the induction of hypnosis. Such effects have been reported by Schneck (397–400). Brenman, Gill, and Hackner (49) have also described these phenomena under the more inclusive heading of psychodynamic manifestations in hypnosis. They include under this heading changes in body awareness, changes in modes of thought, release of emotion, and motor expression. Similar manifestations are also observed during the induction of narcosis. It may be that a common neuromuscular state is involved here. The rise in suggestibility in light narcosis might serve as a basis for the various unverified reports that sleep may be converted into hypnosis. Further support for the belief that the borderline state is a meeting ground between sleep and hypnosis comes from observations of Darrow et al. (88) and of Ravitz (359) concerning drowsy states.

Rapport—Fact or Artifact?

Thus far our concern has been with the physiological aspects of whether hypnosis is related to sleep. We now turn our attention to a somewhat different feature of the problem, namely, the responsiveness of the subject to stimuli when asleep, wakeful, or in hypnosis. This will lead us in turn to consider the basic question of the reality and nature of "rapport."

That there are major differences between the responsiveness of the subject in natural sleep and in hypnosis is only too obvious. The sleeping individual is relatively unresponsive, in contrast to the hypnotized subject who is, if anything, overresponsive in some instances. Usually the hypnotized individual is responsive in a relatively direct and specific manner, whereas the sleeping individual tends to respond in a diffused manner. As a matter of fact, the behavior of the hypnotized subject may be described as purposive, well-integrated and organized, and capable of attaining all of the complexity of waking behavior. This is far from true of the individual who is asleep. Finally, the sleeper can be described as having on the whole a very low level of awareness, if any, as contrasted to the hypnotized person. It is significant that Barker and Burgwin (12, 13) have observed that a large capacity to respond to stimuli may be present in some instances of hypnotic sleep, but that, whenever such a response occurs, the hypnotic sleep passes immediately into the state of hypnotic suggestibility.

It is the usual experience of the hypnotist that his subjects show a selective responsiveness toward him, being seemingly unaware of stimuli emanating from other sources. This is the so-called state of *rapport*, once believed to be a true criterion of hypnosis. Actually, it is found to be a rather fluid state, readily altered by suggestions which may transfer it and make it either more inclusive or more exclusive. Among earlier investigators, Braid, Moll, and Bramwell believed that rapport was entirely the result of auto- or heterosuggestion. Hull (213) has concurred to this. Young (503) tried to investigate the question experimentally and found that subjects could reject heterosuggestions through the influence of earlier autosuggestions || without necessarily coming out of hypnosis. Such a rejection he interpreted as a true break in rapport and concluded that rapport can be broken and is not essential for the existence of hypnosis. An analysis of Young's investigation shows, however, that an alternative conclusion exists which is also more likely. It will be taken up in a later and more appropriate chapter (Chapter 15), but it may be said here that much depends upon what one interprets as rapport. Young appears to take acceptance of suggestions as synonymous with this phenomenon. It is probably safer

|| I have had occasion to witness similar instances as well as situations in which rejection was due to the subject's objection to the suggestions. But even then hypnosis persisted.

to consider (as we shall do here) the extent of an individual's *respon-siveness* to his environment as *the degree of his rapport* with it. The existing data then appear to indicate that *in hypnosis the individual will exhibit a variable degree of responsiveness to a more or less restricted field of stimuli and that overt response is in no way essential for hypnosis.*¶

Erickson (111) has thrown further light onto the question. He reported evidence that awareness in hypnosis is not an all-or-none proposition, but that there are various degrees of awareness and unawareness. Furthermore he was able to demonstrate that it can be highly selective, that a subject may respond to a stimulus and yet not be able to recognize its true nature, and that in many instances the stimulus may be internalized. His investigation appears to indicate that the hypnotic situation, when properly established, *can limit an individual's awareness to the point of completely excluding certain stimuli from it.* Hull (213) suggested earlier that rapport might well be spoken of more correctly as *selective anesthesia,* and as such would have reality. The existence of this phenomenon has been demonstrated rather nicely, for instance, by Erickson (123) in a situation reminiscent of the one existing in the production of rapport. The results obtained by him (111) suggest that an even more correct interpretation might be that *rapport is a form of restricted awareness, associated with a state of hypersuggestibility to some or all stimuli residing within the field of awareness.*

Hypnosis and Dissociation

Finally we might consider the question of hypnotic dissociation. A great many past students of hypnosis have been convinced that hypnosis was a state of dissociation. Thus far the little available evidence has been against this premise. Mitchell (313) has shown for instance that retroactive inhibition is present in successive trance-waking states. Messerschmidt (309) has demonstrated that there is interference between two tasks, even though one is being performed unconsciously by the subject and the other consciously. The conclusion would appear to be that hypnosis is not a state of dissociation if we mean by this that a state of functional independence exists between two aspects of the subject's behavior.

¶ It should also not be overlooked that the appearance of hypnosis *is itself a response* of the subject to the hypnotist and one to which other responses are subordinated. As long as hypnosis persists, one may well question whether there is a break in rapport (assuming one may speak of rapport).

Summary and Conclusions

In summary then, it would appear at present that we must distinguish carefully between induced states of suggestibility and suggested states of sleep * when speaking of hypnosis. The first is a state of hypersuggestibility of primary type † which appears to be physiologically the same as waking. *Within* this state the second one may be produced. The latter cannot be distinguished from natural sleep (at least light sleep) with respect to the psychogalvanic skin reflex and electroencephalograms when ordinary methods of investigation are employed. With special and more sensitive techniques there is some indication that it may be possible to make distinctions in terms of electroencephalographic and of electrometric measurements. For the time being, however, we may call the state of hypnotic suggestibility *hypnosis proper* and the other state *hypnotic sleep.*

There are also indications that the borderline state existing between sleep and wakefulness, and between the latter and (or in) light narcosis, is characterized by similar psychodynamic manifestations which are also to be found in the induction phase of hypnosis. This may be a common factor among all these states.

Finally the reality of rapport appears to depend largely on how we define and use this term. It now appears that the *persistence* of a hypnotic state is not dependent on the acceptance by the subject of all suggestions given to him, or even on his being responsive to the hypnotist *once* hypnosis has been induced. As such then, rapport has no reality. On the other hand, it is quite real as a state of variable and restricted awareness associated with a state of hypersuggestibility.‡ As such, it is a function of both present and past events as they enter into the defining of the hypnotic situation for the subject.

* Or between passive and active hypnosis.

† That is, involving primary suggestibility only.

‡ It is important to understand here that there is rapport in this sense only as long as there is *some* restriction of awareness *above and beyond* the *normal* waking awareness and as long as *hypersuggestibility is present.* An alternative is to speak of *complete* rapport when there is full awareness and hypersuggestibility and of *partial* rapport when awareness is restricted, hypersuggestibility still being present.

·8·

Posthypnotic Phenomena

According to common usage, the expression "posthypnotic" designates action carried out by a subject at some arbitrary future date as a result of and in accordance with suggestions given in a previous trance state. Unfortunately, for purposes of scientific discussion, this is too restricted a meaning for a term that etymologically has a much broader scope. In studying the aftereffects of hypnosis and hypnotic suggestions, we soon come to realize that such effects fall into at least two major categories: (*a*) those phenomena that result from specific suggestions aimed at bringing them about at the appropriate time (delayed hypnotic suggestions), and (*b*) phenomena that are merely characteristic aftereffects of hypnosis per se, that is, are not the result of any specific, directed suggestion. Obviously, either type of effect, taking place as it does after hypnosis, has a "posthypnotic" character. They differ primarily in that one is suggested and the other spontaneous. Accordingly, *a phenomenon will be said to be posthypnotic when it takes place in the waking state, or at least after a period of waking, and when it can be unambiguously associated with, or shown to have its genesis in, a previous hypnotic state.* It will be said to be *suggested* or *spontaneous,* in accordance with the above. One departure from this definition is required by usage, namely, the expression *posthypnotic suggestion,* meaning not a suggestion given after hypnosis, but instead a delayed hypnotic suggestion to be effective at a later date after hypnosis is terminated.

Some Characteristics of Posthypnotic Phenomena

The existence of posthypnotic phenomena has been known for a long time. One of the earliest report of this effect goes back to Mouillesaux in the 18th century. It is probable that certain forms of spell casting reported down through the ages reduce to the giving of posthypnotic suggestions. If this be true, the latter have indeed been made use of from time immemorial. But, without going this far back, there has been since the time of Mouillesaux an abundance of

101

reports of this sort of phenomenon, leaving little doubt of its existence. Little can be said about spontaneous posthypnotic effects. With the possible exception of spontaneous amnesia, of which more will be said shortly, we find little else that can be interpreted as such. Every so often we see or hear of subjects developing a violent headache after hypnosis, or more rarely of feeling confused or drowsy. Only recently I came across a case of hysterical fainting which had been brought about by a subject refusing to carry out a posthypnotic suggestion given by a hypnotist. Inasmuch as these are instances in which the observed phenomena appear to be aftereffects of hypnosis, and not the result of specific suggestions, we can probably speak of them as spontaneous posthypnotic effects.

The situation is altogether different with respect to suggested posthypnotic effects. It has been a common belief that the individual who executes these suggestions is unaware of the cues initiating the posthypnotic act and usually of carrying it out. Erickson and Erickson (112) believe that the posthypnotic act is characterized by a lack of conscious awareness of the underlying causes and motives. How correct this is remains to be demonstrated. Estabrook (128) reported that two of his subjects were able to recognize posthypnotic suggestions in the course of carrying them out. Marcuse, Hill, and Keegan (285) have investigated one aspect of this problem. Their results appear to show the following. There is evidence that posthypnotic acts and suggestions can lie at various levels of awareness. It is possible for some, if not all subjects, to become aware that they are carrying out a posthypnotic suggestion. However, such awareness is usually indirect in nature, the subject reasoning backward after execution of the suggestion. This report, as well as others, appears to indicate that, even when a subject is not aware of the true nature of his action, he may be acutely aware of carrying it out and may go to extremes to rationalize his behavior. Finally, the evidence obtained from the above-mentioned reports tends to show that, even though a subject may be aware of the nature of his behavior as being posthypnotic, he nevertheless will usually carry it out.

According to an investigation of Kellogg (232), posthypnotic suggestions will persist for at least two months, but tend to lose strength in an exponential manner. Strangely enough, he found that, when nonhypnotized subjects (controls) performed the same tasks, suggested under otherwise similar conditions, their performance showed an opposite trend with respect to time. That is, there was a marked improvement in performance in the first few weeks, followed by a leveling off, instead of a decrease in performance as seen in the posthypnotic case. Hull (213) for a number of reasons, however, does not believe that there were significant differences between the two groups.   Patten (334) repeated Kellogg's experiment, taking into account the criticism Hull had made of the latter.   This time, though the nonhypnotized subjects gave a performance superior to that of the hypnotized group, both hypnotized and nonhypnotized subjects were found to show a drop in performance as a function of time.   In conclusion, Patten points out the following: Posthypnotic suggestions can last as long as a month; there is no evidence that posthypnotically suggested reactions will disappear with continuous testing; intervening hypnotization between tests tends to maintain the strength of response which may persist under these conditions for at least eight months.   It might be remarked that neither the suggested act, nor the test used, nor the index of suggestion strength employed in Patten's and Kellogg's investigations were entirely comparable; hence it cannot be said that Patten's work is an absolute substantiation of Hull's criticisms.

Erickson et al. (112) mentioned that posthypnotic suggestions have been observed to last as long as five years without intervening hypnotization, or in fact without any contact between subject and hypnotist.

I have reported (462) that posthypnotic suggestions had been found to last as long as 134 days.   I also found some evidence that the duration of such suggestions is inversely influenced by the difficulty of the task imposed upon the subject.   Wells (469) has also remarked that the results obtained with posthypnotic suggestions should depend on the depth of hypnosis attained.   He reported that posthypnotic amnesia can last for a year.

There is actually nothing unique in the persistence of posthypnotic suggestions.   If individuals can remember after ten and more years incidents that occurred only once, it would be rather surprising if suggestions would not last for a while, even a year.   What surprises people most in this matter is probably not so much the fact that a memory of some sort exists for the content of the suggestion as the fact that the effectiveness of the suggestion as such remains.   This, however, is not necessarily the same thing and will be left to a later chapter for discussion.

Obviously, the persistence of posthypnotic suggestions over time intervals implies the existence of some sort of trace, or engram.   There are no a priori reasons to believe or to expect that the organic state of affairs associated with these traces is essentially different from the one that exists in the persistence of normally acquired (learned) behavior patterns.* The law of forgetting, or temporal decay, which characterizes the latter should also apply to suggestions, as Kellogg and Patten have both shown. That certain suggestions would be less affected than others is in line with the well-known if poorly understood fact that certain types of materials are more easily and better retained than others in actual waking life. Finally, the "learning situation" as it occurs in hypnosis shows itself, upon further analysis, to be less favorable to retention (learning) than the waking situation, largely because it appears to be less likely to give rise to generalization or to cotemporal associative learning. This is in accord with the findings of the above investigators.

The Posthypnotic Trance. Its Nature

Elucidation of the nature of the state of the individual carrying out a posthypnotic suggestion is of considerable importance. In brief, is he hypnotized or not? It is difficult to determine this merely from observation of the subject's general behavior, for the hypnotized individual can behave in a very realistic "waking"-like manner as has been shown in a report of Erickson (111). This entire problem has been approached by Erickson and Erickson (112) who started out with the basic observation that usually the posthypnotic suggestion is given in such a manner that *the waking state becomes in itself a suggested response.* As a result, they remark that the posthypnotic behavior and the supposedly waking behavior become integral parts of a single performance, *both* behaviors being actually *suggested* behaviors. Thus, the subject is actually called upon to carry out at a future time a performance that is *dual* in character. This remark suggests that perhaps after all *the subject is hypnotized when he carries out a posthypnotic suggestion.* Erickson and Erickson as a matter of fact have obtained strong evidence that this is the case! Generally, according to their findings, there is a single, usually brief, spontaneous, and self-limited trance formed at the initiation of the posthypnotic act, this trance being an integral part of the performance of this act. The spontaneous trance may, however, also be multiple and/or prolonged, lasting throughout the entire performance or alternating with waking states. There are *apparent* exceptions to this but no true ones. The formation of this type of trance takes place, according to the two investigators, even for posthypnotic suggestions that become effective as late as five years after they are given. Finally, this spontaneous

* Or of waking instructions in memory form.

trance state shows *a continuation* of the behavior pattern belonging to the original trance. Erickson et al. conclude therefore that the spontaneous posthypnotic trance constitutes a *revivification* † of the hypnotic elements present in the original hypnotic situation.

Admitting the existence of the above spontaneous trance state, it seems a little strange in the first place that its duration should show as much variation as has been reported. Second, it is difficult to understand under these conditions what possible functions such a trance state could subserve, particularly when its duration may be, as reported for some cases, only a small fraction of the time required to carry out the entire posthypnotic response. It is my belief that the spontaneous trance actually lasts the *entire* duration of the post-hypnotic response. If the said response were of such a nature as to require only a strong compulsion to bring its performance about, we might do without this assumption. However, a great many posthypnotic responses are of such a nature as to require considerable trance depth for their execution when called forth under other conditions. It is not reasonable to suppose that the nature of the posthypnotic response would determine the duration and possibly the depth of the posthypnotic spontaneous trance. That is to say, if we admit that in some instances a posthypnotic trance lasting as long as the act is an integral and required part of the performance, there is no reason to suppose that the situation in other cases would be any different, even though less stringent requirements might be satisfactory. As will be recalled, the two investigators in question have remarked that the manner of giving the posthypnotic suggestions usually makes the waking state which follows a suggested response itself. This may well contain the answer for the *apparent* short duration of some of the spontaneous trances. For it is *implicit* in all posthypnotic suggestions that the subject will behave in the posthypnotic situation *as if he were awake.* That a very realistic waking-like performance can be given by hypnotized subjects has already been pointed out. It is then very likely that those instances where the posthypnotic spontaneous trance appears to be missing, or to be very short, are merely cases where a masking effect is present as a consequence of the implicit instructions. This would be particularly effective if the trance were superficial. A careful examination of the data reported by Erickson et al. shows definite aspects that substantiate this point of view.

† By revivification is meant a true return to the psychophysiological state that existed at some particular time in the past of the individual. This will be taken up in more detail in a later chapter.

The existence of the spontaneous posthypnotic trance goes a long way toward helping us understand the character and nature of post-hypnotic phenomena, for, if the trance is a continuation, that is, a revivification, of the hypnotic situation that existed when the post-hypnotic suggestions were originally given, then these suggestions act by virtue of the fact that they are effectively hypnotic suggestions, for which everything that has been and will be said about the general properties of hypnotic suggestions must hold in general. Just how this trance is brought into being by a single cue and how the revivification takes place must be explained, of course, but this topic will be left for the last part of the book. We shall now turn our attention to a special kind of posthypnotic phenomenon which has been the cause of much controversy and can be said to have held a central position among hypnotic phenomena in general.

The Problem of Posthypnotic Amnesia

The reason for the importance of this phenomenon is that many investigators have firmly believed it to be an intrinsic characteristic of hypnosis. Bernheim and Dynes, among others, were so convinced of this that they considered posthypnotic amnesia a criterion of the existence of hypnosis. They failed to recognize that there might possibly be nothing spontaneous about this phenomenon, should it really exist. Bramwell was among the first to voice a doubt about this matter by maintaining that it was an artifact created by either autosuggestion on the part of the subject or unwitting heterosuggestion on the part of the hypnotist.‡ Artifact or not, there is a still more important question, namely: How *real* is posthypnotic amnesia? For a mere assertion by the subject that he cannot remember is certainly no proof of its reality. An objective proof is required. A number of investigators have devoted their attention to this question.

Since this topic is closely allied to the question of the influence of hypnotic suggestion on learning processes, further discussion of the available material will be deferred until Chapter 13, but a few words should be said here about the status of posthypnotic amnesia. It has generally been found that its effectiveness depends on the type of material that is to be forgotten or, rather, on the type of response

‡ For instance, it is rarely realized by investigators that, by suggesting sleep to a subject in order to produce hypnosis, one is suggesting by context all of the characteristic symptoms of sleep (as known to the subject), *including the typical amnesia for sleep events normally associated with the state of wakefulness which follows.*

that is associated with the recall. Symbolic recall is most affected (100 per cent amnesia), and, in general, the effectiveness of posthypnotic amnesia decreases in proportion to the extent to which the recall response approaches that of a simple reflex in nature (no amnesia).§ There is also evidence that some reported cases of posthypnotic amnesia may have been in the nature of compulsive-like inhibitions (or blocking) of volitional activities connected with recall. Although in many instances, if not all, it appears that the presence of posthypnotic amnesia may be ascribed to autosuggestion, or to unwitting heterosuggestion, it has not been shown conclusively that some cases are not spontaneous and intrinsically connected with the state of hypnosis itself. The question of reality or artifact still remains unanswered when all cases are considered. In regard to duration, what has already been said for posthypnotic phenomena in general holds here. It may be added that posthypnotic amnesia is a reversible phenomenon since, when present, it can always be removed by appropriate suggestions. This has considerable significance when we consider the nature of this phenomenon which will be taken up later. Finally, it is now well established that posthypnotic amnesia *is neither a requisite* for the production of hypnosis *nor a criterion* of it.

§ The terminology used here is explained in Chapter 13.

·9·

"Animal Hypnosis"

Until rather recently, the best-integrated presentation of material on "animal hypnosis" had been that given by Volgyesi (452). Since then, however, a briefer but excellent and comprehensive résumé of findings in this field has been made by Gilman and Marcuse (163). In fact, it is nearly impossible to follow the plan of presentation of preceding chapters here without duplicating to some extent this last-mentioned review. Paraphrasing it seems unavoidable; yet any book of this sort would be incomplete if this topic were omitted. There are also a few studies which have not been considered by Gilman et al. in their review. In the pages that follow, the main facts, which we may abstract from the large number of existing studies of the question, will be briefly outlined and discussed. With the exception of a few studies, no specific references will be given. However, for the convenience of the reader, all pertinent studies have been included in the bibliography and their reference numbers are given at the end of this chapter.

To begin with there is considerable doubt concerning the status of "animal hypnosis" as a hypnotic phenomenon in the sense of the material that has been taken up in previous pages. This is well demonstrated by the multiplicity of expressions that have been employed by past authors to refer to states identical or similar to what we have just named "animal hypnosis." Among these one has death feint, cataplexy, conscious simulation of death, immobilization reflex, condition akinesis, hypertonicity, tonic immobility, myotonia congenita, inhibitory states, and just plain inhibition. In fact there is even some question whether these various states are one and the same. This is rather difficult to determine. Certainly they differ in a number of ways. Thus, for instance, some animals show considerable tonicity whereas others do not. With some the state is of very short duration, whereas with others it may last quite a while. Finally, the method of induction is itself very variable. These states do however possess one *common* property, that of being associated with a condition of *immobility* on the part of

108

the animal. This is the true and only valid basis at present for group-
ing all these states under the common class name of "animal hypnosis"
which we shall keep for the time being.

Some Aspects of "Animal Hypnosis"

We might begin by saying that about everything from man to insect
has been "hypnotized" in one sense or another. This includes even
lions! Gilman and Marcuse (163) have listed the following types
of subjects that have been tested: birds, reptiles such as lizards, am-
phibians (crabs), frogs, octopuses, insects such as water scorpions,
cockroaches, and a variety of mammals that includes the pig, monkey,
dog, lion, and man. Such a list seems to indicate that the phenomenon
has quite an appreciable phylogenetic spread.

There appear to be four principal modes of bringing about a state
of "animal hypnosis."

1. *Repetitive Stimuli.* These include stroking or scratching various
body parts, gazing into the eyes of the animal, presenting suddenly a
light stimulus, closing the eyes of the beast, and swinging the animal
back and forth. In general, there are no rules as to the regions of the
animal that must be stimulated.

2. *Pressure on Body Parts.* Pressure on the abdominal region of the
inverted animal is often very effective. Here again the sensitive region
differs with the species. In this connection it should be remarked that
although a number of stage hypnotists have been known to make use
of compression of the carotid sinus to produce states of unconsciousness
under the guise of "hypnosis," such a procedure has no place here.

3. *Inversion.* The sudden inversion of the animal has been found
very successful in some instances. Investigators have gone to the
trouble of building special pieces of apparatus to bring about the
desired rapid inversion.

4. *Restraint of Movement.* This appears to be an essential and
common feature of all experimental productions of "animal hypnosis,"
so much so that one wonders if this may not be after all the main
factor producing "hypnosis." It appears nearly impossible, if not
entirely so, to use any other method without also introducing some
restraint of motion.

Generally speaking there are no fixed rules as to which of these
methods will work best for a given animal, or how it is to be applied.
In fact, the same animal may not even respond twice in the same
manner to a given method. Or, again, one animal may respond well
to several different procedures. In some instances the effect is so

transient that we may doubt whether "hypnosis" was ever produced. Furthermore, in some cases, the state of immobilization that ensues persists only as long as the stimulus is allowed to act.

Various possible characteristics of "animal hypnosis" have been studied. There appears to be little agreement among investigators in these respects. Generally speaking, in regard to *musculature* most workers find that hypertonicity, often associated with a high degree of plasticity, is characteristic. However, states of relaxation or of great rigidity have also been reported. Insofar as *heart rate* and *respiration* are concerned, the available data are inconclusive. Gerebtzoff (155) to date has made the only investigation of the *cortical excitability* and *activity* of "hypnotized animals." He found a depression of both excitability and activity, the nature of the depression depending to some extent on the mode of inducing the "trance" state.

Most experimenters believe that *analgesia* is associated with "animal hypnosis." But this is by no means without exception. Furthermore, Steiniger (424) has appropriately remarked that pain may well be present in all instances but that the animal cannot manifest signs of it because of the immobility associated with the induced state. The same remark applies to the question of general *reactivity* of "hypnotized" animals. The consensus has been that such animals are insensitive to stimuli in general. It might be safer, however, to say that various animals show anything from a slight decrease in reactivity to a complete absence of reaction.

There is little agreement concerning the depth of "trance" obtained in animals. The duration of such "trances" appears to be variable, both from species to species and within species. Furthermore, it is probable that even a single individual also shows variations from time to time. Durations of at least an hour have been reported. In many instances, as already pointed out, the duration of the "trance" is extremely short. Various factors are said to influence it, but in what ways is not clear.

Hypnosis in Animals and Humans

On the whole, we may sum up here by saying that, though there appears to be general agreement that a state of immobility can be brought about by various means in animals, little more can be said besides the fact that there is considerable variation in the degree of immobility, its duration, and its character in general. It appears rather certain, however, that *there is no evidence that this sort of phenomenon is at all identifiable with hypnosis as observed in humans.* This is clearly shown by the results just reviewed and those considered in previous chapters. There exist additional arguments for this point of view. Biologically speaking, we should expect man to show something akin to "animal hypnosis" as described in these pages. Were there no other alternative, we should be warranted in assuming that the type of phenomenon described in past pages under the name of "hypnosis" is the equivalent, or at least the parallel, of the various forms of observed "animal hypnosis." But it should be clear that this would be far from a satisfactory choice, if for no other reason than that immobility is not a true characteristic of hypnosis in humans. As it happens, man does exhibit spontaneous states of abnormal immobility; these are not identifiable with hypnosis but resemble very much "animal hypnosis." Such states are called *cataplexy* in medical parlance. These can best be described as consisting of a sudden loss of muscular tone without loss of consciousness which results in the individual collapsing to the ground. In addition, Hoagland (201) reports having brought about experimentally states of rigid immobility in individuals by means of a technique that has not the remotest resemblance or connection to that employed to induce hypnosis. On the other hand, the technique and results are strongly reminiscent of "animal hypnosis" in general. There is thus an alternative to the above choice. Finally, a very important point of distinction between the two forms of "hypnosis" is the presence of hypersuggestibility in one and its absence in the other. Admittedly it would be difficult to demonstrate suggestibility phenomena in animals, although not impossible. Pavlov (342) has claimed having obtained the equivalent of responses to suggestions in dogs. Just what he did, or how, is not clear from his writings. We must consider this claim rather dubious. On the other hand, if we accept at least Hoagland's cases as being true instances of "animal hypnosis" in humans, then it may be stated that suggestibility appears not to be a characteristic of this sort of state. It may be that the enforced immobility precludes any manifestations of suggestibility of a motor type, even though hypersuggestibility might be present. But even if this were true, such a combination of enforced immobility superimposed over hypersuggestibility is not typical of what we commonly consider hypnosis. Finally, the induced rigidity reported by Hoagland is exactly the opposite of the state of relaxation associated with the usual trance induction. In passing, it is of interest to speculate concerning the possible relation of the classic states of catalepsy described by Charcot and his students to the rigid immobility described by Hoagland. One of the methods Charcot used to induce catalepsy was the violent stimulation of the subject's senses.

States of Immobilization

In the light of all this, there is some question of the advisability of using the term "hypnosis" to describe the phenomena we have been concerned with in this chapter, even when qualifying it as "animal," particularly if, as seems to be the case, the phenomena in question can also be elicited in humans. There is as much or even more objection to using any of the alternative terms which have been listed by various investigators. Now the most characteristic aspect of the entire subject matter is that we seem to be dealing not with one state but with many states possessing a common factor, immobility. That is, we are talking about a *class of induced states of immobility.* What we want is therefore a class name, and what better one can we pick than one that contains the basis of the class, that is, the characteristic immobility? It is thus proposed that all the phenomena that have been considered in this chapter under the name of "animal hypnosis" be designated hereafter as *states of immobilization,* or immobilization for short. Furthermore it will be convenient to use the latter term to designate the process of producing such a state.

In the past, a large number of hypotheses have been offered to account for states of immobilization. As summarized by Gilman and Marcuse, these states have been considered to be reflex response and cerebral inhibition, death feigning, sleep, hypnosis, spatial disorientation, and paralysis of fear. Some of these interpretations can be discarded from the outset: for example, hypnosis and sleep. Others appear rather unlikely. Spatial disorientation, death feigning, and paralysis of fear fall into this category. A brief consideration of these three shows that they are not consistent with the character of many of the animals used in past studies, nor with a number of the techniques employed. In addition, the two last-mentioned interpretations are not acceptable from the viewpoint of an objective animal psychology. If we leave out the possibility that other and better interpretations may be offered in the future, the above considerations pretty much leave us with the first hypothesis listed, namely: reflex and cerebral inhibition. In many respects, indeed, states of immobilization do show aspects that are reminiscent of reflex action. It is very probable that rapid inversion and generalized pressure both bring immobilization about through a reflex-like response. On the other hand, repetitive stimuli and restraint of movement would appear to act through cerebral inhibition. It may thus be that states of immobilization *fall into two subclasses,* each involving a different neurological mechanism.

It may be wondered just what sort of function such a reflex as the above would subserve. Aside from the theory of a protective reflex, it is difficult to find any satisfactory function. *Possibly there is no function.* This may be indicated by the fact that a very large variety of stimuli will elicit the postulated reflex, and also by the fact that all of its characteristics show much variability. It is possible that part of this variability is accounted for by the widespread phylogenetic area in which investigations in this field have fallen. This idea has been suggested by Marcuse (287). There is a further possibility that states of immobilization arise from a *vestigial* reflex, or even that the latter is merely an *accidental* property of the nervous system. There appears to be no reason why either of these two last alternatives could not contain the right answer. I might add that my inclination is in the direction of the accidental property hypothesis.

References

The following numbers refer to the items in the bibliography of this book that are pertinent to "animal hypnosis": 27, 38, 42, 45, 64, 80, 83, 90, 93, 142, 149, 155, 162, 163, 200, 201, 202, 205, 206, 207, 208, 268, 283, 286, 287, 288, 299, 312, 315, 319, 323, 330, 341, 342, 346, 351, 356, 357, 361, 362, 366, 367, 371, 381, 413, 424, 425, 426, 432, 435, 439, 440, 441, 449, 450, 452, 454, 493, 502.

PART

· 3 ·

EXPERIMENTAL
FOUNDATIONS

Extrinsic Characteristics
of Suggestibility and Hypnosis

Suggested Hypnotic Phenomena
General Considerations
Effects on the Motor Functions

With this chapter we begin a survey of those alterations that can be brought about in individuals by means of hypnotic suggestion or hypnosis per se. In contrast to the effects and properties that have been considered in previous pages, and that may be said to be intrinsic to hypnosis and to suggestibility, those to be considered now are more of an extrinsic nature, although some may nevertheless be spontaneous in a sense to be discussed below.

Suggested and Spontaneous Phenomena in Hypnosis

Erickson (113) has shown that two distinct types of psychophysiological and somatic phenomena can be observed. In considering effects induced by means of hypnosis, it is usual to think here of various alterations of behavior which result from specific suggestions directed at obtaining these alterations. However, in addition to the traditional alterations of reaction time, sensory threshold, muscular tonus, and so on, we can also observe, quite independently and as coincidental phenomena, certain other behavioral alterations of a similar nature which appear to be superimposed upon the former. It is therefore quite essential in discussing psychosomatic studies in connection with hypnosis to distinguish between the two types of alterations. This will be done here by distinguishing between *suggested* and *spontaneous* effects. It must be kept in mind, however, that the latter group may not be entirely "spontaneous," in the sense that we would speak of characteristic psychophysiological alterations concomitant with the production of a trance state, such as were examined in previous pages, for they arise in connection with the giving of hypnotic suggestions other than those of sleep. What occurs is that, besides the suggested response, there appear nonsuggested responses in modalities of behavior unrelated to the one in which the change has been

117

suggested. There is thus, effectively, a side effect to the suggestions. Conversely, it is not uncommon to find that hypnotic suggestions directed at a particular behavioral modality may not be effective until alterations have also been brought about in apparently independent and unrelated modalities. Thus, we observe suggestions bearing upon only sensory responses giving rise to motor responses too, and, in other instances, the suggestions being quite ineffective until certain motor responses are also induced.

As Erickson has shown, these side effects are rather variable both within the same individual and among various individuals. Other things being equal, spontaneous phenomena thus observed are largely a function of the nature and character of the suggestions that have been given. To a large extent, they are often masked by the more intense and expected suggested tasks, thus passing unnoticed. This last is probably the reason for the scarcity of reports on this type of phenomenon.

Closely related to the occurrence of side effects is the following common situation, which is particularly true for involuntary responses. Irrespective of the fact that some of these responses may be elicited directly by a suggestion that the actual phenomenon to be observed will take place, they may often be evoked indirectly by suggesting the occurrence of a state that is normally accompanied by the said phenomenon. Suggested emotional states are particularly effective in this respect. Thus, for instance, while a direct suggestion to the effect that a subject's stomach will begin to contract may or may not bring about such a contraction, it can be obtained by suggesting to the subject that he feels hungry, or, again, by making him hallucinate himself in the process of eating an appetizing meal. From a phenomenological point of view the end result is the same, however, as will be seen later, how it comes about is very significant from the standpoint of gaining insight into the nature and properties of hypnosis and suggestibility in general. Since, however natural it may seem, it would be confusing to speak here of direct and indirect suggestions, and yet some means of making a distinction is needed, it is proposed that we employ the expression *direct evocation* when the obtained response is called for by the suggestion, and *indirect evocation* when the elicited response is merely associated as a side effect with the response actually called for.

Classification of Observed Alterations in Hypnosis

Suggested alterations can be classified in a variety of ways. This was done earlier in Chapter 1. For the sake of convenience, one of the classifications will be repeated. As pointed out earlier, the various alterations that may be induced fall into one of the following categories: hyperfunctions, hypofunctions, afunctions, and parafunctions. These in turn may be observed to fall into the following subcategories:

A. Cognitive processes:
   1. Sensation.
   2. Perception.
   3. Attention.
   4. Association.
   5. Memory.
   6. Thought.
B. Motor processes:
   1. Muscular activity in general.
   2. Voluntary acts.
   3. Reflex acts (involuntary).
   4. Habit.
   5. Total behavior.
C. Emotional processes.

Among the most common alterations produced in hypnosis are deafness, blindness, color blindness, amnesia, analgesia, anesthesia, and age regression.

As previously mentioned, certain spontaneous coincidental responses are often observed when the above alterations are induced. These may in turn be classified in a number of ways. According to Erickson (113) one observes:

A. Altered visual behavior:
   1. Decrease in visual acuity with blurring of vision and difficulty in reading.
   2. Contraction of the visual field.
   3. Difficulty in focusing gaze.
   4. Decrease in ability in depth and distance perception.
   5. Subjective sense of color vision, that is, addition of chromatic values to visual stimuli.
B. Altered auditory behavior:
   1. Decrease in acuity.
   2. Inaccuracy in locating sound.
   3. Distortion in perception of sound qualities.
C. Altered motor behavior:
   1. General muscular inco-ordination.
   2. Specific motor disturbances:
      (a) Paresis and paralysis.
      (b) Apraxia.
      (c) Speech disturbances.
      (d) Dysmetria.
      (e) Ocular fixation, pupillary dilation, and nystagmoid movements.

D. Other types of altered behavior:
1. Analgesia and anesthesia.
2. Subjective reactions of nausea and vertigo.
3. Anxiety states and phobic reactions with their various psychological concomitants.
4. Amnesias, usually specific and circumscribed.
5. Revival of forgotten patterns of behavior.

These responses may precede the appearance of the suggested condition, accompany its development, or be a part of the totality of the hypnotic situation after the desired effect has been obtained. It might also be remarked that this group of responses appears to be one of psychodynamic manifestations which may be closely related to various psychopathological alterations of behavior as seen in a variety of mental patients.

The Voluntary Motor Functions

Induced Paralysis. With these few introductory remarks, we shall now begin our survey of hypnotic alteration of the motor functions. Here as in many other areas of hypnosis, much has been taken for granted without actual proof that true motor alterations are present. For instance, it is not uncommon in suggesting say, hand or arm paralysis, that, when the subject is challenged to move the member in question, he asserts he cannot do this, although it is also observed that he has not given any particular indication of having tried. Many persons have been convinced by this type of behavior that paralysis was present. In truth one cannot draw any conclusion from this.

In other cases a somewhat different response is observed. For instance, the subject is told that he is unable to move, that he cannot get out of the chair in which he is sitting, although no definite suggestion of paralysis has been given. When he is challenged to move, as in the above instance he makes no obvious attempt to do so, but instead remarks that he does not want to move out of the chair, is quite comfortable as he is, and sees no reason why he should not stay as he is. Even when more directly and emphatically challenged he will stick to his argument, often remarking that he is sure he can move if he so desires. Or he may simply ignore the request entirely. Such behavior does not necessarily mean that the suggestion has failed. There are fortunately ways of testing the subject indirectly. In my experience such tests have invariably shown the presence of a certain amount of interference with, and often a complete blocking of, the designated muscular process.

With still other subjects, the same situation brings about evident and well-defined muscular effort on the subject's part. In such cases, it is usual to observe that the inability to move is brought about through the simultaneous activation of antagonistic muscle pairs, thus resulting in a balancing of forces with a zero or near-zero resultant.

Clearly then suggested paralysis manifests itself in a variety of ways. It is further evident from direct observations that in most cases suggested paralysis has little resemblance, if any, to paralysis resulting from lesions of the motor neurons or of various motor centers and subcenters. Thus, the last example mentioned could never be confused with true spastic paralysis. In cases of suggested paralysis in which apparent muscular atony is a major characteristic there is no lack of tonus comparable to that observed in lesions of the lower motor neurons. Similarly, with respect to lesions of the upper motor neurons for which the ensuing dysfunctions are more intricate, the typical syndromes have never been completely elicited by suggestions of motor disorders. At least no reports of this have been made to date. It is, of course, not entirely impossible to bring about such syndromes, provided sufficiently intricate suggestions are employed. Presumably, if one suggested all the various symptoms that make up a given motor syndrome, one might bring the syndrome about with as much a degree of exactitude as desired. The importance the form of a suggestion has in the determination of the observed response cannot be over-emphasized, as has been pointed out by Erickson in a number of his papers. This can easily be seen if we consider for a moment the different responses that can be expected in attempting to produce paralysis when one suggests to the subject that (a) he cannot move either arm or hand, (b) his arm and hand are becoming stiff and rigid, or (c) his arm and hand are becoming so completely relaxed that motion will be impossible.*

Strangely enough, although suggested paralysis, or rather inability to move, has been a favorite test and topic for demonstrations, no objective study of it has been made. Perforce we must leave it now and pass on to some other matter.

Muscular Strength. Some investigations have been made on the effects of hypnosis on muscular strength. Wells (469) has reported that hand grip strength as measured with a dynamometer can be increased and decreased by means of suggestions of increased or

---

* It might be remarked here that the observations that have been made in the last few pages are of general application to other phases of induced hypnotic phenomena.

decreased strength, respectively. He also observed that suggested decreased strength is more effective on the whole than a suggested increase. Hadfield (176) has substantiated Wells in regard to increased strength. Hull (213) however considers Hadfield's results doubtful and has received confirmation of his opinion from results obtained by Eysenck (134) and by P. C. Young (504). Neither of these investigators could find evidence of improved performance on the hand grip dynamometer during hypnosis and following appropriate suggestions. Moreover, Mead and Roush (300) and Roush (378) have reported that they could not find evidence of increased strength on the hand grip dynamometer during hypnosis, even though suggestions of better performance and greater strength were given. In contrast, however, they found a statistically significant improvement of 16.8 per cent with the arm dynamometer. In her report, Roush (378) has presented evidence that, when suggestions of "no pain" are given to subjects, in addition to the other instructions, performance on the arm dynamometer and on the hand grip dynamometer are definitely superior in the hypnotic state. She also investigated the effects of such instructions given posthypnotically, and these results show an increase in performance comparable to that observed in hypnosis. On the other hand, the results appear to indicate that less improvement is associated with the hand grip dynamometer than with the arm dynamometer, which is in agreement with the trend indicated in the report of Mead and Roush (300).

In attempting to evaluate these results, we must remember that few of the investigations that have been considered are comparable to one another in procedure.† This in itself may account for some, if not all, of the contradictions and discrepancies existing between reported results.† Only the studies of Wells and Hadfield allow some degree of comparability. Wells's results are definite enough, and there appears to be no reason to question Hadfield's data. Inquiry into Hull's reason for doubting Hadfield's data seems to reveal that it is largely his antipathy against accepting any evidence of what he refers to as "genuine supernormal performance." This of course is hardly a reason for discrediting an investigation. The results of the above two investigations appear to show that an increase of the order of 50 per cent in grip strength is possible. The reports of Young and of Eysenck

---

† This remark will be found to apply in general to the greater portion of the investigations that will be taken up in subsequent pages. This is one of the unfortunate complications encountered in evaluating this material.

must be considered at present on their own merits. Since Eysenck's study was primarily concerned with an investigation of fatigue and the results obtained for strength were arrived at only indirectly, we cannot put too much weight on it. As for Young, actually the suggestions he employed did not amount to more than ordinary instructions (the same for waking and hypnosis). Consequently his investigation cannot be said to investigate truly the possibility of increasing (or decreasing) strength by means of hypnotic suggestion. All it does is consider the question whether hypnosis per se has any influence upon muscular strength. That it does not is entirely in agreement with the fact that hypnosis and waking are apparently similar, physiologically speaking. The results reported by Roush and by Mead and Roush are somewhat puzzling. In view of the excellence of the experimental design employed by Roush, it is not possible to disregard the difference in performance on the two types of dynamometers. This difference may be due, at least in part, to the fact that the two instruments do not lead to comparable dynamical situations. More will be said about this later. A basic weakness in nearly all the investigations considered here is that the strength of muscular contraction is measured by methods that cause the muscles to perform a certain amount of work which may well fatigue them. It becomes then a question whether one is getting a true measure of strength.

In passing, we might mention a spectacular demonstration, long a favorite of stage hypnotists, usually referred to as the "human plank" demonstration. In it the subject's body is rendered rigid by means of appropriate suggestions. He is then used to bridge the space between two chairs, and one or more individuals mount and stand on top of the unsupported portion of the body. A variation of this experiment consists in placing a large slab of rock in a similar position and shattering it with the blows of a sledge hammer. It is rather surprising that no experimenter has yet made an investigation of this demonstration of so-called "catalepsy." A study of the distribution of forces and stresses might well show that it is nowhere near the feat it appears to be. I myself have participated as a subject in the demonstration of this phenomenon, using both autosuggestion and heterosuggestion to bring about the state of rigidity. It was my own experience,‡ much to my surprise, that, when a person of about 200 pounds stood on the epigastric region of my body near the border of the umbilical region,

‡ It might be mentioned that the author, being a medium subject, does not exhibit posthypnotic amnesia.

this person appeared to weigh no more than a few pounds. With an accidental shift of a similar weight over the hypogastric region, I found the situation nowhere comparable, although there still was no difficulty in supporting the weight. In a private communication, a prestidigitator told me some years ago that the "human plank" demonstration could be performed by nearly anybody with a little training in muscular control and without the help of hypnosis. However, there is always the possibility in such cases that some autosuggestion is playing a part, even if unknown to the subject. It is most probable too that there are instances in which hypnosis does enable an individual to act as a human plank by allowing him to attain the necessary degree of rigidity when he cannot attain this voluntarily. In addition, it may be that greater resistance to fatigue and a certain degree of analgesia toward muscular pain are brought about. Both of these would help.

Work Capacity. Another area of investigation has been concerned with the work capacity of individuals. Nicholson (324), Williams (489), and Manzer (284) independently have obtained evidence that hypnotic suggestion will increase the work capacity of individuals. They tested this in terms of performance on a grip dynamometer while various suggestions were given that would presumably alter the performance. Hull (213) has questioned these results on the basis that emotional effects might have been partly a direct cause of the observed increase. It is not entirely clear from his discussion why affective factors should have been present, since the suggestions were limited in general to statements aimed at making the subject perceive the work to be done as harder or easier than it actually was.

In the above investigations, the actual work output was studied directly. Nemtzova and Schattenstein (321, 322) approached the problem from a different angle. They reported that an increase in O_2 consumption and in pulmonary ventilation was observed in the subjects when suggestions of decreased work were given, although at all times the same amount of work was actually given to the subjects. Levin and Egolinsky (261) have also reported that suggested work increases ventilation, O_2 consumption, and pulse rate under various conditions, but mostly when the subject is actually not performing any work, that is, when he is resting. Grafe and Traumann (168) have maintained that suggestions of heavy work will increase the metabolic rate of some subjects, from 6 to 12 per cent.

There is somewhat better agreement among the investigations concerned with work capacity than among those on muscular strength. But here too there is lack of comparability. It is somewhat difficult to decide how to interpret the studies of Nemtzova et al. and of Levin et al. Pulmonary ventilation and even oxygen consumption could be partly influenced by volition. There have also been reports that some individuals can voluntarily influence their heart rate. Since very few subjects were involved in these studies, the results must be weighed carefully. It is very likely that the alterations in respiratory volume and in oxygen consumption have other origins than an actual change in work output. The three other studies are in some respects far more satisfactory. Against Nicholson's work it can be said that he never actually either measured or calculated the work done but based his conclusions on the time required for recovery. According to him, under the influence of suggestion the subjects could perform endlessly. This is in itself a very ambiguous measure! Williams who repeated Nicholson's experiment arrived at a more definite and smaller estimate, reporting an increase in work capacity of only 16.08 per cent. This, however, is a statistically significant value. It should be added that Nicholson's suggestions were more comprehensive that those of Williams and might possibly have caused a greater improvement. A rather important weakness in both studies is that the suggestions employed were aimed, in part or wholly, at eliminating the sensation of fatigue. Though fatigue, both psychological and physiological, does limit work capacity, there is more to the matter than this, as Nicholson was well aware. As these experiments stand, it is difficult to determine whether the increase in work capacity might not have been due solely to inhibition of or removal of the perception of psychological fatigue, rather than to a true improvement in physiological function as seems to be implied by the studies. Of the three investigations, the one by Manzer is probably the most satisfactory. He observed an average improvement of about 6 per cent. The main criticism that may be made here is that, according to the report, the reading on the dynamometer itself was taken as the measure of the work done. Unless the dynamometer was graduated in terms of work done, and not in terms of force exerted as is customary, the work done may not actually have been recorded. Finally, in all these investigations there was failure to take into account the existence of optimal rates of work and optimal loads.§

Fatigue. Though Williams' (489) study was apparently aimed at investigating the work level of subjects in hypnosis, as has just been seen it throws a better light on the possible influence of suggestion

§ This remark does not apply to Manzer's study.

on fatigue. It would appear from his results that hypnotic suggestion can prevent the onset of fatigue, but that merely passing from the waking state to the trance state or vice-versa does not eradicate already existing fatigue. In another study specifically directed at this problem, Williams (490) studied the subject's ability to maintain his arm and hand in a horizontal position when catalepsy was suggested. He reported finding no trance advantage, since fatigue showed up with the same speed and in the same manner as it did in the absence of suggestions. Mead and Roush (300) concurred in this opinion in respect to the maintenance of hand grip, but found an advantage in the maintenance of arm position when an arm dynamometer was used. Roush (378), as was seen, has shown that superior performances are obtained in dynamometer experiments when the awareness of pain is removed. She also studied the ability of subjects to remain suspended by the hands from one of the bars on a stall. She reported that the subjects' endurance in this experiment showed no improvement when superior performance alone was suggested, but showed definite improvement when the absence of pain was also suggested. This was true only for hypnotic instructions and did not extend to posthypnotic situations. As also previously seen, Nicholson's experiment was possibly more of a test of ability to resist fatigue than of actual capacity to release energy. In any event his results probably show increased resistance to fatigue. Riegers (365) also claimed having obtained evidence that hypnotic suggestion can increase the subject's resistance to fatigue in the performance of work. Rather good substantiation of this was found by Eysenck (134), using a hand dynamometer. He reported an average improvement of 43 per cent. It should be noted that Eysenck did not make use of special suggestions aimed at improving the subject's performance or altering his perception of the task, as was done in the other studies. He merely instructed the subjects to perform to the best of their ability. To this list of investigators we might also add a few earlier workers such as Charcot, Bernheim, and McDougall, all of whom reported that appropriate suggestions could decrease muscular tremor presumably caused by fatigue.

All these investigations, however, fail to distinguish properly between physiological and psychological fatigue, not to mention their tendency to confuse strength, energy expenditure, and rate of energy expenditure with one another. Even leaving such matters aside, it is rather doubtful that results obtained in terms of dynamometers or ergographs can really be compared with results obtained from such tests as the one devised by Williams or by Roush (for endurance), in which the ability to keep the arm extended over a period of time is studied. The tasks are hardly comparable myophysiologically speaking. Furthermore, a closer examination of Williams' experiment reveals a weakness that goes a long way toward accounting for his failure to find differences between hypnotic and waking performance in relation to fatigue. Unfortunately, it also invalidates an otherwise excellent study. For an examination of the dynamics and kinetics involved shows that maintaining the arm in the manner and position described by Williams does not depend on rigidity of the arm muscles, but only on rigidity of the shoulder muscles, as the arm in the position described cannot do anything but pivot about the shoulder. Since Williams' suggestions show no features that would allow them to cover this motion, we must conclude that probably Williams never did really study what he proposed to investigate. That is, he studied the production of fatigue in the shoulder muscles, but aimed his suggestions at a totally different set of muscles. My own observations on arm catalepsy would appear to indicate that, for the same suggestions, some subjects show evidence that the muscles of the shoulder joint are affected, whereas others do not. In other words, when the suggestions are too general, the observed results depend to some extent on what the suggestions mean to the subject. Consequently, in all fairness to Williams, we should say that his results may not be totally invalid, but they are definitely ambiguous.

In regard to the results reported by Mead and Roush, Watkins (456) has suggested that there might have been more pain, or at least discomfort, in the hand grip experiment than in the one performed with the subject's arm. Mead (301) agreed that this might be so and that it might account for the apparent contradiction in the results he and Roush have reported. Hull (213) also thought that the results reported by Williams and by Nicholson might have been considerably affected by the suggested analgesia and/or anesthesia toward fatigue pain (or discomfort), and hence that no definite conclusions could be reached from their results, in regard to the effects of hypnosis on fatigue. This agrees with the views presented a few pages back. The results reported by Roush (378) throw additional light on this question. As will be remembered, she showed that, if in the experiment described by her and Mead pain awareness is counteracted by suggestion, the results are changed in two ways: There is a further improvement on the arm dynamometer, and there is now an improvement on the hand grip dynamometer too, although of lesser magnitude. Thus, it is clear that pain and discomfort do affect the results in experiments of this kind. On the other hand, more than this may have been involved in the results of Mead and Roush, because, in spite of the suggested anesthesia, hand grip dynamometer performance appears to have remained superior. Also, these suggestions have even less effect on the results of the endurance test described by Roush.|| One could possibly account for these results by assuming that the anesthesia was not equally effective in the three cases. On the other hand, it seems to me that a more likely solution may be that there are considerable differences in the kinesiology associated with the three situations. With the arm dynamometer, the elbow flexors are "broken" by a steady downward pull exerted by the experimenter. With the hand grip dynamometer, the subject exerts pressure against a spring which resists. In the first instance, the subject is doing the resisting against an externally applied force. In the second, the situation is essentially reversed. As for the endurance test, the kinesiology is too complex to be taken up here. It does not appear to be comparable to either of the two other situations, although it is closest in character to the hand grip situation. It is not surprising therefore that different results were obtained. Of course whether or not the above is the correct answer can be decided only by further investigations of the matter.

Of these various studies concerned with fatigue, in the final analysis the one by Eysenck appears to be the only investigation that comes near to answering the original question. Its main weakness lies in the fact that only two subjects were employed. On the other hand, this is compensated to some extent by the general quality of Eysenck's investigations, and also by the fact that his study of fatigue formed part of a relatively large battery of tests aimed at determining the extent to which hypnosis will influence various mental and physical functions. Since the rest of his results tend to support the ones being presently discussed, they have a definite significance here.

Motor Control and Relaxation. In the above-mentioned study, Eysenck (134) observed improvement of motor control in hypnosis. On the other hand, Young (504, 505) found no such advantage. As Eysenck (134) has pointed out, Young's results are too ambiguous to lead to any definite conclusions. In addition, the tests employed by

|| Roush apparently missed this fact, inasmuch as she makes no mention of it in her report. It may, however, be derived from the data which are included in the paper. Whether or not the differences in this case are statistically significant unfortunately cannot be determined from the reported data. The present analysis is based on the assumption that they are. This appears rather probable.

the two men to study steadiness of motor control were not equivalent by far. Young made use of a V-shaped trough of wires in which a stylus was moved. Eysenck, on the other hand, had the subjects hold the stylus in holes of various diameters. A report of Edwards (106) might also be mentioned here. This investigator suggested greater steadiness to his subjects. He concluded tentatively from his results that body steadiness was not improved. On the other hand, he found that finger and hand steadiness could be significantly increased, but that this increase is greater when the hypnotized subject is told to relax than when he is told that he will be steadier. Unfortunately, the experimenter failed to furnish some rather crucial information in his report, without which it is impossible to evaluate his results.

Suggestions of relaxation form an important part of the usual technique of trance induction. Most hypnotists have taken for granted that suggestions of this kind do indeed bring about a state of relaxation. There seems in addition to be a general feeling that suggested relaxation is greater on the average than nonsuggested relaxation. That this might be so is indicated to some degree by the work of Jacobson (222) which shows that individuals can definitely be trained to relax to a much greater extent than they would ordinarily without training. This, however, is no proof that suggestions have the same effect.

Carhart (63) has made an attempt at examining this proposition. He employed palmar resistance as a measure of general body tonus. His test of 90 subjects of both sexes showed that waking suggestions to relax produce significantly *less* relaxation than the act of just lying quietly without instructions, and less relaxation than lying quietly and receiving instructions to relax. But, as Carhart himself has pointed out, these rather unexpected and somewhat perturbing results need not necessarily be taken to invalidate the effectiveness of suggestions of relaxation: In the first place we know very little about the exact relationship of general body tension to skin resistance. Second, it is certain that some attention must be present during the giving of suggestions and instructions, and it is a known fact that attending tends to lower skin resistance. It might therefore be expected that suggestions and instructions would tend to be associated with lesser relaxation (as measured by skin resistance) than the third alternative of no instructions or suggestions. Finally, Carhart's suggestions were not simply of muscular relaxation, but also of heaviness, numbness, and tactile disorientation. I agree with him when he states that other suggestive techniques might have led to different results, for it has been my experience that suggested heaviness often appears to cause considerable muscular tension.¶

The Involuntary, Semivoluntary, and Nonvoluntary Functions

In contrast to the subject of the voluntary motor phenomena, here is an abundance of experimental material to which we now turn our attention.

Since studies of the influence of suggestion on conditioned reflexes constitute a relatively small group, we might begin with these. Both Scott (405) and Leuba (259) have shown that posthypnotic amnesia does not affect established conditioned reflexes, but that hypnosis appears to facilitate the formation of such reflexes.

Erickson (114), on the other hand, has reported that specific anesthesia of some sense modalities brought about by hypnotic suggestion will affect conditioned reflexes in a manner comparable to that in which organic alteration affect these modalities. He has shown this to be specifically true for suggested binaural deafness. Lundholm (278) has demonstrated a similar effect for conditioned finger retraction to shock. In a later investigation (279) he also reported the conditioning of individuals to hallucinated flashes of light. This was confirmed by Fisher (139) who performed a comparable investigation. Cooper and Erickson (75) also reported an instance of a hallucination becoming conditioned to an affective-like state.

The above about covers what has been done to date in regard to conditioned reflexes. The available literature on alteration of involuntary or quasivoluntary functions, and of natural (spinal and autonomic) reflexes in particular, is by far the more extensive. Some indication that various cardiovascular, gastrointestinal, and respiratory changes can result from the induction of hypnosis, in addition to skeletal muscle responses, has been shown by Schneck (397, 400), Brenman, Gill, and Hackner (49), and Erickson (113). These are, however, spontaneous alterations of functions which have a psychodynamic basis and are better discussed under another heading. We shall be concerned here with more specifically produced effects. Gorton (167) has given an excellent review of this material, and to some extent the pages that follow must of necessity tend to paraphrase his work. The various investigations that have been reported can best be examined

¶ This effect appears in turn to be a reflex action which tends to oppose, that is, compensate for, the fictitious weight increase. It is comparable for instance to the well-known falling reaction in a rotated individual.

by being considered under a number of different headings, although of course a certain amount of overlap is inevitable.

1. *Respiration.* Nemtzova and Schattenstein (321, 322) have been able to alter pulmonary ventilation by means of hypnotic and post-hypnotic suggestions of light and heavy work although the subject performed at all times a constant amount of work. Increases in ventilation of as much as 50 per cent were observed. A similar effect was noted when similar suggestions were given to a subject resting quietly. Astruck (7) has given partial confirmation of this. Similarly, Cohen and Cobb (72) reported appreciable changes in respiratory rate following hypnotic and posthypnotic suggestions of slower breathing in a patient suffering from hyperventilation. Sears (406) reported that respiratory changes accompanying pain are eliminated by suggestions of anesthesia. Dynes (105) and Brown and Vogel (57) have confirmed this. Bier (30) reported that suggestions of rest, happiness, and excitement will cause alterations in respiration. Partial confirmation of this comes from Fulde (150) who reported increase in pulmonary ventilation when excitement is suggested. Levin and Egolinsky (261) observed that pulmonary ventilation is affected most by hypnotic suggestion when the subject is resting. In contrast to all these reports, Bitterman and Marcuse (34) gave evidence that posthypnotic amnesia has no influence on respiratory changes resulting from unconscious recognition of symbolically forgotten words.

2. *Circulation and Heart Rate.* Deutsch and Kauf (95) have reported changes in heart rate through the induction of emotional changes. Wilson (494) and also Astruck (7) both claimed having accelerated the heart by means of suggestion. Whether direct or indirect evocation was involved in these instances is not clear; but Jenness and Wible (227) have insisted in any case that changes in heart rate cannot be evoked directly by suggestion. Whitehorn (486) also reported accelerating the heart of a subject as much as 80 per cent through the induction of anxiety states. In his investigation of hypnotic anesthesia, Sears (406) has observed a considerable reduction in pulse changes normally associated with pain. Bier (30) asserted that hypnotic suggestions of rest, happiness, and excitement will alter the pulse rate as well as electrocardiograms. Again, the results of Bitterman and Marcuse (34) indicate that posthypnotic amnesia does not affect cardiovascular responses associated with the recall of words at the symbolic level. Finally, Benedek (24) reported that he had been able to bring about pulse acceleration by suggestion of an emotional state to his subject.

3. *Metabolism.* Grafe and Traumann (168) declare that in some cases suggestion of depression and of heavy work increases the subject's metabolic rate from 6 to 12 per cent. Grafe and Mayer (169) made similar investigations, suggesting various pleasant and unpleasant experiences. They observed a rise in metabolism of 8 to 25 per cent in some subjects. They concluded that suggested emotions may affect the rate of metabolism and that sorrow-inducing suggestions are more effective than those producing joy.

Further confirmation of the above has been obtained by Whitehorn, Lundholm, and Gardner (485) who suggested a number of moods to their subjects. They concluded that moods of depression, elation, and irritability do not produce any change in BMR, but that moods of anxiety and of apprehension are capable of increasing it.

Both Nemtzova and Schattenstein (321, 322) on the one hand and Levin and Egolinsky (261) on the other found it possible to alter oxygen consumption by suggestions of resting and of light or of heavy work, the subject actually resting or performing constant work. Fulde (150) observed a similar effect when excitement is suggested.

Eichelberg (108) has reported a reduction of hysterical fever by means of suggestion. The decrease amounted to 1.8° C. Gessler and Hansen (156) maintain that hypnotic suggestions can counteract the heat-regulating mechanism of the body. Unfortunately their investigation is of a rather questionable character. Benedek (24) claims to have produced hyperemia through the induction of emotional states in individuals.

Along a different line of thought, Grassheim and Wittkower (170) attempted to influence the specific dynamic action of ingested proteins, using test meals, by suggesting that the meal had not been eaten. They met with no success in this. Conversely, they were not able to bring about the typical specific dynamic action of proteins by suggesting that ingested nonprotein test meals had a high protein content.

4. *Gastrointestinal Muscular Activity.* Frick, Scantlebury, and Patterson (147) observed that, in light hypnosis, hunger contractions are inhibited promptly by the suggestion of food. On the other hand, the contractions are not easily elicited by the suggestion of hunger when the stomach is in a state of quiescence. Nevertheless, in this case restlessness similar to the kind found to accompany hunger in a number of animals is observed. When the same suggestions are given in the waking state, none of these phenomena are observed. The investigators conclude that autonomic processes can be influenced directly by hypnotic suggestion.

In a further study Scantlebury (390) showed that suggestions and sight of food in the waking state did not inhibit hunger contractions, whereas hypnosis and suggestions of eating brought about such an inhibition. Again, Scantlebury, Frick, and Patterson (391) showed that a similar inhibition could be obtained when dreams with food as an integral part are induced.

Lewis and Sarbin (266) reported that, when a fictitious meal was suggested to hypnotized subjects, gastric hunger contractions were inhibited, and a feeling of satiation resulted. They further stated that this inhibiting effect was directly related in magnitude to the depth of hypnosis and could not be elicited in nonhypnotized subjects.

Finally, Heyer (192) reported that hypnotic suggestions directed at altering gastrointestinal motility were able to bring about increases as well as slowing up of this activity, and that for subjects to whom increased motility was suggested defecation took place earlier than for subjects not receiving such suggestions. He reported obtaining changes in the time required for digestion, increased peristalsis, and decreased tonic spasticity of the gut.

5. *Uterine Contractions.* Although in recent years hypnosis has been employed to a considerable extent in childbirth, few data concerning its possible influence on uterine functions have been reported to date. Bonjour (40) reported many years ago that by suggesting to hypnotized pregnant women that normal term had been attained it was possible to bring about premature deliveries as well as abortions. He interpreted these results as arising from induced uterine contractions which are presumably reflex in character. Of more recent vintage is the report of Abramson and Heron (1) that the first stage of labor was appreciably speeded up when preparturient patients were trained to relax by means of hypnotic suggestion. Reynolds (364) also reported tokodynamometric data obtained from a patient in labor who had been successfully anesthetized for labor pains by means of hypnotic suggestion. The records show alterations in the form, rhythm, and intensity of the uterine contractions when compared to records obtained from other patients who had not been influenced in a similar manner.

6. *Vasomotor Effects.* Bier (30) has reported that suggestions of well-being and of excitement will alter blood pressure. White (478) found that unpleasant ideational and sensory situations suggested in the hypnotic state cause changes in blood pressure, the latter being enhanced, while at the same time there is a decrease in psychogalvanic skin reflex of greater magnitude than that observed in waking indi-

viduals.* On the other hand, Doupe, Miller, and Keller (101) have been unable to find evidence that suggestion of warmth or cooling could modify digital circulation. They did observe, however, that suggestions of pain and of emotional states cause such changes. Support for these findings comes from a number of other sources which will not be enumerated.

Sears (406) found that suggested anesthesia decreases the psychogalvanic skin reflex to pain stimulation. This has been partially confirmed by Brown and Vogel (57) and more recently by West, Niell, and Hardy (475). Brown and Vogel (57) also reported increases in this response as a result of suggested hyperalgesia. Levine (265) found that hallucinated pain could increase the psychogalvanic reflex, whereas suggested anesthesia apparently made it disappear.

Talbert, Ready, and Kuhlman (437) maintain that suggested cold produces arm constriction. Eiff (109) finds the opposite for heat.

Benedek (24) reported having been able to bring about an elevation in blood pressure, hyperdrosis of the face and forehead, and elevation in skin temperature, by suggesting emotional experiences.*

Finally, we have a long list of reports on the formation of erythema, wheals, and blisters following suggestions of burns, some rather conflicting data on the inhibition and production of allergic reactions, and reports on the removal of warts by suggestion. Although to some extent vasomotor changes may lie at the root of these phenomena, and certainly do in some cases, because of the particular nature of the material involved, they will be discussed under a separate heading in the next chapter.

7. *Secretion, Excretion, and Tissue Exchange. Electrolyte Balance.* Heilig and Hoff (188), investigating the influence of hypnosis upon secretions, found that pleasant feeling, suggested hypnotically, reduced water, sodium chloride, and phosphate excretion, whereas suggested unpleasant feelings caused an increase in urinary output and a relative increase in chloride and phosphate. Heyer and Grote (193) substantiated this in part by their report that suggested emotional experiences increase phosphate excretion. Marx (292) observed that suggestions of water intake caused increased urinary output with lower specific gravity. Benedek (24), as already mentioned, reported the production of hyperdrosis as a result of suggesting emotional states. He was also

---

* Some of these phenomena may seem to the reader to be out of place here. The reason for mentioning them is that there is evidence that vasomotor changes may be partly responsible for some of their aspects.

able to bring about copious secretion of tears. Since the psychogalvanic skin reflex is a manifestation of sweat gland activity, reports already cited about suggested alterations of this reflex should also be considered as falling under the present subheading.

Delhougne and Hansen (94) found that the suggestion of protein intake causes an increase in pepsin and trypsin secretion, whereas the suggestion of fatty food ingestion causes increased production of lipase. Finally, according to them, the suggestion of ingested carbohydrate brings about an increase in the secretion of maltase. Luckhardt and Johnston (277) observed that the suggestion of food causes a rise in gastric acidity. Both Delhougne and Hansen on the one hand and Luckhardt and Johnston on the other reported that the amount of secretion was comparable to that observed in actual test meals. Furthermore, the first two investigators stated that enzyme secretion was entirely specific. Something along this line was also observed by Heyer (194), who gave his subjects hypnotic suggestions that various foods had been eaten by them. Examination of collected gastric juices showed that (a) the amount of secretions was a direct function of the vividness of the suggestions and (b) the proteolytic activity was characteristic of the food suggested. Langheinrich (252) reported data confirming the above and also showing a similar effect in the secretion of bile.

Heilig and Hoff (189) studied the effect of emotions on gastric acidity. They reported increased and decreased gastric acidity when enjoyment and disgust were suggested, respectively. This was true whether or not the subjects were eating at the time of the suggestions.

Along a somewhat different line of approach, a number of investigators have considered the effect of suggestion on the blood sugar level. Povorinskji and Finne (350) reported that this level can be increased by suggesting that sugar or honey has been ingested. They also assert that suggesting the absence of sugar inhibits the rise in blood sugar level that normally follows when sugar is actually ingested. In contrast, Marcus and Sahlgren (289) were unable to alter the blood sugar level of their subject with and without ingestion of glucose solutions when appropriate suggestions were given. Nielsen and Geert-Jörgensen (325) obtained rather good evidence that inducing changes in blood sugar level is not possible through suggested ingestion of sugar, thus partially substantiating Marcus and Sahlgren.

Marcus and Sahlgren (289) also reported that they have been able to counteract the effects of adrenaline and of insulin injections by means of appropriate suggestions. Stein (423) declared that the blood sugar level of normal and diabetic patients was made to rise or fall by suggesting to them that their pancreas would secrete more or less insulin. Gigon, Aigner, and Brauch (159) confirmed this. These investigators suggested to diabetic patients that their pancreas would produce insulin and that a reduction in blood and urine sugar would take place. They reported that a lowering of blood sugar followed.

Mohr (314) found that the removal and the introduction of emotional factors by means of hypnotic suggestion can cause a change in blood sugar level.

Some workers have also considered the blood calcium level. Kretschmer and Krüger (243) observed that they could change this level by suggesting excitement (increased level) or calming (decreased level), provided the calcium level was already abnormally high. That is, the subjects had to be abnormal in this respect.† Glasser (165) reports that exciting and quieting a neurotic patient by hypnotic suggestion brought about a rise in calcium level.

In connection with hematological changes Cohen and Cobb (72) noted that, when hypnotic suggestions of slower breathing are employed to decrease hyperventilation in patients suffering from this disorder, a reduction in blood pH as well as an increase in pCO_2 was recorded.

Benedek (24) reported that acid salivation resulted from suggesting emotional states. Pronko and Hill (355) have shown that it is possible to alter salivation by suggestions aimed at reversing the action of sweet and acid stimuli on salivation. In a continuation of this study, Bowles and Pronko (44) also found that, when water was given to the subject, salivation could be altered by suggesting to him that it was acid or sweet. The changes in salivation were in the expected direction. These two groups of investigators agree in concluding that the effect of a stimulus can be altered by suggesting that it is another kind of stimulus.

Finally, although this really does not fall under the category of true secretion or excretion and might have been equally well, if not better, considered under uterine functions, we might mention a report of Marcus and Sahlgren (290) to the effect that menstrual flow can be regulated by means of hypnotic suggestion.

We might also mention an interesting study made by Farris, Garrison, and Heintz (137) on the possible effects of suggestion aimed at

† This effect could not be produced in individuals with a normal calcium level.

improving the production of semen in a number of subfertile men. The authors, after examining eight quantitative aspects of the semen samples, reached the conclusion that the suggestions did not bring about any changes.

8. *Other Reflexes.* Thus far, we have been mainly concerned with conditioned and autonomic reflexes. There are some that are primarily spinal in character and a few that involve centers in the brain stem concerning which some data are available. Hakebush, Blinkowski, and Foundillere (178) reported that they had been able to bring about the appearance of neonatal reflexes through hypnotic regression.‡ §

Gidro-Frank and Bowerbuch (157) more recently have offered excellent evidence confirming the above. In particular, these two investigators were able to cause a reversal of the Babinski reflex through hypnotic regression. This change was found to be accompanied by alterations in peripheral chronaxie.

Lundholm (279) reported that, when dysfunctions of various types are induced by means of hypnotic suggestion, some of the associated reflexes are not altered. Thus, hypnotic blindness still allows pupillary contractions to take place in response to light. Conversely, hallucination of a strong light does not produce any changes in pupillary size. On the other hand, winking caused by flashing a strong light directly into the eye is inhibited in suggested blindness. Again, the turning reaction of the eye when a weaker light is flashed in the peripheral region of the visual field is absent during suggested blindness. The same may be said concerning the general avoidance reactions observed when the eye is threatened. This material has been partially confirmed by Dorcus (98) who reported that suggested changes in brightness of a constant source of light do not cause alterations in pupillary diameter, nor does the suggestion of physical rotation influence nystagmus or the fall reaction.

We might also mention here, for lack of a more suitable place,‖ the observation made by Cooper and Tuthill (77) concerning the presence of action currents in the superficial flexor muscle of the thumb of a hypnotized subject who was hallucinating himself in the act of writing.

‡ I have also had occasion to observe this phenomenon.

§ A regression may be stated to be, for the time being, a return of the individual to a past period in his life, both mentally and physiologically.

‖ Since the status of muscle action current associated with imagery as a reflex phenomenon remains a moot question.

Summary and Conclusions

To examine each of these studies critically would be beyond the scope of this book.¶ Many of the reports are found not to stand up under critical examination. Others fail to mention certain details without which it is impossible to evaluate the significance of the reported results. But, even when these are eliminated, there remains an impressive array of data from which certain deductions may be made. In general, there are clear and definite indications that alterations of the motor functions are possible within limits but that these are not nearly so spectacular as popular belief would have them. The rule appears to be that, the less voluntary an activity is, the less easily and the less strongly it can be affected or controlled by suggestion. There is reason to believe that similar alterations can be obtained at times without the intervention of suggestion,* and that in such instances the effects that result may be even greater than those caused by suggestion, although direct evidence for this is lacking.

When attention is turned more specifically to the group of involuntary and semivoluntary motor functions, we find that the majority of reports show that a large number of these functions can be influenced. They appear to be most susceptible to indirect influence arising from the direct evocation of emotional states and of hallucinations. Direct evocation of the changes themselves is least effective. In fact, it is rare that involuntary responses are directly altered by suggestion. It is of considerable significance for a theory of hypnosis that the available information appears to show that, in nearly every reported instance for which alterations of reflex and reflex-like responses were produced by suggestions, the reflex arc most certainly was one that involved higher centers in the cortical and subcortical regions.

¶ However, a number of major experiments mentioned but not discussed in the present chapter will be taken up more critically in later chapters.

* The existence of a large variety of psychosomatic phenomena cannot be denied any longer. It remains to be demonstrated in many cases that some form of autosuggestion was not involved. Until this is done, one cannot assert that hysterical anesthesia (glove anesthesia) is nonsuggestive. Reported instances of the human plank brought about without suggestions must again be questioned in this light, as already remarked.

・ *11* ・

Suggested Organic Alterations

The effects considered in the previous chapter can certainly be considered psychosomatic in character. They are, however, of a rather superficial nature, being mainly concerned with rather transitory *functional* changes. Furthermore, these changes have been for the most part rather specific, involving specific organs or neural paths, as well as relatively well-localized receptors. It is possible, at least theoretically, that repeated production of any of the above alterations of functions would eventually lead to structural organic changes detectable at least at the histological level and having some degree of permanency. There is little question that use and disuse of organs lead to anatomical changes. Radical alterations of muscles result from interference with their innervation. There is, however, another possible group of suggested psychosomatic effects: those in which a single suggestion would bring about definite alterations in tissue structure, such changes being relatively lasting. In this group we might also consider possible changes of a diffuse nature, not involving any specific effectors.

Stigmatization. Suggestions and the Production of Herpes Labialis

The possibility of this sort of action as a result of suggestion is indicated by the existence of various reports of hysterical stigmatization. Though unquestionably many of these reports, if not all, contain gross exaggerations, there is probably some basis for them. Jacobi (221) has reviewed a large number of them and appears to think they were authentic. In this connection, Moody (316, 317) has reported some interesting and rather spectacular instances of stigmatization occurring during abreaction obtained in conjunction with the administration of pentothal. It is to be noted that in these cases no hypnosis or suggestion was involved. Among the various somatizations observed he lists rope marks, bruises, swelling, and petechial hemorrhages. Accumulating data on psychosomatic phenomena in general, such as may be found in Dunbar's work (102), makes the above a strong possibility. Moody cited in support of his findings reports by such men as Alrutz (4), Bolten (39), Doswald (100), Heyer (195), Kohnstamm (239), Kreibich and Sobotka (242), Schindler (393), and Dunbar (102), all of whom reported various psychosomatic effects in the form of skin blisters, urticaria, edema, cutaneous gangrene, spontaneous hemorrhages, and a variety of stigmata. It may be that the steps from dermatographia, through localized psychosomatic allergies, to suggested tissue changes are not so extreme as has appeared in the past.

One of the earliest and most spectacular reports of somatic alterations by means of suggestion was made by Heilig and Hoff (190). These investigators observed that suggestions of itching of the lower lip combined with tactual stimulation of the lip, given in conjunction with the production of strong emotional disturbances through hypnotic suggestion, caused a number of subjects to develop true instances of herpes labialis. Hull (213) has questioned the validity of this study, for it is known that at least two of the three subjects used were prone to developing herpetic blisters whenever under emotional stress. We might add to this the well-known fact (305) that herpes labialis may be brought about by any number of causes—mechanical irritation or trauma, and emotional disturbances, not to mention apparent spontaneous outbreaks without known causes. In the absence of adequate controls, the above results appear ambiguous. However, Heilig and Hoff also reported in the above investigation that direct suggestions of the formation of herpetic blisters, no matter how emphatic or detailed, were not capable of inducing cold sores unless combined with affective experiences of the kind already mentioned. We may therefore strongly suspect that the suggested emotional upsets were probably the main precipitating agent in at least two cases, although we should not discount the possibility that the remainder of the procedure employed by the two investigators may have been a factor in the localization of the eruptions, or/and may have reinforced the effect of the induced emotions. In any event, the results indicate rather definitely that direct evocation of herpetic blisters is unlikely.

Production and Inhibition of Allergies

We turn our attention to a different sort of disorder now, namely, allergies. Hansen (179) has reported that asthmatic attacks may be stopped by hypnotic suggestion and that even status asthmaticus may be ended in this manner.* He also mentioned a case where asthma

---

* Of course, all cases of asthma are not allergic in character. From Hansen's report, however, it would appear that he was dealing primarily with this type.

was caused by an allergy to horse dander; even though suggestions aimed at counteracting the allergy were not able to alter the skin test reaction to the allergen, nevertheless the "sensitivity" of the patient was so reduced that no asthmatic attacks were produced.

The converse situation has been reported by Wittkower and Petow (496). Suggestions were given to a patient that the odor of roses was particularly harmful to her. This was found to make her extremely sensitive to anything related to roses, asthmatic attacks resulting from it. In spite of this, skin tests made with rose extracts consistently gave negative reactions. Notwithstanding the fact that these two investigators believed that they were dealing with an allergic reaction, it is clear that the asthma or a reaction like it could arise in other ways. This coupled with the negative skin tests could indicate that possibly no allergy was ever induced. We shall come back to this presently.

Zeller (508) attempted a similar experiment with a patient suffering from bronchial asthma and with one having no allergies whatsoever. Both were passively and locally sensitized to ragweed pollen, neither being allergic to it before the experiment. It was found that hypnotic suggestion to the effect the subjects would not react to this allergen had no effect. Furthermore, hypnotic suggestion that a nonsensitized area would produce a reaction when the allergen was injected had no effect either. Other patients with a variety of allergies received suggestions that they would show no responses to scratch tests. They were not affected by the suggestions and their positive reactions remained.

Marcus and Sahlgren (290) reported having obtained allergic skin reactions and local dermatographic reactions by means of suggestion, using a psychopathic individual for subject.

Diehl and Heinichen (97) investigated this aspect, using various allergens and patch tests. They chose this particular type of skin test because it affords a means of studying the reactions quantitatively. It might be added that this is the only study of this kind in which quantitative results have been obtained. It is also unquestionably one of the best-controlled studies of its kind that has been performed to date. Before testing for a reaction, the investigators gave the subjects suggestions directed at increasing and decreasing both subjective and objective manifestations. They reported that, though they were not able to obtain qualitative changes in allergic reactions, appropriate increases and decreases in reactions were observed, showing that definite quantitative changes can be produced. The two authors remark that, in the light of the role played by emotional factors in allergic attacks, the type of suggestion they employed probably did not elicit maximal action. This would be partly substantiated by the report of Heilig and Hoff (190).

In attempting to evaluate the results on allergies, it should be kept in mind that the various experiments that have been reported do not appear to make use of hypnotic techniques to their fullest extent, nor in the most efficient manner. In particular, the depth of trance and the amount of preliminary set allowed to form may not have been adequate. As Erickson (111) has pointed out, these are two very important factors which are often ignored in hypnotic experiments. In addition, the degree of participation of the subject in the hypnotic situation is uncertain. It has generally been found that best results in hypnosis can be obtained only when the subject can be made to live fully the suggested situation, even though this may mean that he will have to suffer some pain and discomfort. It should be remembered too that skin tests and general allergy syndromes are not necessarily comparable. One is a localized tissue reaction which occurs quite independently of any emotional upset at the time of the test. In the other the usual allergic attack is a general systemic condition and is often associated with emotional disturbances. Furthermore, recent data show that there is no perfect correlation between allergies and skin reactions. The incidence of positive skin reactions can be as low as 5 per cent with certain allergies. This is in keeping with the fact that allergy is usually the result of local hypersensitiveness of but a few shock tissues. It is therefore understandable that general allergic manifestations could be effected more readily than skin reactions.

Production of Skin Blisters

Many of the early attempts at producing tissue alterations by means of suggestion were aimed at producing blisters. There are unfortunately no recent data on this topic, and we must still rely on rather unsatisfactory and antiquated sources of information. Pattie (337), in reviewing the material made available over a period of 55 years, found only ten reports covering a total of eleven experiments that could be considered anywhere near satisfactory, in that they at least give a fair account of procedures and controls used. My own attempts to survey this field of study led to the same selection. The investigations are those of Fochachon (as reported by Beaunis (22)), Krafft-Ebing (241), Jendrassik (224), Rybalkin (382), Doswald (100), Heller and

Schultz (191), Podiapolskiï (349), Smirnoff (417), Wetterstrand (476), Hadfield (177), and Schindler (393).

Typically experiments in this area consist of hypnotizing an individual into a deep trance and then touching some portion of his skin with a definite object and suggesting at the same time that this act will produce a burn, a blister, an area of redness, or all of these combined. In some instances a period of time was specified for the occurrence of this event, while in others it was not. After the suggestions were given, the subjects were either allowed to wake or, in some cases, kept in the trance state until the end of the experiment. The areas that had been designated were either bandaged right away or observed for a while and bandaged later. In most cases, the object with which the area was touched was allowed to remain in contact with the subject's skin even after termination of the suggestion, being covered and held in place by the bandage. In some instances, however, contact was only temporary. In one instance at least, the area in question was not touched but only pointed at. Usually the objects placed in contact with the skin were of a definite shape, for purposes of leaving a recognizable and specific imprint if possible. Most of the reports were limited to descriptions of the outer appearance of the skin, but a few of the investigators who were dermatologists performed biopsies.

In the eleven experiments under consideration, two subjects were normal but had suffered in the past from hysterical disorders, only three had always been normal, and six were hysterics at the time of the experiment.

The reported time interval required for blister formation ranged from 10 minutes to 24 hours. For erythema formation the time ranged from a few seconds to 7 hours. In two cases the suggested blisters occurred at a place other than the one that had been indicated in the suggestions. In two instances in which biopsies were made, neurotic gangrenous material was reported. In one case the formation of scar tissue was taken as evidence of the past occurrence of something akin to neurotic skin gangrene. In all but one instance absence of pain was suggested. The blisters were reported in general as having been similar in all respects to naturally occurring blisters, including the exudation of clear plasma, and even blood.

In all these investigations the experimenters report definite and rather remarkable effects. Nevertheless, Pattie (337) concluded at the end of his survey that further substantiation is needed as well as more delicate methods of investigation. He admits his hesitancy to accept these results because of the difficulty he has in understanding how such effects could be brought about by suggestion. Gorton (167), on the other hand, in looking over this material, is prone to accept it and to question, with good reason, Pattie's arguments. I am in agreement with Gorton. It is quite true that no clear explanation of the reported phenomena has been given to date.† On the other hand, it must be pointed out that the same situation exists in regard to a number of similar phenomena which nonetheless are real, for example, hysterical echymosis and stigmatization. Furthermore, in conversion hysteria, it is well established that local and generalized vasoconstriction and vasodilatation are observable. In a few cases edematous areas are even seen. Anal and genital pruritus sometimes take place. Again the psychosomatic origin of some allergies has become increasingly well established. Our lack of understanding of such phenomena may merely indicate that we must revise our thinking about involuntary processes.

It may be significant here that the majority of subjects employed in the blister experiments that were cited were either hysterics or had a history of hysteria. Some had even suffered from hysterical vasomotor disturbances of the skin. Even the two subjects that were purported to be normal cannot really be guaranteed not to have had hysterical tendencies. It is entirely possible that there is a special relationship between hysteria and the results of the skin blister experiments. Hysterics might be expected to show a greater facility for this sort of phenomenon.

That the subjects were far from representing a random distribution is again disclosed by the fact that the experimenters in some instances chose individuals showing a delicate skin or other signs that would be expected to indicate a diathesis for the phenomena to be evoked. This also may be significant. I am prone to believe that persons showing a tendency toward dermatographia and special skin sensitivities (as in allergies) may be more likely to respond to suggestions of blistering. It is, incidentally, quite possible that a form of dermatographia was involved in some of the reported instances of blister formation, since in some of these the stimulus object was left in contact with the skin for a while and in others was replaced by a bandage. Consequently, a constant source of stimulation was often present which would favor the production of urticaria factitia. Exactly when a stimulus is neutral and when it is irritating is a moot question.

† A partial solution to this question will be offered in Chapter 22.

The Reduction of Warts

One more topic remains to be considered which in some respects is a little the converse of the previous one. This is the reduction of warts by means of suggestion. There is an abundance of reports on wart cures. Sulzberger and Wolf (434) who have examined a great many such reports concluded that they all have suggestion as a common factor.

One of the earliest reports to which some credence can be given is by Bonjour (41). According to him, warts and condylomas can be removed by suggestion in 95 per cent of the cases. Bloch (37), using a complicated method of indirect suggestion, reported cures of 88.4 per cent of verucae planae juvenilis and 44 per cent of verucae vulgares (he gave an over-all estimate of 78.5 per cent cure out of a total of 179 cases). Bloch's data and method have been criticized by Memmesheimer and Eisenlohr (302) on the basis that they tried his method and obtained about as many spontaneous cures in nontreated patients as in patients who were treated. In rebuttal, Sulzberger and Wolf (434) have remarked that after all a mere examination can in itself act as a curative suggestion. Nevertheless, there is no question but that some spontaneous cures do take place. Among more recent investigators who have reported wart cures by suggestion, are McDowell (296) and Obermayer and Greenson (327). On the basis of their results, it appears that the effectiveness of the suggestions depends in part on the type of wart involved, the number of warts, the age of the patient, and the length of time the wart has been in existence.

It is difficult to arrive at any definite conclusion here. The nature of warts is largely unknown. That a virus is involved seems clear. There is general agreement, too, that vasomotor effects are involved in both the growth and the disappearance of warts. But it is also definitely established that warts have a tendency to disappear spontaneously. It may be better on the whole to leave it to the future to decide the correct answer. This thought applies equally well to the general problem of tissue changes brought about by hypnotic suggestion. There are indications that these are possible and have taken place in the past. It is also probable that direct evocation will usually be relatively ineffective. Beyond this, little more can be said of a definite nature.

· 12 ·

Hypnotic Alterations
of Sensory and Perceptual Functions

As noted in a previous chapter, motor functions can be altered within limits. It is logical to ask next whether this is also true of the sensory and perceptual functions. The investigation of this matter presents certain difficulties for there is a strong possibility that, when positive effects are obtained, these may result from "acting" or "simulating" on the part of the subject rather than from true functional alterations, although it must be emphasized that the subject, when simulating a response, often does so in perfectly good faith. For instance, in studies of hypalgesia or pain anesthesia, facial flinch which is characteristic of pain, can be voluntarily controlled to a certain extent, and quite completely by some individuals. Verbal reports concerning the experience of pain are of course the easiest to "falsify." The absence or decrease of facial flinch and a subjective report that pain was absent cannot therefore be accepted as proof of the existence of anesthesia. What is needed is a physiological reaction over which the subject has no voluntary control. Dilation of the pupil and the psychogalvanic skin reflex are just such kinds of responses and are therefore ideal for examining the "reality" of suggested sensory phenomena. On the other hand, we must not be too anxious to condemn suggested phenomena as fictitious when these same responses fail to differentiate between the suggested condition and the normal state of the subject. For, while the physiological reality of a phenomenon may be lacking, nevertheless the phenomenon may be *subjectively very real* for the subject. Too many investigators have taken the position in the past that the lack of appropriate physiological correlates was proof positive of the nonreality of various suggested phenomena. It seems more rational, and certainly safer, to accept such results as information concerning the nature and mechanisms of hypnotically induced behavior, rather than as evidence of the unreality of such behavior.

146

Auditory Alterations

The belief in the production of sensory alterations has been wide-spread and has existed from the very beginning of hypnosis. Braid believed in it. Bramwell was of a similar opinion. In more recent times, Travis (442) reported a lowering of auditory limen in hypnagogic reverie. Lifschitz (270) has confirmed this. Fisher (140) also observed evidence of increased auditory acuity. Some indication that hypnosis can give rise to sensory alterations has also been given by Schneck (398–400); Brenman, Gill, and Hackner (49); and Erickson (113). For reasons already given, discussion of these last five reports will be left to a later chapter.

On the other hand, Sterling and Miller (428) found indications that auditory acuity could not be improved in hypnosis when it was already maximal in the waking state. This is in agreement with my findings in relation to another sense modality (464). Similarly, Schneck and Bergman (394) were unable to find evidence of improved auditory acuity in the trance state. Eysenck (134) investigated loudness discrimination in relation to hypnosis and could find no difference between performance in this state and that in the waking state.

In none of the above experiments were suggestions of improved performance given to the subjects, although Eysenck did ask the subjects to perform maximally. We are unable to conclude therefore that auditory acuity and discrimination cannot be increased by hypnotic suggestion, although apparently, as we might expect, hypnosis per se does not produce any changes. This last is in keeping with the physiological similarity between hypnosis and waking.

The converse situation of induced deafness has been investigated by Erickson (114) in a very extensive manner. He reported that suggested deafness appears to be in no way different from genuine neurological deafness although it can show a great selectiveness. He also observed that suggested deafness affects conditioned reflexes in a manner similar to that seen or expected in true deafness. Thus, suggested deafness prevents the establishment of conditioning to sound, and, conversely, conditioned responses formed with respect to sound are prevented from occurring by suggested deafness. On the other hand, Brown and Vogel (57) have reported that induced deafness does not abolish certain characteristic physiological reactions associated with auditory stimulation. Pattie (338) has also made a study of unilateral suggested deafness and shown beyond question that the supposedly deaf ear was functioning. Lundholm and Lowenbach (280) have also shown that the alpha pattern in electroencephalograms is not altered by auditory anesthesia.

Some reasons for the differences in results have already been considered in Chapter 9. However, something should be said about the reports of Pattie and Erickson which are contradictory, yet are the result of well-planned experiments, and are in fact probably the two best studies of this kind. The difference of opinion is not entirely unexpected, for the two experiments were not comparable in many respects. From a careful examination of both works the following can be said: It would appear that, when bilateral auditory anesthesia is suggested to a subject who is in the *deepest* possible trance state, who is *fully participating* in the trance situation, and in whom *a specific set* has been deeply and carefully established, one may expect alterations of sensory functions which cannot be distinguished from those resulting from organic causes. On the other hand, when monolateral alterations of the above kind are suggested, and/or the subject is not in the deepest of trance, is not participating fully in the hypnotic situation, and does not have any particular set established toward the phenomena to be elicited, pseudoalterations are observed which can be distinguished from true changes in sensory functions such as would be caused by organic defects. This last form of behavior can be referred to as "malingering," provided the usual opprobrium attached to this expression is left out. It is known from Erickson's report that his investigation falls within the first of the two situations just described. Although it cannot be demonstrated beyond doubt that Pattie's work is of the second kind in all respects, there are rather good indications that this is so, and this has led to the above generalization. In one respect the results obtained by Erickson are puzzling, because it is a well-known fact that hysterical deafness does not affect the formation and elicitation of conditioned reflexes based on auditory stimuli. It may be that hysterical deafness is not so complete a functional deafness as can be obtained with careful techniques under hypnosis. Or, again, there may be more than one mechanism by means of which functional deafness can be brought about, these mechanisms not being completely equivalent.

The Touch and Pain Senses

Early investigators have reported that the tactile sense could be improved by hypnosis. For instance, Bramwell and Moll both asserted that they had observed improvement in two-point discrimination. Berger claimed to have found a lowering of pressure thresholds. None of these reports, however, is at all satisfactory from an experimental standpoint.

P. C. Young (504) has considered the possibility of improving touch through hypnosis. He tested the effects of hypnosis upon the detection of light pressure * in the absence of suggestions of improvement and observed no changes. Hull (213) concurred with Young in concluding that there is no evidence that hypnosis can improve tactual sensitivity. However, there are some inherent weaknesses in this study, and hence it cannot be given too much weight. Gault and Goodfellow (154) report that waking suggestions of improvement increase the vibro-tactile sensitivity of individuals. Unfortunately, they have not made available any details of their investigation; hence one can only take their report at face value.

Brown and Vogel (57) have considered the possibility of lowering the pain threshold by suggestions of hyperalgesia for both pain and indifferent stimuli. They reported observing marked changes in such areas as blood pressure, pulse rate, skin potentials, and respiration. Presumably these changes were in the same direction as those that would have been produced by greater pain or ordinary pain, respectively. The investigators have not made this clear. In any event they also observed that similar changes were brought about when the subjects were requested to imagine hyperalgesia in the waking state. Levine (265) has investigated the response of individuals to hallucinated pain experiences. He reported that overt responses, verbal comments, and the psychogalvanic skin reflex showed evidence of some pain. Unfortunately, neither of these two investigations is too satisfactory from the standpoint of statistical significance. Furthermore, in the light of the remark made by Brown and Vogel that quantitative changes in physiological reactions to painful stimuli are not reliable indicators of painful experience one may wonder somewhat about these results. We will consider this point later.

The converse of the above, namely touch and pain anesthesia, has also been investigated. In view of the increasing use of hypnotic anesthesia in dentistry and childbirth, not to mention the fact that demonstrations of this phenomenon are always very impressive and have played no little part in convincing the common man of the mysterious powers of hypnosis, the extent and nature of hypnotic anesthesia merits considerable inquiry. We might begin with a study of touch

---

* One should of course keep in mind here that light touch and pressure are believed to involve separate sense modalities. If so, Young's results might apply only to one of these modalities.

phenomena. Pattie (339) has conducted the only investigation of this. Actually his intention was to test the genuineness of suggested anesthesia for pain, but analysis of his experiment seems to show that touch alone was all that was considered. He made use of the Japanese illusion in a very ingenious manner in a well-designed experiment. He suggested anesthesia of the right hand and arm to his subjects who were all in a deep trance. This anesthesia was tested under normal conditions by pressing, pinching, and pricking the member in question. When the Japanese illusion was performed, however, the subjects gave the response associated with normal sensation, indicating that anesthesia was not present insofar as the Japanese illusion test was concerned. Pattie consequently concluded that suggested anesthesia is an illusion. Since in performing the crucial test mild touch and not pain stimuli appears to have been the only stimulation employed, we may not necessarily conclude that the results would have held for pain stimuli, although this would certainly be a reasonable expectation. Furthermore there appears to be an unproved surmise at the bottom of this investigation: namely, that, if one hand is anesthetic, the Japanese illusion should break down. But does it? One might ask whether, if the subject were not aware that one of his hands was anesthetic, the illusion would still fail. In any event one control was lacking: namely, a repetition of the experiment with subjects whose hands have been anesthetized by the use of drugs.

Nature and Character of Suggested Pain Anesthesia

One of the better and earlier experiments was performed on the phenomenon of suggested pain anesthesia by Levine (265) who investigated the overt response, the verbal report (subjective responses), and the psychogalvanic skin reflex of two subjects suffering from hysteria. Using the thrust of a venipuncture needle to stimulate pain, he studied the responses obtained when areas that were suggested to be anesthetic and areas that were already anesthetic because of the hysteria were stimulated in this manner. Levine reported the absence of all three types of responses when anesthesia was suggested. In waking hysteria he observed that the psychogalvanic reflex was still active.† On the other hand, all responses were present when the two kinds of anesthesia were absent and when pain was hallucinated. The main criticism that can be aimed at this study, as Hull (213) has

† We might compare this to the remark made earlier in connection with Erickson's results on suggested deafness and hysterical deafness.

pointed out, is that Levine did not check whether there was really complete absence of responses or merely a weakening of these during anesthesia.

Quite fortunately Sears (406), who has probably made one of the most thorough studies of this question, has essentially repeated the work of Levine. He reported that all typical responses to pain are reduced or completely abolished when anesthesia is produced by hypnotic suggestion. The degree of effectiveness appears to decrease in the order voluntary to involuntary. Simulation could of course account for the inhibition of voluntary and semivoluntary responses. It is significant, however, that even involuntary responses such as the psychogalvanic skin reflex showed a decrease! Furthermore Sears had his subjects attempt to inhibit voluntarily the various responses. There was no evidence that they could. Hull (213) has criticized these last-mentioned results on the basis that one would have expected the subjects to inhibit some facial flinch and possibly their respiration. Since they did not, he considers that this invalidates the absence of changes in other response modalities. Such an argument is not tenable, however, since it presupposes in the first place the existence of the very effect that the study was investigating. There are other arguments against it. In my opinion the entire investigation is valid.

Brown and Vogel (57) have made a comparative study of gas anesthesia, Novocain block, imagined anesthesia, and hypnotic anesthesia. Their results confirm those of Sears. Gas anesthesia alone was found to abolish all physiological reactions to mild pain. But even imagining has an inhibiting influence upon these. Besides the psychogalvanic skin reflex, a great many other responses were considered. These authors add that hypnotized subjects are able to withstand pain longer than those who merely imagine analgesia, thus indicating the superiority of suggestion in this respect. By itself this investigation is not entirely satisfactory from a statistical standpoint. There is also some evidence that the stimuli employed may not have been intense enough to bring about physiological responses to a degree that would have allowed a true differentiation. On the other hand, in conjunction with the other reported studies of hypnotic anesthesia, the work of Brown and Vogel gains some weight. It is of interest to note that they employed various pain stimuli. In particular they investigated the effectiveness of suggested anesthesia for continuous pain in contrast to sharp sudden pain. Since there is a certain specificity in this regard on the part of analgesic agents, this is far from being a trivial distinction. There was no evidence of a difference in effect. It is rather interesting that Brown and Vogel obtained evidence that even with Novocain block a definite skin response is observed, as well as other physiological correlates of pain, although these responses were decreased. This and the fact that nitrous oxide anesthesia alone could abolish all responses led the two men to conclude that *awareness of stimulation* appears to be one of the factors influencing the physiological responses to moderate pain stimuli. There has been increasing evidence since then that this is a correct surmise.

On the whole, for pain induced by means of the pressure of a sharp pointed instrument, there is good evidence that suggested anesthesia has more than a subjective reality but is certainly not equal to gas anesthesia. Reports of surgery performed under hypnotic anesthesia confirms the belief that in any case this form of anesthesia is very real at the subjective level. If any single criticism can be made of past investigations, it is that rather mild pain was studied exclusively, and, furthermore, that it tended to be of a single kind. The use of mechanical stimulation with sharp instruments ‡ can be criticized.

The use of a different form of pain stimulation in connection with suggested anesthesia was first used by Wolff and Goodell (499) who employed the method developed by Hardy, Wolff, and Goodell (180) for the quantitative administration of pain stimuli in the form of radiant energy. They reported that in a subject placed in a shallow "hypnosis" the pain threshold was raised by 40 per cent. In other respects, however, this rather superficial study is quite unsatisfactory so far as the present question is concerned and contributes nothing to what has already been said. Fortunately the same technique of stimulation has been employed in a more recent and extremely well-designed investigation of suggested anesthesia performed by West, Niell, and Hardy (475). This group of investigators concluded on the basis of their results that suggestions of anesthesia given to hypnotized subjects can cause an elevation of the pain threshold, hypalgesia, and analgesia,§ thereby influencing pain perception. They also found that under these conditions there is an impairment of the subject's ability to discriminate between different intensities of pain stimulation. Another of their observations was that there is a positive relationship between the depth

‡ Brown and Vogel also employed hot water as painful stimulus.

§ For West et al. the pain threshold is the least intensity of stimulation that the subject reports (perceives) as being painful. Analgesia is a condition in which so-called noxious stimuli are not reported as painful. Hypalgesia, on the other hand, is a condition in which such stimuli are perceived as less painful than they are known to be for the subject in so-called control situations.

of hypnosis || attained and the degree of induced anesthesia. This they found is reflected both in the threshold for pain perception and in the galvanic skin response. The first is raised accordingly, while the second is reduced. However, in most instances, there is no direct correlation between pain threshold and the galvanic skin reflex. In general, they found that a subject with great reduction in the skin reflex might still have a lower threshold than one with a lesser reduction in galvanic skin response, and conversely. In the most extreme cases that they observed the pain perception was not altered, and yet the galvanic skin response was greatly depressed. In other instances the two were found to correlate. Although the average reduction in galvanic skin response in any individual remained less than 100 per cent, there were occasions when the response disappeared completely in some subjects.

Though some of the results of this study are not easy to understand, it is clear that they support previous conclusions. Furthermore, perhaps more than any other investigation, that of West et al. makes it obvious that, although unquestionably the perception of pain and the physiological concomitants of this experience are intimately related, they nevertheless constitute two separate aspects of the problem of pain. Further elucidation of the matter must be left to the future.

Visual Functions

Improvement of Visual Processes. Another area that has proved fertile in the field of investigation is vision. Bergson, d'Abundo, Prince, and many other early investigators, have maintained that visual acuity ¶ could be improved under hypnosis. Unfortunately, the data they have made available in support of this are very unsatisfactory. On the other hand, nothing better has been offered to date in the same line of research. It is true that Sterling and Miller (428) have reported data under the heading of visual acuity, but, as it turns out, they actually studied form and brightness discrimination thresholds, which, as was just seen,¶ is something quite different from what the earlier investigators examined. Sterling and Miller reported that they were unable to find any evidence of lowered thresholds when hypnotic suggestions

|| On the Friedlander-Sarbin scale.
¶ Meaning here the minimum visual angle allowing resolution of two points. The need for specifying what is meant by "acuity" in any investigation is great because of the rather indiscriminate manner in which this term is used. There are serious reasons for doubting that "acuity" measurements obtained in terms of form or of brightness discriminations, for instance, have the same meaning as those obtained in terms of two-point resolution.

154 Alterations of Sensory and Perceptual Functions

of improved vision were given. One cannot, however, come to any final conclusion from their results, because, first, there is some question whether their subjects were adequately hypnotized.* Second, there is a possibility that the suggestions used may have been ambiguous, and even misdirecting for the subjects.

Blackwell (35) has reported data, on the other hand that appear to show that, under *some* conditions, the brightness threshold can be lowered by waking suggestions in the case of *some* individuals.†

P. C. Young (504) also reported negative findings on the improvement of visual functions and perception in hypnosis, after a study of the subject's ability to pick out an object previously seen from among many similar ones. Eysenck (134) in a somewhat similar experiment, confirmed these results. Making a similar investigation, but with an improved technique (464), I obtained results showing that, though such improvement is not possible when the subject is performing maximally in the waking state, improved performance can be brought about in hypnosis, in the differential recognition of certain visual patterns, at least in some subjects. Presumably this group of subjects consists of those who are not performing in the waking state to their fullest capacity. It might be noted that there seems to be some disagreement among investigators as to what the above three investigations were studying. Both Young and Eysenck believe that memory is primarily concerned. I find that actually visual discrimination and memory are both factors determining the subject's performance but conclude that, in the situation under consideration, hypnosis most probably influenced only the discriminatory process. It might also be added that only in my investigation was improved performance suggested to the subjects.

Suggested Total and Color Blindness. By far the majority of experiments on vision have dealt with the nature of negative and positive hallucination. The most extreme form of negative hallucination is of course total blindness. Erickson (115) has found indirect evidence that blindness can be obtained by hypnotic suggestion which sub-

* Only 2 out of the 9 subjects used were in deep hypnosis according to the investigators. But there is even some doubt concerning the actual trance depth of the first two subjects, because the only criteria used for its determination were eyelid closure, arm catalepsy, and the judgment of the observers.

† More will be said later about the role of the underlying conditions in this sort of experiment. In regard to the threshold changes reported in this study, it will be of interest to note that two of the nine subjects used showed an appreciable *rise* in threshold. These may have been two instances of the negative suggestibility mentioned earlier.

jectively is as real as organic blindness. In another report (123) he describes the spontaneous occurrence of blindness for certain specific visual occurrences following the artificial production of minor psychopathological manifestations by means of hypnosis. Pattie (340), on the other hand, made a study of monocular blindness which led him to conclude that there is no evidence for the reality of suggested blindness. Whether this proves "malingering," however, is a question. On the whole, the various arguments that have already been presented against other conclusions drawn by Pattie from his investigations of sensory alterations are valid here too. If any definite fact can be drawn from his present results, it is that suggested blindness is functional, and that suggested monocular blindness is not comparable to the organic kind. This conclusion is confirmed by the findings of Lundholm and Lowenbach (280) which show that suggested and hysterical blindness have no effects on the appearance and disappearance of the alpha pattern in EEG records. Lundholm (279) also reported that suggested blindness does not affect the pupillary reflex. This has been confirmed by Dorcus (98) in an experiment equivalent to suggesting partial blindness. On the other hand, Lundholm has also observed in the above study that the wink and avoidance reactions to sudden light are inhibited. The significance of this fact will be seen later on. Lemere (258) has partially substantiated the above results in regard to EEG records and alpha activity for the case of a hysterically blind individual.

On the other hand, Loomis, Harvey, and Hobart (273) claim that they have observed the appearance of alpha activity in the records of a hysterically blind person when his eyes were closed, the alpha patterns being absent when his eyes were open. It is very probable that conversion hysteria syndromes take on all degrees of completeness in their manifestations, so that this last report is not really a refutation of the results of Lundholm and Lowenbach, but helps us to realize that we should not expect perfect confirmation of results in regard to physiological changes associated with hypnotic phenomena, when after all this is not the case for well-established disorders.

Young (504) was one of the first to investigate the possibility of interfering with color vision. His results are ambiguous, however, and he himself does not consider them significant but regards his data rather as a "curiosity." The first real investigation of this question we owe to Erickson (115). It is unquestionably one of the best studies of its kind, being extremely carefully done. He tested his subjects with the Ishihara test for color blindness after causing them to become

color-blind through the use of hypnotic suggestion. His results lead
him to conclude that induced color deficiencies are comparable in
degree and character with those found in organic cases of color blindness. Grether (172), however, has pointed out a number of weaknesses in Erickson's work. The validity of many of his criticisms seems
to be dependent on the relative merit of his interpretation versus Erickson's. In any event, this led Harriman (181, 182) to repeat Erickson's
work while taking into account Grether's criticism. At the same time
he expanded the study by including a number of other tests of color
blindness besides the Ishihara test. Since he followed Erickson very
closely in the procedures used, the two investigations are comparable.
In their general aspects, Harriman's results verify the conclusion reported by Erickson: namely, that color vision anomalies can be induced
by suggestion. On the other hand, he showed rather plainly that
induced color blindness is not entirely the same as organic color blindness. He considers that his results show that the alterations resemble
attitudinal changes more closely than true changes in sensory content.
In any event, there are wide differences between organic and suggested
anomalies of color vision as obtained by Harriman. A rather significant outcome of Erickson's investigation is his observation that he
found that direct suggestions of color blindness were not effective in
producing this phenomenon. Not only was it necessary to remove the
subject's *perception* of the color in question, but the *conception* of the
color itself had to be eradicated. Harriman has not confirmed this
finding, but the fact that he employed the technique which Erickson
had designed on the basis of this observation would seem to indicate
that he agrees with Erickson. It might be added that Harriman also
showed that the suggested color vision anomalies could be carried over
into the waking state through the use of posthypnotic suggestions.

Suggested Color Experiences. On the side of positive hallucinations,
a number of inquiries have been made into the nature of hallucinated
colors. Binet and Féré appear to have been the first ones to consider
the possibility that negative afterimages might result from the hallucination of colors. They report finding positive evidence of the existence
of appropriate afterimages. It should be clear that whether or not
such images occur is of considerable theoretical importance in more
than one respect. Erickson and Erickson (116) were the first modern
investigators to touch upon this problem. In a very carefully designed
experiment they essentially duplicated the earlier study of Binet and
Féré. They reported that subjects form the correct afterimages corre-

sponding to various suggested colors, thus confirming Binet and Féré. Hibler (196) attempted to verify these results but was unable to do so, beyond confirming the fact that subjects report experiencing after-images, or at least appear to indicate that they do when tested for this. More precisely, Hibler's results show that some sort of afterimage results, but they do not duplicate the results obtained by the Ericksons. In addition, Hibler does not agree with them about the type of after-images obtained or the nature of the hallucinations which he disclaims to be sensory. This particular report has led to a series of criticisms and countercriticisms which the scope of this book does not permit us to detail. There is something to be said for either side, although for the most part Hibler's criticisms have little to back them up. By and large, analysis of both sides of the question seems to favor the Ericksons. It must be kept in mind that Hibler did not try to duplicate the investigation of the Ericksons but designed his own variation of it. Consequently the way was opened for discrepancies in results arising from a divergence in techniques. Possibly the most crucial factor, which may well account for the bulk of the disagreement between the two studies, is that Hibler's suggestions instructed the subjects to *act as if* the situation were as described, instead of to *experience* the newly defined situation, as was the Erickson procedure. Hibler's suggestions also suffer from brevity and possibly too much simplicity. In addition, there is reason to believe that his subjects were not in so deep a trance state as those of the Ericksons. On the whole, Hibler's investigation shows primarily what happens when hypnosis is not so deep as it could be, when the subject is not completely naive, and does not participate fully in the hypnotic situation. Under these conditions, mere verbal agreement seems to result more than any alteration of sensory or perceptual processes. On the other hand, the Ericksons' results would appear to indicate what one might expect in the converse situation, namely, a functional alteration.

Dorcus (97) attempted an experiment partly similar to Hibler's in which the subjects were shown colored disks that were suggested to be of another color. He could not find this to have any influence on the afterimages. This study, however, is not comparable to the one performed by either the Ericksons or Hibler, if in no other respect than the task difficulty presented. Furthermore, in the light of the criticisms presented by the Ericksons and Hibler of their respective work, Dorcus' report appears to be rather inadequate. Thus, for the time being the conclusions reached in the previous pages hold.

Kinesthesia, Temperature, and Gustation

Still other sense modalities have been studied in relation to the influence of hypnosis. There is a small amount of evidence indicating that kinesthesia can be improved in this manner. Eysenck (134) has reported an improvement of 27 per cent in the judgment of weights under hypnotic influence. Actually more than kinesthesia is probably involved here so that we cannot take this as definite evidence. Dorcus (98) attempted to influence vestibular phenomena such as nystagmus and the falling reaction, both when the subject is actually rotated and when he is standing still. He was unable either to inhibit or to bring about these responses by appropriate suggestions. It is said that Berger lowered the temperature threshold of subjects by suggestion. Bramwell also reported improved temperature discrimination following suggestion. Eiff (109) claims that perception of cold can be altered by suggestions of warmth. The various reports on the production of blisters by suggestions of burns can possibly be taken as evidence that the perception of temperature changes can be influenced by suggestion. The same may be said perhaps for the studies of Brown and Vogel (57), Wolff and Goodell (499), and West et al. (475).

Bowles and Pronko (44) and Pronko and Hill (355) have made some interesting and significant observations on gustation. They have shown that with hypnotic suggestion it is possible to equalize the taste of sweet and sour to an appreciable degree and that a neutral stimulus can be made to acquire the quality of sweet and sour, all of this to an extent sufficient to bring about measurable changes in salivation.

Time and Space Perception

A small number of investigations have been concerned with the perception of time. This is certainly one of the more interesting areas of study. It is one in which there is also considerable disagreement on the nature of the perceptions involved. The experience of time would appear to depend on a complex interaction of sensory processes and to be primarily a percept. It has been postulated by various authors that the basis for temporal judgments is to be found in certain rhythmic processes in the body. In rather recent times, Hoagland (199) has shown that temporal perception is a function of body temperature, time moving faster for individuals when their body temperature is raised above normal. A mathematical treatment of his results led him to conclude that some relatively simple chemical reaction taking place in the body probably acts as pace setter or master clock.

Lecomte Du Noüy (254) also presented evidence, on the basis of studies of cicatrization rates, that in regard to physiological processes time appears to flow faster the younger an individual is. This led him to postulate a physiological time, as contrasted to clock time, and to subjective time.

That subjective time can be considerably altered is evident from normal everyday experience. The effects of pleasantness and unpleasantness on the perception of duration are only too well known. The contraction of time in dreams is another well-known phenomenon. Also certain drugs are known to cause alterations in the perception of the temporal flow. Among other possible methods of achieving this hypnosis seems particularly indicated. Many earlier investigators appear to have been struck by the "punctuality" with which posthypnotic suggestions are carried out. A closer examination of results seems to show that this "punctuality" may not be quite so remarkable as it is claimed to be. Bramwell (45) makes numerous references in his book to various experiments in which improved performance in temporal judgment was supposedly obtained. Unfortunately all these reports are entirely lacking in satisfactory controls. However, Stalnaker and Richardson (421) have performed a well-controlled investigation of this problem. They reported that hypnosis shows no effects on the perception of time intervals of 1, 2, and 3 minutes. Hull (213) reported that Ruth Eken made a similar investigation for 16-minute intervals and found the same sort of results. On the other hand, Eysenck (134) obtained definite evidence that individuals can judge intervals of 5, 10, 15, and 30 seconds better in hypnosis than in the waking state. In evaluating these results, we may disregard Eken's experiment since the details have not been made available by either her or Hull, and it is therefore not possible to ascertain its validity. It is somewhat regrettable that Eysenck did not furnish details of the manner in which he measured temporal judgment, since in this regard his work may not be comparable to that of Stalnaker et al., thus accounting at least in part for the discrepancy in results. It is highly probable, however, that the order of magnitude of the test intervals employed is the main reason for the disagreement between the two investigations. As will be seen later, there is evidence that the difficulty of the task imposed by a suggestion tends to oppose the influence of hypnosis in a direct relationship. It is reasonable to assume that judging a time interval accurately increases in difficulty with increase in duration. Consequently, for the present it would appear as though there is no essential contradiction in the two sets of results, the conclusion being that hypnosis improves temporal judgment for intervals of less than one minute but has no influence on the perception of intervals of one or more minutes' duration. It may be noted that, in the light of this, Eken's results acquire a certain confirmatory value.

Both Erickson (118) and Welch (466) have reported strong evidence of the existence of temporal condensation under the influence of hypnosis. Further elucidation of the nature of such condensation has been furnished by Cooper (74, 78), Cooper and Erickson (75), Cooper and Rodgin (76), and Cooper and Tuthill (77). In the first and third of these studies the investigators suggested to their subjects a large variety of hallucinated activities. In some cases these activities were suggested as performed within a definite amount of time (subjective time) whereas in other instances no references were made to the subjective time. Also in some cases a certain amount of clock time (objective time) was allotted to the hallucinations, these being therefore terminated by the experimenter; in other situations no specific objective time was allotted, and the subject himself terminated the hallucinations. Finally, the last group was divided into two: those that progressed until a certain state of affairs had been reached, thus completing the activity, and those that did not progress to such a limit. In the first instance the activities were referred to by the investigators as "completed activities," and in the second as "incompleted activities." In all of these experiments allotted time was never less than 10 seconds and subjective time never more than 30 minutes.

One of the outstanding features observed was that, whenever a completed activity is hallucinated with no definite time allotted, there is invariably a distortion of time in the direction of condensation, although this may not have been suggested. When a certain time is allotted but no subjective time suggested, the hallucination is always adapted to the allotted time, regardless of how short it may be. In all instances the subject completes the hallucinated activity, always using an amount of objective time less than his reported subjective time. Clearly a completed type of activity determines once and for all the amount of action that will be present. This is not true of incompleted activities. If no subjective time is suggested, the rate of action is found to be dependent on the allotted time and the rate with which the subject decides to act. If, however, the subjective duration of the activity is suggested, the subject seems to make every effort to fill this interval with activity. As a consequence some rather phenomenal results have been observed. Such for instance was the leisurely counting of 664 hallucinated cows in 65 seconds objective time, the subjective time being in this case 30 minutes.

The investigators also report having found that the ability to distort time shows considerable variability among subjects. This ability can be improved by practice. Losing contact with the physical world appears to be a requisite for optimal temporal distortion. In general, the hallucinations were found to be very real for the subjects, the action in them showing excellent continuity. On the basis of the subject's reports, these hallucinated experiences are definitely different from those of nocturnal dreams. Although mental processes during temporal distortion appear to the subject to be progressing at a normal rate, these processes were found by the investigators often to be taking place at an extremely fast rate with respect to objective time. In some ways these thoughts were found to be superior to waking thoughts. No data were obtained on the influence of temporal condensation on problem solving. Relearning and practice appear to take place very effectively in distorted time, which shows, in this respect, evidence of an advantage over objective time. That there is a gain in learning ability under such conditions was shown by Cooper and Rodgin (76) for nonmotor learning of nonsense syllables. Cooper and Erickson (75) have also reported indications that motor learning might be improved by hallucinated practice associated with temporal condensation. On the other hand, in a more recent investigation of motor learning, in which subordinated handwriting was learned under similar conditions, Cooper and Tuthill (77) found no improvement. These experiments will be taken up at greater length in the next chapter.

The main criticism that can be made about the first two studies, which are otherwise excellent, is that the crucial data consist mainly of subjective reports. However, as the investigators have remarked, when one examines the entirety of the results, it is difficult not to agree that a most interesting aspect of the problem of temporal distortion has been uncovered. Besides, even objective time appears to have its origin in subjective time. Additional weight is also given to these two reports by the findings of Cooper and Rodgin, these results not being subject to the above criticism. Although in this instance we might question whether with only one case we can deduce anything safely, it may be remarked that, while the authors did not evaluate the statistical significance of the difference in waking and hypnotic performances, this difference appears to be large enough to insure significance. As will be seen in the next chapter too, there is reason to believe that temporal distortion and not some other effect was the cause of the observed improvement in learning.

Any speculation about the meaning of these results most probably would lead into the domain of philosophy,‡ but it is preferable to stay away from this field for the time being. One of the very interesting observations made by Cooper and Erickson (75) which offers considerable food for thought is that real sounds were often able to penetrate into the hallucinations of the subjects. When this happened, continuous sounds were found to be prolonged. Such a merging of objective reality with subjective reality has fascinating possibilities. The possibility of falsification has been considered by the investigators. They find no evidence for believing that the subjects might have reported falsely. There is, however, a puzzling feature to these experiments—in the case of completed activities, when a definite duration of time is allotted by the experimenter, not only is this fact unknown to the subject, but also the subject obviously does not know what the duration will be. Nevertheless, he is apparently always able to select the correct rate of activity, in spite of the fact that the necessary information for doing so is not available to him! Possibly, as soon as the subject perceives the beginning of the signal to stop, his temporal frame of reference becomes drastically distorted, and the remainder of his experience takes place at a speed not even dreamed of by Cooper and Erickson. It is a well-known fact that in nocturnal dreaming an individual may be wakened by an external stimulus which also becomes an integral part of the dream and gives rise to a sequence of events that appear to precede the dream event corresponding to the external stimulus. Something similar to this retrograde action was observed by the two investigators in at least one instance.

One would expect that, if time perception has been studied to the above extent, there would be available at least a similar amount of material on alterations of space perception. Actually hardly anything exists on this question. Eysenck (134) has made the only investigation in this area worth mentioning. He reported in regard to two tests of space perception that this function can be improved at least 33 per cent by hypnosis with no suggestion of improvement being given. Welch (466) believes that space is distorted in suggested hypnotic dreams, but he furnishes no empirical evidence to substantiate this in any conclusive manner.

‡ Cooper (78) has attempted to explain his results by means of semantic considerations. To say the least, his entire treatment of the matter is rather naive, particularly from a psychological standpoint.

Summary and Conclusions

A review of the material covered in this chapter reveals that reports on improvement of sensory functions are for the most part negative, while in contrast those concerned with decreases in sensory functions are positive. The evidence also seems to point in these instances to the *genuineness* of the subject's experiences of suggested deafness, blindness, pain anesthesia, and other afunctions. On the other hand, there is no evidence to show that the alterations are anything more than functional. Various critics have looked with some suspicion on the fact that the influence of hypnotic suggestion is greatest on voluntary functions and decreases rapidly as the functions considered tend to be involuntary. This has led many to declare that the subject merely pretends and acts out the suggestion. There is an alternative interpretation: namely, that the above simply expresses the fact that cortical and subcortical integration play a crucial part in hypnotic phenomena. This is considerably substantiated by the fact that, on one hand, suggestions appear to have considerable effect on conditioned reflexes but not on natural reflexes, and, on the other, it is now well established that conditioned reflexes involve association pathways in the cerebral cortex. Rosen (375) has indeed pointed out the resemblance of some forms of suggested anesthesia to the effects of frontal lobotomy in the reduction of persistent pain. Erickson (115) has remarked that the results he obtained on the effect of suggestion on color vision demonstrated the importance of cortical processes in color blindness. In any case, anyone who has observed surgery under hypnotic anesthesia can verify the fact that it is hardly possible that the subjects in question were pretending. In addition, since there is evidence that even the most involuntary types of physiological responses are affected to some extent, the hypothesis that the hypnotic behavior is just an "act" loses considerable weight. One should not, however, lose sight of the fact that there are probably instances when the subject does pretend. It is the job of the experimenter to weed out such instances.

One should also keep in mind in this connection the fact that it is now established that conditions other than hypnosis lead to what appears to be functional threshold alterations. Neurotics, for instance, have been found to have lowered visual and auditory limens.§ A list of pertinent studies of this question has been given by Miller (311).

Gault and Goodfellow (154) have pointed out that factors such as motivation, instructional set, muscular tension, and even the presence

§ Form and brightness discriminations were primarily involved in these studies.

or absence of the experimenter can affect the subject's sensitivity. Furthermore they report that certain methods of measurement are more affected than others by these factors. In particular, results obtained with the method of average errors are most affected by suggestion. Blackwell (35) has confirmed this view in the case of brightness threshold studies. He has shown that in these instances there is an optimal psychophysical procedure which leads, among other things, to (1) a minimum influence of threshold data by variables which are not specifically sensory, and (2) the lowest possible thresholds. Inasmuch as Sterling and Miller used the method of limits in their determination of brightness thresholds, it is clear that their negative findings need not hold in general.

Two other factors should be kept in mind in analyzing data on the influence of hypnosis on sensory phenomena. One is the role of subliminal stimuli. For instance, a subject who allows himself to be influenced by such stimuli in responding to test objects in a threshold determination experiment should tend to show a lower threshold than a subject who is not influenced thus. Blackwell (35) has made an extensive study related to this question. The other factor is that muscular tension can apparently influence threshold values. According to Gault et al. (154), this would at least be true for vibrotactile, auditory, visual, and tactile sensitivities which are all increased.

·13·

Influence of Hypnotic Suggestion on Memory and Learning

Learning and memory are two very intimately related concepts which are often very difficult to separate at the experimental level. In many situations the two appear to be synonymous, in others only memory per se appears to be present, and in still others more than memory seems to be involved. As will be seen presently, learning experiments are often employed to investigate memory. Which of the two processes is the more fundamental is very hard to tell. Probably neither is, and the distinction is arbitrary.* In any event no attempt will be made here to distinguish between them. Many if not all of the experiments considered in the next pages can be interpreted as furnishing data on both memory and learning, and many of the conclusions derived from them will hold for both. We will begin by considering the question of hypnotic improvement of learning and memory, after which we will turn our attention to the converse problem of suggested amnesias.

Learning, Remembering, and Hypnosis

Morton Prince is one of the earliest investigators to have reported improvement of memory under hypnosis. Unfortunately his experiment was quite crude and can be given little weight. Stalnaker and Riddles (420) have made a much more satisfactory study. They investigated the ability of 12 subjects in deep trance to recall logical (meaningful) material learned while in the waking state a year or more before the test. Emphatic suggestions were given that recall would be easy. The two workers report that they observed an improvement of 53.7 per cent over the waking performance. Another

---

* It is usually said that learning consists in the measurable changes in behavior that result from practice. It also includes the conditions accompanying practice. In contrast, retention (or memory) refers to the persistence of the measurable changes in behavior that have been acquired through practice. That is, learning is measured during acquisition, whereas memory is measured after acquisition.

study of interest was performed by Huse (218) who, making use of nonsense material learned in the waking state 24 hours before the test, could not find any evidence of improved recall in hypnosis. In addition, this experiment was designed to test the hypothesis that there exists a threshold of recall which might be lowered in hypnosis. Whether such a threshold exists is not shown by the results, but, if there is one, the results indicate that it was not lowered. Mitchell (313) made a similar experiment, using three-place numbers, the recall test taking place 7 minutes after learning. No evidence of superior trance recall could be found. He also found that retroactive inhibition is not affected by the presence of hypnosis. Young (504) made a rather extensive study of this matter, testing memory for digit span, nonsense material, adjective-noun associates, miscellaneous associations, remote events (childhood memories), and memory span for names. In all cases the initial memorization was made in the waking state. Young found improvement in one case only, that for remote memories. Gray (171) has investigated learning to spell in hypnosis as compared to the same done in the waking state. He reported finding only a small improvement in hypnosis. There may, however, be some question of the general validity of his results since he used subjects who were known to be weak in spelling. Whether or not hypnosis could improve their spelling ability would depend in part upon what caused the weakness. This is particularly important in view of the small number of subjects that were used.

Eysenck (134), like Young, made an extensive study of memory which included learning of nonsense syllables, memory span for digits, recognition of playing cards (both face and reverse sides being used),† and recognition of cards on the basis of dots marked on them. He too was unable to find any difference between waking and trance performance. Although he employed only two subjects, the quality of his investigation as well as the large number of tests and trials used tends to overcome this weakness.

Thus far the results appear to be against the possibility of hypnotic facilitation of memory and learning. White, Fox, and Harris (482) were the first to show that such a facilitation actually depends on the type of material involved, although it should be stated that Young's results were indicative of this. White et al. tested recall for nonsense material, meaningful verbal material, and meaningful nonverbal material (scenes from movies). All learning was done in the waking state.

† As remarked in the last chapter, results on this type of test may be more a function of improved discrimination than of improved memory.

They reported no gain in hypnosis for nonsense material but found a definite gain of about 50 per cent for meaningful verbal material and a gain of around 80 per cent for nonverbal meaningful material. Along a similar line of thought, Rosenthal (377) made a comparative study of recall in hypnosis for material consisting of meaningless and meaningful items and also of the influence of emotional disturbances on such recall for meaningful material. He reported finding that, in the absence of affective factors, hypnosis does not favor recall of meaningless material, or of meaningful material which is not a part of an organized, meaningful context. On the other hand, he finds hypnotic hyperamnesia for some experiences of an emotionally disturbing nature and for meaningful connected material.

Finally to this list we must add the reports of Cooper and Erickson (75), Cooper and Rodgin (76), and Cooper and Tuthill (77). As was indicated earlier, this group of investigators have shown evidence that in some instances hypnotically suggested temporal condensation, combined with hallucinated experience, leads to an apparent facilitation of learning. Thus, Cooper and Erickson reported an instance in which hallucinated violin practice with temporal condensation was reported by the subject and a witness as having been remarkably effective. Cooper and Rodgin undertook to investigate the question more carefully for the learning of nonsense syllables. In terms of average learning time (for 100 per cent recall), and in terms of both the number of serial presentations required and the amount of material found to be recalled in each presentation, their data indicate that trance learning was considerably superior to learning in the waking state. Thus, the average learning time per letter group, not including presentation time, was decreased by about 76 per cent in the trance state. The increase in material found to be retained in the various individual trial runs averaged about 23 per cent and in some trials ran as high as 44.5 per cent. Complete recall (100 per cent) occurred one trial run earlier in the trance state than in the waking state. On the other hand, in terms of retention and relearning (in the waking state) 24 hours later, the trance state showed only a 4 per cent superiority in retention and a decrease in relearning time per letter group pair of only about 20 per cent. Clearly the effectiveness of learning here is partly dependent on the method of measuring learning effectiveness. Since no information is made available concerning the statistical significance of the differences reported in this study, we cannot conclude quite so definitely as the investigators did that hypnosis with temporal distortion led to greater effectiveness in this instance, although they appear to have a good case for it.

Cooper and Tuthill studied the effects of hallucinated practice of subordinated handwriting with temporal condensation upon the acquisition of this skill. When their subjects' performances were compared with the reported performances of amputees trained to use subordinated handwriting, they found evidence for the superiority of the trance training. Since they felt that the amputee group in this instance was an unreliable control group, they also compared the results for the trance subjects with the performance of another group of subjects who had been allowed to do an amount of subordinated handwriting equal to the "nonpractice" writing ‡ done by the trance subjects. In this instance they found that such "nonpractice" writing constitutes in itself a learning situation which can account for the observed trance superiority. They therefore concluded that there is no evidence of facilitation, in spite of the fact that the subjects felt they had acquired practice and that there was an increase in the ease of performance in a subsequent waking trial. This particular study, however, has a number of weaknesses in its design so that the results just considered cannot be considered conclusive. To this the authors themselves agree, adding that the data are merely preliminary.

To the above, certain remarks should be added. Although we have spoken here of a facilitation of learning in connection with temporal distortion, it should be clear that this group must be considered apart from the other investigations that have already been considered because of the totally different approach to the problem. As a matter of fact, it may be questioned whether we can really speak of facilitation in this case, for, if we condense by a factor of N the temporal flow of a person who is memorizing, this is really equivalent to allowing him to memorize during an interval of normal time N times longer than the control period. Obviously, under these conditions we should expect an increase in learning, simply because of the longer time allowed for this, and not because of any special facilitation of the learning process itself. As seen earlier, nonsense syllables learned in the waking state are not recalled better in hypnosis. If this should also be true when the learning is done in hypnosis, then we should have definite proof that the time condensation was indeed the sole source of improvement in the present situation. There is reason to believe on

‡ By this is meant such subordinated handwriting as was done by a subject in order to provide a sample of the initial performance for comparison and later to provide samples by which the degree of progress could be determined.

theoretical and experimental grounds that the absence of improvement in learning nonsense syllables does extend to the case of learning in hypnosis. Thus it is probable that temporal condensation was the cause of the observed increase in recall. In any event, in this investigation learning is done in the hypnotic state, as contrasted to most of the other studies reported here. Hence the two sets of data would not be entirely comparable.

Leaving this work of Cooper and Rodgin aside, the investigations of White et al. and of Rosenthal cast considerable light on the entire matter of learning and recall in relation to hypnosis. Clearly the key to understanding the reported results lies in the association of meaningfulness and the memorized material. In general, the experiments in which negative results were obtained are those in which meaningfulness was lacking. Mitchell's results, which at first appear odd, are readily understandable when we realize that numbers as employed in this experiment represent essentially nonsensical material. Gray's results are quite in accord with the above, for learning to spell is equivalent to memorizing material that possesses only a small degree of meaningfulness and certainly is not integrated within a meaningful context. On the other hand, it is clear now why Young observed improved recall in one instance. In spite of the fact that this is probably the answer in this case, we should keep in mind that there are indications that Young "regressed" his subjects. As will be seen later, there is probably a close relation between ordinary recall and regression, but the two are by no means identical. Consequently, Young's results cannot be taken as a substantiation of the work of White et al. or of Rosenthal. It may be that hypnotic facilitation and regression were combined in this instance.

In regard to Huse's finding that retroactive inhibition was not prevented by hypnosis, it should be remarked that there is really no reason to expect anything radically different, provided the additional learning is done *during the waiting* period. This must not be confused with the entirely different situation in which the subject is in a passive trance during the same period. As is well known, retention is improved under such conditions because retroactive inhibition is prevented from taking place. As things stand, the results reported by Huse are neither unexpected nor particularly incompatible with the notion of improved memory in hypnosis.

In evaluating situations in which the hypnotized subject is asked to remember childhood experiences (remote material), it is important to know how much is really actual recall. Stalnaker and Riddles (420) found that there is a tendency for subjects to reconstruct or even partially fabricate material that they cannot recall entirely in the trance state. This is particularly significant for those aspects of psychotherapy in which remote memories are evoked by means of suggestion. From the standpoint of psychotherapy it is also of interest to know to what extent hypnosis may be expected to facilitate recall, through either lowering of the recall threshold or actual improvement of the recall function as a whole, rather than through an inhibition, removal, or bypassing of blocking agencies. The report of White et al. (482) sheds a little light on this. The nonverbal test they employed appears to be a fairly good approximation of the conditions involved in standard recall situations taking place in psychotherapy. From their results, it appears that, wherever abnormal blocking is not involved, recall processes for nonverbal material of this type are favored by hypnosis. Hull (213) also pointed out, in connection with the work of Stalnaker and Riddles, that in the waking state subjects may set their own standards and refuse to report material that does not meet their own personal criterion of satisfactory recall. In hypnosis, on the other hand, such inhibition is presumably absent. Consequently, hypnosis would tend to lead to spuriously high scores for recall in contrast to those obtained in the waking state. This obviously applies to other experiments too. While it is true that various reported observations do seem to indicate that individuals are less inhibited in hypnosis, Hull's arguments are largely unsubstantiated. In any event, even taking this possible effect into account does not alter the general conclusions.

At this point we should possibly mention an observation of Young (504) which reminds us of Williams' (488) finding that simulated responses to suggestions lead to effects similar to those resulting from true responses. Young used for a control group nonsuggestible individuals, that is, nonsusceptible to hypnosis. They were made to submit to exactly the same procedures, including trance induction, as the experimental group. According to Young, not only did the control group at times show slightly better performance in what we may call pseudohypnosis, but also in at least one instance their performance was definitely superior to that of the experimental group. There is always a possibility that the pseudohypnotic state did partake somewhat of hypnosis, instead of being, as assumed, identical to the waking state. This would not, however, explain the reported superior performance of the control group over that of the hypnotic group. In view of the bulk of the available data, it may be assumed that Young's results, though interesting and worth further investigation, probably have nothing to do with hypnosis. It is to be noted that Young himself did not appear to think that this was overly significant, as appears from the wording of his conclusions.

In final evaluation of this material, the data show a very definite trend. That there is not always full agreement between reports individually considered is not particularly surprising since the various studies in question are not entirely comparable. For instance, learning to spell and memorizing paired nonsense syllables can hardly be considered the same task, or even similar tasks. Comparability is even harder to establish when we consider the time intervals that were allowed for forgetting. These ranged from years to minutes. Assuming that hypnosis can affect recall, can it be said to be equally effective for all time intervals elapsing between the time of acquisition and the time of recall? Had it not been for the investigations of White et al. and of Rosenthal, we might indeed have suspected that this was not the case, since recall of remote material had been found superior to that of recent material. Hull (213) had in fact proposed that retroactive inhibition weakens with the increasing passage of time, thus giving credence to the above. The true explanation, however, appears now to lie in the relative degree of meaningfulness and integration in a context that the respective materials possessed in the investigations.

We might inquire at this point whether improvement in recall is entirely restricted to hypnosis. The answer to this query must be in the negative. Recall can be helped in a number of other ways in the waking state. Abstraction, relaxation, free association, and other mental states are effective. "Twilight" sleep, crystal vision, and automatic writing are also instrumental in facilitating recall. Some of these may be suspected to involve hypnosis or states akin to hypnosis. All, however, are characterized by the common factor of a state of relaxation. This is a significant fact, for there is evidence that relaxation does favor certain mental functions, particularly creative reconstruction and processes. In summing up, we may say that recall in hypnosis is superior to recall in the waking state for certain types of material memorized in the waking state; namely, it would appear that the material must possess some degree of meaning and organization. For nonsense syllables, numbers, and single words, hypnosis offers little advantage or none at all. On the other hand, for such material as prose and poetry, hypnosis shows a gain of as much as 50 per cent. There appears also to exist in hypnosis a superior recall for past individual experiences. In such a case, however, there may also be present considerable distortion due to fabrication on the part of the subject. Finally, some evidence exists to show that hypnosis also favors recall of experiences associated with affect, this being equally true for verbal and nonverbal material. Along a different line of thought, there are indications that learning may be indirectly increased by temporal condensation.

Amnesia, Paramnesia, and Hypnosis

As Hull (213) has remarked, the reversibility of hypnotically induced amnesia makes it unlikely that the underlying mechanism should lie either at the level of retention or at that of registration. This leaves the level of reproduction to be considered. All investigations to date have been aimed at the last. Hull (213) has outlined three methods of study which have been exclusively employed in investigating the reality of posthypnotic amnesia. They make use of learning situations, measuring the degree of amnesia in terms of the extent of recall present. These methods are simple reinstatement, reinstatement by learning, and symbolic reinstatement. It will be convenient to denote amnesia detected by these methods as simple amnesia, learning amnesia, and symbolic amnesia, respectively.

Young (503) reported that he could find no evidence of spontaneous amnesia. When, however, amnesia was suggested in the form of an emphatic order to forget, he observed complete symbolic amnesia for trance events. On the other hand, he never found better than 50 per cent amnesia in simple reinstatement recall tests. He concluded the following from his observations and data: (a) Posthypnotic amnesia varies greatly with the subject; (b) there is probably never total posthypnotic amnesia; (c) the extent of posthypnotic amnesia is a function of the method of testing; (d) the extent of posthypnotic amnesia is inversely related to (i) the amount and similarity of the materials learned in waking and hypnosis and (ii) the length of time since learning. Finally, on the basis of these results, he concluded that posthypnotic amnesia is not a criterion of hypnosis.

Strickler (431) made a similar and very careful investigation of this problem. He also observed 100 per cent symbolic amnesia for nonsense syllables. For the same type of material he found 81 per cent simple amnesia and only 50 per cent relearning amnesia. This study is of considerable importance because of the care with which it was designed to eliminate a number of sources of errors which Hull (213) had indicated would lead to faulty conclusions. As can be seen, it agrees very well with the one performed by Young. Strickler also obtained figures for the normal degree of amnesia one must expect to occur in the absence of posthypnotic amnesia. This was 16.35 per cent for the simple reinstatement situation, while it was only 1.82 per cent for the relearning situation. Hull (213) has remarked that this brings up the interesting question of how much of the reported amnesia, particularly of simple reinstatement, is caused by the natural process of forgetting. This could be the full 16 per cent or nothing at all. The question remains unanswered to date. Interestingly enough, neither Hull nor Strickler noticed that the decrease in amnesia in going from simple to learning amnesia parallels a similar decrease in normal forgetting. This would seem to indicate that a common mechanism underlies natural forgetting as well as posthypnotic amnesia.

Wells (470), also using this type of approach, studied suggested amnesia for all three types of recall, indicating specifically to the subjects which type was to be involved. This point is well taken, for other investigators left it pretty much up to the subject to interpret just what was desired by the suggestion of amnesia, thus leading to possible variations within and between studies. Conceivably a subject might understand the suggestion to mean that he would be unable to recall only certain types of material, and hence erroneous conclusions might be reached. Wells also made use of nonsense words. He found not only complete symbolic amnesia as other investigators did, but also *better than 100 per cent amnesia* for simple and learning amnesia. In addition to this, in his work he showed beyond question that the suggestions were entirely responsible for the amnesias. It is most probable that, were it not inherently impossible for symbolic amnesia to be greater than 100 per cent, the same would have been reported for it as for the other two kinds. The meaning of greater than 100 per cent amnesia is probably that there was a compulsion present which prevented the subject from initiating the recall mechanism. Analysis of the manner in which each subject did respond in the tests shows evidence of strong blocking or inhibition. Furthermore, analysis of the suggestions used by Wells shows that this is what should have taken place since the suggestions contain definite instructions of inhibition of the act of recall. Thus, whatever amount of true amnesia was present, it was associated and masked by this additional effect. In conclusion, it therefore does not appear that Wells's results are a contradiction of others.

Since verbal responses are a form of symbolic behavior, it cannot be inferred from the investigations just examined that the results and conclusions apply to all types of memorizing. Coors (79), aware of this fact, tried to study the influence of posthypnotic amnesia on behavior as far removed from symbolic processes as possible. For this purpose he chose stylus maze learning as testing material and tried to duplicate Strickler's study as closely as possible. As Hull (213) has remarked, this was not entirely possible since it is difficult to find a large number of mazes that are comparable, as would have been required if each subject ran a control and an experimental series as in Strickler's experiment. Instead an additional control group was employed. Also Coors limited himself to reinstatement learning in his investigation. His results agree rather well with those of Strickler for learning reinstatement, there being some amnesia, but by no means complete.

Patten (335) approached the problem in a different manner, considering the influence of posthypnotic amnesia on practice effect. For the purpose of the investigation he made use of mental addition for testing material. He reported that, when 100 per cent symbolic amnesia is found present, practice remains unaffected. Life (269) carried Patten's experiment a step further by studying the fate of generalization of practice when posthypnotic amnesia is present. This experiment was in general design similar to Patten's, although in this respect it leaves something to be desired. In spite of this and the fact that the results show considerable variability, it may be said that they show no effect of posthypnotic amnesia upon generalization when 100 per cent symbolic amnesia is present. We may take this, in a sense, as confirmation of Patten's findings.

Since conditioned reflexes are believed to be basic to learning, possibly the simplest and most primitive form of learning, a study of the effects of posthypnotic amnesia on this type of phenomenon seems indicated. Such a study was done by Scott (405). He considered the conditioning to a buzzer sound of responses to electric shock applied to the finger. Besides finger and hand retraction, he also took into account typical changes in heart action, respiration, and galvanic skin reflex, which are found associated with strong electric shock. He observed that, when such reflexes were established during hypnosis, they persisted into the waking state, in spite of the fact that symbolic amnesia was complete. These reflexes were, however, much weaker. Unfortunately we cannot tell from this investigation to what extent experimental extinction may have been present. This is quite capable of accounting for part or all of the reduction in reflex strength. Leuba (259) has also reported the persistence of conditioned hallucinations when the subject passed from hypnosis to waking. Thus Scott is partially confirmed. Whether the reflex was also decreased in Leuba's experiment is not clear.

Bitterman and Marcuse (34) preferred to use responses of the autonomic system in studying posthypnotic amnesia. Using subjects showing complete symbolic amnesia for specific words as a result of suggestions to this effect, they demonstrated by means of a Keeler polygraph that the subjects nevertheless retained the ability to recognize the words at the "unconscious" level.

From the various reports considered so far, it appears *that the extent of posthypnotic amnesia is a function of the material recalled and of the response associated with the recall.*§ It is clear that the more like a natural reflex the response is, the less effective is posthypnotic amnesia, or, conversely, the greater the amount of cortical involvement, the more effective is the amnesia. This is very similar to the picture for motor and sensory functions presented in the last two chapters.

On the duration of posthypnotic amnesia, when it is present, not many data are available. Strickler (431) attempted to consider this problem, but the information he reported is ambiguous. Wells (470) stated that posthypnotic amnesia can persist for at least a year. Unfortunately, considering the criticism made earlier of this study, we must take this figure with some reservation. Since, however, there is no reason to assume that the duration of posthypnotic amnesia would be different from that of other kinds of posthypnotic effects, it appears safe to accept the evidence reviewed in Chapter 8 as applicable in the present instance, particularly since it agrees with that found by Wells. On this basis, we may say that *suggested posthypnotic amnesia will last several months and probably longer.*

What the nature of amnesia is that is suggested and tested within the hypnotic state has not been considered by investigators. We might make a guess here that the results would probably be very much like those just considered.

Whether or not spontaneous posthypnotic amnesia exists is not known in any definite manner. Hull (213) has concluded from the results considered in this chapter that posthypnotic amnesia is not a primitive physiological mechanism distinct from suggestion, that is, intrinsic to and characteristic of hypnosis, but instead the result of some form of suggestion, be it autosuggestion, implied, or other. He argues that the results of Strickler, Coors, and Patten all point to this. This conclusion does not appear to me to be entirely justified, for all that

§ That is, the indicator–response or response used to test for recall.

these investigators have actually demonstrated are the properties of posthypnotic amnesia when the latter is suggested. Actually, their experiments *do not* give evidence *either for or against* the existence of spontaneous occurrences of the phenomenon. However, as pointed out in an earlier chapter, this is not a requisite for the production of many, if not all, hypnotic phenomena. This is even true for post-hypnotic suggestions themselves. It is my personal belief that post-hypnotic amnesia is probably a natural concomitant of very deep hypnosis, whereas in the lesser depths it appears either as a generaliza-tion from such deep states or as a result of some form of suggestion, the last being more generally the case.

Before leaving the question of amnesia in relation to hypnosis, a few words should be said about *paramnesia*. The existence of this type of phenomenon is of some importance in evaluating results on sug-gested amnesia, for, if it is present, it is evidence of the persistence of some recall. If it is overlooked, this can easily lead to faulty con-clusions concerning the amount of recall present, which will be judged to be smaller than it actually is. It may also cause the subject to be misled in reporting recalled material. As will be remembered, Stal-naker and Riddles (420) found that subjects tended to fabricate part of the recalled material. There is also a possibility that instead of fabricating they were experiencing various paramnesias. Banister and Zangwill (10, 11) have investigated the production of paramnesia fol-lowing suggested amnesia for visual and olfactory material. Their method of testing combined recognition and symbolic recall. They reported results showing that paramnesias do take place quite exten-sively and that under the conditions of the test they did not appear to differ substantially from normal occurrences of paramnesia. To what extent this factor modifies already existing data on recall and amnesia in relation to hypnosis cannot be said. There are some reasons for believing that the alteration is probably not too serious. First of all, the above two investigators have remarked that, to their knowledge, paramnesias are particularly pronounced only for olfactory and visual material (presumably scenes). This minimizes the above-mentioned possibility. Second, as Banister and Zangwill have noted, the term "recognition," which was employed in the suggestions, was not defined for the subjects. Just what it signified to them when they were told they would be unable to recognize the test stimuli is not known. If they considered it to mean the exclusion of detailed recognition alone, then the observed paramnesias "would represent mainly those aspects of the recognition process which had not been made subject to an artificial repression" (11). They also suggested that possibly activities of cognitive mechanisms outside of consciousness may have been evoked. Finally, they remark, too, that their observation of paramnesia may have resulted from the fact that the trance depth used was not so great as it might have been and from the particular kind of material employed for their tests. It is certain that scenes and nonsense material are not at all comparable. From other sources we know that post-hypnotic amnesia affects different material in different ways. The topic certainly bears further investigations, but, as already stated, it does not appear to necessitate a revision of the conclusions already reached in regard to suggested amnesia and recall in hypnosis.

· 14 ·

Suggested Emotions and Moods.
Alteration of the Personality

The expression "mood" is probably one of the vaguest terms used in psychology. To say, as some have, that it is a state of mind is just as vague. Similarly, the statement that it is a complex state of feeling is of questionable superiority. But, whatever it is, there is general agreement that it refers to an aspect of individual behavior that has a highly affective tone. According to Warren (455), a mood is "an enduring, but not permanent emotional attitude." Be that as it may, for lack of a better definition we shall make use of the one given by Warren.

Suggested Moods and Emotions

As elsewhere, the main problem in relation to hypnosis is (a) Can one bring about overt responses characteristic of various moods, and (b) how real are these changes? The same questions may be asked about emotions, which will be taken up with moods in view of the fact that the two appear to be intimately related. It was seen earlier that Benedek (24) reported the production of a copious secretion of tears by reproducing an emotional state in a subject through suggestion. Presumably the state was one of sadness. Since lacrimation is far from being involuntary in many individuals, we may question the significance of this report. The same investigator also reported bringing about in the same manner elevation of blood pressure, acceleration of the pulse, and hyperdrosis of the face and forehead. The sketchiness of the report makes it difficult to attach much weight to the results. Other reports of physiological changes caused by suggested emotions have been considered in other connections in Chapter 10. Thus Bier (30) and Fulde (150) have shown this in connection with respiration. Deutsch and Kauf (95), Whitehorn (486), Bier (30), and Benedek (24) reported similar results in regard to heart rate. Grafe and Traumann (168), Grafe and Mayer (169), Whitehorn, Lundholm, and Gardner (485), and Fulde (150) have observed changes in metabolism

178

resulting from suggested emotions. Bier (30) and White (478) have reported changes in blood pressure. Heilig and Hoff (188) and Heyer and Grote (193) found some effects of suggested emotions upon the excretory functions. Heilig and Hoff (189) reported effects on gastric acidity. Mohr (314), Weber (460), Kretschmer and Krüger (243), and Glasser (165) observed various blood changes in similar instances. At the level of muscular responses we have the report of Edwards (106) who observed a considerable increase in finger tremor when subjects were made to recall, under hypnosis, emotional experiences such as of anger and fear. Finally, there is the account of Heilig and Hoff (190) of the production of herpes simplex through the suggestion of emotional states. As has been mentioned earlier, many of these reports must be taken with a grain of salt, largely because of inadequate experimental design. Yet it should also be clear that as large a number of positive reports as listed here must indicate that some physiological changes do take place when emotions and moods are suggested. In the light of present-day developments in psychosomatic medicine we can hardly doubt any longer the truth of this matter.

More satisfactory investigations, from the standpoint of design, have been made on the psychological correlates of induced emotions and moods. Fisher and Marrow (141) concerned themselves with reaction times for words with strong mood associations, pleasant mood associations, unpredictable mood associations, and unpleasant mood associations, using subjects who were in a normal mood, in suggested elation, and in suggested despondency. They observed definite differences in the word responses as well as the reaction times which were in keeping with the three moods. It must be remarked, however, that, though this investigation shows that free association is appropriately altered by suggested moods, it does not demonstrate that suggested moods and real moods are the same, since no waking controls were studied by the investigators. Levine, Grassi, and Gerson (262, 263) made a study of the effects of suggested moods on Rorschach scores. The Rorschach test was given for the following conditions: normal waking, normal hypnosis, suggested situational depression, elation, hypochondria, depression, sexual concern without anxiety, and apprehension. The investigators obtained results showing that hypnosis per se does not differ from the waking state in regard to the Rorschach test. On the other hand, the various suggested moods caused definite changes in both the overt behavior of the subjects and in their Rorschach scores, these changes being consistent with the suggested moods. The scores as well as the overt behavior of the subjects revealed some interesting aspects. In the first place, the scores as a whole showed a considerable amount of similarity, which may be taken as an indication that the underlying personality did not suffer any essential alterations. Second, the records disclosed characteristic features of mental and personality disorders contiguous with an absence of the so-called "normal" aspects. Now it is true that the investigators designed the instructions in such a way as "to parallel some of the most common emotional disturbances found in mental and personality disorders." On the other hand, examination of the suggestions used shows no wording that would be likely to lead the subject to neurotic behavior, regardless of the said parallelism. That the suggestions did lead to a tendency on the part of the subject to exhibit neurotic traits seems to indicate that suggested moods, at least in the present instance, are more closely related to functional alterations of the affective life than to the changes brought about by actual events of everyday life. Levine et al. have pointed out that it appears evident from their results that the basic personality of the subject will largely determine the responses that are seen. Their experiment is weak in that it made use of only one subject.

Counts and Mensh (82) have considered the influence of hypnotically induced hostility upon the Rorschach scores. The hostility was brought about presumably by means of the creation of an artificial conflict. They found indications of a trend of changes in responsiveness, intellectual control, fantasy, activity, emotional control, and level of hostility, all in the expected direction. On the other hand, there were actually no significant differences, and the underlying personality of the subject appears to have been unaltered. To what extent the observed trend is the result of the conflict-induced hostility is not clear, for unfortunately the investigators also suggested or rather instructed the subjects directly in regard to some of the specific feelings they would experience while being tested. In other respects the above study is quite satisfactory.

Lane (251) has also reported obtaining an appreciable shift in Rorschach responses, particularly in those of movement, in such a direction as to show an increase in introversion. The technique used to bring this about involved the combined effects of suggestions of a mood of satisfaction (and even of elation) and of earlier suggestions aimed at creating introversion, striving, imagination, and productive thinking. Since only one subject was used and since it is not entirely clear what role the suggested mood played in bringing about the reported results, we cannot place too much weight on this report.

On the whole then the evidence shows that emotion-like and mood-like phenomena can be brought about by hypnotic suggestion, and that these have a reality which manifests itself in the overt behavior of the individual, in his responses to projective tests, and in his physiological responses. On the other hand, the identification of these phenomena with emotions and moods as they occur in everyday life is not clearly demonstrated, and in some instances a parallelism rather than an identity has been shown to be present. In view of this, it may be preferable for the time being to speak of pseudoemotions in this connection. It must be remarked, however, that this is not the consensus of opinion. Gidro-Frank and Bull (158, 61) for instance believe that in their studies of emotions, which they induced by means of hypnosis, the emotions resulting are true ones. They based their arguments for such a belief on the fact that most of the affective states thus produced gave rise to overt behavior and to subjective reports which were the same as those associated with the corresponding naturally occurring emotions. They pointed out that in the past most investigators have suggested not only a given emotion but also the types of responses desired. Under such conditions one may well expect artificialities to be present. Excellent as are the studies of Fisher et al. and of Levine et al., it is to be feared that the suggestions they employed may have dictated the reported responses to some degree. This may account in particular for the lack of "normal" aspects in the responses observed by Levine et al. Gidro-Frank and Bull eliminated this undesirable feature by using a stimulus word alone in inducing the emotions, leaving the elaborations to the subject. Such stimulus words were "joy," "fear," "anger," etc. It is possible that under such conditions more realistic behavior patterns are obtained. It remains for earlier experiments to be repeated, using this method, in order to ascertain the correctness of the surmise. In the meantime it may be remarked that even Gidro-Frank et al. unwittingly may have determined in part the direction of the subject's behavior, for the instructions they gave their subjects in hypnosis contain definite guiding statements about the manner in which they will behave. In addition to this, they admit having discarded a number of visceral reactions which they observed to accompany induced emotions, on the basis that these constituted a group of changes that are correlates of general muscular activity and not specific to any given emotion. Changes in heart rate and breathing were among these. In view of the present status of our knowledge about emotions, the validity of doing this may be questioned.

Pasquarelli and Bull (332) have extended and repeated in part the investigation of Gidro-Frank et al. and have been able to confirm their results. Pasquarelli et al. have also obtained some other interesting results which have a bearing on the topic just considered. They attempted to induce emotions by suggesting the usual reactions observed to be associated with the type of stimulus word employed by' Gidro-Frank and Bull and by themselves in an initial portion of the study (332). That is, various postural sets and organic sensations, which were representative of the overt behavior and of the subjective reports of subjects when actual affect was suggested, were used. The investigators reported that the subjects responded by assuming the appropriate emotional attitude and by even naming the original affects. Finally, when a contrasting affect was suggested (stimulus word) simultaneously with the chosen affective expression, Pasquarelli and Bull found that the suggested affect had no influence. From this they concluded that affect is primarily dependent on bodily changes. If this is true, some of the criticisms that have already been made of experiments on induced emotions might have to be revised. It is to be noted, however, that this investigation of Pasquarelli et al. is deficient in controls. Also there may be a question of the extent to which the suggested expressions of affect may have been stereotypes.

In an effort to ascertain the reality of induced emotions, True and Stephenson (445) conducted the following experiment in a very careful manner. By means of an intensive study of the personal histories of six subjects they determined the psychic stimuli most appropriate for bringing about positive (love) and negative (fear) emotions. In a series of preliminary sessions these emotional states were repeatedly induced, and eventually the subjects were conditioned to produce these states at a given signal. In the experimental sessions the subjects were regressed to the time when they had experienced the given emotions and made to relive the emotions by means of the prearranged signal. Concurrently EEG records and pulse rates were obtained. The investigators reported that they were not able to change the subject's EEG in the direction of the EEG's typically observed with the corresponding emotions in the waking state.* However, as they pointed out, it may be that these typical characteristics are really artifacts and that emotions per se do not produce EEG alterations even in the waking state. In pulse rates they observed a clear-cut change (increase) only for the negative emotions. On the whole they believe

---

* That is, when these emotions occur naturally.

that their results are far from conclusive, particularly in regard to pulse rates.

Personality Alteration. Multiple Personalities

The induction of moods and emotions in individuals might be considered as a sort of attempt at altering the personality of the individuals. From the standpoint of overt behavior, individuals in whom moods and emotions have been induced appear to show a definitely altered personality. But, as has been seen, there is evidence that the personality structure is not actually altered. It might be thought that part of the reason why this is so is that the suggestions have been aimed at altering only certain factors that enter into the determination of the personality. We might ask, for instance, what would happen if a subject were told that he was some other person? Sarbin (386) considered this question. Having suggested to an individual that he was some other person, Sarbin then administered the Rorschach test to the subject. He reported that the results show evidence of external and self-imposed *Aufgabe* which alter the Rorschach responses to some extent. There were no indications of changes in the basic personality structure.

An obvious line of investigation in this connection is the production of multiple personalities. Harriman (183) reported having obtained triple personalities by means of hypnotic suggestion. Leuba (260) also produced secondary personalities by such means. None of these investigators attempted to study the exact nature of the induced personalities. It remained for Leavitt (253) to do this. He studied a case of induced triple personalities by means of the Thematic Apperception Test and the Rorschach test. His results show that, with respect to structure and content, the induced personalities are quite real, but that they are also *substructures* of the normal waking and total personality of the subject.

The topic of multiple personalities brings up an important matter, namely, the question of dissociation. Earlier investigators such as Janet and Prince performed experiments that led them to conclude that dissociation was present. Unfortunately the design of their experiments is far from being satisfactory. In addition they employed subjects who were suffering from hysteria and who were prone to develop spontaneous secondary personalities. We cannot of course identify such cases with hypnotically induced multiple personalities in normal individuals, at least not with the available data. Burnett (62) and Messerschmidt (309), however, investigated the question of dissociation in a more satisfactory manner. Although neither answered the question directly in regard to secondary personalities, they did consider it in connection with a closely related phenomenon, and hence their results have some bearing on the problem. Using suggested automatic writing in the waking state, Burnett found that there is less interference between simultaneously performed tasks when one of these tasks is made unconscious through suggestion (automatic writing). On the other hand, Messerschmidt found interference present in a similar situation. There was even some indication that the amount of interference might be greater than it would have been if the two simultaneous tasks had both been performed consciously. Messerschmidt's investigation is by far the superior of the two, being the only one in which the amount of interference was accurately measured. It would thus appear that dissociation, in the sense of functional independence, is not a characteristic of secondary personalities, as shown in the case of cryptesthesia. There is a possibility that Messerschmidt's subjects were not so deeply hypnotized as they might have been, and that, had they been, a totally different picture would have resulted. This would be a relatively easy matter to determine.

Induced Regression

One of the most interesting types of apparent alteration of personality is the so-called "regression" in which the subject exchanges his present personality for one he had when he was younger, usually a childhood personality. Gill (161) has reported a case of spontaneous regression during hypnosis, and he adds that a limited number of similar instances have been recorded in recent times. Keir (230) tested a spontaneously regressed subject with word association tests, intelligence tests, and the Rorschach test. He found evidence that the personality is essentially unaltered but that the MA changes in accordance with the regression age. Hakebush, Blinkowski, and Foundillere (178) induced regression by means of suggestion and then tested the subjects with drawing, association, intelligence, and Rorschach tests. They reported having found appropriate responses for the various regressed ages and also claim to have been able to elicit neonatal reflexes during the regression. I have also observed this last phenomenon in a number of regressions.† Leeds (257) studied a subject regressed to various age levels (2 to 12), using variations of the Goodenough Draw-a-Man Test and of the Stanford-Binet test. He reported

† Unpublished data.

finding appropriate alterations in the observed responses. Platonow (347) made a somewhat less complete study of several cases of regression, also using intelligence tests. He found that, though overt behavior and handwriting were appropriate to the suggested ages, the MA was not. Young (506) repeated this investigation with a number of subjects. He also had his subjects simulate in the waking state the responses they believed were appropriate for the various regression ages. He reported that simulation is just about as effective as actual regression and that IQ's were not entirely consistent with the regressed ages. Young concluded from his data that subjects cannot regress to before six years of age, for reasons unknown, and that regression is an artifact. Spiegel, Shor, and Fishman (419) have also reported variations in MA and in IQ that are not always in the direction of the regressed age. This observation came out of a very extensive study of a case of regression. They found, however, that *such variations can be ascribed to aspects of the personality development of the subject and that the variations are rather consistent with the latter.* Further evidence for this has been presented by Bergman, Graham, and Leavitt (26) who administered the Rorschach and the Goodenough Draw-a-Man Tests to a regressed individual. This very extensive and well-designed investigation showed the existence of very definite changes in personality which were entirely consistent with the subject's case history. Mercer and Gibson (304) also studied a regressed subject, using the Stanford-Binet vocabulary test, the Goodenough test, and the Rorschach test. They concluded from their data that changes occurred that were consistent not only with the characteristic productions of the age levels to which the subject had been regressed but also with the known clinical data. Kline (235) with the Otis Test of Mental Ability tested a fairly large group of subjects who were regressed to three different age levels. He reported results consistent with the regressions. He found that the IQ remained constant while the raw scores showed appropriate changes. He concluded from this that "when an individual is regressed in age through hypnosis his mental ability assumes a functioning level consistent with that age. Changes in intellectual functioning reflect losses in maturational power and not in capacity or brightness." Finally, Sarbin (387) repeated Young's (506) study on nine subjects, being careful to eliminate certain weaknesses that were characteristic of Young's experiment. First, Young paid no particular attention to the fact that the depth of trance might have some influence on the results, and, second, he made no attempt to check objectively whether or not the scores on the intelligence test duplicated those made by the subjects when they had actually been of the age to which they were being regressed. The results found by Sarbin showed that none of the subjects gave performances identical with those they actually had given at the corresponding chronological ages. In all instances, they made higher scores; that is, they overestimated.‡ However, compared to the scores they made when simulating the regression ages in the waking state, their hypnotic approximations were much superior. Making use of a computed regression index,§ Sarbin found a positive correlation of 0.91 (significance not given) between the degree of approximation in regression and depth of hypnosis as measured on the Friedlander-Sarbin scale. From these results Sarbin concluded (a) that in regard to intelligence tests the regression to earlier "age-roles" is neither complete nor "authentic," (b) that regression is more "authentic" under hypnosis than when simulated in the waking state, and (c) that there is a definite correlation between the depth of hypnosis and the "authenticity" of the regression.||

In accordance with the concept of "role-taking" and the part it plays in the determination of hypnotic behavior as developed by Sarbin (385), the latter interprets his results as showing (a) that regression is the result of role enacting,¶ and (b) that it is the more precise as

‡ This appears to have been also true in the studies of Platonow (according to Sarbin) and of two other investigators (as reported by Orne (328)).

§ The regression index specifically designed for this investigation is given by the expression

$$\left[\frac{\text{MA simulated regression}}{\text{MA original test}} - \frac{\text{MA hypnotic regression}}{\text{MA original test}} \right] \times 100$$

|| A few words might now be said concerning role-taking and associated concepts. According to the point of view held by Sarbin and others, society consists of a system of interrelated positions held by its members. A *position* is the place occupied by an individual in the social system to which he belongs. Every individual holds at least one and usually many such positions (as when he is, say, a father, husband, lawyer, member of a bridge club, each of these being a position). A *role* is the behavior prescribed by the society for any individual holding a given position. *Role taking* (or *role playing*) consists in an individual behaving as prescribed for any given position. In particular, the prescribed behavior for a child of, say, age 4, is an *age role*. Behaving accordingly, regardless of actual age, would be taking an age role of 4. Such other notions as role perceiving and authenticity of role playing are self-explanatory.

¶ This should not be misunderstood to imply simulation. According to Sarbin, Farberow, and Orne (to be discussed presently), much of this arises from true changes taking place in regression. But it is also their claim that there is no replication, at least in totality, of an earlier life stage as others have asserted.

role-taking aptitude increases, the latter being measured in terms of the Friedlander-Sarbin scale of hypnotic depth.

Sarbin and Farberow (388), continuing the study of Sarbin, reported data obtained from the use of the Rorschach test and the Goodenough Draw-a-Man Test with six subjects regressed to the ages of 3, 6, 13, and 18. Their data appear to show inconsistencies in the regressions in the sense that the Rorschach records disclosed that none of the subjects was responding fully as a child of the corresponding regression age would have responded. The investigators feel that in all instances the results showed some influence of the subject's adult personality. The same thing was also revealed by the various inconsistencies in the general overt behavior of the regressed subjects: In a great many respects they behaved very much like children of the regression age; yet at times they did or said things that were atypical of children but typical of adults. The investigators also reported evidence that the individuals who are more mature, are better adjusted, and have a more adequate personality tend to be less capable of approximating the typical performance of children and give responses that are less stereotyped. Sarbin and Farberow concluded that their evidence supports the hypothesis that regressions are the enacting of a child role ¶ by an adult, in which the latter integrates his perception of the child role into his perception of the self from an adult viewpoint, and that the more congruent the two perceptions, the greater will be the approximation.

Orne (328) has also studied the performance of six subjects regressed to the age of six, using the Rorschach and the Goodenough Draw-a-Man Tests. The results on these were compared against accepted norms for age six. In one instance original drawings made by the subject at six years of age were available. Comparison of the regression drawings with the original drawings in this case revealed no resemblances. Study of the drawings for the other subjects showed that, although the drawings contained childlike concepts, the manner of execution tended to be adult. They were, in Orne's own manner of speaking, "sophisticated oversimplifications." He found that approximations attempted in the waking state tended to be superior to regressed ones; and that, in some instances, when the subjects imagined that they were six years old, they produced results in no ways distin-

¶ This should not be misunderstood to imply simulation. According to Sarbin, Farberow, and Orne (to be discussed presently), much of this arises from true changes taking place in regression. But it is also their claim that there is no replication, at least in totality, of an earlier life stage as others have asserted.

guishable from those brought about by the regressions. As for the Rorschach data, although it tended to reveal marked childish elements in the regressions, it also showed, mingled with these characteristics, many others that should not have been present. In general, the formal characteristics of the Rorschach results were not of a kind that is specific to the six-year-old level. Finally, it may be said that there were no consistent trends toward the Rorschach criteria typical of children, particularly of the six-year-old level. If any consistent change can be said to have been present, Orne considers that it was in a decrease in the Rorschach characteristics reflecting intellectual capacity and critical ability (form level), rather than in any features reflecting personality organization. He also reported having observed many inconsistencies in the subjects' behavior showing clearly that the adult personality was influencing the responses in the regressed state. In addition, he found evidence of confabulation.

On the basis of the results Orne concluded that hypnotic age regression is not a phenomenon of re-enacting an earlier phase of developmental history, but that it is a "role-taking" on an emotional level in which random memories are combined and supplemented by appropriate confabulation. This creates a hallucinated environment of which the subject is an integral part. The two constitute a true field which is so structured as to approximate as well as possible the field that was prevailing at the suggested age.

The Problem of Revivification. Regression Types

Before continuing with this matter, we must now examine an aspect of regression that was probably first brought out by Erickson and Kubie (119). These writers called attention to the fact that so-called "regressions" do not form a homogeneous group of phenomena, but instead fall into two groups. One which they name *regression* consists in the subject recalling and dramatizing (or acting out) past events in the light of the present; the other is *revivification* in which the subject actually returns to the psychophysiological state he once was in (at the age of regression), there being at the same time a reversible ablation of all experiences subsequent to the age of regression. In support of this, the above-mentioned investigators cited a number of instances of both types of situation, although they did not give any formal proof of the nature of the cases in question. Erickson and Kubie emphasized that the conditions for obtaining revivification are much more exacting than those needed for regression. Of particular significance is the need of obtaining a sufficient depth of trance and of allowing the subject a sufficient time to reorient himself into the suggested situation. That the depth of hypnosis is an important determinant here has already been shown by Sarbin's (387) work. This is confirmed indirectly by many of the investigations considered in previous pages. In particular, we might cite here the report of Lewis and Sarbin (266) in Chapter 10, in which these workers showed that the extent to which gastric contractions are inhibited by suggestions of fictitious meals was proportional to the trance depth. There is also the report of West et al. (475), showing that the degree of suggested anesthesia that can be obtained is directly related to the depth of hypnosis. Finally, as will be seen, Mazer (294) found a direct relationship between trance depth and the extent to which suggested dreams took on a symbolic character, and hence were like nocturnal dreams. Evidence of the reality of revivification as an actual physiological change comes from a number of investigations and reports. Erickson (118) reported a patient who became unconscious (using this term in the clinical sense) upon being regressed to a time in his life when he had been rendered unconscious by drugging and a blow. There seems to be no reason for questioning the authenticity of this reported state of "unconsciousness." I was a witness some years ago to a similar incident. Kupfer (249) has reported observing preconvulsive normal EEG records when regressing an epileptic patient to a period before his first attack. Ford and Yeager (143) described an interesting case of a patient who, when regressed to a period of time preceding an operation which had corrected a visual disorder, once again exhibited the same disorder of vision. Lewis, as reported by Gidro-Frank and Bowerbuch (157), observed the appearance of a positive Babinski reflex during hypnotic regression. These two authors have themselves confirmed this in a number of cases. In addition they mentioned having found changes in peripheral chronaxie which are associated and consistent with the reversal of the plantar reflex. This last, though in itself good evidence that psychophysiological changes are brought about by suggestions of revivification, is not quite so strong a proof of the reality of revivification as might at first appear. The reason for this is that the plantar reflex can be reversed in the adult individual in a fairly large number of instances, none of which is in the nature of a regression. Nonetheless, combined with the rest of the evidence just listed, the observed reversal of the Babinski reflex gives strong support to the reality of revivification.

Evidence for and against the reality of revivification has been reported by True and Stephenson (445) who performed one of the best and most careful investigations of age regression. They too observed a reversal of the plantar reflex in five out of six subjects who were regressed to the age of 1 month. The sixth showed an equivocal reflex in all states. They also observed the sucking reflex in two subjects and the Moro reflex in one. On the other hand, they could find only a trend toward a rise in pulse rate with progressive regression.* They do not consider that any conclusions can be drawn from this observation for the present. True et al. also studied the subjects' EEG's. They were unable to find any change in EEG patterns with regression, particularly in relation to the alpha component.† Thus, the results support as well as deny the existence of physiological changes concomitant with age regression, which all in all is a rather ambiguous situation. In evaluating these results it should be kept in mind, however, that, in two situations other than regressions which True and Stephenson investigated, they were unable to observe the expected alterations in EEG. One of these was discussed earlier in connection with the induction of emotions. The other consisted in the fact that the alpha activity was found to persist in situations presumably involving attention fixation.‡ It should also be kept in mind that alterations of the electrical activity of the brain would be most difficult to bring about by suggestion. In spite of the high quality of the above investigation, it is entirely possible that hypnosis was not so deep and/or the regressions were not so complete as was possible. Thus the results are not so negative as might at first appear. True and Stephenson themselves agree that their report must be considered as preliminary.

Further support for the reality of revivification comes indirectly from the already mentioned report of Moody (316, 317). He observed somatic changes of a highly localized and rather complex nature taking place in drug-facilitated abreaction, in such a way as to duplicate original and past somatic trauma. His observations also tend to show that revivification is not specific to hypnosis alone. Moody has mentioned a number of similar reports of somatization observed by other investigators. These have been listed in Chapter 11. The notion of revivifi-

* As is well established, pulse rate is highest at birth and decreases progressively with age.
† It is generally believed that brain waves change progressively from a very slow, arrhythmic pattern to a 8- to 12-cycle alpha wave as the individual passes from childhood to adulthood.
‡ As is well known, the alpha wave vanishes in such situations.

cation gains additional strength from the fact that it helps to account for what appears at first to be disagreement among the results surveyed in the last few pages. As remarked earlier, writers have unfortunately been prone to use the term "regression" in an indiscriminate manner. But even the classification of observed phenomena given by Erickson and Kubie is not entirely satisfactory. The main reason is that conceivably one could have a mixed condition of "regression" and "revivification" which would not be either of these. Actually examination of reported cases of so-called regression show evidence of just this. I should like to propose a somewhat different terminology. We will agree to denote instances of strict dramatization, or acting out, by the expression *regression type I* and instances in which there is a true psychophysiological return to a past state as *regression type II*. More generally, however, the subject's *total* behavior will be determined partly by acting out and partly by a shift to an earlier psychophysiological state. This will be referred to as *regression type III*.§ The process by means of which such a psychophysiological shift is brought about in association with a temporary ablation of certain "future" events will be called *revivification*. Thus far, no instance of regression type II has been reported, all cases falling in either of the other two categories. It might be added that other investigators have recognized the existence of mixed states in regression. Among these may be mentioned True (444). What has not been recognized, however, is that all instances of so-called "revivification" that have been described in the literature are really regression type III. In fact, whether or not type II regressions are possible is a moot question inasmuch as a complete ablation of "future" events implies cessation of the hypnotic state and of the action of the suggestions of regression themselves. In addition, the hypnotist must obviously cease to exist as such. We shall return to this topic later.

As has been seen, every position from a full belief in "regression" to a complete denial of it has been taken by different investigators concerned with regression phenomena. The question must be asked, however, whether they are all speaking of the same phenomenon. Examination of the procedures and results that have been reported leads us to conclude that a great many of these examples represent instances of regression type I, or type II with a very small amount of revivifica-

§ In general, the term "regression" by itself will be used in this book to designate any apparent or true return of the individual to an earlier age as manifested by his general behavior.

tion present. This is particularly true of the investigations of Orne and of Sarbin and Farberow. There is no question but that both groups performed careful investigations. It is also my opinion that, on the basis of the description they gave of their respective procedures, they most probably did not meet the most stringent requirements for the production of maximum revivification. This is definitely indicated in Sarbin's (386) earlier report. The techniques employed by these investigators show no comparability with those employed by Bergman, Graham, and Leavitt or by Mercer and Gibson. Both these groups of investigators followed a technique that meets much more satisfactorily the conditions believed to be necessary for the production of revivification. As we know, their results show a very different picture from those of Sarbin et al. or of Orne. But, even were we to accept at face value the results obtained by means of intelligence and personality tests, we should still have to take into account data concerning physiological changes in regression experiments. These are a kind of data that role taking, simulation, and other theories do not account for very well if at all. Strangely enough, both Sarbin et al. and Orne have completely ignored these phenomena in their discussion of regressions. Young's finding of a limiting regression age of six may possibly be related to the fact that children enter the first grade of school at about this age, at which time they receive their first impetus toward the acquisition of a verbal symbolic type of recall. As we shall see later, regression type II is probably very dependent on symbolic recall. Here then may be the explanation. In any case the limit appears to be an artifact.

On the whole, the majority of reports seem to show definite evidence of revivification being present. This appears true even in the case of Keir who stated that he did not believe revivification was present in his investigation. It is more probable that he meant by this that he had not obtained regression type II, for he certainly appears to have brought about regression type III. The same remark probably applies to many of the studies that claim to disprove the existence of "regression," such as those of Sarbin et al. and of Orne. A close examination shows that what is really meant is that regression type II could not be obtained. And indeed, for reasons already mentioned, we must look with doubt on any report that claims that "revivification" has been obtained. Such reports will invariably show on examination that regression type III was actually present.

Progression

Kline (237, 238) has attempted an interesting experiment, namely, to bring about the opposite of regression. This he calls an "age progression." Thus far he has reported data on only one case. These data were obtained, using the Wechsler-Bellevue Intelligence Scale Form I and the Terman-Miles Attitude-Interest Analysis Test. The subject, a young woman of 22 years of age, was progressed to the age of 65.|| Her responses on the Wechsler-Bellevue scale, when compared to those given in the waking state, showed alterations in time, accuracy, and total achievement. According to Kline, these alterations were at a clinically significant level. At the same time there was no decline in comparative Wechsler IQ. The investigator summed up these results by stating that the pattern of decline in mental ability observed in the progression was essentially similar to that reported in studies of senescence. A similar picture was found to be true for the Terman-Miles M-F Test, there being a shift to femininity paralleling that seen in late maturity. Kline found that the most significant changes took place on the following subtests: Word Association, Information, Emotional, and Ethical Attitudes and Opinions. He concluded that here too the changes were consistent with those that have been recorded for individuals of this age. As controls, Kline administered the Wechsler-Bellevue Scale in the waking and in the hypnotic states (at the chronological age) and found no essential differences between the two sets of scores. He had the subject take the Terman-Miles test while simulating the age of 65. The results showed no essential deviations from those obtained in the waking state without simulation. Thus, the responses appear to have been authentic.

It is difficult to evaluate this interesting investigation in view of the fact that the data were obtained from only one subject. In addition, Kline failed to give certain details, such as the depth of hypnosis and the actual suggestions that were employed. To this we must also add two criticisms of the controls. First of all no data are available concerning the subject's ability to simulate old age in the waking state (or the hypnotic state) in respect to the Wechsler-Bellevue Scale. It is conceivable that simulation could have given rise to scores comparable to those resulting from the progression. Second, there is no information concerning the subject's performance on the Terman-Miles M-F Test when simply hypnotized (chronological age). This may be

|| Kline also regressed her to the age of 8 and obtained results that were consistent with those reported for this age.

an important defect in the study for the reason that it is known, on the one hand, that there is a positive correlation between femininity and introversion on this test, and, on the other hand, as mentioned in Chapter 5, there is some evidence from Rorschach studies that hypnosis per se may produce introversion in at least some individuals. Lane (251) has also furnished evidence that specific suggestions can increase introversion considerably. It is therefore entirely possible that Kline's results on the M-F test are artifacts.¶ In addition, we should remember that it is well established that the Terman-Miles test is definitely susceptible to faking. It is therefore rather surprising that the simulation scores reported by Kline showed as little difference as they did from the waking nonsimulated scores,* particularly in the light of the rather low reliability of the separate exercises of the test. In other words, we may wonder if this control was a valid one in this particular instance. In any event, in view of the above-mentioned weakness of the Terman-Miles M-F Test, the progression scores might well have arisen simply because the subject was able to role-play in a superior manner, was better motivated, or possibly was able to better abstract the essential characteristics of senescence, when in hypnosis.

Assuming, however, that Kline's results would hold in general, what may these indicate? Kline was led to do his experiment by inferring that, if psychobiological changes can be produced in regression experiments, then it should necessarily follow that the same would result from progressions. In this surmise, however, it seems to me that he is wrong since the situations involved in the two cases are not equivalent. In regression, the subject has *experienced* the condition that is suggested, and hence presumably traces of some sort or other are present. On the other hand, in a progression the subject is asked to assume a condition that *he has never experienced,* but will experience in the future. There is therefore no parallel between these two conditions. Contrary to Kline's belief, the nature and validity of age regression need not be affected by the possibility or impossibility of inducing progression.

The one fact that appears to be established by this study, within limitations, is that suggestion of progression can cause a perceptual reorganization very similar to that seen in aging individuals. This might be an indication that the characteristics that were studied are

¶ Which does not necessarily signify that the results on the Wechsler-Bellevue are not evidence of progression, since we are dealing here with two very different tests.

* That is to say, the profiles were practically identical.

less dependent on physiological senescence than on a perceptual frame of reference having little to do with the physiological changes concomitant with aging.† This, however, is a mere supposition. Actually no further conclusions will be possible until more definite experiments are made in this area.

Summary and Conclusions

As we review the results that have been described in this chapter, it would appear, in general, that suggestions aimed at altering the personality of the subject can bring about changes in overt responses, in responses to such tests as the Thematic Apperception Test and the Rorschach test, and, to a certain degree, at times in physiological reactions. Evidence increasingly shows that the subject can exhibit two types of behavioral responses. In one, he "acts out" the suggestions, or, to use the words of Erickson and Kubie, dramatizes his present understanding of the suggested situation and of related facts.‡ In the other, the subject undergoes actual changes of a psychophysiological nature which affect his personality structure and content. In such instances his responses, instead of being the result of acting, are genuine responses to stimuli as organized by the new personality structure and content. It should be understood that even in these instances nothing new is really brought into being in the sense that elements of the personality already present are utilized. Thus, in induced multiple personalities the secondary personalities are found to be substructures of the total waking personality. Again, in regression type III, and presumably in type II, the younger personality is constructed out of elements that are part of the older personality. The extent to which psychophysiological changes can be brought about, and hence to which the changes may be made genuine, appears to depend directly on the depth of trance attained, an observation that is not entirely unexpected.

† We should not overlook the possibility of psychosomatic effects.

‡ Although this formulation was made by Erickson and Kubie in a more restricted sense in reference to regressions in general, it appears to have a much wider application.

· 15 ·

The Will and Hypnosis

Possibly no single aspect of hypnosis has been more controversial in the past than the relation of volition to hypnosis. Superficial examination of hypnotic phenomena would tend to lead to the belief that a subject can be forced to do anything by the hypnotist. For many years, indeed, this was a common conception, even among hypnotists of standing. Not only was it thought that in hypnosis the subject's will is entirely subjugated to that of the hypnotist, but also many investigators of old advocated that the induction of a trance was nothing more than the imposition of the hypnotist's will over that of the subject. Consequently, many of the older treatments of hypnotic technique contain special sections on the art of developing will power and concentrating the will, including various exercises. This particular viewpoint appears to be tied up with a belief that some sort of telepathic rapport is created between the subject and the hypnotist. Setting this last question aside, we see that certainly more than will is involved in the induction of hypnosis. A little reflection would have revealed to even early investigators that this was true, since neither mesmerism nor Braidism involve in any manner the question of willing the subject to sleep. Historically speaking, this latter view appears to be a relatively recent development.

There seems to be hardly any need for discussing this particular aspect any further. All available modern data on hypnosis show clearly that any theory advocating that hypnosis is an imposition of the operator's will on that of the subject is obsolete. The best refutation of this theory lies in the efficacity of modern techniques for the induction of hypnosis. These techniques show no evidence of being dependent on the relative will power of subject or the hypnotist, and even less on any mysterious extrasensory influence.

There are, however, three admissible questions that fall under the topic of the relation of the will to hypnosis: (*a*) Can a person be hypnotized against his wishes; (*b*) can an individual be hypnotized without his knowledge of this (but not necessarily against his wish);

196

(c) can a person be made to do under hypnosis something contrary to his will?

Will, Awareness, and Trance Induction

Watkins (457, 458) has reported that some subjects cannot resist the induction of hypnosis. Both Schneck (395) and Estabrook (128) have confirmed this. Eysenck (135) has also observed something of the sort. In contrast, Wells (471) maintained that subjects can resist induction of hypnosis.

Schneck (395) seems to conclude that it is possible to hypnotize an individual without his being aware of it. I myself can vouch for at least one instance in which an individual was accidentally hypnotized under conditions that precluded his awareness of this fact. In fact, the thought of hypnosis at the time was remote from the subject's mind. We also find, in the literature on psychic phenomena and related material, reports that seem to indicate that individuals have practiced self-hypnosis without being particularly aware of doing so. Further confirmation that awareness of being hypnotized is not a requisite for its taking place comes from the work of Adler and Secunda (2), Erickson (119), Sargant and Fraser (389), and Rosen (376), all of whom have used techniques aimed at preventing the subject from knowing that he was being hypnotized. They reported having obtained trances comparable to those induced by the usual methods. Finally, we might also cite the not too infrequent mention by various authors of the use of natural sleep to bring about hypnosis. The most recent paper on this is that of Fresacher (145).

Dehypnotization and the Will

We might also consider at this time a topic that could have been taken up earlier but that usually comes up in a context relevant to the matter at hand. This is *dehypnotization,* or what in lay language is usually referred to as "waking" the subject from the trance state. Aside from Krueger's (244) investigation which is not particularly relevant to this chapter, no other specific study has been made of dehypnotization.

Normally, one dehypnotizes a subject by suggesting to him that at a given signal he will "awaken." There are no reasons to believe that this type of suggestion is different in nature from other hypnotic suggestions, and hence anything that is true for these should also be true for it. It is for this reason that dehypnotization has not been made the subject matter of a separate chapter. It is also generally agreed that besides suggestions one can always dehypnotize a subject by allowing him to "wake up" spontaneously, which he will do if he is left alone. It is believed that under this condition the subject usually passes into a state of natural sleep from which he awakens naturally within a reasonable amount of time. In view of this, the consensus of opinion is that a hypnotized subject *will always "awaken."*

The relevance of dehypnotization to the present chapter lies in the fact that every so often a hypnotist encounters a subject who refuses to be dehypnotized when told to "awaken." I have myself witnessed two instances of this. Unfortunately, little attention has been paid to this question, so that, although one hears of such cases, nothing definite can be found reported on them in the literature.

In general, the reasons for refusal of a subject to be dehypnotized appear to be varied, and often of a complex psychodynamic nature. It is usually possible to find out what these reasons are by simply questioning the subject about his refusal. In most cases he is quite willing to give the desired information. Armed with such knowledge, a skilled hypnotist can then nearly always get the subject to accept the suggestion of waking, or at any rate can circumvent the subject's resistance. The only instance known to me in which such an approach has failed was a case in which a subject had been given a posthypnotic suggestion that when a certain hypnotist used him as a subject the former would not be able to dehypnotize him. In this instance, the hypnotist had to resort to letting the subject come out of the trance of his own accord. This particular case is, incidentally, a rather good example of one of the laws of precedence that are taken up later in this chapter.

As was just stated, usually, when a subject is left alone to dehypnotize spontaneously, he does so within a relatively short period of time. It is within the realm of possibility that, because of some particular psychodynamic aspect of the situation, or possibly other factors, a subject will take an inordinately long time to come out of the trance, conceivably several days. There have been reports of such instances, mainly in newspapers. It is my belief that this sort of happening would be a rather rare event and that those cases which have been the object of news reports in the past arose most likely through a hypnotist making use of suggestions specifically aimed at producing a prolonged trance. Actually, although no satisfactory data are available on it, it is generally believed that hypnosis *cannot* be prolonged for great lengths of time without additional suggestions being given every so often during the prolonged trance.

Suggestions and the Will

In considering the subject's ability to resist hypnotic suggestion, it is well to take up non-noxious and noxious suggestions separately, since such factors as emotions and superego influences may enter into play to a much greater extent with noxious than with non-noxious suggestions.

Young (503) reported results, in another connection, that would tend to show that subjects can resist suggestions of a non-noxious nature. However, on repeating this investigation, Wells (471) was unable to substantiate the above. On the contrary, he found that subjects cannot resist suggestion.

The majority of investigations concerned with the problem of free will and hypnosis have been directed at situations involving noxious stimuli. Rowland (379), Wells (472), Brenman (50), Schneck (396), Watkins (457), and such older investigators as Bernheim all agree, after having investigated the question by means of various experiments, that subjects can be made to commit crimes and other antisocial acts. On the other hand, Bramwell (45), Schilder and Kauder (392), Hollander (204), Hull (213), and Erickson (120) disagree with the above conclusion, finding evidence to the contrary.

Finally, there is some evidence, such as may be found in a report by Erickson (111) that hypnotized individuals are anything but blind automatons. Gidro-Frank and Bull (158) pointed out that "subjects kept in a permissive atmosphere are capable of considerable independence of judgment as far as description of their emotions are concerned." Similarly, Adler and Secunda (2) remarked that in hypnosis the subject is neither defenseless nor passive. At worst his ego may be more permissive than in waking, but in any case it remains in active control.

Evaluation of the Experimental Data

Trance Induction. If we review the material available on these various questions, it must be admitted in answer to the first query, whether a person can or cannot be hypnotized against his wishes, that the data are unsatisfactory. Watkins' attempt to test the subject's ability to resist hypnosis unfortunately tells only one part of the story since his subjects had all been hypnotized previously at least once and some had even been trained to go into a trance at a signal. Schneck's report suffers chiefly from the fact that it does not represent a critical experimental investigation of the question, the results having been obtained incidentally in the course of practicing psychotherapy. Estabrook's report is nothing more than an anecdote and suffers from the usual weaknesses of this form of reporting. Eysenck's data have direct bearing only on resistance to waking suggestions of postural sway, and hence little can be inferred from them for hypnosis. This particular report brings to mind Baudouin's (20) famous law of reversed effort, according to which, the more the subject tries to resist a suggestion, the stronger he is compelled to carry it out. Unfortunately, this law has never been tested experimentally. It is to be suspected that, in many if not all instances in which it is found to hold, it is the result of autosuggestion, or of implied heterosuggestion. There remains Wells's investigation. It tends to be unfortunately rather inconclusive because of too many uncontrolled factors. Furthermore, it involves a considerably artificial situation brought about through the use of a previous trance induction. In it Wells instructed his subjects that they could not be hypnotized in the future unless they wrote and signed a statement to the effect that they were willing to be hypnotized by a specified individual. It should be clear that, however desirable such protective measures are, the only way to settle the question satisfactorily is to investigate it without such an adjunct. On the whole the entire question remains largely unanswered.

The matter of awareness in relation to trance induction is in a somewhat better status. Though there has been no direct investigation of the problem, there is at least considerable evidence confirming that awareness is not essential in the induction of hypnosis.

In connection with the above two questions an interesting point arises. By means of posthypnotic instructions, a hypnotist can train his subject to go into a trance nearly instantaneously (in a fraction of a second) at a prearranged signal. This type of phenomenon has done much toward giving credence to the idea that a subject could not resist trance induction in some situations. As a matter of fact, this method was employed by Watkins (457) in his investigation of the reality of the above belief. As has already been pointed out, the use of such a method of induction limits considerably the conclusions that may be derived from the results. Although the above situation does give an observer the impression that a subject can be hypnotized against his will and without his awareness of being hypnotized, it is more probable that the subject is never given a chance to use his will and muster up effective resistance. Things happen much too fast and unexpectedly for this, and he is taken by surprise, so to speak. For similar reasons it is quite probable that he is hypnotized before he has fully evaluated the situation, and hence become aware of its true nature. But even here we cannot be certain, for, in view of the work that has been reported on temporal condensation, it is clear that cognitive processes can apparently take place and be carried to completion in extremely brief intervals of time.

Antisocial Acts—the Laws of Precedence. Comparison of the procedures used by Young and by Wells, respectively, in their studies of the subject's ability to resist non-noxious stimuli leads to the observation of an important difference in technique between the two. All of Young's subjects *gave themselves autosuggestions before being hypnotized,* the autosuggestions being aimed at counteracting the hypnotist's own suggestions. There is no evidence that this expedient was used in Wells's experiment, although his subjects were asked to *decide* before hypnosis which one in a list of suggestions they would resist. Considering what is known about the nature and properties of suggestion, the use of autosuggestion can hardly be said to be *equivalent* to making a decision, or even to stating subvocally to one's self the desired outcome of an experiment. The rather definite difference in procedure seems to hold a possible key to why the two sets of results are diametrically opposed, and also points to a possible rule about the interaction of antagonistic suggestions, namely: *All other things being equal, when two antagonistic suggestions are given, the one that is given first has precedence over the later one.* If we accept this rule as valid, on the assumption that Wells's results are also valid, we can easily account now for Young's data. Arnold (6) has offered a different explanation. She believes that, in Wells's experiment, some autosuggestion was also present, but, in Young's investigation, the experimental situation favored the subjects' *imagining* their chosen patterns of resistance, this not being true for Wells's investigation. Since, according to Arnold, the effectiveness of a suggestion is a direct function of the intensity with which the subject imagines the response, the difference in results must perforce follow. Though there is some basis for Arnold's postulated relationship between imagining and the strength of response to suggestions, as will be seen later, her explanation in the present instance breaks down, for a close examination of the two investigations shows that the very factor that Arnold declares is responsible for the superior imagining in Young's study is also present in Wells's investigation. On analyzing these two investigations further, she remarks that the outcome in either situation depends primarily on the fact that the activity focused on first is the one carried out. She refers to this as the "primacy of focus." It is my belief that this is nothing more than the law that has just been stated.

This law can be called the *law of temporal precedence*. There is some rather indirect evidence to be found in the literature on hypnosis, as well as from everyday experience with hypnosis, that two similar laws probably hold. These I have called the *law of depth precedence*, and the *law of impressional precedence*. The first of these states that, *all other things being equal, of two conflicting suggestions, the one associated with the greater trance depth will be carried out*. According to the second law, *all other things being the same, of two antagonistic suggestions, the one impressed * the most strongly through factors other than trance depth has precedence over the other*. These two laws and the one mentioned earlier constitute the three *laws of precedence*. In general, all three are simultaneously effective and give rise to a resultant that determines which suggestion is to be carried out, and probably the strength of the response to it. It must be emphasized, however, that all three laws have been derived in a very indirect manner and that they should not be given too much weight until more definite evidence for them has been obtained. This is particularly true of the last two.

We may now pass on to the case of noxious suggestions. For the sake of convenience, we will use the expression "antisocial act (or behavior)" to denote behavior causing harm either to others or to the subject himself, or, in general, behavior of which the subject or society as a whole would strongly disapprove. More specifically we will be concerned with what would be called criminal and injurious actions.

As was just seen, among those who have investigated the production of antisocial acts in hypnosis, some obtained evidence that this could be accomplished, whereas others obtained opposite results. This second group of investigators has generally held that reported instances of criminal action induced in hypnosis could be accounted for on the basis that the subjects: (*a*) believed that there were protective measures, (*b*) trusted the hypnotist, (*c*) had confidence that there were legitimate reasons for the hypnotist's requests, or (*d*) had latent needs or criminal tendencies. It is difficult in most instances to establish with certainty the absence of any one of these very reasonable possibilities. And, as a matter of fact, there is good evidence that one or more of these were present in various reported instances. On the other hand, when we consider all the experiments that have been reported, particularly certain very similar ones which have led to diametrically

---

* Meaning by this the degree or extent, complexity, stability, and permanence of the associations formed between the suggestions and already existing determinants of behavior.

opposite results, it becomes rather evident that the above four alternatives can be only part of the answer.

As I have indicated elsewhere (463) there exists still another alternative which may be derived from a study of the methodology of the reported investigations. Leaving out those instances of induced antisocial behavior which have pretty clearly been brought about in one of the four ways just outlined, analysis of the data shows that it is possible to divide the remainder of the experiments into two distinct groups. This is done on the basis of whether or not the suggestions that were used were of such a nature as to produce *perceptual alterations* in the subjects.† Furthermore, with the possible exception of one experiment, all those in which such suggestions were used contain strong evidence that the perceptual alterations that resulted were of such a nature that the subjects *would not perceive themselves* as behaving antisocially. This is to be contrasted with the cases in which perceptual distortions were not induced. In these, the subjects presumably perceived their behavior in a frame of reference common to other observers present, that is, as antisocial. All of this is of course edifying, but not particularly significant until we observe a rather remarkable fact: If the two classes of experiments thus arrived at are compared with the two classes of experiments obtained on the basis of negative and positive results, we find that a nearly perfect congruence exists. More specifically, the investigators who reported success in inducing antisocial acts were also the ones who distorted the subject's perceptions, whereas the negative reports came from experimenters who did not produce perceptual alterations in their subjects (with possibly one exception). This sort of congruence could hardly be a coincidence!

The conclusion seems clearly at this point to be that (*a*) whatever intrinsic compulsive power or property hypnotic suggestion may possess, this alone is incapable of causing individuals to commit antisocial acts, and (*b*) subjects can be induced to act criminally if they are made to perceive their actions as occurring in a situation (or context) in which they are not antisocial.

It needs to be emphasized here that the above is not meant to exclude alternative explanations for the dichotomy in the reported results. In many of the reported instances of successful induction of antisocial acts, we find not only that perceptual alterations of the kind just mentioned were present but that one or more of the conditions

---

† The types of alterations that were produced in these instances consisted of illusions, hallucinations, and paramnesias.

listed earlier were also there. In such cases it may be that all of these factors influenced the subjects rather than any single one. It is my opinion, however, that the perceptual alterations in these instances most probably played a major role, possibly to the exclusion of the other factors.

Furthermore, it must be emphasized that no claim is made here that, of the possible perceptual distortions that may be induced, only those causing the subject to perceive his behavior as acceptable can account for the positive results under consideration. It is conceivable, for instance, that in some of the reported experiments violent emotions arising as a consequence of hallucinations or other perceptual distortions might have been the motive agent behind the subject's action rather than the fact that the hypnotic situation was so structured by suggestion as to make the behavior appear legitimate. This interpretation is applicable for instance to several of Watkins' experiments. Either view is acceptable.‡ What is significant, however, for the present analysis is that, even if we choose affect as prime agent, the fact remains that in the experiments under discussion *a perceptual alteration was invariably induced first.*

It should not be thought either that the manner in which perceptual alterations may be affecting the subject in these experiments is always clearly defined. One of the experiments reported by Watkins appears at first examination to have been a case where a subject was made to carry out an antisocial act while being fully aware of its nature and of the gravity of her action. Briefly, a WAC in the intelligence service was hypnotized and compelled to divulge secret information in spite of the fact that the seriousness of the action was impressed upon her. Leaving out various details, it will merely be said here that the information was forced out of her through what seems to have amounted to hallucinated torture (combined possibly with some induced motor disturbances). As it happens in this instance it is possible to argue that, quite independently of any suggestions, the subject never considered the situation as involving a serious breach of confidence and that her efforts to resist the suggestions grew out of her accepting the situation as a challenge of her ability to resist suggestions. There is also some justification for taking the view that the subject's action was

‡ Thus, for instance, in one of these experiments we can ask whether an enlisted man who was made to attack an army officer with intent to kill did this because it had been made a matter of life or death for him or because he was made to see his action not only as commendable, but also as his duty [he was made to hallucinate the officer as a Japanese soldier about to kill him (the enlisted man)].

really the consequence of the arousal of emotional elements.§ None of these possible solutions can really be denied. On the other hand, it must also be remarked that divulging information under the influence of drugs, hypnosis, or torture may have a certain amount of legitimacy. These are circumstances that tend to exonerate an individual for perpetrating what would otherwise be a serious crime. There may be a certain amount of shame and guilt feeling attached to such a situation, but this does not have the same valence as acting criminally without extenuating circumstances. Thus we can also take the position that in the experiment under examination the subject eventually yielded to the suggestions because, when the hallucinated situation finally became unbearable, the crime of divulging the information really became nominal. If then this was really what happened, the experiment also reduces to one in which perceptual distortions led to the subject seeing herself as *not* committing an antisocial act. In any event, whichever point of view we take in this case, it is clear that suggested distortions of the subject's perceptions came first.

On the whole then, the dichotomy in the reported results concerning the hypnotic production of antisocial acts appears explainable in terms of the presence or absence of suggested perceptual alterations, and more particularly of such alterations as lead the subject to perceive his actions as taking place in such a context that his behavior does not appear to be antisocial. Furthermore, it may now be remarked that such factors listed earlier as trust in the hypnotist, confidence in the legitimacy of the suggestions, and belief in the existence of protective measures are themselves of a perceptual nature and function essentially by neutralizing the antisocial aspect of the suggested behavior. Thus, it appears possible to state in rather general terms, on the basis of the present data and leaving out the possible influence of latent needs or criminal tendencies,|| that (*a*) *it is unlikely that one can compel a hypnotized individual to commit antisocial acts by virtue of any inherent compulsive power the suggestions may possess per se; but that* (*b*) *it appears entirely feasible to do this by distorting the subject's awareness in various ways.* In particular, if the subject is made to

§ We must remember too the fact that the interrelation of affect and perception is quite complex. It may well be asked whether the fear impelling a man to kill in order to survive may not itself alter the individual's awareness of right and wrong. Society does after all consider killing in self-defense as justifiable homicide. This may be compared to the material that follows.

|| It may even be that some perceptual distortions are a prerequisite to evoking such needs and tendencies.

perceive his actions as not being antisocial, he most probably can be induced to perform antisocial acts.

Summary and Conclusions

In general, the picture we obtain from the available information is that hypnosis in no way abolishes or alters the will of the subject,¶ nor does it represent a contest of will between hypnotist and subject in which the former wins. The subject never behaves in any other way than the one which is most appropriate for the total situation as defined by the suggestions themselves. Whatever the subject does is done consciously, under the guidance of his critical capacities, the power to choose still being available to him. However, in making use of his capacity for self-expression, the subject is forced by the hypnotic situation to behave within the limitations of the frame of reference imposed by it. Such a frame of reference may be totally different from that existing for an observer. Whether or not a subject can resist or circumvent such limitations as are imposed by the hypnotic situation appears to be the real problem. Under certain rather special circumstances it appears possible for the subject to do so.

It is probable that awareness of being hypnotized is not a requisite for the induction of a trance state. This conclusion, however, has still to be tested in a crucial manner. To the question of whether or not a person can be hypnotized against his will no definite answer can be given. On the basis of Watkins' report, it would seem that a person who has been previously hypnotized *cannot easily* resist trance-inducing suggestions given by a competent hypnotist, nor can such a person usually prevent himself from going into a trance at a signal after having been trained to do so by posthypnotic suggestion. On the other hand, on the basis of Young's results, it would appear that a subject can effectively resist suggestions by means of prior autosuggestions. Presumably he could do the same in regard to trance-inducing suggestions, provided no posthypnotic suggestions had been given aimed at increasing his hypnotic susceptibility and ante-dating the autosuggestions.

¶ There may of course be occasions when through transference, or otherwise, the subject develops a dependence on the hypnotist and appears to show through it an apparent weakening of his will. This type of reaction is, however, not specific to hypnosis.

The Transcendence of Normal Voluntary Capacities in Hypnosis

It has often been said that hypnosis bestows on the subject powers that transcend his normal voluntary capacities. The appeal and fascination that hypnotism exerts on many persons lies in the belief that somehow it endows individuals with extraordinary powers, enhancing their normal faculties and skills, and allowing them to perform superior feats. To what extent this is true can be determined from the material of the previous chapters, and from a few other studies to be mentioned in the present chapter. We will not present new material here, for the most part, but instead will attempt to examine material already presented from a different and over-all viewpoint.

General Remarks Concerning Transcendence

It is essential for us to understand clearly just what we are looking for. We may say first that by "voluntary capacity" will be meant the ability of an individual to *initiate voluntarily* and to *control* various manifestations of his neuromuscular apparatus. The extent of this ability, as well as the quality of these manifestations, will be considered to constitute his *level of performance,* or simply his performance. This last is usually ascertained by means of a specific test situation. The performance in terms of the test situation (such as increase in strength) becomes the performance with respect to the given voluntary capacity (being a measure of the extent to which strength is controlled).

An individual will be said to *transcend* his voluntary capacity in hypnosis if hypnosis per se or certain hypnotic suggestions enable him to bring about in his performance alterations that he is not capable of bringing about voluntarily in the waking state. Transcendence will usually be found to fall into one of the three following categories:

1. Initiation and/or control of neuromuscular manifestations, over which the individual has no influence in the waking state.

2. Production of a performance exceeding *maximal* voluntary waking performance in specific test situations. This is the usual sense in which "transcendence" is considered.

3. Other alterations.

In relation to the production of transcendence, it is rather important to distinguish among several situations:

(*a*) The alterations are specified, that is called for, by suggestions:

(i) Part of which are aimed at producing a set favoring the appearance of such alterations (repeated emphasis that it is possible, that the hypnotic state confers special powers, etc.). Such suggestions will be called *set-producing* or *preparatory* suggestions.

(ii) Without attempts to produce a set.

(*b*) The alterations are not specified in the suggestions, but are found to accompany, as *side effects*, other changes called for by the suggestions.

(*c*) The alterations are associated with the presence of hypnosis per se as side effects and irrespective of suggestions other than those used to induce the trance (the subject is then merely given instructions of a nonsuggestive nature in regard to the test situation).

Thus for instance, one could make an individual blush by suggesting that he was doing just this (direct elicitation) or merely that at a given signal he would blush (direct elicitation). Or he could be given extensive suggestions to the effect that he had acquired or would soon acquire conscious control of some of his vasomotor processes and would be able to blush when told to do so (direct evocation with preparatory suggestions). On the other hand, one might arrive at the same end result by suggesting an embarrassing experience (indirect elicitation as side effect of a suggestion). Finally, flushing of the face might happen to be a normal accompaniment of the trance state (indirect elicitation as side effect of the trance state). It will be clear to the reader that these various instances are not comparable with each other.

Hypnotic transcendence may be sought in any one of the four categories of alterations of functions which have already been considered (Chapter 10): hyperfunctions, parafunctions, hypofunctions, and afunctions. On the basis of the topics that have actually been investigated, we may consider the hypnotic transcendence of voluntary capacities under the following headings:

Motor functions: voluntary.
Motor functions: semivoluntary, involuntary, and nonvoluntary.
Somatic alterations.
Sensory and perceptual functions.

Other cognitive functions and skills.
Personality alterations.

A few words need to be said concerning the fourth of these categories. Under it are included such phenomena as hypnotic blindness and deafness. The production of these phenomena is taken here to be a transcendence of the individual's normal capacity for voluntary *inhibition* of the functions involved.

Influence of the Task Character on Transcendence

As mentioned at the beginning of the chapter, nearly all the material needed for the present discussion is to be found in earlier pages. There are, however, a few pertinent studies that remain to be mentioned. These are of such a nature that it was thought best not to try to classify them under earlier headings on functional alterations, none of which seem to be entirely suitable. The studies in question are concerned with the improvement of various skills. Young (504) investigated the hypnotized subject's capacity for the following skills, no suggestions being given except those of trance induction,

> (*a*) Spelling backwards.
> (*b*) Saying the alphabet backwards.
> (*c*) Cumulative adding.
> (*d*) Logical associations.
> (*e*) Free associations.

Young concluded on the basis of his results that hypnosis per se does not bring about any improvement in performance in the above skills. There may be some question whether the last two tasks could be expected to show improvement under the conditions in which they were given. In the test of logical associations, the subject was limited to the use of certain word associates selected by the experimenter beforehand. There is little question but that what is a logical association for one individual need not be for another. This might well tend to interfere with the subject's attempt to make the "correct" association in Young's test. Also, even in logical association there is probably a certain amount of influence from free association taking place concurrently. This would be particularly true in a time-limited test, the kind employed by Young. Finally, in my opinion, some of the "associated" words the experimenter chose seem to have had only a remote logical association with the corresponding key words. As for improvement of free association, it must be remembered that this is significant only insofar as it can reflect the psychodynamics of the individual. Obviously, and as is shown empirically, some words have a neutral quality while others have a high affective content, and which words fall into which group is a function of each individual. Responses in free association tests depend largely on the nature of the associated context and the psychodynamic patterns evoked. The matter of the influence of hypnosis on free association will be taken up more appropriately in the next chapter. It may be remarked here, however, that there was no reason to have expected "improvement" in free association in Young's study, particularly since the notion of "improvement" in this connection is somewhat ambiguous.

Considerable light is thrown on the entire question of task performance in hypnosis by the work of Eysenck (134). He considered a large number of skills which he had subjects perform both in hypnosis and posthypnotically, no suggestions of improvement having been given. The following tasks were used:

(a) Reaction time to sound.
(b) Drawing one line equal to another.
(c) Muller-Lyer illusion.
(d) Equating two color mixtures.
(e) Differentiating between color mixtures.
(f) Repeating a demonstrated arm movement.
(g) Dotting as rapidly as possible in a small square.
(h) Multiplying numbers.
(i) Adding and subtracting (combined operations).
(j) Crossing out certain letters in a given list.
(k) Adding numbers.
(l) Continuing an incompleted beehive pattern.
(m) Counting in threes.
(n) Tapping.
(o) Sorting out cards.
(p) Placing rings on a pole.
(q) Writing continuously the letters SZ.
(r) McDougall's dotting test.

In general, Eysenck found less variability in the performances done in hypnosis than in the waking performances (as measured by the standard deviations of the scores). All his results show some evidence of improved performance in hypnosis. However, *such improvement is not the same for all tasks.* He reports improvements ranging from 12 to 77 per cent, with an average of 38 per cent. The situation was similar for the posthypnotic case, the average increase in scores being somewhat smaller and evaluated at 28 per cent. The most significant aspect of Eysenck's results, however, is that they show a very definite trend, according to which the greatest improvement was associated with the "simpler" (more mechanical) tasks and the superiority of hypnotic performance decreased with the increased complexity of the tasks. Other factors, of course, are expected to influence such a performance and must be taken into account. Thus, special aptitudes, training, etc., can very much affect the results. Eysenck was careful to take these into consideration before evaluating his observations. It may be noted that Young also remarked that task difficulty could affect task performance in hypnosis, but he never clarified this remark in a satisfactory manner. My own data (462, 464) confirm Eysenck's observations on the relation of task difficulty to performance in hypnosis, as well as after posthypnotic instructions. In reference to the improvement of performance following posthypnotic suggestions, Koster's (240) investigations, cited earlier, should be mentioned.

In the light of Eysenck's and my findings, it can now be stated that Young's results are essentially in agreement with the observations made by Eysenck and that, if Young had employed a greater and more diverse battery of tests, he probably would have reached a different conclusion. As it stands, his concluding remarks are valid provided we do not take them to be of general application. In evaluating these two investigations, we should not overlook the possibility that the subjects may not have been so deeply hypnotized as they could have been. Furthermore, we may wonder whether giving specific suggestions of improvement might not have caused greater improvement in at least some instances. In one respect Young's study is superior to Eysenck's in that he made use of a larger number of subjects. But, as has already been brought out, other factors give Eysenck's investigation considerable statistical weight.

Conditions for Transcendence

Examination of the various investigations that have been considered in past pages shows that experiments may be divided into two classes: those *in which various suggestions are employed to bring about the desired effects,* and those *in which such suggestions are absent,* hypnosis alone being present. No attempt will be made to review the pertinent material, since in all examples that have been discussed it has been indicated which of the two classes the investigations fell into. It might be remarked, however, that attempts to bring about alterations of involuntary functions were invariably made by means of suggestions. For additional details the reader may refer to my paper on transcendence (465). When the various investigations are considered, it may be observed that, in general, *hypnosis per se does not produce transcendence, but the addition of various suggestions can bring it about.* Furthermore, the effectiveness with which transcendence is brought about is found to depend on very definite factors. In order of decreasing effectiveness these are:

1. Alteration of the perceived stimulus situation by suggestions.

2. Suggested emotionally toned experiences.

3. The degree to which the altered capacity or function is itself normally amenable to voluntary control: the more it is, the greater is the influence of suggestions on it.

4. The presence of other factors specific to the given test situation (such as meaningfulness of material recalled).

5. Set-producing (preparatory) suggestions.

6. Difficulty and nature of the task: simpler, less difficult tasks favor transcendence.

It would appear that the effects of the first three factors are not so much specific to hypnosis as that they are merely allowed to manifest themselves more fully in hypnosis than in the waking state. Other conditions can, or presumably could, disclose the same effects.

However, a different situation seems to exist with the last three factors. Generally speaking, we find that direct suggestions of alterations are not effective unless associated with set-producing suggestions. In some instances where direct suggestions alone are given, there may actually be a reinforcing or set-producing effect due to the context surrounding the suggestions, thus leading to an incorrect impression of the power of direct suggestion. It is an important feature of effects associated with set-producing suggestions that to date none of these suggestions has ever been shown capable of making an individual perform at a level superior to the best performance levels that can be obtained from waking controls. It is probable that set-producing suggestions act upon the subject in no different a way from what ordinary instructions of maximal performance do. Exceptions to this are set-producing suggestions which, in addition, are responsible directly or indirectly for alterations in the perceived stimulus situation or for the appearance of affective tone. The powerful influence of perceptual alterations appears to be best understood in relation to Kantor's (229) notion that stimuli are functional in nature. The question of the influence of factors specific to the task situation appears to be closely connected with the extent of cortical and subcortical involvement present in any given instance.

Thus, on the whole, the reality of hypnotic transcendence is fairly well established. There can hardly be any further doubt that hypnosis per se can improve some functions or capacities and that suggestion can cause extensive alterations in nearly all organismic activities. How such a transcendence can come about will be considered in more detail in the next part of the book. It might be suggested tentatively that *transcending phenomena elicited in hypnosis are potentially present in the waking state, but are not able to manifest themselves. Hypnosis and suggestion are factors that make such manifestations possible.* We can find considerable support for this viewpoint in data obtained both in the area of hypnosis and in general neurophysiological investigations.

The Genuineness of Hypnotic Phenomena

Before concluding this chapter it may be well to consider two questions of considerable significance here. Certain investigators, particularly Pattie (338, 339, 340), have raised the question of the "genuineness" of induced hypnotic phenomena. Pattie's basis for this has been that it is possible to demonstrate in many instances that the reported functional alterations have no organic basis. This seems to be rather like begging the question, for, with a few exceptions, changes at the organic level are the last phenomenon that has been claimed in connection with the above alterations. To question the genuineness of suggested functional alterations is to question the genuineness of a great many known psychopathological manifestations. It is indeed very difficult to deny the reality of suggested phenomena that are capable of influencing neuromuscular processes at the reflex level. Furthermore, in many instances the altered behavior that results from hypnotic suggestion is certainly "genuine," in the sense that the subject's responses are appropriate to the suggested situation, are an integral and consistent part of his total response system, and have a certain degree of permanency. The confusion seems to have arisen, in my belief, in the fact that we must first of all make a clear distinction between *objective* and *subjective* reality or genuineness. Second, we should never make the mistake of believing for one instant that suggested and organic alterations of sensory modalities must of necessity have the same or similar objective realities. It is certain that both the causation and the mechanisms responsible for the two classes of alterations are fundamentally different in a number of respects. It cannot be too much emphasized that the objective manifestations of suggested and organic phenomena have never been found to be similar in degree or quality; therefore there is no point in testing the genuineness of the former in terms of the latter.   Finally, it must be remarked that, even if there were no objective reality to suggested phenomena, we still could not discard their subjective reality.   Such phenomena are very real for the subject!

The Extent of Transcendence

The second question that arises has to do with the measurement of the *extent* of transcendence.   A number of erroneous conclusions have been drawn from often improperly obtained data through a lack of understanding of what is really involved.   Generally speaking, every individual can be assigned a *potential maximal performance level*. This is the highest performance that the individual could attain in any given area of endeavor under optimal conditions.   It is strictly an "ideal," which may or may never be exhibited by the individual.   In contrast, we may speak of an individual's *manifest maximal performance level*, this being the performance level attained by the individual under conditions calling for maximal performance, but not necessarily optimal for it.   For any given individual, task, and set of other conditions,* his *manifest* maximal performance level may or may not equal his *potential* maximal performance, but in any event, the former can never be greater than the latter.   In general, the question considered in connection with hypnotic transcendence is *whether manifest maximal performance in hypnosis is superior to manifest maximal performance in the waking state*.   If it is, this only means that the waking individual is not performing at his *potential* maximal level and that hypnosis is a condition that allows him to progress in this direction. Whether he ever attains the potential level cannot, of course, be determined.   This leads to an important consequence: namely, that "transcendence," whether hypnotic or otherwise, must always be understood in terms of an individual's *own* performance itself measured under a standard set of reference conditions.   That is, each individual must furnish his own personal standard for comparison.   Since individuals who normally perform near their potential maximal level can show only a small improvement in hypnosis, one can be led to erroneous

---

* As has been seen, trance depth is a very important condition in determining the final results.   Unless it can be shown that the results are independent of the former, negative results in respect to transcendence can often be suspected of having arisen from an inadequate depth of trance.

conclusions concerning the effectiveness of hypnotic suggestions aimed at producing transcendence. Thus the necessity for establishing beforehand the range of performance that can be expected on a particular task under specific conditions. This also helps us to understand why the extent of transcendence seems to be an inverse function of task difficulty. Obviously, the more difficult a task is, the more likely it is that a subject will normally perform it near his maximal potential level; consequently the smaller would be any improvement in performance in hypnosis.

· 17 ·

The Production of
Psychodynamic Manifestations
through Hypnotic Suggestion

According to Warren (455), "psychodynamics" is the branch of psychology that deals with the development of mental processes and the changes that occur in these. It is contrasted to "psychostatics" which considers only the elements of such processes, that is, their contents.

Psychoanalytically speaking, the expression "psychodynamics" has a somewhat different meaning. Hinsie and Shatzky (198) state that "it is related to the forces of the mind." Amplifying this, they add: "Ideas and impulses are charged with emotions, to which the general expression *psychic* energy is given. For example, delusions of persecution or obsessions or compulsions are described as psychodynamic phenomena in that they are said to represent the results of activity of psychic forces."

Hypnosis, Free Association, and Ego Function

As can be seen, a large portion of the material treated in previous chapters has been of a psychodynamical character in the sense used by Warren. The material we shall now consider is also of a psychodynamical nature, but more in the sense employed by Hinsie and Shatzky. It should be noted, however, that, in many instances of hypnotically induced phenomena resembling standard psychodynamic manifestations, much of the affective tone usually associated with the latter may be largely if not totally absent. This is particularly true when the suggestions are aimed at directly bringing about the overt manifestations rather than creating the type of factors normally responsible for these.

We might begin by considering a minor manifestation of the subject's psychodynamics, namely, free association phenomena. It is often said that hypnosis facilitates free association. Wolberg (498) is certainly of this opinion, and equally so is Lindner (271). Kubie (248) found evidence that this is true for hypnagogic reverie. As seen earlier, Young (504) was unable to find any difference between free association in the waking and in the hypnotic states. However, as was pointed out, the particular list of stimulus words employed may not have been adequate. One may also question the depth of hypnosis of the subjects. More recently Kline and Schneck (236) have performed a well-controlled study of this, using Rapaport's (358) list (actually designed by Orbison) and the technique he describes, with minor variation. Under these conditions they obtained definite evidence of improvement in hypnosis in the sense that (a) there was a greater incidence of associative alterations; (b) the percentage of fast reaction times was increased while conversely the percentage of slow reaction times was reduced; and (c) there was an increase in the percentage of serious disturbances to traumatic stimuli. They added that their findings showed that in the case of patients the associative alterations brought about by hypnosis were qualitatively meaningful within the framework of hypnotherapy and hypnoanalysis. There seems therefore to be little doubt but that hypnosis does facilitate free association.

The possibility of bringing about psychodynamic manifestations by hypnosis is indicated in the results reported first by Brenman, Gill, and Hackner (49), according to which spontaneous alterations of the state of the ego often take place during hypnosis. Erickson (113) has reported the appearance of spontaneous psychosomatic alterations under similar conditions. Further instances have been described and discussed by Schneck (397–400). These four reports are of particular interest because they show some of the mechanisms underlying these manifestations. In all the cases just mentioned the observed phenomena were spontaneous, and it remains to be shown that the same or similar phenomena can be brought about at will by means of suggestion.

A step in this direction can be found in a second report by Erickson and Brickner (121), in which they studied the production of aphasia-like states. Not only were they able to bring about such states, but also these were found by the investigators often to lead to strong affective disturbances.

Suggested Dreams and Cryptesthesia.

Still somewhat indirect in nature have been the investigations of the production of artificial dreams and cryptic writing through the use of suggestion. Both these effects have been employed for some time now as part of standard hypnotherapeutic methods. An excellent account of the techniques of induction as well as of the ways of using these phenomena has been given by Wolberg (498). In the experimental field, some of the earlier studies on the production of dreams through hypnosis were made by such men as Schrötter (403) and Roffenstein (372). More recent are the works of Welch (466), Siebert (414), Klein (233), Hoff and Pötzl (203), Farber and Fisher (136), Brenman (51), and others. As a result of these investigations, it may be said in general that there exist a number of ways of inducing dreams. The subject may be told to dream during the hypnotic session, or after it (posthypnotic). He may be given part of the dream situation, all of it, or none at all. When the induction is successful, the suggested dream takes on all the appearance of a spontaneous dream, particularly in regard to bizarre and pictorial character.

In general, the character of the dream, when produced, is determined by the nature of the stimulus employed in bringing it about, the structure of the subject's personality, and his relationship to the experimenter. In many instances, the subject may incorporate considerable material from his own past experience, substituting at times such material for suggested items because of resistance arising from past traumatic experiences.

It has been the belief of many investigators that hypnotized individuals have a remarkable ability for translating their own dreams as well as those of others. Farber and Fisher (136), investigating this, found that the belief is partially correct. The ability appears to be far from universal, since only 20 per cent of their subjects could translate dreams in a satisfactory manner. When they did, the translations were found to show a remarkable consistency both with each other and with translations obtained by other means.

The reality of suggested dreams has been considered by Brenman (51), who concluded that they are not in all cases the same as nocturnal dreams. Instead, on the average, a hypnotic dream takes a position somewhere between the conscious daydream and the night dream. Many so-called hypnotic dreams are what she refers to as "quasi-dreams." Along this line of thought, it is interesting that Sirna (415) was unable to find any difference between EEG patterns of hypnotized individuals who were made to dream and the patterns obtained from them in the absence of dreaming or in the waking state.

The entire matter has been further clarified by the excellent study of Mazer (294) who undertook to re-examine the whole problem in the light of the work done previously. He found first of all that responses of subjects to dream suggestion (stimulus) fell into three categories: no dream, nonsymbolic dream (or paraphrases of the stimulus), and symbolic dream. The significant observation here, however, is that whichever one of these types can be produced depends on the depth of hypnosis attained. In general, to get any dream at all, the subject must be in a light trance.* His dreams are then mainly of a nonsymbolic nature. Symbolic dreams may be produced in a few subjects who are in the medium trance but normally do not appear until a somnambulistic trance is attained.

Second, from his examination of 333 suggested dreams obtained from 26 normal adult subjects, of whom only 59 were nonsymbolic, Mazer concluded on rather sound grounds that

(a) Questions of falsification can be eliminated in evaluating his results.
(b) Hypnotic dreams are essentially the same as natural dreams in regard to character. In support of this he presents five points of similarity:

(1) Both are hallucinatory experiences taking place in nonpsychotic individuals and in conjunction with certain states of altered awareness.
(2) Both are produced below the level of awareness.
(3) The two types of dreams reveal information about the subject's personality.
(4) The two can express these revelations in a symbolic language.
(5) Both types of dreams contain the same Freudian distortions.

(c) Hypnotic dreams are not precise duplications of natural dreams in regard to function and structure, but the differences between the two kinds are primarily quantitative and not qualitative.

On the whole Mazer presents a rather convincing picture—the more so as it is the result of a carefully planned investigation. In this respect his conclusions must be given more weight than those of Brenman who appears to base hers mainly on clinical experience gathered in a nonexperimental setting. In spite of this, it cannot be denied that such material often contains much truth, particularly when gathered and reported by such an investigator as Brenman. It is my opinion that we cannot disregard Brenman's conclusions and that perforce it may be necessary to find a way to reconcile these and Mazer's results. Such a reconciliation may be sought for the time being in (a) the characteristics on which the two investigators have based their respective analyses, and (b) an observation made by Mazer that the dream symbols are determined by cultural and educational experiences, that they are usually highly specific (not common) to the dreamer, and that

* On the Davis-Husband scale.

a given dreamer may use the same symbol differently on different occasions.

In regard to cryptic writing there is little available of an experimental nature. Erickson and Kubie (122) have reported a very interesting instance of this which shows the same puns, elisions, plays of words, and so on as are found in dreams. They also reported that a second individual was able, when hypnotized, to give an accurate translation of the writing of the first subject. Much earlier, Messerschmidt (309) had shown that suggested cryptesthesia does not involve a functional dissociation insofar as interference between simultaneously performed tasks is concerned.

Induced Personality Disorders

Of a definitely more ambitious nature have been attempts at producing artificial complexes, neuroses, and even psychotic behavior. It should be stated from the outset that the literature does not always distinguish too clearly among these three. This is particularly true of neurosis and complex formation, where either designation may be given to essentially the same group of induced phenomena by two different authors. Generally speaking, neuroses and psychoses are in one sense the outward manifestations of the presence of certain complexes. They are the syndromes, in contrast to the complexes which are the causative agencies of the syndromes. The term "complex" is used here in the sense employed by Hinsie and Shatzky (198), to mean "a group of repressed ideas interlinked into a complex whole, which besets the individual, impelling him to think, feel, and perhaps act after a habitual pattern." In general, such a group of associated thoughts constitutes a complex only if it is associated with a conflict. In the final analysis, the entire matter would appear to resolve into whether one wishes to emphasize the syndrome itself or the causation instead. Whatever the case may be, a number of investigators have presented material under one heading and others under the alternative heading. This distinction will be preserved in the pages that follow.

Quite early in the history of psychiatry, a number of writers had noted the resemblance between neurotic compulsive behavior and post-hypnotic behavior. Ferenczi had particularly emphasized this aspect. However, no actual experimentation in this direction had been made.

One of the first studies on artificially induced complexes was done by Luria (282) who reported success in it. Huston, Shakow, and Erickson (219) have substantiated his results. In both instances, the "complexes" were in the nature of a paramnesia having to do with a traumatic experience and suggested to the subject, being at the same time of such a nature as to bring about affective disturbances. The Luria method for the detection of complexes was employed after the suggestions were given.

In a later paper, Erickson (123) reported having succeeded in producing a large variety of manifestations of "everyday" psychopathology. Here, too, paramnesias were employed. According to the investigator the various manifestations fell into the following categories:

(a) Unconscious determinants of the causal content of conversation.
(b) Manifestations of unconscious ambivalent feeling in conversation about a person.
(c) Lapsus linguae and unconscious irony.
(d) Unconscious resentment expressing itself in masked forms through a smoke-screen of overcompensatory courtesy.
(e) Ambivalence. Manifestation of unconscious conflict about smoking in the distortion of simple, daily, smoking habits.
(f) Unconscious conviction of absurdities with rationalization in support of the belief in them.
(g) Automatic writing. Unconscious obliteration of visual impressions in order to preserve an hypnotically ordered amnesia.
(h) Crystal gazing. Hallucinatory vividness of dream imagery embodying anger displaced from hypnotist unto dream person.
(i) Implantation of a complex.
(j) The assumption of another's identity under hypnotic direction, with striking unconscious mimicry and the assumption of unconscious emotional attitudes.

In still another study, concerned with the production of a neurosis, Erickson (124) obtained even more spectacular pathological manifestations through a similar technique. Brickner and Kubie (53) in another interesting investigation reported the production of what they have described as a "minor psychotic storm." In this, various manifestations of a conflict over the subject's allegiance to contending superego figures were clearly present. A number of induced neuroses have also been reported in connection with the treatment of psychopathological conditions. Erickson (117) and McDowell (297) have made such reports. Wolberg (498) described a case in one of his books. We should also mention here the pioneer work of Eisenbud (110) on the use of induced conflicts in the treatment of migraine headaches.

The approach to experimental psychopathology has taken a very different turn in the hands of Lundholm (279, 281) under the description of "laboratory neuroses." His method parallels essentially the classical technique employed in the production of neuroses in animals, in which the animals are presented with conflicting stimuli to which they are equally compelled to respond.† This is very much in contrast to the conflict situation previously described which is created by means of a suggested complex. That is, in Lundholm's approach, the neurosis is brought about by having the subject come face to face with a situation in which conflicting forces are at work. It is up to him to resolve the situation as best he can. In contrast, in the other approach, the neurotic behavior is brought about by means of paramnesias. Lundholm declares that he was able to bring about in this manner the symptoms of various functional disorders. He reported that the resulting behavioral responses paralleled not only hysterical symptoms, but also a great many obsessional ones, and even such symptoms of the major functional psychoses as delusions, moods of elation, moods of depression, irritability, and apprehension.

Summary and Conclusions

There seems to be little reason to doubt that psychopathological manifestations can be brought about by means of hypnotic suggestions. Whether they may be identified with the various manifestations that make up the domain of abnormal psychology and that are found to occur spontaneously in waking individuals is another matter. It is difficult to answer this question with any certainty, mainly because the whole area is pretty much virgin territory. As was seen, there is some question whether suggested dreams are always the same as nocturnal dreams. Hypnotically induced complexes appear to have properties similar to those of naturally occurring complexes, insofar as free association and other techniques of a similar nature are concerned. In fact, it is clear from the report of Huston et al. (219) that there is a tendency for natural and hypnotic complexes to merge into each other when the Luria method is employed for their detection. Again, Erickson's (123) demonstration of various manifestations of "everyday" psychopathology shows no essential differences from similar manifestations taking place in nonhypnotic situations. At worst, one has a slight impression of artificiality, but, after all, the entire situation is artificial in the first place. The most natural-like instance reported thus far is the case of cryptic writing described by Erickson

† With the difference here that the conflicts are, of course, brought about by means of suggestions.

and Kubie. However, in this instance no complex in the strict sense of the word had been induced. As for the neuroses induced by Lundholm, we must ask, as in past cases of "experimental neuroses" in animals, whether the situations in question are entirely comparable with those that in practice give rise to neurotic and psychotic behavior in humans. To some extent this same question must also be asked of the cases in which paramnesias are employed.

PART

· 4 ·

TOWARD A THEORETICAL FORMULATION

·18·

Past and Present
Theories of Hypnosis

A great number of attempts have been made to formulate theories
to account for the phenomena of suggestibility and hypnosis. Some
of these theories have had to be discarded completely in the light of
modern data. Others remain because of a lack of decisive evidence
against them. Few if any to date have been able to give a satisfactory
unified explanation of all the known phenomena.

The Theories

It will be convenient, although quite arbitrary, to classify, as Wolberg (497) has done, the theories according to the kind of manifestations they interpret hypnosis to be. Accordingly we have these classifications.

HYPNOSIS AS A PATHOLOGICAL MANIFESTATION. This view was held
by such prominent investigators as Charcot (68, 69), Binet and Féré
(32), and Janet (223). They believed that hypnosis was pathological
in nature, being a symptom of hysteria. Few support this notion today.
Among modern investigators who do we might mention W. Brown
(60).

HYPNOSIS AS A NEUROPHYSIOLOGICAL MANIFESTATION. Under this
heading we find a variety of theories contending that hypnosis is
associated with physical changes in the cerebral cortex and in adjacent
regions. It is clear that the close relationship between mental and
neurophysiological events must of necessity lead to overlapping between this view and others presented in these pages. The basis for
the present classification lies in the fact that different investigators
appear to emphasize different interpretations and even aspects of the
same manifestations. Actually, the next three groups to be taken up
also fall under the present heading.

Bennett (25) for instance considers hypnosis as a suspension of activity in the white substance of the cerebrum, accompanied by increased activity of the remainder of the brain. Heidenhain (187) believed that there is an inhibition of the ganglion cells of the brain. Vincent, as reported by Wolberg (497), interpreted hypnosis as the inhibition of one set of mental functions and the acceleration of others. For Sidis (412) there was a functional dissociation between nerve cells. Hart (184) on the other hand thought in terms of cerebral anemia. McDougall (295) saw in hypnosis a shift of nervous energies from the central nervous system to the vasomotor system. Similarly Volgyesi (452) spoke of hypnosis as a vasomotor decerebration involving anemia of the frontal lobes. Finally, Eysenck (131, 135) who favors the ideo-motor hypothesis proposed that hypnosis is a property of the synaptic nerve junctions. According to him, it involves a limiting of the nervous energy into a smaller number of channels.

HYPNOSIS AS A STATE OF IMMOBILIZATION (CATAPLEXY). A number of investigators, particularly European ones, have held that hypnosis as found in man partakes of the nature of states of immobilization as seen in animals. Since the latter states are strictly physiological in nature, involving apparently a tonic recumbency reflex, hypnosis would thereby acquire a similar nature.

In more recent times Schneck (401, 402) has proposed that a relationship existed between hypnosis and states of immobilization on the basis of his observation that some subjects equate "hypnosis" with "death." This, he suggests, is comparable to the view that so-called "animal hypnosis" is a "death-feint."

HYPNOSIS AS SLEEP OR SLEEP-LIKE STATES. According to a relatively large number of older investigators, hypnosis is a modified form of sleep. Pavlov (342) made the claim that sleep and hypnosis were similar, involving a spread of cerebral inhibition in both cases. More recently Kubie and Margolin (247) have presented a theory in which hypnosis results from the creation of a focus of central excitation with a surrounding area of inhibition. A similar notion seems to be held by Wolberg (497) and by Barker and Burgwin (12, 13).

HYPNOSIS AS A CONDITIONED RESPONSE. It might be remarked that this view overlaps considerably the one just considered. Here we find the postulate that hypnotic phenomena are of the nature of a complex conditioned reflex. The work of Cason (65) and of Hudgins (212) on conditioned pupillary reflex and of Menzies (303) on conditioned peripheral vasomotor effects have been used in support of this hypothesis. Similarly with Jacobson's (222) demonstration of the association of specific patterns of action currents with thoughts related to muscular activity.

Pavlov (342), Bechterew (23), and Platonow (348) have attempted to carry reflexology into the domain of hypnosis on the basis that words can become conditioned to both internal and external stimuli and may in turn cause organic reactions. In hypnosis, the word becomes a stimulus which sets up conditioned reflexes of a physiological nature. These reflexes are copies of organic innate reflexes. Suggestion, Platonow insists, is a typical conditioned reflex. Welch (467) and Corn-Becker, Welch, and Fisichelli (81) have presented evidence for the existence of "abstract" conditioning and propose that hypnosis is nothing else but a form of abstract conditioning.

If we are to accept the consensus of opinion that habit formation is a conditioning process, we must include Hull's (213) view that suggestions are habit phenomena. As a matter of fact, by virtue of Hull's interpretation of monoideism and of ideomotor action as habit phenomena, these two also come under the present heading, and hence so does any theory of hypnosis based on either of them. But, even if Hull's proposition is rejected, the ideomotor theory of suggestibility finds a place here on the basis that ideomotor action is best understood in terms of conditioned reflexes. According to Young (507) and to Eysenck (131) suggestibility is the result of two forces: ideomotor action and inhibition.

Finally, we should also consider Arnold's (6) theory that suggestibility is merely an expression of imagining actualized through ideomotor action.

HYPNOSIS AS A STATE OF DISSOCIATION. According to Janet (223), hypnosis consists of the production of a secondary dissociated consciousness, that is, the formation of a group of unconscious memories and activities which temporarily appropriate the stream of consciousness. Prince (353), Burnett (62), and Sidis (412) also favored this hypothesis. According to it, depth of hypnosis is directly associated with the degree of dissociation. All the phenomena of hypnosis are accounted for in terms of a splitting off from each other of the various functions governed by the cerebrum.

Also a part of this theory is the concept of automaticism. According to it, behavior manifests itself at two levels: the purposeful, volitional, striving level, and the reflex activity level. Hypnosis is theorized here to abolish volition, resulting in the automatic appearance of a reflex-like type of behavior which is dissociated from consciousness.

HYPNOSIS AS A FORM OF SUGGESTION, OR OF SUGGESTIBILITY. It is generally agreed that hypnosis is a state of hypersuggestibility. Hull (213) believes that all hypnotic phenomena can also be brought about in the waking state. Wells (473) is of a similar opinion. According to this point of view, ideomotor action manifests itself as increased suggestibility brought about in response to a prestige relationship. This point of view does not distinguish between hypnosis and waking except in respect to the degree of suggestibility present.

HYPNOSIS AS A FORM OF TRANSFERENCE. Ferenczi (138) believed that susceptibility to hypnosis depended on the extent of transference formed between subject and hypnotist. According to him, there is involved a parent-child relationship. Jones (228), Freud (146), Schilder and Kauder (392), Speyer and Stokvis (418), and Lorand (276) all see erotic components in hypnosis and offer theories along the line of erotic gratification, manifestations of the Oedipus complex, masochistic tendencies, and so on. Wolberg (497) conceives hypnosis as resulting from the subject's desire to obtain pleasure goals in the form of security and avoidance of pain, this serving as motivation for the subject to submit to the hypnotist. Kubie and Margolin (247) also agree that transference phenomena are part of the trance induction and carry over into the hypnotic state; however, they do not make it the basis of hypnosis as others have done.

HYPNOSIS AS A GOAL-DIRECTED STRIVING. Closely related to the above is White's (483) theory that the phenomena of hypnosis result from the subject's motive to behave like a hypnotized person as defined by the hypnotist and as understood by the subject. As Jenness (225) has remarked, others before White have voiced a similar interpretation, but perhaps not in quite so clear-cut a manner. In the same line of thought, McDougall (295) has proposed that subjects satisfy an "instinct" of submission when they pass into the hypnotic state. Rivers (368) considered hypnosis as the result of a "herd instinct." Finally, Sarbin (385), developing White's hypothesis further, adds that hypnosis is a form of general social psychological behavior which he calls "role-taking." According to this, the subject strives to take the role of the hypnotized person as prescribed or expected by the culture to which he belongs. How well he succeeds in this depends, according to Sarbin, on his favorable motivation, role-taking aptitude, and his role perception. As will be seen later, there is probably no fundamental incompatibility between Sarbin's theory and the theory that will be developed in the next chapters.

HYPNOSIS AS A PSYCHOSOMATIC MANIFESTATION. Wolberg (497) is probably the first to have proposed in so many words the view that hypnosis is psychosomatic in character. Others, however, have implied as much in earlier writings. Among contemporary writers, Kubie and Margolin (247) have been particularly emphatic about this. Basically the above group of investigators regard hypnosis as being both physiological and psychological in character. From the physiological standpoint, Wolberg believes hypnosis is a spreading of inhibition over the higher centers in the cortex. Kubie and Margolin speak of the hypnotic state as involving a limitation of sensorimotor channels in a manner resembling that which takes place in sleep. On the psychological side of the theory, Wolberg conceives hypnosis to be a transference phenomenon. Though Kubie and Margolin admit the presence of transference in hypnosis, they give it a less important role. As a substitute for it they propose that hypnosis involves an extension of the subject's own psychic processes so as to include the voice of the hypnotist.

Evaluation of the Theories

With these few remarks about the various theories that have been propounded to date, we will now pass on to the examination of their major weaknesses. Some of these theories can be discarded in a summary manner. Thus, for instance, the hypothesis that hypnosis in humans is identical with states of immobilization as seen in animals is no longer tenable, even when Schneck's (401, 402) "hypnosis-death" concept is taken into account.*

Similarly, there is now ample evidence to contradict any proposal that hypnosis is a form of natural sleep. Even if Pavlov's theory of generalized inhibition should turn out to be correct for both sleep and

* The evidence and arguments presented by Schneck in support of his view are extremely flimsy, and in any event quite superficial. Unquestionably some individuals do equate death with hypnosis, but, like erotic components, and transference in general, this act is to be conceived more probably as taking place in a contemporaneous and quasi-independent manner than as being an expression of the true nature of hypnosis.

hypnosis, it is now clear that one or more additional factors must be involved in one of the two states. Nor are there any reasons today to believe that hypnosis and suggestibility are symptomatic of a pathological condition, or even associated with one. Although it is correct that hysterics are more suggestible than normal individuals, this fact does not by any means imply the converse, namely, that high suggestibility is a sign of hysteria, or even of susceptibility to hysteria. On the other hand, we should not lose sight of the fact that hypnosis and hysterical manifestations may involve one or more mechanisms which are partly or entirely similar. As Wolberg (497) has remarked: "The ability of the individual to invoke vegetative mechanisms is certainly not unique for hypnosis, since, in emotional illness, too, the motivation to escape anxiety causes the elaboration of various symptoms, the development of which is outside the range of normal volition."

Physiological theories, particularly early ones, are for the most part extremely weak. There is in nearly all instances little specific experimental evidence to support them. Although they may account for the hypnotic state per se, they cannot account satisfactorily, if at all, for the majority of phenomena found to be associated with hypnosis.

A rather peculiar situation exists in connection with those theories that consider hypnosis to be a form of suggestion, for certainly it is a suggested state. The fallacy is that these theories beg the question. They presuppose that the nature of suggestion has been fully clarified, which is hardly true. The same charge can be made against trying to explain hypnosis in terms of a state of hypersuggestibility. There only remains to explain how this hypersuggestibility comes about, what its nature is, and how it can bring about all of the phenomena known to be associated with hypnosis!

Refutation of the psychoanalytical theory of hypnosis causes some difficulties, largely because transference phenomena are still poorly understood in terms of the more elementary concepts which constitute the basis of psychology. In the present state of our knowledge of transference it is entirely conceivable that it can account for hypnosis. Still, if it does, we will unquestionably have to revise some of our notions about it, if we are to account for such phenomena as *self-hypnosis*. Also, instances of trance induction have been reported that appear to preclude any appreciable transference. Finally, as Wolberg (497) has remarked, it is rather clear that transference by itself does not account for the complex phenomena produced by hypnosis. As intimated in Chapter 6, transference phenomena most likely are incidental to hypnosis, possibly being facilitated by this state, but are by no means intrinsic to hypnosis. It is true, as psychoanalytically minded investigators have asserted, that hypnosis very likely does involve a special and close relationship between subject and hypnotist. This is very characteristic of rapport and leads us to ask what possible relationship might exist between rapport and transference. Actually, in the psychoanalytic interpretation there is little evidence that the two effects are to be distinguished from each other. On the other hand, "rapport," as traditionally defined and as defined in Chapter 7, appears to be a much broader concept. As Christenson (70) has remarked in this connection: "It does not seem desirable to abandon this term in favor of *transference*, since the observed dynamics of the subject-agent interaction suggest that rapport is present regardless of whether transference is positive or negative, and may thus be considered a more comprehensive construct." Alternatively, we may even think of rapport as inclusive of transference and possibly reducing to it in some instances.

The arguments for and against the need theory of hypnosis follow along lines similar to those just given for transference. Consequently, no attempt will be made here to take these up in more detail. It might be remarked, however, that Sarbin's theory has the additional weakness that it makes hypnosis a phenomenon defined by society. There is no question but that the behavior of subjects is often influenced by what they believe is (perceive to be) expected of them. On the other hand, certain phenomena of hypnosis and suggestibility, in general,† are hard to picture as having such a genesis, primarily because they are of a type for which it is doubtful that there have been any well-defined societal attitudes; and also because, even if there are such attitudes, it is hardly conceivable that the subject could have brought forth the phenomena only through a desire to do what society wished him to do.

The dissociation theory has had a good many supporters in the past and still has an appreciable number. To a large extent, however, contemporary investigators use the concept of dissociated states more as a descriptive term for certain aspects or manifestations of hypnosis than as a complete theory. As was seen, the general theory has been that the induction of hypnosis brings into existence a secondary dissociated consciousness which controls the subject's behavior. Such an interpretation unfortunately tends to beg the question in some respects. In addition, as Hull and his co-workers (213) have shown, the pre-

† Such for instance as homoaction, or some of the physiological changes reported in cases of revivification, and in conjunction with hallucinations.

supposed autonomy of dissociated elements is primarily more apparent than real. The related hypothesis of automaticism fares no better in the light of the facts now available about the part that volition and critical (or rational) thinking can play in hypnosis.

Nevertheless, after everything has been said, we cannot throw overboard the notion of dissociation so easily. For there is little question but that, as Freud and others have shown, a large portion, if not most, of an individual's mental activities takes place outside of his consciousness, to the extent that even complex and precise elaboration of thought may take place at a nonconscious level. There is considerable evidence that dissociation of some sort plays a part in hypnotic phenomena. This, however, does not necessarily indicate that dissociation is the cause of, or is, hypnosis. It may be more correct to state with Christenson (70) that "hypnosis does not produce *dissociation* of itself, but rather makes use of the existing dissociation between conscious and subconscious phenomena in the subject."

The major defect of the conditioned reflex theory of hypnosis as presented by the Pavlovian school is that, although it describes hypnosis fairly well in broad general terms, it fails to account for the many phenomena associated with it. This criticism of course can be directed at nearly all, if not all, theories presented so far, but it appears even more true of the conditioned reflex theory. There are no experimental situations in the field of classical conditioning theory that approach anywhere near the complexity of the usual hypnotic situation. Some of those in favor of the theory have cited the famous experiments of Cason and of Hudgins in support of their contentions. Though these experiments are highly suggestive, they certainly do not by any means prove the reflex nature of hypnosis. One does not necessarily follow the other. An important argument against the hypothesis is that in many instances the time factors involved in the hypnotic situation are at variance with those required in conditioning phenomena. Thus far we have been concerned here with the strictly Pavlovian interpretation of hypnosis. There are, however, other aspects of conditioning theory which when applied to hypnosis cannot be discarded too easily, if at all. Both in studies of suggestibility and in the physiology of the neuromuscular system very strong arguments can be found for believing that ideomotor action is indeed the basis of primary suggestibility and of homoactive hypersuggestibility. These arguments will be presented in the next chapter. For the time being, let it be simply remarked that the most acceptable interpretation available is that ideomotor action is a complex conditioned reflex. Thus, in this

wise, conditioning would account at least *in part* for hypnotic phenomena. Again, Hull (213) has concluded that hypersuggestibility
(of primary type) follows the same laws as habits. This can be taken
either as evidence supporting the ideomotor theory or independently
as indication that conditioning does play a part in suggestibility phenomena. But neither the strict ideomotor theory of hypnosis nor the
habit theory are found to account satisfactorily for all observed phenomena. They both break down in the face of some of the properties
of suggestibility reported at the beginning of this book. We will
discuss this in the next chapter. There has been presented fairly
recently a conditioning theory of hypnosis to which serious thought
must be given. This is the one advanced by Welch and by Corn-
Becker et al. in which abstract conditioning is made the basis of
hypnotic hypersuggestibility. Though there is no question but that
further confirmation is needed in regard to abstract conditioning, it
does explain a number of phenomena that have been observed in relation to hypnosis, and particularly for certain properties of suggestibility
which have not been or cannot be accounted for by other theories.
Closer examination of this new theory seems to indicate that, like the
ideomotor theory, it can account for hypnosis in part, but not for the
entire phenomenon. In particular, it may be pointed out that there
are situations in which suggestions are effective, yet in which it is
unlikely that abstract conditioning would take place. Again it is
doubtful whether the picture of hypnotic induction described by
Welch and his associates is representative of all instances that take
place in practice. Further discussion of the matter will be left to the
following chapters.

The psychosomatic theories of hypnosis remain to be considered.
Actually, as should be evident by now, there is really no single theory
that can be said to belong exclusively to this category. The only
reasons for speaking of this group are that there are some theories that
really represent a merging of two or more theories belonging under
one of the other headings and also that these theories tend to emphasize more than others the double nature of hypnosis as a physiological
and a psychological phenomenon. Of this there is little doubt any
more. But these theories have the same weaknesses as others that
have been examined, for, in general, they merely combine several existing theories without attempting to eliminate the weaknesses that these
already possess. It is true that Wolberg has offered the novel hypothesis of a neurophysiological regression (revivification) being part of
the hypnotic state. However, this is extremely speculative in nature,

there being little evidence for it. Also, in the light of the difficulty of bringing about revivification after hypnosis has been induced, it seems unlikely that the induction itself would consist of revivification. Kubie and Margolin have also introduced some novelty in their theory, in the form of a hypothesis that there is a dissolution of the boundaries between the subject's ego and the external world, and an extension of the subject's psychic processes to include the voice of the hypnotist. Unfortunately for this hypothesis, the mechanism which is proposed to account for the dissolution and extension fails to be convincing in its entirety. It also fails in other respects, particularly in accounting for the phenomena of waking suggestibility. Nevertheless it has some merit and can be justified in certain respects, as will be seen shortly.

A number of references have been made in previous pages to the fact that some of the theories under discussion were unsatisfactory because they failed to account for certain general properties of suggestibility. Mention was made of these instances because it is of particular significance in their evaluation. Actually, however, this is a general weakness of all the theories that have been considered. Not that they all fail to take into account the same properties of suggestibility, but each does fail in one or more respects to do so. They all tend to overemphasize hypnotic phenomena at the expense of such fundamental properties as the existence of several types of suggestibility, and of such basic phenomena as homoaction and heteroaction, to mention only a few. Yet, it should be clear from the material that has been covered that hypnosis has its foundation in these very properties. In the next chapters an attempt will be made to outline a theory that takes such facts into consideration.

The Nature of
Primary Suggestibility
and Hypnosis

In the last chapter a number of theories of hypnosis were considered and, for the most part, discarded. Yet, unsatisfactory as they may have been, many of them seem to contain some elements of truth. Up to a certain point they account quite well for certain known facts, but sooner or later they fail in the face of other facts. In many instances, this failing is unquestionably a result of the fact that much of the experimental material available to us today was not accessible to former investigators. To some extent this is true even of the investigations of Hull and his associates. The same thing cannot be said for the more recent theories, for which plentiful data have been available. Here the weakness seems to lie in another direction. Some investigators, like Sarbin for instance, have made use of notions so general and abstract as to explain little if anything. Others, like Lorand and Wolberg, have centered their theories around a phenomenon that is itself poorly understood and that also tends to be too general. Still others, like Corn-Becker and associates, have picked on a specific and tangible enough phenomenon, but have limited themselves too much to the general, over-all aspects of hypnosis and suggestibility. This has been a common weakness of nearly all modern theories of hypnosis, and of not a few of the older ones. A theory, to be satisfactory, must not only take care of the general, but must also account for the particular. In any event, whatever truth may be found in these various theories will have to be taken into consideration by any new theory if the latter is to endure. It goes without saying, of course, that, in addition, such a theory must meet the criteria of the scientific method. It is the purpose of this and of the next two chapters to attempt the formulation of a more satisfactory theory and to examine the extent to which it may account for the various phenomena of suggestibility and of hypnosis.

Homoactive and Heteroactive Hypersuggestibility

In attacking the problem of the nature of hypnosis we must keep uppermost in mind that, at the outset, the subject *is in the waking state.* Thus, whatever processes are initiated by the trance-inducing suggestions, they are, at first, *responses of the waking subject to waking suggestions.* Logically, then, we should begin our search for the nature of hypnotic hypersuggestibility and other characteristics of the trance state with a consideration of the properties of waking suggestibility. This inquiry should also be guided by the fact that hypnosis usually does not appear to involve a sudden transition from waking to hypnosis. Instead, we find what appears to be a continuum from normal suggestibility to hypersuggestibility, although in some instances the gradient of suggestibility may be so steep as to give the impression of a discontinuity. Thus we are led to seek either a single process, which possesses continuity from waking to and into hypnosis, or a number of processes, some of which may be limited entirely to the waking state but which are so interrelated as to have an over-all continuity.

Let us begin by reviewing a few basic and elementary properties of waking and hypnotic suggestibility. We saw earlier that Hull and his co-workers had found that (*a*) *positive homoaction* is characteristic of suggestibility to postural sway suggestions, *both* in the waking and in the hypnotic state; (*b*) the magnitude of homoaction in either state is the same; (*c*) homoaction is cumulative; (*d*) *heteroaction is not characteristic* (is absent) of suggestibility to postural sway suggestions; and (*e*) though with suggestions other than postural sway suggestions the results for heteroaction are the same, there is considerable variation in the degree of homoaction associated with different suggestions. Homoaction is found to range from highly positive to none at all, and even to slightly negative.

To clarify the picture further we must refer back to the work of Eysenck, of Furneaux, and of their associates. They found that postural sway suggestions are associated mainly with primary suggestibility and hence can be said to be of *primary* type. Their results also show that, aside from trance-inducing suggestions, the other suggestions studied by Hull and his associates for the most part were connected with secondary (and tertiary) suggestibility and hence can be said to have been of *secondary* (and tertiary) type. Again, from the work of Krueger combined with that of Eysenck and Furneaux, we now know that a high degree of homoaction is observed when trance-inducing suggestions are employed, and that a number of the items making up these suggestions are themselves suggestions of primary type. It is unfortunate that the investigations of Hull's laboratory concerned with homoaction did not cover a greater number of primary suggestions. In spite of this, it appears probable, on the basis of the evidence just discussed, that *homoaction is mainly characteristic of primary suggestibility*. Now, if we examine a standard induction of hypnosis, we will see that the pretrance period, that is, the initial portion of the procedure that precedes the appearance of the trance, consists of suggestions mainly of primary type. Such for instance are the suggestions of relaxation, heaviness of limb, ocular fatigue, and eyelid closure. A word of explanation seems to be in order here. Although this was not specifically pointed out earlier, an examination of such suggestions as are known to be of primary type, from actual investigations, shows that suggestions calling forth muscular responses in a direct manner are probably always of primary type. This is the reason for making the above statement. In some instances of trance induction, the suggestions employed for this purpose include even those of arm and hand movements. Furthermore, all these suggestions, except possibly those of eyelid closure, are *waking* suggestions; and certainly the action of eyelid closure suggestion appears to be, in its early phase, of a waking character.

At this point we might pause to give some consideration to the theory recently proposed by Welch and by Corn-Becker et al. These investigators, as well as others, have pointed out that the general situation normally accompanying this early phase of trance induction tends to favor the spontaneous occurrence of the events that are called forth by the suggestions. They have contended that the subject's responses at this stage are caused by this factor and not by suggestibility. We shall come back to this point later, and for the time being we will concern ourselves with a further aspect of the above theory. Welch and Corn-Becker have made this contention the basis for postulating that hypnotic hypersuggestibility is merely an expression of a form of generalized conditioning. As seen earlier, Corn-Becker et al. have indeed found evidence which, at least, makes the actuality of the hypothesis possible. On the other hand, as Sarbin (385) remarked, it still remains to be shown that hypnosis can actually be induced in an experimental situation comparable to the one Corn-Becker and his associates studied. To this we should add that it also remains to be demonstrated that *no other* mechanism can account for waking suggestibility and for hypersuggestibility.

Strong arguments and evidence against the above as well as for the existence of an alternate mechanism do indeed exist. To begin with, all the suggestions involved in the early stages of trance induction are relatively simple waking suggestions, which can be elicited singly in a great many individuals under conditions that preclude the possibility of a generalized conditioning taking place, and for which the critical helpful factors listed by Corn-Becker and by Welch are absent. But this is not all. More specific arguments can be found against the acceptance as a whole of these investigators' theory. First, although it could account in certain cases for primary hypersuggestibility, it is not readily applicable to secondary suggestibility, not to mention tertiary suggestibility. Second, these various suggestibilities can be evoked under conditions that are anything but favorable for the establishment of a conditioned response. Finally, to jump a little ahead, the nature of posthypnotic phenomena does not entirely fit into a theory that makes hypnotic hypersuggestibility nothing more than the generalization of a conditioned response, even when abstract and delayed conditioning are taken into account. In spite of all this, we must not discard too hurriedly the results and the theory of this group of investigators. They have opened the way to a promising field of inquiry and, as will be shown later, have after all furnished a *partial* explanation for hypnotic hypersuggestibility.

The results reported by Hull, Eysenck, and their associates lead to a tempting alternative theory, according to which hypnotic hypersuggestibility would be nothing more than a cumulative effect. As a matter of fact, Hull's thoughts have followed along this line. It is not difficult to conceive that hypnosis is merely an expression of hypersuggestibility brought about by a combination of homoaction and heteroaction resulting from the successive responses of subjects to a series of graded waking suggestions. One of the weaknesses of this hypothesis is that it offers no explanation for the subject's initial responses to the suggestions. However, the main stumbling block is heteroaction itself. For, as has been seen, the bulk of the trance-inducing suggestions are primary in nature, particularly in the early waking phase of the induction. Then too, there is the observation that hypnotic suggestibility is primary, and hence should not show heteroaction. On the other hand, it is not possible to solve the question by identifying hypnotic hypersuggestibility with a cumulated homoaction alone, for there is no question that *heteroactive hypersuggestibility is as much a characteristic property of hypnosis as is homoaction.*

As stated a moment ago, the bulk of the trance-inducing suggestions consists of items that are primary in nature. There are, however, a number of items that for the time being remain unclassified in this respect. We do not know whether suggestions of drowsiness or of sleep are primary, secondary, or tertiary. Is it then possible that these few items might be responsible for the production of heteroaction in the case of trance-inducing suggestions? Both this property and the possession of these items seem to be unique to them. There is a reason to believe that this is an unlikely solution, for, as has also been seen, primary suggestions, which otherwise never show any appreciable heteroaction, have a unique heteroactive influence on trance induction, in spite of the fact that they do not include the above items.

The problem therefore remains, and we must continue to question how we can account for the appearance of heteroaction in an instance when homoaction alone can be expected.

Let us approach the matter in another way. Two things can be said with certainty in regard to the existence of heteroaction and homoaction. Hull and his co-workers showed (*a*) that homoactive hypersuggestibility could be produced; and (*b*) that heteroactive *and* homoactive hypersuggestibility could be created together. But it has never been shown whether heteroaction could occur independently of homoaction; whether, in fact, it did or did not depend on homoaction for its existence. Nor have its specific properties been investigated. Since homoactive hypersuggestibility appears to have an independent existence, we may think for the time being, as we have done implicitly in previous pages, of hypnotic hypersuggestibility being made up of two *components*: a homoactive and a heteroactive component. However, there are better reasons than the one just mentioned for believing this. First of all, Krueger reported that, after the subject woke from the trance state, his hypersuggestibility dropped fairly rapidly to the 20 per cent level of hypersuggestibility (that is, the subject was only 20 per cent more suggestible than normal) and remained there for an indefinite time. Because of the design of the experiment, this fact applies only to the homoactive aspect of hypnotic hypersuggestibility. What happens to the heteroactive aspect was not investigated. Now, interestingly enough, and rather suggestive, according to the work of Hull and his men, cumulated homoactive hypersuggestibility produced in the waking state appears to have a ceiling value that also corresponds to just about the 20 per cent level. In effect then, upon the waking from hypnosis, the subject's suggestibility *falls back to the maximum attainable with homoaction in the waking state*. It is as if trance-inducing suggestions raised the subject's suggestibility up to a certain point (the 20 per cent level) by means of homoaction, *and then beyond this* (the 60 per cent level or better) through some other mechanism, presumably heteroaction. Second, it is rather significant in this connection that, as we saw in Chapter 4, the drop in hypersuggestibility which follows waking reaches the 20 per cent level in about 60 minutes. Actually, half of the total drop has taken place in about the first 7 minutes, and better than two thirds of it in the first 20 minutes. In contrast, the decay of homoaction produced in the waking state causes a decrease of only 9 per cent in 24 hours, a negligible amount compared to the above loss. This, in itself, would indicate that whatever portion of hypnotic hypersuggestibility is lost in the first 60 minutes after waking is not homoactive in nature. Last, but not least, is the fact reported by Williams and others that the homoactive effect can be produced equally well in waking as in hypnosis. In fact there appears to be no qualitative or quantitative differences. If, however, hypnotic hypersuggestibility was merely cumulated homoaction, would it be possible to produce further homoaction in it, particularly in amount equal to that possible in its absence? It is not logical. In the light of Krueger's results, we can be even more categorical and state that, theoretically, *it is not possible.* For, if his results are taken to apply to homoactive hypersuggestibility, and since according to them suggestibility most probably reaches its *maximum* when hypnosis appears, *further homoaction in hypnosis is precluded.* But, if, as has been proposed, part of hypnotic hypersuggestibility is not the result of homoaction, then there is place for further homoaction, in spite of an apparent maximum in suggestibility. Since there is still some question whether hypnotic suggestibility remains at its maximum level during the trance or drops slightly below this value shortly after closure of the eyelids, this last bit of evidence cannot be considered irrefutable. Fortunately the first two arguments are very strong. Consequently there seems to be little doubt regarding the hypothesis that the homoactive aspect of hypnosis is distinct from its heteroactive aspect, although it does not necessarily follow that they are completely independent of each other.

Besides the above direct evidence, other facts exist which also lend support to the hypothesis. These are worth mentioning briefly. If we examine the reports of Hull, Eysenck, and their associates, we find certain facts that appear to be at variance with our common everyday knowledge of hypnosis, a knowledge well established by nearly a century of practice. So much so that we might be led to conclude that these investigators did not always induce the same state as the one we have come to call hypnosis by usage. For instance, Krueger showed that hypnosis appeared to reach its maximum depth shortly after closure of the eyelids. It is a known fact, however, that this same depth can usually be materially increased after this response. Also, as we have seen, Eysenck and Furneaux have shown that, although there is a high correlation between response to postural sway suggestions, or, more generally, suggestions of primary type, and susceptibility to hypnosis, primary suggestibility accounts for only a little more than 50 per cent of the susceptibility. This is fully in line with the well-known fact that in practice many individuals respond poorly to such suggestions and yet turn out to be excellent hypnotic subjects, and conversely. Again, Krueger observed a sharp decline in hypersuggestibility following waking. But from practice we know that many subjects will maintain a high level of waking hypersuggestibility if they are so instructed in the trance. Finally, there are some indications that in practice a greater homoactive effect and a particularly broader heteroactive effect are obtained following trance induction, than the results reported by Hull and his associates would appear to indicate. Since the explanation for these discrepancies will be presented in the pages to follow, no further attempts at accounting for them will be made at this time. It will be stated simply that the resolution of the differences evolves directly out of the hypothesis that hypnotic hypersuggestibility possesses at least two separate components.

The Generalization of Suggestibility

It is therefore my belief that, when all the facts concerning hypnosis and suggestibility are considered, they point to one basic conclusion: *Hypnosis is the outcome of not one but of several temporally overlapping and interacting processes.* Homoaction is one of these processes. Another is a process that can best be described as a *generalization of suggestibility* because of the outward resemblance it has to a spreading or generalization of an initially specific effect to a more inclusive field of action. A preliminary and incomplete picture of the mechanism responsible for hypnosis which may now be proposed along this line of thinking is as follows: Initially, waking suggestions bring about an increasing state of homoaction as well as some generalization. As the trance-inducing suggestions progress, more generalization and homoaction are produced with the additional influence of already existing generalization and homoaction now facilitating this growth. As this progression proceeds, generalization becomes more and more predominant and eventually *masks* the ever-present homoaction. When this happens, a characteristic state of heteroactive hypersuggestibility appears to be present. For the time being, this last-mentioned state may be referred to as "hypnosis." As a help in visualizing this complex

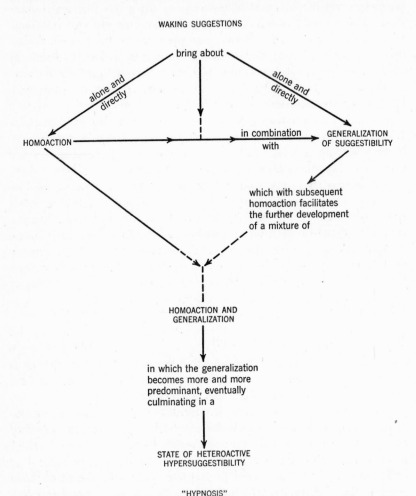

FIG. 4. The Production of Heteroactive Hypersuggestibility or "Hypnosis"

pattern of actions and interactions, the diagram in Figure 4 is offered.

It may be well to remark that in this schema certain observables are postulated to be highly variable. Thus, the place in the sequence of events where generalization first appears and that at which homoaction ceases to be distinguishable from generalization are strictly functions of each individual subject and of the conditions under which the induction is carried out (this includes the environment of the subject). The same may be said of the degree and quality of generalization reached at the termination of the induction. Some individuals may show very little generalization but considerable homoaction. Others may show neither. Still others may show generalization of a high degree right from the start. Again, after homoaction ceases to be distinguishable from generalization, some individuals may develop generalization much further or may never show more than just enough to mask the homoaction. A little thought will show the reader that this describes rather well the various situations encountered in practice.

It also helps us to understand why, although trance-inducing suggestions are largely, if not entirely, of primary type, and are not expected to produce heteroaction, yet they do just this. Theoretically, as will be seen later, any waking primary suggestion should be capable of inducing some generalization. In fact this is true also for other suggestion types. However, for reasons to be taken up later, trance-inducing suggestions, besides causing homoaction, are particularly effective in causing generalization. We are then faced with an instance of waking suggestions being capable of bringing about *both* homo-action and a relatively high degree of generalization.

The Physiological Basis of Homoaction and of Generalization

The reader should not think at this point that this is the end of the matter. There is much more to be said. However, at this time we must turn our attention toward an examination of the physiological mechanisms that might be postulated as responsible for suggestibility, homoaction, and the generalization of suggestibility.

Clues concerning the nature of suggestibility come from a variety of sources, including the investigations of homoaction itself. Possibly the first of these clues comes from the demonstration by Hull (213) that having the subject imagine a response instead of suggesting it to him is equally effective insofar as postural sway suggestions are concerned. This has been further substantiated, as we know, by Berreman and Hilgard (29), Arnold (6), and Schultz (404). The work of Schultz is of particular interest here because he did not limit himself to postural sway only but claimed to have brought about a great many of the phenomena associated with hypnosis through imagining alone. On the basis of these various reports, Arnold (6) has suggested that imagining is the key to understanding hypnosis and has developed a theory in which the two are essentially equated. In the light of existing data, this may be a somewhat premature conclusion. It might have been more correct if Arnold had said that the two appear to have some common factors.

Another clue to a solution of the problem is derived from the investigation of Williams (488), who showed that, when an individual simulates, that is, carries out voluntarily the responses expected to result normally from suggestions, this action apparently facilitates further simulation to a repetition of the suggestions. It would seem as though homoaction had its genesis in the act of responding per se or, again, that it is a property of the neuromuscular apparatus itself. This has also been the contention of a number of investigators, foremost among them Eysenck (131), who concluded that primary suggestibility is an expression of *ideomotor action*. His arguments for this, derived from his studies of primary suggestibility, are not overly convincing. More satisfactory reasons for supporting this point of view can be obtained from the existence of homoaction itself. For, as will be shown in a moment, if there is such a phenomenon as ideomotor action, it is possible to predict and account for homoaction entirely in terms of existing physiological data on neuromuscular processes.

Let us consider first the question of the existence of ideomotor action. If we disregard temporarily the problem of the exact nature of this phenomenon, there appears to be little reason to doubt its reality. Schultz (404), Vandell et al. (447), Lee (256), Max (293), and Jacobson (222), among others,* have shown quite satisfactorily that thought can give rise to specific patterns of muscular tension and activity, particularly in those muscles that are symbolically represented in the thought in question.

In order to account for homoaction, we must consider, in conjunction with ideomotor action, certain phenomena characteristic of nervous and muscular tissues, namely:

(*a*) *Summation effects* such as spatial and temporal summation, quantal summation, latent addition, treppe, recruitment, fusion, and tetanus.

(*b*) Effects such as reinforcement, augmentation, afterdischarge, spread, and rebound.

(*c*) Certain facilitating effects of spinal and cerebral origin, as well as some similar effects of interneuronic nature, all of which may or may not be distinct from the above-listed phenomena.

(*d*) The existence of trains and volleys of nerve impulses.

* Further references will be found in Eysenck's book (131).

(e) The increase of the strength of muscular responses by the presence of tonus.

One of the most significant aspects of the present theory which arises out of the known physiology of neuromuscular processes is that the various phenomena just listed for muscles and nerves are definitely known to be responsible *for the transformation of directly unobservable tissue changes into gross observable muscular contractions.*   Furthermore, they are known to be responsible *for the enhancement of muscular response.*

In particular, microscopic contractions of muscles are built up by these means into macroscopic contractions.†   For any given situation, there will be a great many possible combinations of the various effects that have been listed, all leading to the above end result.   The entire process is a *general* neuromuscular phenomenon and property which may be appropriately called *neuromotor enhancement.*

As it is understood today, normal muscular action itself is the result of asynchronic summation combining the various phenomena that have just been considered.   That is, the basis of normal muscular action is the building up by various summation effects, hence by neuromotor enhancement, of very small and even *latent* muscular contractions into large sustained contractions.   Normally, muscular responses associated with thinking can be expected to be minute and not to give rise to overt motion.   If, however, it is true that thoughts of muscular action, not specifically directed at producing actual muscular movements, nevertheless do cause the same tissue changes in the muscles concerned as are initiated by voluntary action, then are we led to infer that, under favorable conditions, *the minute responses initiated by thoughts can be built up to relatively huge proportions through neuromotor enhancement.*

This statement contains in essence the entire physiological basis of primary suggestibility.   Briefly we may suppose that the initial statement of the suggestion implants or, better, evokes, certain specific thoughts in the subject's mind.   Concurrently, small changes occur in appropriate muscle fibers.   These changes may be no more than the formation of a local state of excitation, or may consist in an actual propagated state of excitation.   Again, a single muscle fiber may be involved, or many.   In any event the ground for a contraction has been laid.   With subsequent repetitions, the local state of excitation, if one

† It is beyond the scope of this book to delve into the intricacies of nerve and muscle physiology.   The reader will find excellent discussions of these topics in Fulton (151) and in Houssay (211).

has been produced, builds up until a critical value is reached, where-upon a wave of contraction appears. We must not forget, however, the contributions of the nervous system to the over-all enhancement. The production of quantal summation, tetanus, and asynchronic summation are very much dependent on neural activity when taking place in situ. At first a single nerve impulse, a very small train, or more probably a small volley is initiated. With repetition and/or with increase in intensity of thoughts, the volley grows, and trains either appear or increase (within limits) if already present. In addition, the frequency of impulse also rises. All this leads to greater complexity and magnitude of the induced muscular effects. In this wise, *homoaction appears to be merely a form of neuromotor enhancement combined with ideomotor action.* It should be kept in mind that homoaction is defined *in relation to suggestions.* For this reason it is not merely enhancement.

In brief, we need only substitute the word "suggestion" for "thought" in the definition of ideomotor action to obtain a physiological basis for suggestibility and homoaction. It is possibly significant in this connection that very often, especially with subjects of relatively low suggestibility, suggestions of muscular movement (such as levitation of the hand) lead at first to slight twitches, then to trembling, and, finally, to abortive and partial responses. With continuation of the suggestions, these muscular responses are usually found to increase in strength and frequency of occurrence, and tend more and more to fuse, eventually giving rise to the full response. It is as if one were watching enhancement in the making.

Further evidence supporting this interpretation of the nature of homoaction comes from a number of sources. Thus, for instance, Arnold (6) has demonstrated that the effectiveness of suggestions of postural sway is a direct function of the subject's vividness of imagery. Finally, there is also the basic observation that repetition is an essential factor in the production of suggestion phenomena. Nearly all investigators agree on this last point.

Concurrently with the various physiological processes that have been described, the general situation usually associated with the administration of suggestions, especially those aimed at producing hypnosis, possesses factors that, I believe, favor the development of ideomotor action and its overt expression. There are three principal factors. First is the focusing of the subject's attention on certain ideas contained in the suggestions. This has a double effect. It tends to maintain the suggested thoughts in the mind of the subject and also tends to prevent the formation of extraneous thoughts. The net effect is a stronger, steadier stream of nerve impulses to the muscles and the elimination of other patterns of muscular tension which might either oppose or at least mask the desired effect. Second, once a definite state of contraction has been established, there follows a state of tonic contraction over and above the normal resting level. This, as is known, tends to favor subsequent responses. Finally, a condition of relaxation usually accompanies the suggestions. Data reported by Barry et al. (14) have indicated that relaxation has an influence on suggestibility, although in what direction is not clear. One would expect it to (a) equalize tonus, while allowing it to remain, and (b) tend to bring about a state of uniform muscular tension equivalent to a muscular "tabula rasa." Consequently, any pattern of muscular tension that may be impressed will tend to stand out, however small it may be. In addition, being alone, it will be in a better position to bring about actual contractions. Thus relaxation may be expected to facilitate suggestibility.

There remains one fundamental question. If we admit that ideomotor action is the basis of suggestibility, what is its own neurophysiological nature? This is a difficult question to answer in the present state of our knowledge. The most satisfactory explanation at present seems to be that ideomotor action is a *complex conditioned response,* or *habit* phenomenon. Certainly, as Hull (213) has indicated, suggestibility (at least of primary type) shares many of the traits that have come to be associated with habits—so much so that Hull has proposed that hypersuggestibility is nothing more than habit formation. There would seem to be some truth in this, at least insofar as ideomotor action is concerned. In any event, ignorance of the exact nature of this phenomenon does not warrant its denial. Ideomotor action is too well established now as a phenomenon to be reckoned with for us to ignore it. The reader may find the diagram in Figure 5 of some help in visualizing the above material.

All of this has taken us up to the generalization of suggestibility, for which we must now account. The situation here is fortunately simpler. In brief, generalization of suggestibility to date can best be identified with what Welch (467) and Corn-Becker et al. (81) have called *abstract conditioning.* The ideas and facts behind this notion have been adequately presented by these investigators, and the reader may best be referred back to the original articles for the details. However, to state the matter briefly, conditioning can apparently become generalized to a complex stimulus situation as a whole on the basis of a very *general structural resemblance* instead of on the usual basis of specific content and/or specific elements. Applied to the

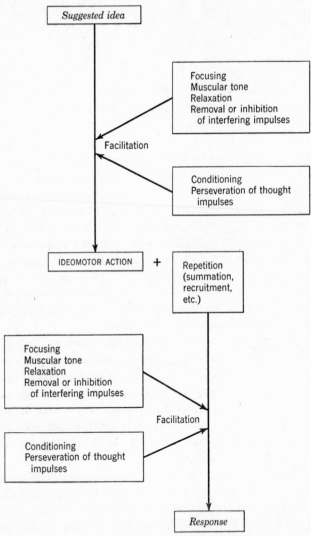

FIG. 5. How Suggested Ideas Produce Motor Responses

induction of hypnosis, this would result from the fact that at first the suggestions given suggest and coincide with events that would take place anyway; that is, there is a natural tendency for individuals to give the response because of normal physiological events called forth by the situation. The above investigators refer to the use of such natural events as "hocus-pocus." This last really seems uncalled for. Be it as it may, a conditioning situation is thus brought into existence. In each instance, the fact that the statements made by the hypnotist in his suggestions always turn out to be correct acts as the basis for the generalization. Eventually, a tendency is created in the subject to carry out suggested responses, even for situations in which they would not normally take place of their own. It should be emphasized that the above is the interpretation given by Welch and his associates. There is definite evidence that something of this sort does take place. Furthermore, it fits rather well into the present theory of hypnosis. There is some question in my mind as to how great a part the so-called "hocus-pocus" plays in the production of generalization, that is, in bringing about abstract conditioning. It is true that one can trick the subject into giving the desired responses for certain suggestions and that one often does so as part of the trance-induction technique. However, it is my contention that *ideomotor action and homoaction are far more basic and that, alone, they can give rise to responses that may serve as a basis for bringing about abstract conditioning.* In practice, "hocus-pocus" does help, but it is not essential. Furthermore I am inclined to believe that a large portion of the so-called natural tendency to carry out responses independently of true suggestibility effects may actually be in part the result of true ideomotor action and homoaction.

As was pointed out a little while back, abstract conditioning (if this be generalization) theoretically can take place anywhere in the process of trance induction. It has been stated by some learning theorists that conditioning can occur as the result of a *single* trial. If so, it is clear that "hypnosis" viewed as a conditioning phenomenon in the above sense could take place in the absence of trance-inducing suggestions as a mere consequence of the subject's responding to a suggestion planned to be a waking suggestion. There are indications that this does happen. But whether as the result of one-trial conditioning is another question.

In summary, thus far, "hypnosis" is seen as resulting at first from ideomotor action (suggestibility) and neuromotor enhancement (homoaction), possibly helped along at times by natural tendencies (hocus-pocus). As the induction progresses, abstract conditioning (generalization) makes its appearance and gives rise eventually to a state of heteroactive hypersuggestibility—"hypnosis."

Awareness and Hypnosis

One might hope that homoaction and abstract conditioning fully account for the nature of hypnosis. Unfortunately, this does not appear to be so at present. In the first place, a very extensive and powerful generalization sometimes takes place under conditions that appear to preclude any conditioning. Second, the complexity of some of the phenomena that may be evoked is not entirely consistent with conditioning alone. Finally, and foremost, the general behavior of the hypnotized individual shows a degree of individuality and of independent mentation that would not be observed if conditioning were the only motive and directive force.‡ The recognition of this last fact is of paramount importance in my estimation.

There is ample evidence that hypnosis involves activity of the higher centers. As Sarbin (385) has remarked, it is rather widely accepted today that hypnosis and its associated phenomena involve integration at the cerebral level. This is nicely demonstrated for instance by the work on the effect of hypnosis on memory and learning. We might have been led to such a conclusion from a mere consideration of the nature of suggestion. For the latter involves imparting intelligence to the subject by means, usually, of a highly symbolic verbal language. Such a process must of necessity involve higher-center activities. The importance of suggestions seen *as a form of communication* cannot be ignored. One of the more difficult aspects of hypnosis to explain is the *persistence* of the influence of suggestions or commands long after they have been given. Obviously a more lasting *substitute* for the suggestion stimulus maintains the sequence of events that has been initiated until the concluding step has been reached. It may be of significance here that nothing at all comparable to hypnosis in man can be produced in animals, as may be gathered from Chapter 9. Although the details of the mechanism by which this persistence is accomplished are not available at this time, there would seem to be indications that *hypnosis is a unique property of language, of man's ability to use symbolic processes, and of their actual existence in man.*

Many of the data existing today show beyond a doubt that the behavior of the hypnotized subject is determined not only by the content of the suggestions given to him but also by his own personality structure, content, and dynamics, and finally by various situational factors. Any or none of these factors may be predominant for a given

‡ Unless one takes the position that all behavior is strictly determined and is entirely accountable in terms of conditioning.

hypnotic situation. Thus the great diversity of aspects under which hypnosis appears in the literature.

The molding of the subject's responses by his personality is so striking at times that a number of investigators, among them White (483), have interpreted hypnotic behavior as resulting from a goal-directed striving in which the subject behaves the way he does because he tries to act in the manner defined for him by the hypnotist. Sarbin (385), recognizing this aspect, has chosen a different interpretation, seeing in hypnosis a form of "role-taking." There is another alternative interpretation which is very attractive for its simplicity: *The subject behaves the way he does because it is the only pattern of behavior consistent with his present perception of his environment.* To state this another way, if the subject behaves in a manner apparently at variance with the existing state of affairs in his actual environment, the reason is that he does not perceive the latter in its true color. *His awareness has been altered.*

This alteration of awareness in hypnosis is especially well demonstrated in the production of antisocial acts under hypnosis. Here we find the subject behaving strictly *in accordance with his perception* of a situation that has been defined for him by the hypnotist. Again, it may be of no little significance, for instance, that part of Erickson's (115) very effective technique for the production of color blindness by suggestions was aimed at removing the "meaning" of specific colors from the mind of the subject. The close relationship between "meaning" and awareness suggests that an alteration in awareness is indeed fundamental in the production of suggested color blindness. As a matter of fact, Erickson is very emphatic, in this study as well as elsewhere, about the need to allow the subject a sufficient amount of time to become fully integrated into the hypnotic situation if typical results are to be obtained. This is understandable in view of what has just been said. Excellent support for the claim that awareness is or can be altered by hypnotic suggestion also comes from data by Barker and Burgwin (12, 13). As will be remembered, these two investigators were able to demonstrate that EEG patterns typical of sleep could be produced during hypnosis by giving suggestions specifically aimed at bringing about a state resembling sleep.

To understand how the alteration of awareness comes about, we must now turn to still another characteristic of the trance-induction situation. As is well known, the process of producing hypnosis usually involves focusing the subject's attention on a very restricted range of stimuli, keeping it there, and progressively narrowing it down further.

In this manner, both internally and externally initiated impulses, hence activities, are reduced to a minimum, with the exception of those initiated by stimuli from the area of focused attention. Normally the subject would be expected to fall asleep, were it not for this one center of cerebral activity which effectively keeps him "awake" in a limited way. There is thus a constriction of consciousness, which in essence involves a *dissociation of awareness from* the majority of sensory and even strictly neural events that are taking place.

It may seem strange that dissociation should be introduced here, in the light of the history of the dissociation theory of hypnosis. As the reader will recall, the evidence obtained from experiments led Hull (213) to conclude that hypnosis is not a state of dissociation, in the sense that functional independence could not be demonstrated.

One may, however, argue against the acceptance of Hull's evidence as being conclusive. We know that some nonhypnotized individuals exhibit a phenomenon that certainly is best described by the term dissociation. Its resemblance to hypnosis in certain respects was originally responsible for the genesis of the dissociation theory of hypnosis. It is a fact, however, that *it has never been demonstrated that a functional independence is present in spontaneous dissociation.* Rather, certain experiments performed in connection with cases of conversion hysteria appear to indicate that the contrary is true. If we agree, for the time being, that the phenomenon just alluded to is properly labeled, then Hull's results do not demonstrate that hypnosis is different in nature from spontaneous dissociation. What these results do indicate is that either the latter state is improperly labeled or that we must revise our notion of "dissociation."

A better reason yet exists for asserting that there is no inconsistency in speaking of dissociation of awareness, as has been done in connection with the present theory, even though the arguments against Hull's interpretation should prove invalid. It is that we are not speaking here of quite the same thing as Hull and his co-workers considered. The term "dissociation" is capable of describing a number of different psychophysiological states or phenomena, and as employed in the present discussion *does not presuppose functional independence.* To be more specific, the dissociation in question is one of awareness *from* those events that otherwise would form part of its content. In contrast, Hull and his associates appear to consider dissociation as being entirely *within* the content of awareness itself. That is, they see it as a breaking up of connections between groups of elements forming this content, each group thereby acquiring autonomy. No such a separation is postulated in the present idea. Furthermore, whereas the older dissociation theory connected hypnosis with a pathological, or at least an abnormal, condition, this is not done here. On the contrary, the type of dissociation we are concerned with is a phenomenon to be found in normal everyday life. Whatever else awareness may be, it can be said to be a very plastic, even fluid, transitory quality which is attached to various groups of psychophysiological processes. It may be all-inclusive, or seemingly absent. From moment to moment its content changes. One instant events are in our awareness, in the next moment drop out of it, and at a still later time reappear in it. This dissociation and reintegration of events from and into awareness is a constant characteristic of every waking moment of our life. But, characteristically, whether or not we are aware of specific psychophysiological events taking place in us, these go on unaltered. Thus no functional independence needs to be postulated here, insofar as the elements that form the content of awareness are concerned. In hypnosis the situation presumably remains very much the same as in waking, the only difference being that the dissociation from awareness in this case takes on the form of a more permanent and drastic constriction of awareness.

In any event, whatever name we use to describe the observed narrowing of consciousness in hypnosis, the over-all picture would appear to indicate that the *full* development of hypnosis depends on a *last stage* consisting of the following elements: There is a narrowing of consciousness brought about largely by the hypnotic situation itself, and of such a magnitude and nature as to limit to the voice of the hypnotist the source of stimuli to which the subject is responsive. Generalization adds to this effect by introducing a situation in which each assertion of the hypnotist acquires the value of nonsymbolic (that is, actual) stimuli such as are normally acting on the subject. Finally, helping to make this last action more complete, we have the well-known phenomenon of sensory projection. In the final analysis we have an induced situation in which the subject's normal awareness has been largely displaced by the voice of the hypnotist. This is essentially the picture arrived at by Kubie and Margolin (247) when they describe hypnosis as a dissolution of the boundaries between the subject's ego and the external world, in such a way that the voice of the hypnotist becomes an "extension of the subject's own psychic processes."

To sum up the full process of trance induction by the standard technique, the following may be said: It appears to involve for certain at least two distinct phases, with very strong possibilities in favor of a third phase. All of these complement each other, and are interwoven, although each appears to have a different mechanism of action and different end results when considered singly. There is an initial period during which the primary suggestibility of the subject is made to manifest itself and to increase through homoaction. This is *phase I*, culminating and ending approximately with actual closure of the eyelids. It may be called the *pretrance period*. Overlapping this and

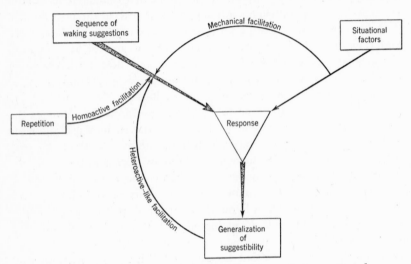

Fig. 6.   The First Phase of Trance Induction or Pretrance Period

continuing it, we have the *period of trance induction proper*, or *phase II*, characterized mainly by generalization of suggestibility and increasing dissociation. Finally, with the full appearance of dissociation and termination of phase II, we have the *third* and final phase, *hypnosis proper*. These various phases will be found diagrammed in Figures 6 and 7.

Generally speaking, the speed of trance induction will depend largely on how early the generalization and dissociation make their appearance. Similarly, the depth of trance attained will be a function of the degree of generalization and dissociation obtained. Some individuals never become dissociated (or very little) but nevertheless may show a strong generalization. Others may become dissociated without showing any evidence of much generalization. Possibly these are the so-called "passive"-type subjects. It is clear that, if dissociation in the form of constriction of awareness takes place but generalization does not, we will have a subject who is largely unresponsive, since the only source of stimulation to which he is sensitive has not acquired the power to act as a source of surrogate stimuli, that is, in the capacity of an adequate stimulus.

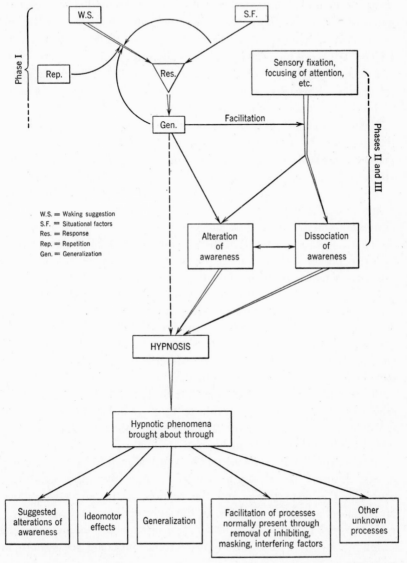

Fig. 7. The Complete Induction of Hypnosis. Production of Hypnotic Phenomena

Before concluding this chapter, we should consider so-called "*waking hypnosis.*" Wells (473) more than any other investigator has been a firm believer that all phenomena obtained when hypnosis is induced by means of suggestions of sleep can be brought about without recourse to this technique (which may be called the sleep technique). That the idea of sleep is not essential in the production of the classical trance state has been shown by such investigators as Adler and Secunda (2), Schneck (395), Sargant and Fraser (389), and by Rosen. (376). All these men have devised techniques of induction which do not necessitate the use of the notion of sleep but instead emphasize relaxation. Rosen has suggested that we might designate this form of trance induction as the *sensorimotor method.*

A comparison of the material described by these investigators with that reported by Wells shows no essential differences, aside from the greater complexity of the induction suggestions and the fact that they are specifically designed to bring about hypnotic hypersuggestibility in the former case. Thus, the sensorimotor method may be said to bring about "waking hypnosis" too. The question still remains to be answered whether this type of hypnosis is different from classical hypnosis. It is my belief that there is no essential difference between hypnosis proper and "waking hypnosis," particularly when induced by the sensorimotor method. For the theory that has been presented in the preceding pages admits of this very possibility, that is, of inducing hypnosis without recourse to sleep suggestions. Primary suggestibility, homoaction, and generalization are not at all dependent on the presence of specific references to sleep or relaxation, or even eyelid closure. In addition, the techniques described by Wells, and particularly by Rosen, Adler and Secunda, and others, can be expected eventually to lead many subjects into a state of dissociated awareness, since they involve elements comparable to those found to favor the same event in the sleep technique. It must be emphasized that, no more than the other three steps in hypnotic induction, does dissociation of awareness specifically depend on the suggestions of sleep, relaxation, or eye closure. The theory as a whole implies that other conditions could do the same thing, and the reports of the above-mentioned investigators are proof of this. In the light of these facts, it appears valid to speak of hypnosis in either type of situation, taking the sleep technique merely as the prototype of trance-inducing suggestions or techniques.

Summary and Conclusions

It might have been pointed out at the beginning of this chapter that in approaching such a topic as hypnosis and hypersuggestibility there are two alternatives. It may be assumed that a single mechanism or process is responsible for the observed phenomena, as has been assumed in past theories; or the opposite view may be taken, as was done here, that the *observed phenomena have a multiple origin,* that hypnotic hypersuggestibility is not a unitary phenomenon. More specifically, the theory advanced in the previous pages proposes the following principal ideas:

1. Suggestibility phenomena have a multiple origin. They are the expression of a number of different mechanisms or processes which at times act in unison and at times act separately. In particular, during trance induction pretrance phenomena, especially in the early stages, have a different origin from those of later phases of trance induction.

2. Hypnosis itself is a state of hypersuggestibility arising from an orderly sequence of psychosomatic and somatopsychic interactions. It is a psychic as well as a physiological state and differs from the normal waking state in a number of respects. The characteristic hypersuggestibility itself arises through two different mechanisms, one causing homoactive hypersuggestibility, the other producing heteroactive hypersuggestibility.

3. Psychologically speaking, hypnosis is a state of altered awareness, the character of which is the chief determinant of the subject's behavior when hypnotized. That is, the subject behaves the way he does because it is the most consistent form of behavior for him in terms of his actual perceptions.

4. The psychophysiological basis of suggestibility is *ideomotor action,* itself a form of conditioning.

5. The physiological bases of hypersuggestibility are (*a*) *neuromotor enhancement* (homoaction), and (*b*) *abstract conditioning* (generalization or heteroaction).

6. The psychophysiological basis of the hypnotic alteration of awareness is a combined selective inhibition and excitation of various cerebral regions leading to a dissociation of awareness *from* all stimuli except the voice of the hypnotist, unless otherwise specified by suggestions.

7. Through hypersuggestibility and dissociation of awareness, the words of the hypnotist acquire the value of actual stimulus objects. His voice becomes an extension, so to speak, of the subject's psychic processes. This opens the way to a large variety of perceptual alterations.

It should be emphasized that the above applies only to primary suggestibility and hypnosis. To what extent, if any, it also applies to secondary and tertiary suggestibility will be the subject matter of the next chapter.

·20·

The Nature of
Secondary and
Tertiary Suggestibility

In the previous chapter primary suggestibility was identified with ideomotor action. Since Eysenck and Furneaux (129) have shown that secondary suggestibility has a very low correlation with primary suggestibility and hypnosis, a totally different theory may be required to account for the former than was presented in Chapter 19. Tertiary suggestibility poses still another problem because of its "in-between" character.

One of the major difficulties in attempting to determine the exact nature of secondary and tertiary suggestibility is that relatively little is known concerning their properties. There is much ambiguity in their case, even in regard to homoaction and heteroaction. The little that is known with some certainty may be summed up as follows:

(a) Secondary suggestibility tends to give rise to bell-shaped distribution curves, whereas primary and tertiary suggestibility tend to bring about U- and J-shaped distributions.

(b) On the Matrix test for intelligence, secondary suggestibility has a negative linear correlation with intelligence as contrasted to the possibly curvilinear correlation observed for primary suggestibility.

(c) There is little correlation, if any, between secondary suggestibility and primary suggestibility (or hypnosis). There is some correlation between hypnosis and tertiary suggestibility. In contrast, primary suggestibility is highly correlated with hypnosis.

(d) The suggestions involved in primary suggestibility on the one hand and in secondary suggestibility on the other hand *are very different in character.*

These various distinctive characteristics are not of equal weight. Eysenck and Furneaux (129) have presented arguments in support of the claim that the U and J character of the distributions obtained for tests of primary suggestibility is an artifact superimposed upon distributions that are basically Gaussian. Briefly, these authors account for the observed distributions mainly by assuming the existence of a threshold and a ceiling for the tests of primary suggestibility that were employed. It remains to be shown, however, that this is a property of the tests and not of primary suggestibility itself. Eysenck and Furneaux have attempted to demonstrate that it is a property of the tests, but their proof is not absolute, and alternative modes of reasoning leading to the opposite conclusion exist. Eysenck (131) has also questioned the curvilinearity of the correlation between primary suggestibility and intelligence, declaring that this is an artifact. According to him, the latter has its genesis in the degrees and distribution of psychoneurosis and also in the distribution of sex among the subjects employed in the investigation. If this be correct, it remains to be explained why these same groups of subjects gave a linear correlation in secondary suggestibility. The fact that in this instance the presence of the very same factor did not lead to a curvilinear correlation prompts us to conclude that secondary suggestibility must involve additional rectifying influences and hence must still be differentiated from primary suggestibility in respect to intelligence. In any event, the sign and values of the linear correlations reported by Eysenck for primary suggestibility are ambiguous.

Fortunately, we do not have to rely entirely on these two features. There is little question but that primary suggestibility (and hypnosis) has a very low correlation with secondary suggestibility and that tertiary suggestibility has a somewhat larger, but still small, correlation with the former. Insofar as secondary suggestibility is concerned, and assuming that the theory of the last chapter is valid, this leads us to conclude that either (a) ideomotor action plays no, or very little, part in it, or (b) ideomotor action is a determinant, but its action is masked by one or more additional factors (two opposing trends tending to neutralize each other). As for tertiary suggestibility, if the latter really exists as a distinct type, it clearly must depend on one or more factors common to hypnosis and to secondary suggestibility. It does not follow, however, that the common factors are determining processes themselves, such as ideomotor action would be.

We may hope to uncover further information by studying the character of the suggestions that elicit each type of suggestibility. Suggestions that cause primary suggestibility to manifest itself are "direct" in nature; that is, they consist of direct statements of the expected (desired) responses that they describe. On the other hand, in secondary (and tertiary) suggestibility, "indirection" * appears to be characteristic of the suggestions.   This last group of suggestions appears to take three main forms:

(a) The subject is led to expect by direct or implied statements that a certain class of stimuli will be presented to him, his task being either to discriminate between successive stimuli of this class or to detect their presence.   Subsequently, he is presented with actual stimuli which may either constitute a progression in respect to some characteristic as in the progressive line test or are various members of their class in respect to their common characteristic, such as in the odor illusion test.   Presently, however, in the first instance, the progressive series is changed to a succession of identical stimuli.   In the second case, the characteristic of the stimulus on which the subject's attention has been focused is removed.   Thus, in the progressive line test, first a series of progressively longer or shorter lines is shown to the subject; then it is replaced by a series of lines of identical length.   In the odor illusion test, actual samples of odorous solutions are presented to the subject, to be subsequently succeeded by a series of neutral substances (usually plain water).

(b) The subject is allowed to experience a stimulus associated with a very specific set of conditions.   Subsequently, the same set of conditions (insofar as the subject is concerned) are presented once more, but the occurrence of the stimulus is prevented, unknown to the subject.   The heat illusion test is typical of this situation.   Here the subject is allowed to see for himself that turning the knob of a dial causes a progressive rise in the temperature of a heating element.   He is usually requested to run a series of trials purportedly to determine his temperature threshold.   At some point along the test, a switch is thrown, unknown to the subject and in such a way as to prevent the element from heating.   It may be thought by some readers at this point that the heat illusion test and the odor test belong to the same category, but there are at least two reasons for making a distinction.   First, the two tests give rise to different correlations with a number of identical variables.   Second, the odor illusion test involves a *class* of stimuli, whereas the heat illusion test involves only *one* stimulus (that is, it involves a class with only one member).   This may seem to be a rather fine point.   It should be kept in mind, however, that the nervous

---

* Although dictionaries make the expression "indirection" synonymous with "trickery" and "deceit," the usual opprobrium attached to these should not be carried over to the present use of the word, since nothing like this is meant.

system is a very delicate instrument capable of making differential responses to differences of this kind.

(c) The subject is first presented with a complex stimulus and then asked a number of descriptive questions about the stimulus after its removal. Some of the questions are leading questions containing references to nonexisting elements or characteristics of elements of the stimulus. The picture report test is of this kind. In it a picture is shown to the subject. After he has been allowed an appropriate amount of time to study it, the picture is removed, and questions are asked about the contents of the picture. Some of these will be concerned with elements that were not present, such as "What color was the dog?" when actually there was no dog in the picture.

If we compare the general situation involved in the first group of suggestions (a) with the situation described by Welch (467) and Corn-Becker et al. (81), in connection with their interpretation of hypnosis as a form of abstract conditioning, it becomes apparent that we have here exactly the sort of circumstances they described. On the other hand, there seems to be little in the character of the situation that would lead to any amount of ideomotor action. As it happens, the group of suggestions described in (a) has been primarily the one employed in the past to demonstrate the existence of secondary suggestibility. Of the two alternatives considered earlier, it now appears that the one that assumes that secondary suggestibility is not ideomotor in character is probably the more correct explanation for the absence of correlation between secondary and primary suggestibility. Furthermore, it would seem that a generalization process accounts for this form of suggestibility.

The second group (b) consists of the kind of suggestions that Eysenck and Furneaux (129), among others, maintain will elicit an intermediate form of suggestibility which they have named tertiary suggestibility. Here no more than in the first group (a) does there appear to be a place for ideomotor action. This last remark is in agreement with the fact that the heat illusion test has a low correlation with the various tests for primary suggestibility, hypnosis excepted. The relatively high correlation with hypnosis seems at first to be a contradiction. Since the theory presented in Chapter 19 postulates that other processes besides ideomotor action are determinants of the hypnotic state, however, there is really no problem. The type of phenomenon brought about by the heat illusion test is suggestive of conditioning. The situation in this respect is far simpler than it presumably is with abstract conditioning. It seems reasonable to assume, if the latter not only can take place but is actually partly responsible for hypnosis, that we may well expect that conditioning takes place in the heat illusion test.

It is tempting at this point to conclude that this last accounts for the observed correlation of the test with hypnosis, by inferring that it is plausible to assume that susceptibility to abstract conditioning is positively related to susceptibility to other forms of conditioning. In addition, since the standard tests of waking suggestibility do not involve any conditioning, we have a possible explanation of why the correlation of these tests with the heat illusion test is so low—provided of course the theory evolved in this book is accepted. Unfortunately, a major difficulty presents itself in that, if the explanation for the nature of secondary suggestibility just given is correct, then we should also infer a relatively high correlation of the heat illusion with the latter. This last is contrary to fact. There is an alternative interpretation. We might expect that the heat illusion test is the sort of test for which responses are favored by a strong imagination. As has been seen in the last chapter, strength of ideomotor action and strength of imagination appear to be positively related. There should therefore be a correlation of the heat illusion test with both hypnosis and primary suggestibility, but not with secondary suggestibility, assuming of course that no other factors are involved. If, however, conditioning is also involved, we should expect to find some correlation with secondary suggestibility, a low correlation with tests of primary suggestibility other than hypnosis, and a relatively high correlation with the latter. This is quite in agreement with actual observations.

The last group of suggestions (c) is a rather puzzling one since it does not appear to be of a nature that would give rise to either ideomotor action or conditioning in any form. Certain features of the data reported by Eysenck and Furneaux (129) point to the possibility that we may be dealing here with a type of phenomenon that does not belong fully, if at all, to any of the suggestibility groups already mentioned. Examination of these data show that, though factor analysis places group (c) in the category of tests of secondary suggestibility, the distribution of responses to the picture completion test and to the ink blot test nevertheless give rise to J-shaped distributions which, as we know, are characteristic of primary suggestibility. Quite aside from the question of artifact in this instance, the above observation suggests that tests of primary suggestibility and the present group of tests have more in common with each other than the latter has with other tests of secondary suggestibility. This, however, is not all. It is also observed that responses to these two forms of suggestions show an extremely wide range of correlation with the responses to other members of the secondary suggestibility group. This sort of variability is not typical of tests of secondary suggestibility when the above-mentioned tests are excluded. Thus we obtain again an indication of a possible basic difference between the picture completion test (and other similar ones) and the more typical tests of secondary suggestibility. Finally, there are some indications that the picture completion test and the ink blot test are the more dependent on imagination as a factor. Thus, imagination would appear as a plausible common factor responsible for the observed correlations in this case. Another alternative which presents itself in accounting for the nature of this third group of suggestions is that the response to the picture completion test and other tests of a similar nature depends on the formation of a "set" and/or "expectancy." This admittedly is not a very satisfactory explanation since neither of these phenomena is well understood.

Thus far we have been concerned only with primary, secondary, and tertiary suggestibility. As pointed out quite early in this book (Chapter 2), the existing literature speaks of various kinds of suggestions in a manner that might be thought to imply that corresponding suggestibilities exist different from the above three. It behooves us therefore to consider this matter to some extent.

One classification, it will be recalled, groups suggestions as *direct* and *indirect*. Examination of such suggestions shows that the first are suggestions of primary type while the second are of secondary type.

Another widely used classification lists *prestige* and *nonprestige* suggestions. Aveling and Hargreaves (8) as well as other investigators have shown that prestige suggestions give rise to U- and J-shaped distributions. In spite of the possible artifactitious nature of these distributions, it is fairly safe to assume that they are an indication that prestige suggestions belong to the group of primary suggestions. Further evidence of this is found in an examination of the character of the various suggestions in question. The character of prestige suggestions is essentially the same as of those found in tests for primary suggestibility. As a matter of fact, some of the suggestions are the same in the two instances. A similar observation can be made of nonprestige and secondary (or tertiary) suggestions. It should be noted, however, that the so-called "prestige factor" is not entirely restricted in practice to suggestions falling in this class; it is present to various degrees in all sorts of situations. It is true though that prestige suggestions probably allow the prestige factor to play a greater part when it is present.

Lastly, suggestions have been classified as *personal* and *impersonal*. One group of investigators appears to employ this designation synonymously with the prestige-nonprestige classification. Another group headed by Hull (213) appears to use these terms to denote also whether or not the suggestions are given directly by a suggestor, present in person. In either instance no further discussion is needed.

Just which of these various designations to use seems to be largely a matter of personal preference. There is some evidence that in general they are not entirely equivalent because of overlapping between them. This is probably caused by the fact that "directness" and "prestige" are not themselves equivalent, nor does one either preclude or imply the other. Furthermore, these two characteristics do not always lead to clear-cut situations. In these respects, the classification of suggestions into primary, secondary, and tertiary, as in the past pages, seems to be more satisfactory for the time being. It might be remarked, however, that, had any one of the alternative classifications of suggestions been used in the previous pages, this would not have materially altered the arguments presented in the last and the present chapter.

In conclusion, it appears that it is entirely possible to include secondary and tertiary suggestibility in the framework presented in Chapter 19 for primary suggestibility and hypnosis. When this is done, it appears that the three types of suggestibilities have their genesis in the postulated *multiple nature* of hypnotic suggestibility. That is, hypnosis acts as a unifying phenomenon which is itself neither primary, secondary, nor tertiary suggestibility but yet involves elements basic to all three of these types of suggestibilities. These would seem to denote a *class* of phenomena rather than any single phenomenon. But, it must be emphasized, many data are still lacking concerning the entire matter, and future investigations may show that secondary and tertiary suggestibility are totally different classes of phenomena. The existence of common factors giving rise to correlations is by no means an absolute proof of the contrary. In the meantime, the actual status of secondary and tertiary suggestibility would not appear to present a major obstacle to the acceptance of the theory presented in the last chapter.

The Nature of Suggestion

There have been a great many attempts at defining "suggestion." In ordinary discourse, to suggest means to hint or to start a chain of ideas, and possibly to initiate actions too. This expression has also been used synonymously with "association of ideas." Thus we speak of one idea suggesting another. Or it may refer to the tendency an individual has to act under the influence of another individual, whether as a result of direct communication, instructions, or otherwise. It is instructive to consider briefly some of the meanings that have been ascribed by past investigators to the term "suggestion."

For instance, Wundt considered suggestions as associations connected with an external impression and characterized by a narrowing of consciousness and an absence of inhibitory influences. Hart thought along similar lines. For Sidis, suggestion is an intruding idea which is realized unreflectively in a semiautomatic manner. Titchener had a similar definition. McDougall conceived of a suggestion as a process in which a proposition is accepted with conviction, irrespective of any logical reasons. Janet saw it as the influence of one individual on another without mediation of voluntary consent. Thorndike had a somewhat different approach and considered suggestion as an ideo-motor process according to which, in the absence of interference, every idea tends to realize itself. This viewpoint was also held by Hilger and by Bernheim. According to Lipp, suggestions are some particular psychical experience which is called forth by the arousal of ideas. This is in direct opposition to Munsterberg's views. He thought that the belief in the idea and not the idea itself is created by the suggestion. He visualized the suggestion as creating an attitude and need in the individual which led him in turn to accept imagined impressions as reality. He was strikingly modern in this respect.

Quite in contrast, Woodworth took the position that a suggestion is merely a term describing a situation in which the suggested idea happens to be the only stimulus at the time. Like Woodworth, Otis also considered suggestions an expression of a stimulus-response relation in which no interference has a chance to enter.

Freud took a still different approach to this topic. According to him, suggestions acquire their character by virtue of the production of transference. Similarly Ferenczi has declared that suggestions are an expression of submission arising from a child-parent relationship between subject and suggestor.

Although Binet was one of the first to point to the fact that suggestibility involves at least five phenomena which must be distinguished from one another, and he demonstrated the reality, if not the independence, of these phenomena, his contemporaries and successors continued to focus on single aspects. More recently Coffin (71), recognizing that these aspects might indicate that more than one kind of suggestion exists, proposed a rather complex classification which distinguishes eight kinds of suggestions in terms of the processes that are presumably responsible for their characteristics. Without going into unnecessary details, it may be said that, according to Coffin's analysis, suggestions fall into two major categories: ideomotor suggestions and prestige suggestions. The influence of the first group arises through the formation of perseverative tendencies, sets, or expectancies. That of the second group results from the presence of certain emotional factors in the social situation associated with them.

In brief, suggestions have been everything from association of ideas, ideomotor action, and an expression of transference to an unimpeded stimulus-response process. It is rather clear that there is no unity among psychologists on this topic.* To some extent this may be ascribed to the fact that different bases are used for the definitions. Janet, for instance, defined verbal suggestion in terms of its apparent outward action. Wundt, on the other hand, seemed to be more concerned with internal effects. Other investigators attempt to give an operational definition. And so on.

---

* Possibly a qualification should be added here. Looking from our present-day understanding of psychological phenomena at the various views just considered, we are tempted to believe that many, possibly all, of these can be reconciled, and that probably their proponents did not intend these to mean different things. Unfortunately, short of reading between the lines (which I am loath to do), the correctness of this supposition cannot be ascertained. Since there are instances in which it seems rather clear that different meanings were intended and others in which there is little ground for agreement, the above presentation has been preferred. That is, it has been considered safer to group and contrast points of view on the basis of their manifest rather than their latent contents.

Further reason for this lack of unity is that *suggestion has many facets,* as already remarked, and that various investigators have been concerned with only a few of these aspects at a time.

But, regardless of the variety of opinions on what it is, *the reality of suggestion is a well-established fact.*

The Definition of "Suggestion"

It is not difficult to find arguments against the various definitions that have been offered in the past. It does not seem particularly worth while to spend time enumerating such arguments. A more constructive approach is to attempt to find a suitable definition of suggestion, if such is possible. This is the task we shall now undertake.

It must be kept in mind that a definition is largely an arbitrary matter. It is something that can be neither proved nor disproved. At best we can only say that a definition does or does not meet the needs for which it was intended, and even this is usually more a measure of degree than an absolute criterion of value. Nor are there any set rules for making a definition.

However, there are certain guiding principles that can be followed to good advantage. First, any definition we choose will have to be applicable to all forms of "suggestion," regardless of specific individual differences among them. Second, it will have to be capable of discriminating unambiguously between what is a "suggestion" and what is not.† In other words, "suggestion" will be a class designation. Third, the definition should be consistent with the facts and theory presented in the previous pages. Finally, the delimitation of the concept of "suggestion" should be guided by the content of present-day psychology. These two last points are important because they imply that, when other psychological considerations leave undecided whether a certain event should be conceived as a "suggestion," the material of the previous chapters may allow us to make a clear-cut decision. Similarly, what may have once been considered a "suggestion," for lack of a better designation, today may fall in a different category.

A case in point is the notions of direct, indirect, mediate, and immediate suggestions, as employed by Sidis (412), who performed the following experiment among many others of a similar nature.

Sidis let his subjects observe for a brief moment a number of strips of paper on which were pasted a linear series of squares. Except for being different in color, these squares were otherwise identical with

† This means in particular that the phenomena included under this designation must be rather well defined at the empirical and/or theoretical level.

each other. All but one were given similar positions on the strips.‡ The exception was given a different orientation (usually a 45° rotation). The subjects were instructed to name the first color that came to their mind immediately after each strip was exposed. Sidis found that (*a*) the color of the square with altered orientation was named significantly more often than it could have been by chance alone, (*b*) this was true also of the adjacent squares, but (*c*) the effect was stronger in the first than in the second case. According to Sidis, both types of response were the result of the orientation of the one square functioning as an indirect suggestion to the subject to pick the colors of the squares in question. He believed that in the first instance orientation had acted as an immediate suggestion and in the second it had functioned as a mediate suggestion. Finally he concluded that orientation was stronger as an immediate suggestion than as a mediate one. It was this sort of data that Sidis offered as evidence for the existence of these various kinds of suggestions.

But are we really dealing with "suggestions" in this situation? Without going into detail, it may be remarked, first, that modern psychology offers alternative interpretations which are equally acceptable, in fact more so in the light of material to follow. Second, the information available on the above phenomenon does not seem to indicate that it has much relation, if any at all, to suggestibility (as understood in the present text). This is not to say that further investigation may not show the last observation to be wrong. However, until this occurs, it seems reasonable to state that, whatever "suggestion" is to denote, it should not include mediate, immediate, and indirect suggestions, at least in the sense that Sidis used these terms.

Another phenomenon that must be considered at this time is "empathy." As seen earlier, there is considerable evidence that empathy, among other phenomena, has properties similar to those of accepted "suggestions." There are certain reasons, however, why the boundaries of the definition that is being sought should exclude "empathy" from the class of "suggestions." A main one is that "empathy" is too indefinite a concept and is very poorly understood. Hull (213) employed it mainly to denote a type of response that in his own terms can be designated as unconscious imitation or mimicry. Others like Hutt and Miller (310) view the phenomenon as a form of nonverbal com-

‡ That is, they were equally spaced and given the same orientation. It is clear that their respective positions in the series were themselves a differentiating factor. Sidis was aware of this and had quite a bit to say about the influence of position in his study.

munication, thereby denoting by "empathy" a mode of interpersonal relating. More extreme views have gone so far as to speak of "empathy" as a form of telepathic communication. Another reason for the proposed exclusion arises from a remark of Hull (213) that Köhler found evidence that "empathy" (in the sense of unconscious mimicry) could take place in apes. Since there is no evidence that the majority of suggestibility phenomena, if any at all, can be evoked in animals, to include "empathy" under "suggestion" would lead to a rather lopsided definition of the latter. Thus, it seems desirable, at least for the time being, to exclude "empathy" from the class of suggestions; although it might be remarked that the phenomena associated with the two notions probably do share a common basic mechanism, ideomotor action being the most likely candidate for this.§

With the establishment of these rough limits, we can now begin to construct a definition of "suggestion" by observing, as some older investigators did, that all suggestions have the common property of being *stimuli*. For they are events that initiate as well as alter behavioral patterns in individuals; and this is exactly what stimuli are by definition. Furthermore, "suggestions" may be said to belong to the class of stimuli that establish *determining tendencies*.

Such a description, however, is not sufficient to characterize suggestions uniquely. For a great many stimuli have this last-mentioned property but yet could hardly be called "suggestions." Furthermore, in practice, one and the same stimulus does not always act in the capacity of a suggestion. Whether it does depends largely on the conditions under which it is used. Thus, something more is needed to differentiate suggestions from other types of stimuli.

A possible solution to this problem appears to be derivable from a comparison of the responses produced by suggestions and those resulting from stimuli other than suggestions. If this comparison is made, the following picture is obtained.

When a *normal* individual is placed in a specific situation,|| and is confronted with a specific stimulus,|| he makes a certain response which is *appropriate* to the stimulus *in* the situation in question. Furthermore, under *identical* conditions, all other things being equal, this

§ Hull appeared to identify "empathy" and ideomotor action, which is in line with this thought. It should be noted, however, that all manifestations of ideomotor action are not necessarily manifestations of suggestibility.

|| The situation and the stimulus as known to an observer other than the subject will be called the *objective* stimulus and situation.

response is replicable. That is, it can be predicted, provided, of course, we have ascertained ¶ what it should be.

Now, where a suggestion, seen as a stimulus, differs from a non-suggestive stimulus is that it always gives rise to a response that, from the standpoint of an observer other than the subject, *is not appropriate* to the present objective situation, but instead is appropriate to another *nonpresent* (i.e., absent) but possible objective stimulus situation. That is, the subject reacts to the suggestion *as if* it were some other stimulus. Or, again, the suggestion acts as an *inadequate stimulus* for the particular observed response. Effectively then, a suggestion is a stimulus that, in combination with a general present objective stimulus situation, becomes equivalent to, or acts as a *surrogate* for, another nonpresent objective stimulus situation. For instance, the statement, "A force is pulling you backward. You are falling backward," is an auditory stimulus which normally is not of a kind to cause individuals to respond as if they were pulled backward by a force. Yet, under appropriate conditions this same statement, acting in the capacity of a suggestion, is capable of functioning as if it were such a force. We may now restate all this in a more formal manner as follows:

A suggestion is a stimulus S which, when added to a present objective stimulus situation A, evokes a response not appropriate to either A or S, but which is entirely compatible with another possible objective stimulus situation B and of which S is not a part.[*]

This definition is still too inclusive, for it is possible to interpret it in such a way that the phenomena selected earlier for exclusion would have to be considered as suggestions.

To get around this, we need to return to an examination of the general situations in which suggestions are given, that is, in which suggestibility phenomena are evoked. We find first of all that an interpersonal relation is always involved. There is always one individual presenting the suggestion to another individual.[†] Furthermore, the stimulus presented to the subject has always *"meaning"* attached to it

---

¶ This is usually done by means of a test situation, better known as a control experiment. In some instances, it may be predicted on theoretical grounds. But even this presupposes an empirical foundation somewhere along the line.

[*] That is, the actual stimulus situation $(A + S)$ functions as a substitute for the nonpresent situation B, A being the apparent situation.

[†] In the case of autosuggestion the interpersonal relation becomes one of intrapersonal relating, so to speak. The meaning of this will become clearer to the reader if he thinks of autosuggestion as subvocalization (this last, however, is not meant to imply that thought is equated to subvocalization).

or to a part of it.‡ It was remarked in Chapter 19 that there are indications that hypnotic phenomena might be intimately related with the properties of language. It is therefore not so strange that the notion of "meaning" should appear in connection with the notion of suggestion.

The above remarks lead to our adding two provisions to the definition just given: that a stimulus, to be a suggestion, (*a*) must be initiated by a given individual, the suggestor, and *directed by him* at another individual, the suggestee, or subject; and (*b*) must convey some *meaning* to the subject.

With this in mind, it is now possible to restate the formal definition in a somewhat simpler form: *A suggestion is a group of ideas proposed by one individual, the hypnotist (or suggestor), to another person, the subject, such as to cause the subject to react as if the phenomenon for which the ideas stand were actually present.*

This definition of suggestion, viewed particularly as a stimulus, leads quite naturally to a rational classification of suggestions along lines similar to those outlined in Chapter 2. Thus, in terms of the origin or *source* of the stimulus, we may speak of autosuggestion and of heterosuggestion. If we consider the psychophysiological *state of the respondent*, we can talk of waking and hypnotic suggestion. Finally, by considering the *processes set into action* by the suggestions, we are led to the more fundamental of the categories, namely, the division of suggestions into primary, secondary, and tertiary types.§

This much then for the matter of definition.

The Nature of Suggestions

If we consider suggestions from the above standpoint, a rather strange situation develops. When we examine the available data carefully, we discover that apparently any and all stimuli capable of conveying meaning can function as suggestions, although quite obviously they do not always function in this capacity. This raises the question: What endows these stimuli that we call suggestions with the capacity to manifest themselves through an individual's suggestibility?

‡ It must be remembered here that certain situations have been excluded from consideration. It would be difficult to make such a statement in connection with, say, the "orientation" of a square considered as a suggestion. As a matter of fact, it would be even a problem whether the "orientation" as such could be called a stimulus.

§ The various other categories mentioned in Chapter 2 can also be derived in this wise. This has not been done here for obvious reasons.

So far as hypnotic and posthypnotic suggestion are concerned, this presents no problem since the hypnotic state is a necessary and sufficient condition for the existence of suggestion. Any stimulus satisfying the last definition given must of necessity be a suggestion in this instance.

The situation in regard to waking suggestion is another matter. We may seek the answer in either the structure or the content of the suggestion, or in both. Now, although the content of a suggestion will certainly determine the direction that the response to it will take, it cannot be a major factor, since, as pointed out earlier, any stimulus imbued with meaning has the potentiality to be a suggestion. Clearly, meaning and content are essentially the same thing; || hence, if content were the dominant factor in making a suggestion out of a stimulus, all meaningful stimuli would automatically have the power to evoke suggestibility phenomena at all times. This is not the case. This leaves, then, structure for consideration. And indeed, part of the answer, at least, appears to lie in it.

Consider the following three statements (and suggestions):

S1 Your eyes are closing.
S2 Your eyes are closing–closing–closing–closing. Your eyes are closing. . . .
S3 You are relaxed–Your eyes are becoming heavy–heavier–very heavy. You are getting drowsy–sleepy–very sleepy. Your eyes are tired–they are closing–closing–more and more. Your eyes are closing. You cannot keep your eyes open any longer. . . .

In practice we tend to speak loosely and indiscriminately of all three of these statements as suggestions without any particular attention to the fact that they might possess some basic differences. A simple analysis does indeed show that such a difference exists, not only at the level of statement construction, but also at the level of the suggestibility effects that are induced.

The first, S1, is a simple statement possessing only one referent and of such a nature that it cannot be reduced to a simpler expression without the meaning it carries being destroyed. A suggestion of this type can be called a *unit* suggestion. The second suggestion, S2, is a compound statement which has for its only referent the same one as S1. It may, however, be reduced to a simpler form (namely a unit suggestion) without losing or suffering alteration in its meaning. Also

---

|| At least to a first approximation.

it carries the additional factor of situational repetition.¶ This type will be called a *simple* suggestion. Finally, the third and last statement, S3, is also compounded, but in contrast to the others possesses more than one referent (four in this instance). It cannot be reduced to a simple or a unit suggestion without its total meaning being altered. Besides, possessing the factor of repetition, it also has what we might designate as multiple modes of stimulation. It may be called a *compound* suggestion.

As we know from previous chapters, S1 will usually bring about only weak ideomotor manifestations. On the other hand, S2 will lead to cumulated homoaction and possibly some generalization. Finally, S3 will usually produce definite generalization and probably dissociation.

Clearly then, although eye closure is the direct aim of all three suggestions, they are by no means equivalent in the manner in which they attain this end. As was just seen, this difference is to be found reflected at the psychophysiological level. As a matter of fact, on the basis of the analysis alone we could rank the three suggestions in order of decreasing effectiveness from S3 to S1. Empirical data support this.

It would appear then that the capacity of a stimulus * to evoke suggestibility phenomena in the waking state, hence to be a waking suggestion, lies primarily in the reflection of its structure into the environmental conditions in which the subject is placed. Content usually plays only a relatively minor role. Nevertheless, the full potency of a suggestion must be conceived as arising from a combination of both structure and content.† It is entirely conceivable, too, that for a given individual one could find unit suggestions of particularly high ideomotor potency, thereby allowing content to gain a more dominant position. Effectively, this is what seems to happen when an individual's suggestibility for a given suggestion is increased by training, and particularly through the use of posthypnotic suggestion aimed at accomplishing this.

¶ We say "situational" here because in respect to the subject a new environmental situation is actually created by the factor of repetition.

* It should be kept in mind that while verbal statements have been taken as examples in the above discussion, the analysis applies equally well to other kinds of stimuli employed as suggestions. In a similar manner we may speak of unit, simple, and compound stimuli. It might also be added that the analysis as presented here is by no means intended to be rigorous. The main concern has been to present roughly certain basic ideas necessary for the final development of the thesis presented in this chapter.

† Particularly since content usually influences the structure.

Actually our analysis is greatly oversimplified. In practice, a suggestion tends to be much more complex than has been outlined in the last few pages, because, in addition to such basic elements as words, such factors as voice inflection, intonation, gestures, facial expressions, general or specific body movements, etc. can and usually do have a definite effect on the final outcome of the suggestion. These can be considered either as marginal suggestions or as a true part of the total suggestion. As implied in footnote * on page 275, there are no reasons why word-gesture complexes or other combinations cannot be used as basic elements of suggestions. In reality this is probably nearly always, if not always, the case. In spite of this, the general analysis which has been given in these pages still appears to be applicable.

· 22 ·

The Nature of
Induced Hypnotic Phenomena

In essence and in at least one respect, the theory developed in the last two chapters considers the responses of hypnotized individuals as falling into the same category as those of waking * subjects. Namely, they are responses to *stimuli* and are part of the general behavioral pattern specific to the individual; that is, as stated earlier, the suggestions act in the capacity of an adequate stimulus. Thus a clear understanding of hypnotic behavior presupposes a clear understanding of waking behavior itself, and in particular of normal behavior.

Although the formulation thus far presented *does not* preclude the possibility that suggested responses might in other respects fall outside of the domain of waking responses, it does lead us to expect that a great many suggested responses would be in other respects essentially the same as waking responses. It is indeed a fact that, of those phenomena brought about through suggestion that have been reported and may be considered as scientifically valid, thus far none has fallen outside the domain of already known waking phenomena. More specifically, a survey of the various investigations in question shows that nearly all, if not all, hypnotic phenomena can also occur in the absence of hypnosis or of any suggestions. In fact, a great many of these phenomena are of common everyday occurrence. In nearly all instances, the existing differences between hypnotic and waking phenomena are found to be more of *degree* than of *quality*.

---

* "Waking" will be used here as synonymous with "nonhypnotized"—more specifically, it will denote an individual who is under the influence of neither hypnotic nor posthypnotic suggestion, "hypnosis" being understood in the sense employed in Chapter 19. The class of "waking" subjects will, however, comprise the subclasses of *normal* and *abnormal* persons. Since in one sense hypnosis can be called an abnormal state, an alternative will be that "waking" is the class of subjects who are normal and abnormal but who are not under the influence of hypnotic or posthypnotic suggestion.

There are no a priori reasons to expect that phenomena in hypnosis should result from physiological or even psychological mechanisms radically different from those responsible for similar phenomena in the waking state. Consequently, we should first attempt to understand hypnotic phenomena in terms of waking functions and mechanisms, and, only if we fail beyond question to find a satisfactory explanation in this wise, should we seek an approach along other assumptions. Just when a categoric failure of this kind should be declared to exist is a moot question, for of necessity, if hypnotic phenomena have essentially normal processes at their foundation, then our understanding of hypnotic phenomena themselves must be *limited* by our own inability to account for waking phenomena of a similar kind. The uncertainty in our knowledge and understanding of normal processes must necessarily reflect itself in a corresponding uncertainty in the domain of hypnosis. For these very reasons we must be wary in interpreting any failure that may arise in accounting for hypnotic phenomena, lest we wrongly place the blame on whatever theory of hypnosis we accept instead of on the existence of inadequate data and theories for waking phenomena.

If then we are to take the attitude that the basic psychophysiological processes underlying hypnotic phenomena are, for the most part, responsible for waking phenomena too, it may be well to state at the outset certain considerations of general waking behavior that have considerable bearing on the problem at hand, viz.:

(*a*) Man is an organism that reacts to its environment mainly through its neuromuscular apparatus. Man is stimulated nearly entirely, if not entirely, through direct and indirect action on his nerve endings, and particularly through stimulation of groups of specialized cells, or receptors.

(*b*) All *effective stimulation* leads to a response of some sort, provided the neuromuscular-glandular apparatus, or that portion of it that is involved, is intact: that is, is normally functioning.

(*c*) Nearly all *responses* of the individual, especially those initiated by stimuli from his external environment, *are mediated by his nervous system*.

All this is another way of stating the *central and dominant role* in the human organism of the *nervous system* which constitutes the main agent of co-ordination and integration of all activities of the organism. This is even more particularly true of the cerebrum and, within the latter, of the cortex and certain subcortical centers located in the diencephalon.† The essential role of these regions in the psychical activities of man appears to be beyond question. Of considerable importance for us are the following established facts:

1. There exists a projection system of afferent and efferent nerve fibers connecting the cortex with underlying parts of the central nervous system, that is, with the spinal cord, medulla, pons, mid-brain (thalamus)—and the autonomic system.

2. There exists an association system of nerve fibers interconnecting one part of the cortex with the other.

3. There exists a commissural system consisting of nerve fibers interconnecting the parts of the cortex of each cerebral hemisphere.

4. There appears to exist projection areas for the autonomic functions which are nearly as well defined as the somatic areas, although there is a tendency for the corresponding cortical foci to be less definite than in the somatic case. As Fulton (151) remarked, this is in agreement with the more diffuse nature of autonomic activity.

5. This cortico-autonomic representation tends to overlap somatic areas known to be related to behavior, personality, and the more complex emotional responses.

6. Cerebral control extends to the level of the spinal reflexes.

7. Conditioned reflexes ‡ are for the most part *mediated* by the cerebral cortex. In any event, subcortical conditioning is rather limited in its range of manifestations and can be extended and perfected only through associations with cortical areas. Penfield and Rasmussen (344), in summing up recent work on this topic, concluded that the locus of conditioning must itself be an association pathway.

Thus it is found that *the nervous system in man possesses all the essential characteristics that are prerequisites for the various phenomena reported to occur under hypnosis.* We might then be led to expect similar phenomena to take place under other conditions than hypnosis. As already pointed out, this is exactly what happens. There is then at least a physiological basis for an understanding of suggestion phenomena. From this standpoint, the problem becomes largely one of determining, first, to what extent the hypnotic situation differs from the equivalent waking situation and, second, in what ways the general

† The reader may be referred here to the various excellent physiology texts and related books that are available on the market, and more particularly to Fulton (151). A book of special interest is one by Penfield and Rasmussen (344) dealing with the cerebral cortex.

‡ Whether "conditioned reflexes" are really reflexes may be questioned for their minimum latency is found to be more than 100 milliseconds. This is longer than the latency of true reflexes and happens to be also just about equal to the latencies for voluntary activities.

conditions underlying the observed phenomena have been changed in order to bring about such differences.

The Universality of (Primary) Suggestibility

That suggestibility, as is observed, should be found to be rather highly developed in a large number of individuals, and present to some extent in nearly all persons, if not all, is a foregone conclusion if we agree to accept ideomotor action as the basis of primary suggestibility. Theoretically, we would expect that all individuals are suggestible to the degree in which ideomotor action can develop in them. Unquestionably, however, various factors can be expected to interfere with the manifestations of this action. Thus individuals with extremely low suggestibility § have been observed. Conversely, we may also expect that some factors might facilitate ideomotor action, as has been seen already for the case of imagery.

The observed widespread distribution of suggestibility not only is characteristic of the normal group of individuals, but, with certain provisions, also applies to the abnormal group. This has been clearly shown in Chapter 3, where the reasons for certain features of the reported data were taken up. The high correlation between neurosis and suggestibility to postural sway suggestions leads us to presume that ideomotor action is the main factor involved in this instance. A number of alternatives could account for the increase in suggestibility: (a) Increased ideomotor action is characteristic of and is more strongly manifested in neurotic behavior; (b) factors such as "attitude" which normally tend to operate against ideomotor action or its manifestations lose their potency and vanish; (c) factors favoring ideomotor action or its manifestations become predominant. Unfortunately no data are available at present that would allow us to decide the issue.

The explanation of the lowered suggestibility of psychotics would seem to lie in a similar direction. It is certain that in the more extreme cases there may be a definite problem of communication. But this is not by far the entire answer. Wilson, Cormen, and Cole (491) have reported considerable success in hypnotizing a large variety of psychotics of all categories, although they remark that the technique used must be custom-made for each individual case. There is also evidence

§ In the present chapter we shall be concerned nearly entirely with primary suggestibility, and henceforth, unless otherwise specified, "suggestibility" will be used synonymously with the former. It is clear that hypnotic phenomena and phenomena of waking suggestibility normally encountered are mainly a function of primary suggestibility insofar as their initiation is concerned.

that in schizophrenics there is a correlation between the degree of suggestibility present and the type of schizophrenia involved. Further elucidation of this matter will probably have to wait until a better understanding of abnormal personalities has been reached.

Hypnotic Susceptibility and Trance Depth

Susceptibility to hypnosis has been traditionally measured in terms of response to waking suggestions of primary type. Obviously, if ideomotor action and homoaction are the basis of hypnosis, or at least of the first stages of its induction, the above should follow. However, it is also clear that a test limited to measuring an individual's capacity for ideomotor action and homoaction would not necessarily give a true index of hypnotic susceptibility if other processes are involved. Thus the need for a battery of tests. This is also probably the reason why many so-called standard tests of hypnotic susceptibility often fail to give accurate estimates. The probable reasons for the particular place the heat illusion holds in the prediction of susceptibility have already been examined and need no further explanation.

It has been customary to describe the trance state as possessing various degrees or depths. There is no particular difficulty in accounting for these in terms of the present theory. The correspondence follows:

Insusceptible	Poor ideomotor action or/and homoaction; or/and presence of interfering factors
Hypnoidal	Primarily homoaction—possibly a small amount of generalization
Light trance	Homoaction and definite generalization
Medium trance	Primarily generalization ‖—possibly some dissociation
Deep trance	Dissociation fully established

To put it another way, the existence of a continuum of hypnotic suggestibility, as well as the fact that it merges with waking primary suggestibility (itself a continuum), is predicted by the theory.

Factors Affecting Suggestibility and Hypnotic Susceptibility

In considering factors influencing suggestibility it must be kept in mind that their influence can arise through both direct and indirect action, upon the manifestations of ideomotor action, neuromotor en-

‖ Of course in every instance, it is assumed that all other earlier processes in the sequence leading to hypnosis are also present. In this instance ideomotor action and homoaction are assumed also present.

hancement, generalization of suggestibility, and dissociation. The basic processes can be inhibited or facilitated; or their expressions can be affected in a similar manner through other phenomena. In general, the greatest difficulty encountered here in trying to account for the observed influences lies in the lack of basic information concerning the nature of the interactions that the factors under consideration have with normal psychological processes themselves. The exact distribution of many of these factors is itself often not well known. With these few words of introduction we shall now consider some of the factors in question.

Age. As was seen, suggestibility appears to reach a maximum at around the age of eight in both males and females. Several agents are probably responsible for this. We may presume that before the age of eight verbalization ¶ is proportionally smaller and more poorly defined as the individual is young. At the same time, the conditioning process responsible for ideomotor action is probably also proportionally less well established. Finally, the attention of a child appears usually to be rather transitory. All this would contribute toward a decrease in suggestibility below the age of eight. On the other hand, there are indications that, with increasing age, after eight years individuals tend progressively to lose their capacity for vivid imagery, particularly of the sensory type. This faculty appears to be especially well developed in younger children. Concurrently, there are also both a progressive growth in critical thinking and the formation of more and more definite attitudes. A net drop in suggestibility would be expected to result, particularly if the attitude of the subject toward suggestion is negative.* Thus, these two groups of changes taking place might well establish an optimal age for suggestibility.

Sex. Women and girls have been found to be slightly more suggestible than men and boys, respectively. It has been said that women and men differ in the predominant type of imagery they use (131). This could account for differences in the extent of ideomotor action present in the two sexes. Possibly there is also a difference in capacity

---

¶ By verbalization is meant the use of words in any form: spoken, heard, seen, written, visualized, and so on, as substitutes for actual objects, events, or experiences. "Word" is being employed here in a very general linguistic sense.

* Conversely, a strong positive attitude toward suggestion would be expected to compensate in some instances for the loss in suggestibility caused by other factors. As a matter of fact, this sort of thing is not too uncommon among adults. More will be said about this matter in a later section on attitudes and their influence on suggestibility.

for dissociation between the sexes. It is unlikely, on the other hand, that sex is directly linked to ideomotor action, capacity for conditioning, or neuromotor enhancement.

Intelligence. In view of the somewhat uncertain status of Eysenck's results with intelligence measured on the Matrix test, we shall restrict ourselves here to the data reported for intelligence measured on Binet-type tests. It is rather unfortunate that no attempts have been made to correlate suggestibility with the various items of the tests in question, since this would probably shed considerable light on the observed relationship. In the absence of such information, we may speculate that superior imagining and attention are to be found associated with superior intelligence and are responsible for the positive correlation that has been reported. Possibly, too, intelligent individuals tend to have more favorable attitudes toward suggestibility phenomena. Any or all of these conditions would tend to favor the expression of ideomotor action and homoaction.

Personality Traits. Possibly less than anywhere else can anything definite be said here. The classification and measurement of personality traits remain one of the biggest problems in psychology. Understanding the exact nature of such traits offers even less promise at present. Probably because of these factors, the correlation between suggestibility and the majority of personality variables remains in general quite confusing, showing no definite trend in any given direction. Exceptions to this are intelligence and a *group* of traits characteristic of neurosis and psychosis. These last have already been considered.

Attitudes, Expectation, and Motivation. Transference. The data concerning expectancy are very inconclusive. It seems clear, however, that whatever influence expectancy may have is easily masked by more potent factors. Attitudes would appear to be among these factors. Eysenck (131) has postulated that the outcome of suggestions of primary type is dependent on the interaction of ideomotor action and attitude. The relationship of favorable and unfavorable attitudes to suggestibility has been further established by White (481), as was seen. Without more complete knowledge of the nature of attitudes, we may presume that, neurophysiologically, they have the equivalent properties of facilitating and inhibiting cerebral centers.† That such centers exist is a well-known fact of neurophysiology. There is no

---

† Of course such centers must be conceived not as having a specific locus, but more as a mosaic, or rather as a net-like arrangement interwoven with a multitude of other net-like arrangements of neurons.

particular difficulty in accepting the idea that ideomotor action can be and very probably is altered by impulses from various centers when it is a fact that reflexes themselves come under such influences.

It has been generally held that certain patterns of need dispose the subject toward accepting or rejecting suggestions, and more particularly influence his susceptibility to hypnosis as well as the depth of hypnosis that he is likely to attain. Most probably the influence of needs is mediated through mechanisms similar to those involved in attitudes. This is particularly indicated by the fact that needs and attitudes appear to be very closely interrelated. As in the case of transference, it is very likely that certain needs appear to be correlated with suggestibility and hypnosis, not because they are instrumental in bringing about suggestibility phenomena, but because both have some common factors. Little more can be added here to our earlier discussion of transference, hence this topic will not be carried further.

Drugs. As has been seen, hypnotic and anesthetic agents facilitate suggestibility, provided subanesthetic doses are employed and the subjects possess some suggestibility to start with. The first of these conditions would seem to indicate that suggestibility and the initial phase of hypnosis depend on a relatively high level of cerebral activity. It may be inferred from this, too, that, when drugs are employed as an adjuvant, suggestion remains the main agent causing hypnosis and related phenomena. Clearly there is no reason for inferring the presence of a new mechanism. In spite of this, however, it is not possible to tell for certain how the above effect is brought about. If ideomotor action is basically conditioned reflex in nature, and if it is, as postulated, the basis of primary suggestibility, we could account for the results of Eysenck and Rees (133) if the drugs in question have the appropriate action on reflexes. Unfortunately information concerning the effect of narcotic drugs on conditioned reflexes and conditioning in general is rather inadequate.

There are really two aspects to the problem which are not always clearly differentiated in the literature. One is the effect of drugs on conditioned reflexes after they have been formed. The other is the effect of drugs on the process of conditioning itself. There is some evidence that caffeine facilitates conditioned reflexes and decreases inhibition (500). Hypnotics, particularly the barbiturates, and anesthetic agents might be expected to have the opposite action. This appears to be true of hypnotics such as sodium isoamylethyl barbiturate, chloral hydrate, and sodium bromide ‡ (500). A phenomenon that has been reported in this connection and is of particular interest is that, when large doses of sodium amytal are used, a brief phase is observed in which conditioned reflexes are facilitated § (500). In general then, narcosis tends to decrease conditioned reflexes and to increase inhibition. In regard to the actual process of conditioning (and inhibiting), Settlage (409) has reported finding indications of the existence of a critical anesthetic dose of Nembutal below which it is possible to establish conditioned reflexes even though the organism may be too depressed to give any overt responses during the process (409). Sterling and Miller (429) have substantiated this, finding at the same time that conditioning can take place at a much greater depth of anesthesia. Their data seem to indicate that the critical depth may be an individual characteristic. Since they used cats, whereas Settlage used dogs for his study, there may also be a species difference in regard to critical depth. In general, it is said that the bromides decrease the rate of conditioning and increase the rate of extinction (186). Nembutal also appears to decrease the rate of conditioning (186).

All these data can be supplemented by the extensive information that exists concerning the effects of central nervous depressants on unconditioned reflexes. Generally speaking, depression of nervous activity is obviously one of their main characteristics, there being usually a progressive descending action. Conditioned reflexes might be expected to follow suit. On the other hand, when central nervous depressants are administered, there often is an initial period of stimulation which again might be expected to manifest itself at the level of the conditioned reflex. As was just seen, there is evidence that this takes place. There are thus three ways in which subanesthetic doses of hypnotics and anesthetics could cause enhanced suggestibility: through enhanced conditioned reflexes (or conditioning) resulting from initial stimulation, through decreased (or decelerated) inhibition arising in the same way, or through both these effects capitalized on by a judicious use of suggestion. Leaving out the possible influence of suggestion aspects inherent in the administration of drugs intended to produce sleep-like states, and also those inherent in the subject's

‡ Actually in the case of the bromides, the evidence would seem to indicate that this is true primarily for large doses, whereas with a lesser dosage inhibition alone is decreased (211).

§ Whether or not inhibition is also decreased, as might be expected, has not been made clear.

subsequent subjective experiences, there is in hypnosis another factor that could be responsible for the increased susceptibility. Namely, the subject appears to be brought by the drug into a state that can best be described as one of dissociation, in which cortical functions appear to be altered to some extent, leading to a certain amount of mental confusion (this may in itself be a symptom of dissociation). Eysenck and Rees (133) have proposed that there is an inhibition of attitudes in narcosis, thus allowing ideomotor action to have a greater influence. It is my belief that, in addition, the state thus induced tends to favor generalization, and particularly the dissociation of awareness, if by doing nothing more than bringing about an alteration of awareness through a purely pharmacodynamical action, thus laying the ground for more of the same. Unquestionably a fuller account is needed of the action of light doses of appropriate drugs on psychophysiological processes in general before a more conclusive picture can be reached.

Finally, even small doses of hypnotics and anesthetics eventually lead to a certain amount of relaxation. If this last facilitates suggestibility, as has been proposed earlier, this at least would furnish part of the answer we are seeking.

Alterations of Motor and Sensory Functions in Hypnosis

We shall now turn our attention to those phenomena that can be brought about by means of hypnotic suggestion. Alterations of the motor and sensory functions will be considered first. Though it is now clear that such alterations are not nearly so spectacular as was once believed, nevertheless they do exist. There is, however, some question as to just how many of these effects are really specific to the hypnotic state and how many are not. There is considerable evidence that similar alterations can be brought about without hypnosis. There is also reason to believe that no hypnotized person has ever significantly surpassed in a given function the best performance obtainable from nonhypnotized (and nonsuggestible) individuals taken from a sufficiently large random population. All this is at the basis of the earlier assumption that *functions in hypnosis are essentially normal*. At most, hypnosis appears merely to allow the individual to make better use of his potentialities. But even this is no small feat, and it remains to be explained how hypnosis can do this. Thus, the first step in examining the entire problem would seem to be to determine the exact part played by hypnosis in these alterations.

In many instances, it is possible from the outset to eliminate certain aspects of the observed phenomena. Aspects that result only indirectly from hypnosis have little bearing on its nature. Thus, for instance, for the present we may safely assume that the influence of suggested emotionally toned experiences on sensorimotor functions should be looked for in the nature of the affective processes and not in the nature of hypnosis. On the other hand, the manner in which hypnosis brings such affective responses into being is quite another matter. A similar situation exists in regard to the effectiveness of suggested perceptual alterations on sensorimotor functions. The resulting responses are probably only consequences of the fact that, in general, individuals tend to respond primarily to the *perceived* stimulus rather than to the actual stimulus giving rise to the perception. As Kantor (229) has remarked, a stimulus is functional in character.‖ Consequently, our concern in such instances is mainly with the manner in which hypnosis can bring about such alterations of perception, and not so much with the actual response.

It is not without significance that, all other things being equal, the degree of hypnotic control an individual can exert over any given function appears to be directly related to the extent to which this same function comes normally under waking voluntary control. As noted in Chapter 19, a suggestion is a communication of intelligence, usually by means of a language. It must of necessity act through the cerebrum in which it initiates various activities. There is also much evidence to show that cerebral activity, especially when conscious, has its strongest influence on voluntary functions, and the least on involuntary acts.¶ We are thus led to conclude that the site of primary action for hypnotic suggestion must be in the cortex and in certain subcortical centers. This is further substantiated by other observations; some have already been discussed, and others will be taken up later.

Additional insight into the manner in which hypnotic suggestion can alter functions comes from the observation that it is generally impossible to bring about changes affecting general reflex action by means of direct evocation. The same appears to be true of the production of organic changes. Analysis of the nature of suggestions and of the general situation associated with direct and indirect evocation leads

‖ It might be remarked in line with this that there is increasing evidence that such notions as those of stimulus and threshold as well as others need badly to be redefined.

¶ There is a direct relationship between strength of influence of suggestions and extent to which the function is involuntary. Conversely, for a function to be susceptible to a high degree of voluntary control, it is a requirement that it be influenceable by cerebral activity to a high degree. If we define a voluntary action in these terms, the above is merely a consequence of the definition.

to a rather simple interpretation of the above facts.   Namely, direct evocation is relatively ineffective with reflexes and certain other proc- esses because the suggestions are always in the form of orders or in- structions which must be put into effect by cerebral activities differing in no way from those normally involved in voluntary acts.   As we know, reflex phenomena and the like are not easily controlled by such activities.   On the basis of the present theory of hypnosis, there is no reason to expect the trance to cause changes in this respect.   The observed facts substantiate this.   In contrast, we can expect indirect evocation to succeed where direct evocation fails because the sugges- tions involved are aimed at bringing about phenomena that are them- selves normally and directly related to the group of responses under consideration.   That is, the type of cerebral activity thus produced is the sort that is normally connected with reflex activity in a very inti- mate manner.   Thus, here too we find no evidence that anything differing from normal functioning is involved.   Pushing the analysis a step further, we easily discover that the suggestions are of a type that reduces to the kind which in one fashion or another brings about alterations of the subject's perceptions.*

Positive Hallucinations.   This last observation leads us directly into a discussion of *suggested hallucinations.*   These appear to fall into three main categories: (*a*) the individual is made to perceive *non- existent* sensory impulses (positive hallucination); (*b*) he is led *not to* perceive actual sensory impulses (negative hallucinations); (*c*) the subject experiences a mixture of negative and positive hallucinations.†

---

* "Perception" is considered here as the subjective experience associated with any given stimulus or group of stimuli acting as a unit.   The basis of perception is therefore largely sensory data associated with a pattern of awareness.   Some readers may object to this reference to perceptual phenomena, on the basis that introspection is not a valid scientific method of study.   For such a group of readers, it may be pointed out that "perception," as considered in these pages, denotes that sensory data appear to be molded by various internal influences in such a way that the pattern of nerve impulses entering the final common path is not the same by any means as the original pattern of receptor impulses which were directly initiated by the stimulus pattern in question.   The resulting behavior is therefore dependent on more than the stimulus pattern which elicits it, as is well known in fact.

† There may be a fourth group.   One in which actual sensory impulses are perceived and no fictitious ones created, but where the general interrelationship of the sensory components is perceived in a different manner from what it would normally be (altered perceptual matrix).   For this reason, although by usage we speak of hallucinations in this case, the term *paraperception* might be more appropriate.

There has been some concern in recent years regarding the reality of suggested hallucinations, the assertion being made that subjects merely act out the suggestions. There is little question but that this does occur in some cases. However, when we have discarded all instances that might in the least manner fall into this category, there still remain a number of examples of suggested hallucinations which bear all the characteristics of genuineness, to the extent of being associated, presumably as causative agents, with various functional alterations. As much as this was implied earlier.

It is interesting to note that even Orne (328), who maintains that regression phenomena are not "real" in the sense that, according to him, they are only age-role enactments, emphasizes the reality of hallucinations. He has analyzed and summed up the situation in this regard rather nicely. He points out that available data show that hallucinations tend to follow a course of their own and to remain constant in the absence of further suggestion. This, he remarks, is one of the more outstanding facts leading to the inference that we are dealing here with a field.

If the subject and the hallucinated environment constitute a field, he adds, certain general field properties should be evident. For instance, it should follow that any reorganization of the field structure will automatically change the subject's behavior without such changes being suggested directly. Also, in the face of disturbances in any of its parts, a field has the capacity for self-maintenance of its equilibrium by means of a minimum number of changes involving all other parts, thereby reaching a new equilibrium in this wise. Finally, if the subject and the hallucinated environment constitute a field, then, when such a field is established, it should have the same subjective validity as an objectively real field. Orne presents interesting evidence that the hallucinated situation does indeed possess these various properties, and that in particular the hallucinated reality possesses many of the characteristics of the objective reality.

The lack of adequate information about perceptual functions in general is an especial drawback here when we try to account for the observed role of hypnosis in perceptual functions. But, slender as this knowledge may be, it would require us to go too far afield to take up the topic in any detail. Fortunately, it appears possible to present a rather simple but adequate theory of at least the production of *positive hallucinations* by means of suggestion.

As already expressed in footnote * on page 288, an individual's behavior at any instant appears, in its final stage, when considered at the neurophysiological level, to be determined by the *final common path*, which is entered at that instant by the pattern of nervous impulses initiated at the receptors. Because of mediation and supplementation by the CNS as a whole, the impulse pattern which enters this final common path usually bears little resemblance to the original receptor impulse pattern. That is to say, the actual origin of a pattern of impulses is not so much a determinant of behavior as is the pattern of impulses associated and determined by the final common path. Thus, *all stimuli that give rise to a response through the same final common path are equivalent.*‡ If hypnotic suggestions can bring about in some instances neurophysiological patterns of activity which are *identical* to those produced by stimulus situations other than verbal ones, it would be expected that the behavior of the subject would be identical in both instances. For example, a hallucinated light can become, as reported by Lundholm (279), a conditioned stimulus. This is understandable if it corresponds to the same equivalent neurophysiological activities which constitute the basis of both the perception of the hallucinated and of the real prototypical light. Such an equivalence would arise naturally if the hallucination were built out of activated *traces* (*engrams*) of previous experience. In other words, if the basis of positive hallucinations were recall,§ we should have the above-postulated situation. This I believe is the case.

A few facts available at present favor this point of view. In normal everyday life we encounter certain phenomena that bear a close resemblance to positive hallucinations. Such are eidetic images, so-called memory images, and imagining in general. Extremely vivid images can be produced in these circumstances. It has been shown experimentally that voluntary imaging can lead to images so realistic that

‡ Actually the very nature of the nervous system leads to an equivalence which can take on all degrees from full identity to a very distorted resemblance. This important property might be called the *principle of special neural equivalence* (since there may be a more general effect).

§ The term "recall" has been given a variety of meanings by psychologists. It will be taken here to denote the operation of reviving a former experience in the absence of appropriate stimuli, the content of the revival being an exact duplication (copy) of, similar to, or a symbolic representation in part or in whole of the original experience. The second of these cases is what Warren (455) refers to as "memory images." In accordance with M. Prince (353) it will be assumed that recall can be made up entirely of physiological elements lying at a non-conscious level (physiological memory), only of psychic elements lying at a conscious level (memory proper), or a combination of both (psychophysiological memory). This is a somewhat different classification from the one employed in earlier pages which was based on the method of testing recall.

they cannot be distinguished by the subject from real objects. Woodworth (501) concluded on reviewing such experimental evidence that there is no absolute difference between an image and a percept and that there is no sure criterion by which one can be distinguished from the other. The essential difference between images of the above kind and hallucinations appears to be that the individual is aware of the true nature of the experience in the first instance while he is not in the second. If this analysis is correct, then clearly *awareness* becomes once more a very important factor in the determination of the final outcome. To this we will return later. Whether voluntary imaging and recall images lead to the same kind of image or not has not been shown empirically. However, consideration of the problem, of the facts available, and particularly of the properties of the underlying nervous system strongly favors the notion that all imaging is basically a recall phenomenon. Mental images, whatever else they may be, must have an experiential origin. We may disagree concerning the exact nature of engrams, but it is widely accepted that they exist. Images that arise in the absence of specific sensory stimuli appear to have an engrammatic basis. In particular, aside from distortions of present images produced by actual stimuli, whatever the subject hallucinates must be made up of recall elements from past experiences. That this is so can often be demonstrated by questioning the hypnotized subject about his hallucinations. Since there is no reason to expect that recall is a function fundamentally altered by hypnosis, a surmise substantiated by the facts reported in Chapter 12, if the above is correct the production of hallucinations is essentially a property of the normal individual.

Clues as to how hypnosis may come to have the control it has over the production of positive hallucinations can be obtained from examination of certain aspects of recall images and voluntary imaging || in normal life. It is generally agreed, although actual specific data are lacking, that the capacity for vivid imagery is particularly well developed in children and seemingly decreases with increasing age. This

---

|| A mental image (or simply image) is usually understood to be an element of experience that has a *central* origin and possesses all the qualities of a sensation. It differs from a sensation in that the latter has a *peripheral* origin (thalamic pains being possibly an exception). Some images act in the capacity of a substitute for some particular experience which they represent. Such images may be called *symbolic* images. All others are then *nonsymbolic*. A group of images of particular interest are word images which may be called *verbal* images. Symbolic verbal images are of the highest importance in human behavior.

is especially true of eidetic imagery. Furthermore, children appear to experience readily complex and extensive imagery bearing all of the aspects of reality if we may judge by their behavior. In seeking a differentiating factor which would account for the marked difference in this capacity between adults and children, we are led to the observation that one of the biggest differences characterizing the ideational processes of these two categories of individuals is the availability of a language,¶ and the degree to which it is used by each group. The child, particularly before the age of six, uses a minimum of language in his thinking which presumably tends to be largely in terms of nonverbal images. The predominance of this form of thinking may well be expected to be inversely proportional to age. In particular, recall would tend to be increasingly in the form of nonverbal images as the individual is young. Beginning with infancy, the individual, with increasing age, acquires a more and more complex language, while training and circumstances concur to impose on him the habit of thinking and remembering in terms of symbolic verbal images rather than reliving past experiences as a whole, or experiencing events created from a variety of recalled sensory elements. In other words, with increasing age there seems to be a shift from nonverbal to symbolic verbal images. It is, however, pertinent to the present problem that even symbolic verbal images can become conditioned to somatic changes, as has been made clear by the experiments of Cason (66) and Hudgins (212).

The capacity for ideation in terms of nonverbal images alone is not entirely lost, however, in most adult individuals. They can at times regress, so to speak, to this more "primitive" mode of thinking. Drugs, sleep, dreaming, and daydreaming all seem to be able to bring about, or at least appear to be associated with, conditions favoring this form of ideation. As a matter of fact, it would appear that most states involving a dulling of consciousness tend to have such a facilitating influence on nonverbal imagery. Evidence comes from the study of the psychic changes associated with the descending action of most hypnotics and anesthetics that verbalization probably involves nervous centers which are first to go under the influence of inhibiting agents. In addition, in the waking individual verbalization appears to have precedence over nonverbal ideation, and presumably tends to prevent

¶ "Language" is used here in a more extended sense than is usual, for, though it is considered as a medium of communication between individuals, it is also made to include symbolic systems used in "thinking," this latter being conceived as *self-communication*.

a more extensive use of nonverbal imagery. The hypnotic state, particularly in its last phase, that is, of dissociation, might be expected to be associated with an inhibition of verbalization, thus allowing nonverbal processes to emerge. Certainly, if it is agreed first that centers involved in verbalized ideation succumb to generalized inhibition (or depression) and second, that the hypnotic situation leads to this last condition, then the above picture is an excellent possibility. It may be objected that, since suggestions are verbal in nature, it is strange they should evoke nonverbal rather than verbal material. However, if we consider the fact that the suggestions are only stimuli, this difficulty is removed. For the kind of nervous activity the suggestion will initiate is dependent on the psychophysiological state of the individual. If through selective depression the subject is rendered incapable of giving internal verbal responses, then we can presume that the next best and most available form of internal response will result— in this instance—in a nonverbal response.

In any event, the production of positive hallucinations does not lead to any incompatibility with the theory of Chapter 19.

Negative Hallucinations. The question of the place of awareness in the above scheme comes to the fore when we turn our attention to *negative* hallucinations. It is very unlikely in the first place that suggestions could prevent sensory impulses from arising at the receptors or from ascending the various spinal tracts that are involved. On the basis of our present knowledge of the neurophysiology of sensation, it is more likely that any inhibition of sensation would take place at the level of the cerebral cortex or of the thalamus. This is particularly indicated by the fact, already mentioned, that the initial action of suggestions most probably takes place at these levels. There are further reasons, however, for taking this view. Harriman (181, 182) for instance has indicated that suggested color blindness resembles attitudinal changes more closely than these resemble true changes in sensory content. Erickson (115) has also pointed out that cortical function must play a definite role in color perception. Also, as has been seen in previous chapters, when negative hallucinations affect reflexes, they are most effective with conditioned reflexes, and relatively ineffective with natural reflexes. Since the main neurophysiological difference between the two types of reflexes appears to be that the former depends on cerebral mediation, in contrast to the latter, it seems evident that the primary action of suggested negative hallucinations probably begins at the cortical and subcortical levels.

Now it is clear that many voluntary and semivoluntary responses will not appear if the individual is not aware of the stimulus.* For instance, we do not expect the subject to address a person of whose presence he is unaware. Absence of awareness would obviously account for responses observed at the voluntary level of such a nature as to indicate the presence of a negative hallucination.† The influence of involuntary phenomena by suggestions is, on the other hand, a very different matter.

A feasible solution offers itself if we accept the possibility that *awareness itself can become conditioned.* This is not so difficult a notion to accept as may at first appear if we look at it from a neurophysiological standpoint. Granted that we do not know what awareness really is; nevertheless, its existence is a fact ‡ about which there is rather general agreement among psychologists, as well as among physiologists. Furthermore, there is some agreement that it probably has a distinctive physiological basis, whether this latter be anatomical or functional in nature.§ If then we consider a given stimulus acting on an individual for the first time without his being aware of it, and acting on him on some other occasion with his awareness (all other things being the same), it is reasonable to assume that the over-all pattern of impulses ‖ which results in each case and which initiates activity in the final common path is not entirely the same in the two instances. Now, conditioning associations take place not so much between effector impulses (response) and receptor impulses (stimulus), as between the former and the over-all pattern of impulses which have been brought into being (percept). Theoretically, it is possible then, on the basis of these premises, to have conditioning take place in which the aware-

* It is assumed that the subject is not acting.

† Rosen (375) has proposed that since the results that followed suggested anesthesia were in some instances similar to those observed in prefrontal lobotomy, we may well be dealing in such cases with what he calls a "psychological lobotomy." Whether this is the same as what was referred to in Chapter 19 as "an alteration of awareness" remains to be determined. There would, however, seem to be at least some overlapping.

‡ At the behavioral level we may say that awareness denotes an individual's capacity to communicate about his experiences provided, of course, that a suitable apparatus and medium for communication is available.

§ That a neurophysiological feature can have its genesis in the anatomy of the nervous system is well shown for instance by the sympathetic division of the autonomic system in respect to its diffused, massive action.

‖ Alternatively, one can speak of patterns of CES and CIS, neuron networks, mosaics, and so on.

ness factor becomes an essential *element* serving as a basis for discrimination.¶ If it is assumed that hypnosis possesses greater discriminatory capacity in this respect,* it is now possible to account for the fact that negative hallucinations in hypnosis can influence conditioned reflexes in the manner described by Erickson (114), since the stimulus in the waking state is not equivalent, from the standpoint of conditioning, to the stimulus in hypnosis.

As for natural reflexes, if a definite influence is exerted on them by negative hallucinations, this influence is small. It can be accounted for in a number of ways. The action may be of the same nature as that involved in other instances of inhibition of natural reflexes (knee jerk, sneeze reflex, etc.), or, since it is probable that a certain amount of conditioning takes place throughout life between our natural reflexes and various perceptions, a small amount of inhibition might arise through such conditioning. Still other alternatives are possible.

Whether the above is the answer or even part of the answer must be left for the future to decide. It does, however, fit readily into the theory proposed in Chapter 19, since, according to it, one of the main properties of hypnosis is its power to bring about an alteration in awareness, this latter being a fundamental characteristic of hypnosis.

It is beyond the scope of this book to consider all the various alterations of functions that have been reported. There is, however, one type of change related to the production of positive hallucinations that merits some discussion because of its significance for psychosomatic medicine. This is the production of blisters by hypnotic suggestion. Though admittedly the evidence for the existence of such phenomena is far from satisfactory, it was seen earlier that it is still difficult to deny it entirely. The neuromuscular system appears to possess all of the necessary elements and characteristics for the production of this type of phenomenon, and, even if available data are unsatisfactory, the possibility of its reality is worth examining.

Somatic Alterations. There are two basic problems in considering organic alterations leading to blister formation: (a) the production of somatic changes capable of giving rise to blisters in some arbitrary region of the body, and (b) the specific localization of these changes. There are some indications in some of the reported cases that these

¶ Effectively, the stimulus plus awareness is equivalent to a new stimulus different from the stimulus alone.

* Though actually this is not a necessary condition, it does appear that, if this sort of discrimination is possible, the above situation very probably exists.

may indeed be two separate problems.† As we understand it today, blister formation is a rather nonspecific reaction found to take place under a variety of conditions. Tissue destruction is by no means a prerequisite. There is rather convincing evidence that the release of a histamine-like substance at the site of blistering can initiate the process. It is probable that there is a close relationship between blister formation and the triple response, particularly the two last phases of the response. Since the triple response is in part neurogenic, there exists a possibility that it can be brought about wholly, or at least in part, as a result of activity of the central nervous system, and more particularly of the higher nervous centers.

If we assume for the time being that blister formation and the triple response are connected, it follows from the above that there is also a possibility of initiating blisters through cerebral influence.‡ It is most likely that, if this can really be brought about, it is made possible through conditioning. That is, blister formation as the result of suggestion is probably a conditioned response, in which the re-experiencing of sensory or other elements associated on past occasions with situations causing blisters brings about reflexedly the somatic changes that were once associated with these same elements.

While this rather broad statement accounts fairly well for the production of blisters without reference to specific localization, the latter aspect requires further refinement. The possible nature of such refinement is suggested by the neurogenic theory of herpes zoster. This disorder, which involves the formation of localized hyperemia and of vesiculation, arises presumably from the production of antidromic impulses causing cutaneous and subcutaneous vasodilation.§ Such a

† In some reported instances, blisters were formed as the result of suggestions but failed to localize in accordance with these same suggestions.

‡ It must be remarked that, even if there should not be any relation between the triple response and blistering, the fact that somatic changes such as are involved in the response have a neurogenic nature to at least some degree makes it plausible that blistering might also partly be under nervous control. There is little question but that it does involve vascular changes, and those we know are under the influence of the autonomic system. Further, we know that there exists a central division of the autonomic system which is closely connected with the central nervous system and that the autonomic system has cortical representation. The possibilities of inducing blisters by suggestion are therefore quite good.

§ The fact that herpes zoster appears to be definitely connected with a virus infection does not necessarily invalidate this theory, for the exact role of the virus in this instance remains to be elucidated. There is evidence that emotional disturbances can bring about herpes labialis, a condition clearly associated with a related virus infection, yet obviously partly influenced by the nervous system.

mechanism is exactly what we need to make suggested blistering and hyperemic reactions a strong possibility. In addition, we also have the rather suggestive facts that (*a*) antidromic impulses in general appear to go mainly to the vessels of the skin, causing these to dilate; (*b*) the sensory fibers predominantly involved in the conduction of antidromic impulses appear to be those subserving the sensation of pain (protopathic).

Let us then try to visualize, in terms of these facts, what may take place when suggestions are given to an individual that he will hallucinate the experience of being burned at some specific point on his body. There will be first the activation of quiescent traces identifiable with the various elements of the suggested experience. The only elements that would not be present would be those involving impulses originating at cutaneous receptors and traveling up the sensory fibers connected with the pseudotraumatized region. However, given the average individual and the average reported situation, it can be assumed that in the past he has had sensory impulses, particularly pain and temperature impulses, traveling up the same paths, which were able to bridge the various synapses that must now be involved. Thus, the trace elements that are activated include central synaptic connections, motor and sensory fibers connected with the exact locus of pseudotrauma. So we have a situation in which a path of low resistance is open to impulses traveling along the sensory fibers joining the area of pseudotrauma with the central portion of the nervous system.

The feature of particular significance here, however, is that *some of these fibers are capable of conducting antidromic impulses.* Consequently, activity arising in the central division of the trace will give rise to an outflow (antidromic) of impulses going to the area of pseudotrauma and giving rise to vasodilation and vesiculation. Since in all but one reported instance tactual stimulation was employed to localize the pseudotrauma, it is possible that another effect was also present which would have facilitated the formation of a path of low resistance between the central nervous system and the pain fibers going from the pseudotraumatized area. For, if the convergence (irritable focus) theory of referred pain is correct, we are led to expect that, under appropriate conditions, the stimulation of touch receptors in some part of the body may create a central excitatory state, which in turn favors the flow of impulse along certain paths, these impulses and paths being other than those involved in bringing about the facilitation.

In this manner, the localization and production of organic changes, as the result of suggesting the formation of blisters (directly and indirectly), becomes primarily an expression of natural neurological manifestations initiated and facilitated by recall. There are still a number of problems in this connection that remain unsolved but that have no direct bearing on the nature of hypnosis or suggestibility. For instance, hyperemia is easily accounted for by vasodilation alone. But the change in permeability of the vessel walls, presumably accounting for the formation of vesicles and blisters, is another matter. Is it a direct consequence of the vasodilation itself, or is a chemical factor first produced which in turn changes the permeability? It has been suggested by Lewis (267) that hyperalgesia results from the production of a chemical substance (Lewis P-factor) by specialized nerve fibers and that this same mechanism is responsible for herpes zoster. It may be added that the same chemical might also give rise to any observed vasodilation under comparable conditions. Are we then dealing with a similar situation here? We may safely assume that, besides the production of antidromic impulses, hallucinations bring about other physiological changes of such a nature that they very possibly sensitize the various tissues to the action of certain nerve impulses. Pain is always a signal for the body to prepare for a situation of stress. As we know, this usually results in considerable and widespread changes at the physiological level.

If the above is the correct explanation of the formation of blisters under the influence of suggestion, a number of consequences must follow. First, for the suggestion to be effective the subject must have previously experienced traumatic situations leading to blister formation. Second, the success of the experiment would depend considerably on the subject's re-experiencing vividly such a past experience, or at least some of the elements involved in it. The actual re-experiencing of pain would be particularly indicated. These considerations may in turn explain why experiments with the influence of suggestion on allergic reactions have failed to produce qualitative changes. Such reactions are not associated with past sensory experiences, at least with any comparable to those accompanying burn trauma. Furthermore, allergies are usually tissue-specific. Nevertheless, there is good evidence that some allergies have a psychosomatic origin. Possibly, if we can eventually discover the exact manner in which nervous impulses give rise to localized allergic lesions in such instances, we will then be able to induce these by means of suggestions more direct than those that have previously been reported successful in causing allergic effects.

Temporal Distortions. Another topic upon which we might touch briefly is the fascinating work of Cooper and his co-workers on temporal condensation, particularly in connection with learning. We are probably dealing here with a very complex perceptual alteration which cannot be fully understood until our comprehension of time perception itself is increased. Nevertheless, certain general remarks can be made which may help us to a better understanding of the results reported by the above investigators. It is pretty well agreed that we may speak of objective and subjective time. Normally these two forms are congruent. This is probably brought about through use by the individual of various external cues,|| this congruence being necessary in normal everyday life if the individual is to be able to interact consistently with his environment.¶ In situations where the press of the environment does not exist or has been minimized, the necessity for congruence vanishes, and the individual is free to live according to his personal (private) temporal scale. This sort of thing is seen to occur in individuals under the influence of certain drugs, who are somnolent, dreaming, psychotic, and so on.

Now it seems reasonable to assume that, if we disregard any other limiting factors, the maximum speed at which mentation can take place is determined by the rate at which neural activity can proceed. We have definite evidence that some of these activities can take place at rates much higher than might be inferred from observations of human activity. In normal everyday living there are of course limiting factors which do not allow the expression of neural phenomena at their highest possible rate. There is again evidence that some, if not all, of these limiting factors are variable, and certainly can be either bypassed or eliminated in one way or another. One of the limiting factors is the need for congruence of subjective and objective time. As long as it is present, the individual's neural events must take place at a speed that maintains them in phase with external events. Of necessity, speed of learning, which presumably depends on neural processes, may be expected to be limited by this congruence. When the subject is under hypnosis, this necessity is removed, or rather the individual's subjective time is matched against a new temporal frame

|| We may think here of a phase matching and interlocking of neural events and external events, in such a manner as to keep these in phase, the external events setting the pace, so to speak.

¶ This is analogous to the situation thought to exist in retinal inversion. The congruence is then considered here to arise through learning processes. Evidence from studies of children seems to support this.

of reference (defined by the suggestions), and mentation and learning in particular become free to take place at a new rate—a higher one in the present instance. From the discussion of previous pages, it is clear that hypnotic suggestion would be particularly effective in bringing about the postulated change in temporal reference frames. Since experimental data on this question are still meager, no attempt will be made at this time to consider the phenomenon in more specific terms. Furthermore, it must be emphasized that the above material is offered only as a tentative hypothesis and that no attempt has been made to give a rigorous presentation.

Simulation and Hypnotic Phenomena. Since the problem of "acting" in response to suggestion will come up again in the material to follow, it may be well to consider it in more detail at this time. There is little doubt but that the subject, in many instances, merely acts out a part consistent with the suggested hallucinations but does not experience these. When questioned as to why he behaved as he did, he usually replies that he did so because of his desire to co-operate, although some subjects admit that they felt compelled to do so, and finally some answer that they do not know why. That the subject should behave accordingly when he does hallucinate is a logical outcome. He is going through an experience that to him has all the reality of one caused by adequate stimuli. If we admit that the hallucinations are possible, then the rest follows. But, when hallucination is absent and compulsion is nevertheless present, what does this compulsion to act originate from? To gain insight into this problem, we must first examine why hallucinations may fail to take place. Two possibilities present themselves: The subject is not sufficiently hypnotized, or the subject is sufficiently hypnotized but cannot or can only partially hallucinate for various reasons.* In the second of these alternatives, the hypnotic state possesses the power of compulsion through its very own nature which is in turn derived from the generalization and the dissociation that has taken place. However, it must be noted that the subject will act out the missing hallucination only if he interprets the suggestion as requiring this of him. Where he has only a partial hallucination, it should be a natural tendency for him to fill in the gaps, so to speak.† Consequently, his behavior would

---

* This might occur if the subject is innately possessor of weak imagery mechanisms or if he lacks the necessary traces (engrams)—clearly in the second instance he cannot be asked to *re*-experience something he never has experienced.

† This has been referred to by some investigators as "confabulation."

tend to appear at times as if he were acting, although actually he is having hallucinatory experiences to some extent. In the first alternative, if the subject is not sufficiently hypnotized to produce hallucinations, he may still be sufficiently hypnotized to be compelled to carry out the suggestions according to his own interpretation of them. In still other instances, a subject with a high capacity for imagery may have hallucinations although he is in a relatively light trance, dissociation and even generalization being absent. In such a case, we may expect that the subject will fail to react appropriately, realizing for one thing that he is indeed suffering from a hallucination. Finally, in other situations, the hallucination may be present for similar reasons, but the degree of dissociation is not sufficient to make the hallucination the sole reality. As a result, while the subject has a true experience and is particularly compelled to react to it, at the same time his awareness denies its reality. The net result can be expected to show a certain amount of artificiality which makes it resemble acting.

In terms of these considerations it is now possible to see more clearly what the status of Sarbin's theory ‡ is in respect to the theory that has been developed in this book. Briefly, it constitutes in essence a sub-theory. Sarbin has chosen to construct a theory that focuses attention on the group of suggestibility phenomena that are most often seen to take place in practice. In doing so, he ignores those very phenomena that go to the root of suggestibility.§ In the present theory, the attempt has been made to take into account all phenomena.

Recall, Learning, and Hypnosis

We shall now leave the topic of sensorimotor alterations and examine those alterations that were considered earlier in connection with memory and learning. In the next section alterations having to do with moods, volition, and the personality in general will be taken up. As will be seen shortly, all these topics are actually related to the material just considered.

Investigations of hypnotic hypermnesia have furnished clear evidence that learning and memory can be improved under the influence of hypnosis in proportion to the extent to which the material learned has meaning or is a part of a well-integrated and meaningful context,

---

‡ The same remark will also apply to Orne's (328) views on regressions.

§ In reading Sarbin's papers, we get the rather definite impression that this attitude has arisen from the fact that he is unwilling to admit the existence, or even the possibility of homoaction, and particularly of suggested physiological changes as well as certain other phenomena.

and also in proportion to the extent of the affective content associated with it.   To evaluate these observations correctly, we should first consider that the relationship of improved performance to meaningfulness and integration in a context is also a well-known characteristic of material learned and recalled in the waking state.   Thus, hypnosis does not appear to have any exceptional properties in this respect. The same is true of affective factors.   Second, in respect to the fact that performance in hypnosis can be superior to waking performance, all other things being equal, analysis of the data seems to show that the observed hypnotic improvement is not particularly superior to similar improvement brought about by other means in the waking individual.   For instance, relaxation appears to favor recall, and in fact might account for a large portion of the reported hypnotic facilitation.   Besides relaxation, greater attending resulting from the constriction of awareness associated with hypnosis, the possibility that hypnosis can act as a source of motivation, the removal of interfering conscious ideation through constriction of awareness are all additional factors that would be expected to favor learning and recall.

In regard to the report of Cooper and his associates about the influence of temporal condensation combined with hallucinated experiences on learning, as has already been remarked, if the suggested condensation is truly present, this is effectively increasing the subject's amount of practice, and hence hypnosis would not be directly affecting the learning processes themselves.   In addition, we must consider the possible effect of the hallucinations themselves on learning.   It appears to be a common belief that practicing a skill in imagination contributes to the acquisition and perfecting of the skill; that is, it constitutes a learning situation.   Hallucinating a practice situation should therefore be expected to constitute a comparable situation.   In the case of motor skills, at least, this might be explained as resulting from the activation of the muscles concerned through ideomotor action.   The reports of Cooper and Tuthill (77) concerning their observation of action potentials in the flexor muscles of the thumb of a subject who was hallucinating that he was writing is evidence in support of the above.   In any event, the indication is that we are not dealing, in the case of learning with time distortions, with a specific property of hypnosis.

On the whole then the "superiority" of hypnotic recall and learning is probably not especially significant insofar as the nature and the theory of hypnosis are concerned.

In general, results of investigations on the production of amnesia by suggestion appear to indicate rather clearly that the effectiveness of posthypnotic amnesia (the only kind studied) is a direct function of the amount of cerebral and, particularly, of cortical involvement associated with the material to be forgotten. More specifically, it seems to be a function of the degree and extent to which awareness is an integral part of the recall process. A similar situation is found in regard to forgetting and remembering in the waking state; hence there is no particular reason to expect or believe that hypnotically induced amnesia, with one exception to be considered, involves anything out of the ordinary. On the basis of these considerations, it seems reasonable to conclude for the time being that posthypnotic amnesia is to be identified with a lack of awareness of the material that is forgotten. Results obtained from studies of hypnotically induced paramnesias support this thesis. Since, according to the theory of Chapter 19, control of awareness is a major characteristic of the hypnotic state, we might expect that this state would be particularly effective in bringing about amnesic phenomena.

In some cases suggested amnesia takes on more the form of a compulsion not to recall or an inhibition of voluntary recall than a true inaccessibility of material to the field of awareness. This type of "pseudo-amnesia" is well demonstrated in Wells's (470) investigation. The question of hypnotic compulsion has already been examined; hence no further comment appears necessary here, except possibly to point out the analogy existing between this type of amnesia and certain types of functional amnesias which are observed in practice.

Personality Alterations

Suggested Moods. As with hypermnesia, the study of induced moods has led to no development of particular significance in this area. The results appear to indicate that suggested moods are more akin to functional alterations of affective life than to those that arise in normal everyday life. This might have been predicted without difficulty, since all evidence points to the fact that hypnotic suggestion must act at a functional level. The fact that the basic personality structure of the subject seems to remain unaltered is consistent with the general picture obtained with waking individuals. Thus, on the whole the reported data are pretty much as they should be, although we might have expected that some instances of suggested moods would have shown themselves to be more realistic than they have. If hallucinatory phenomena are of the nature postulated in previous pages, it should be possible to reinstate previously experienced moods and therefore obtain considerable realism. Examination of the reported investigations would seem to indicate that the hypnotic situations in question were not sufficiently structured in the appropriate direction for this to take place. As seen in an earlier chapter, instances of regressions have been reported which meet this condition and which appear to have indeed led to realistic mood changes.

Volition and Hypnosis. It hardly seems necessary, after what has been said, to take up the actual mechanisms underlying suggested mood changes. Instead, we shall turn our attention to the problems of volition in relation to hypnosis. Actually, a large portion of the observed facts has been adequately explained in past pages and need not be of further concern to us at this time. A few additional words might be said regarding the three laws that were given for antagonistic suggestions. The role of trance depth as a deciding factor is pretty much self-explanatory since the force of a suggestion is, within limits, a direct function of trance depth. The matter of impression is really not specific to hypnosis or suggestion in general, but is itself a general psychological factor which, among other things, is found to play a basic role in motivation and in the acquisition and manifestation of habits. The temporal factor is the least understood of the three postulated factors. Possibly the first of two suggestions that are given establishes a set which favors it subsequently. Or it may be that the time factor allows the first suggestion to become more impressed, and is therefore not an independent condition as was stated earlier. There is unquestionably need for further study of this matter.

Multiple Personalities and Regressions. By far the more complex of the alterations under consideration are those having to do with personality changes. By the very nature of "personality" we have already touched, on many occasions, on various aspects relating to the entire question. However, thus far, only aspects of personality rather than the total personality have been considered. In the next few pages our main concern will be with personality as a whole. Quite apart from the reality or artifactitious nature of reported personality changes, we may summarize the type of situations that will be dealt with in the following manner:

A. Mutiple Personalities
   (a) Several personalities are created. These show no knowledge of each other's existence, the same being true also of the normal waking personality.

(*b*) Some or all created personalities know of each other and have access to all or part of the memories of the others. This is also true for the normal personality.

(*c*) The personalities in the above (*a*, *b*) are assumed to exist at different times. A third possibility is that the personalities coexist and may or may not be aware of each other or be capable of interacting. The normal personality may once more be one of the personalities in question.||

B. Regressions

(*a*) The individual is made to recall incidents of his past life and in some cases enacts these.

(*b*) The subject is presumably made to re-experience past events fully in a physiological sense, all experiences caused by events future to the period of regression being temporarily obliterated insofar as their capacity as determinants of behavior is concerned.

We shall begin the discussion with the production of multiple personalities. Interpretation of this is further complicated by the fact that creation of multiple personalities takes on several *nonequivalent* forms as follows:

1. The subject is told that he is some other person known to him more or less well. Either (i) he may be told that he is in some specific situation, or (ii) no situation is specified.

2. The subject is told that he will execute two different (and of course compatible) tasks at a predetermined time. (i) He may be told that this condition will be brought about through the existence of two personalities present in his body, but otherwise unspecified, or (ii) nothing is said in this respect.

3. The subject is told that he will behave as if he were possessed of a certain personality which is well defined for him.

One outcome of any one of these situations, in the case of multiple personalities as well as regressions, is that the subject merely acts out the part that has been suggested. In such an outcome there is no problem, except possibly for the reason why the subject acts at all. What was said earlier about hallucinations and acting applies equally well here. Another outcome involves the subject hallucinating as a result of the suggestions, but not showing any true personality alterations. This can account for some of the reported artificialities observed in former studies. A further analysis of this situation appears unnecessary. A third possibility is one in which no response at all is elicited. This last is too trivial to merit more than a passing mention. Finally, we have the instance in which a bona fide personality satisfying the

|| Personalities here are conceived as members of a *class* of personalities.

criteria for a secondary personality ¶ is produced. This situation will now be our primary concern.

A great many of the results obtained in such instances are understandable if we remember that hypnosis never elicits anything that is not already present in the subject. As a matter of fact, studies of suggested personalities have given us one of the best proofs of this fact. Thus, for instance, when a subject is told to be some other person known to him in some detail, the underlying structure of the new personality invariably shows the same character as the subject's normal personality. That is, the original personality structure persists. In other instances, when a subject has been induced to produce multiple personalities, the results have led to the general conclusion that suggested personalities are merely subpersonalities of the subject's total normal personality, and, conversely, the latter is a composite of the various suggested personalities that can be obtained. Finally, the results obtained appear to indicate that, the less the suggested personalities are defined by the hypnotist, through suggestion, the more they tend to show in their make-up manifestations of the psychodynamics specific to the subject's normal personality. Actually, we could have predicted this to a large extent from simply recognizing the fact that any new personality the subject may show must be built out of the same psychophysiological elements that form the basis of his normal personality. Some of these elements may be left out or given a secondary role, while others that play a minor role in the normal personality may become dominant as a result of the suggestions. However, no new elements have been created, and we must at best deal with subpersonalities.

The above considerations are important in attaining an understanding of suggested personality changes, for, if we tell a subject to be some other person known to him more or less extensively, it is clear that he can exhibit a change in personality only to the extent that he can match elements of his own personality with elements in the proposed personality. The success of such a matching depends on the subject's possessing such elements, and also on his being able to identify these elements from his knowledge and understanding of the other personality. The final problem of course is the integration of the abstracted elements into the model personality. None of this takes

¶ One of these criteria is rather important for this discussion and should be stated, namely: the secondary personality must be an autonomous entity; hence all other elements of the subject's waking personality not common to the secondary personality must be at least functionally isolated from the latter, that is, ablated.

place at a voluntary conscious level. Such an integration depends on the subject's ability to abstract the given structure and to duplicate it. Thus it becomes clear why it is extremely unlikely that a subject could take on the personality of Mae West, for instance, to the extent of eliminating any trace of his own waking personality, even when actively hallucinating a suggested specific situation.*

The degree to which the suggested model personality has been defined for the subject should make a big difference in the observed results. The more poorly it is defined, the more likely the new personality will tend to deviate from the suggested personality and resemble the subject's normal personality. That is, the smaller the imposed degree of constraint, the more possibilities there are opened to the subject and the more elastic is the situation for him. In studies made of cryptesthesia, for instance, all the subject is usually told if he is told anything at all about this matter, is that a new personality will manifest itself through his writing. Except for the compulsion to produce a new personality, the dynamics of the subject's personality have full sway in defining the new personality; hence the analytical value of induced automatic writing and related techniques in psychotherapy.

Before considering further the mechanisms responsible for the production of personality alterations as outlined above, we will now look a little more closely at certain features of regression phenomena.

Revivification. The situations we shall deal with primarily are those in which revivification, partial or complete, takes place. Although complete revivification is theoretically conceivable, there is no evidence that any instances of it have ever been observed. As remarked in an earlier chapter, there is good reason for this, since the notion of complete revivification leads to an apparent paradoxical situation. By its very nature, it demands that the very conditions which bring it into existence and make it possible should cease to exist so far as the subject is concerned—in fact, these conditions must take on the appearance of having never existed. To state this another way, complete revivification would appear to imply that the subject must reach a condition in which, so far as his psychophysiological processes of the moment are concerned, *he has never been revivified or even been hypnotized.*

---

* Whether this could ever be possible remains a rhetorical question. Theoretically, it is possible that, through training, extensive study of the model personality, and proper suggestive techniques, such a matching of personality elements and the resulting changes could be effected. There is some basis for this statement in the results obtained from regressions, provided of course we accept the reality of regression phenomena, particularly that of revivification.

A possible way out of this dilemma may be suggested. If we agree that any process seen in hypnosis can also take place in the waking state, then we can conceive the possibility that, once the process of complete revivification is initiated through the use of hypnotic suggestion, it can become self-sustained and does not require the presence of the conditions that were necessary for its initiation. Thus the subject could pass back to the waking state and yet remain revivified. The truth of this matter remains to be demonstrated. In the meantime, since regression types I and III do not involve complete revivification, we can discuss them without having to worry about any paradox.

In regression type I, the subject is presumably made to *remember* † past events in his life but does not re-experience these to the fullest extent, if at all. Furthermore, he remains under the influence of later experiences. In regression type III, on the contrary, there is by definition a certain amount of recall of the type that Prince (353) called physiological, whereby a past psychophysiological state is fully re-established. Such a recall can best be understood as an activation of quiescent traces, or as the reintegration of already active traces which have been isolated. That is, part of the revivification process is what we may call a *reinstatement* process.

The remainder is of course an *ablation* process.‡ But it is clear that, if part of revivification is an activation of experiential traces, then we have nothing more here than the production of a hallucination. This is substantiated by the behavior of regressed subjects who often conduct themselves in a manner no different from that observed of hallucinating individuals. The main difference in this respect between revivification and ordinary hallucination appears to be that in the former the subject hallucinates a *total single* and integrated past expe-

---

† "Remembering" is used here to denote recall in a symbolic form, that is, usually but not necessarily in terms of verbal images.

‡ An *ablation* is the apparent obliteration, or removal, of the neural equivalent (representation, trace, etc.) of specific experiences in such a manner that these experiences can no longer influence the individual's behavior. *Reinstatement* is the opposite of ablation, being the reincorporation of isolated experiential units and elements into the general pool of available experiential material. This is a more general notion than recall. The latter is a term designating the activation of quiescent traces which are otherwise fully incorporated in the body of present neurological determinants of behavior. On the other hand, an ablation involves the functional isolation of active elements, as well as the inactivation of neural pathways. Thus the greater inclusiveness of reinstatement.

rience whereas in the latter *elements* of *many different* past experiences are integrated into a single fictitious experience.

Revivification bears some resemblance to another phenomenon already considered, namely, the production of secondary personalities. There is a striking similarity between the two. Both in revivification and in the production of secondary personalities, elements of the individual's total personality are segregated and reintegrated into a subpersonality. It makes little difference whether the subpersonality is built out of those elements that are mainly characteristic of the present aspect of the total personality or out of those that are primarily characteristic of an older aspect. The process is the same. At least there is no reason to assume that it would be different. From an observer's standpoint, leaving the presence of hallucination out, there seems to be no essential difference between the production of secondary and of regressed personalities. From the standpoint of the mechanics involved, the main difference appears to be that in a regression the subject does not have to match elements of his personality with those of another personality as he must do when secondary personalities are induced. Instead, he has only to select those elements in himself that were exclusively present in an earlier stage of his life and integrate these into a structure similar to the one that existed then. These last remarks might explain at least partly why regression on the whole has led to more realistic changes than have the attempts to induce secondary personalities.§

This similarity extends further. One might at first object that the presence of ablation in revivification is a distinctive mark which differentiates the two phenomena. There is, however, something very similar to it in the production of secondary personalities. In fact, this is probably what led earlier investigators to speak of dissociation in this connection. Stated somewhat differently, both in revivification and in the production of secondary personalities, certain experiential traces as well as certain whole patterns of neural activity appear to be prevented from having any influence on the subject's behavior of the

§ Sarbin and Farberow (388) speak of regression phenomena as an enacting of age role which depends for its effectiveness on the accuracy of role perception, the role-taking aptitude of the subject, and favorable motivation. The perfection of a regression is mainly a function of the degree of congruence that can be brought about between the subject's perception of self and of role. The reader might compare this view with the above one. As has been pointed out, it is my belief that there is no fundamental disagreement between the theoretical approach presented in this book and that proposed by Sarbin.

moment. Nevertheless they are potentially present, as is well demonstrated by the observed facts. Seen in this light, ablation and the ablation-like process found in the production of multiple personalities appear more like a reversible severance process, or, to use an older but essentially correct term in the present context, like a dissociation.

In brief, then a possible way to look at revivification is to consider it as a composite involving (a) the production of hallucination, and (b) the production of a secondary personality.

The production of hallucination has already been discussed and needs no further comment. We need thus concern ourselves only with the second phenomenon. Though in some respects the partial reduction of regressions to the production of secondary personalities may be considered an improvement, it must be admitted that it does not help to elucidate the nature of multiple personalities nor the mechanism by which they are produced when suggestions are employed for this purpose. There is the advantage of having to deal with one problem instead of two. This problem itself leads to two fundamental questions. First, assuming that the interpretation that has been given is valid, how do hypnotic suggestions bring about the segregation, matching, and integration of personality elements into a secondary personality? Second, if there is an ablation-like effect present in the sense that elements of a secondary personality cannot interact with the remainder of the elements of the total personality, what is the nature of this ablation, and how does it come into being?

It must be admitted that no satisfactory answers to these questions are available at present. As was seen in an earlier section of this book, evidence was offered some years ago by Messerschmidt (309) showing that, whatever dissociation of personality was, it did not involve a functional severance. It was remarked in Chapter 9 that this does not preclude the existence of a dissociation of awareness *from* the substratum of neural events associated with the act of experiencing. As shown earlier in this chapter, this would account for certain aspects of negative hallucination. There is a strong outward resemblance between negative hallucination and ablation in that both negate certain experiences. This resemblance suggests that possibly dissociation of awareness can account for ablation as manifested in revivification and secondary personalities. It is entirely possible, on the other hand, that such a dissociation is not at all necessary and that ablation is merely an expression of a natural tendency for personality elements to integrate themselves into autonomous or quasi-autonomous units, or subpersonalities, whenever there is a weakening of the forces holding together these same elements in the waking personality, such as presumably may be accomplished by awareness. Furthermore, it is entirely conceivable that a slight "push" in any given direction, such as might be given by suggestions, would be all that is necessary to cause these elements to fall into a specific personality pattern. Certain concepts of modern physics are very suggestive in this connection. Such are the principle of minimum energy and the notions of quantum states and of atomic (or nuclear) shells. It would be beyond the scope of this book to pursue this matter to any extent, and we must leave it at that. After all is said, ablation may be simply an amnesia, or an aphasia-like phenomenon. It should also be remarked that it has never been clearly demonstrated by means of the technique employed by Messerschmidt that a functional isolation does (or does not) exist in revivification. The evidence against dissociation which is available at present holds only for secondary personalities as manifested in cryptesthesia, and in regard to the hypnotic state itself. Finally, it is possible that, in revivification, the recalled elements are so extensive, predominant, and well integrated into a unit that they override, mask, or tend to exclude the more recent material belonging to the forbidden periods of the subject's life. The simplicity of this solution makes it worth investigating. In any event, although the problem of how revivification comes into being as the result of suggestion remains partly unsolved, and similarly the problem of certain aspects of secondary personality production, the fault appears to lie less in the theory of hypnosis than in the lack of basic information about these two groups of phenomena.

Posthypnotic Phenomena

One more topic will be touched upon before concluding this chapter, that of posthypnotic phenomena. These have already been discussed rather extensively in Chapter 8. Two points remain to be elucidated. How does the posthypnotic signal acquire its capacity to produce any sort of trance, and, more particularly, a revivification of the kind shown to be present by Erickson et al. (112)? No complete answer is available at present, largely because too many fundamental data are still missing in regard to this problem and phenomenon. It would appear, however, that the posthypnotic signal acquires, somehow or other, at the symbolic level the equivalence of the entire process of trance induction as discussed in Chapter 19. Generalization of suggestibility is most likely at the root of this effect. If this is so, it should be possible to bring about posthypnotic phenomena for which the fully developed trance state is lacking (dissociation absent). There is evidence that this may take place in practice. The observed revivification itself may be a side effect caused by the tendency of the subject to seek a frame of reference. In the posthypnotic situation, a most natural frame of reference would be the situation in which the posthypnotic suggestion was initially given.

Summary and Conclusions

We have examined some of the important phenomena that can take place as the result of hypnotic suggestion. Possibly the most outstanding feature of the material considered, as pointed out earlier, is *that the differences between hypnotic and waking phenomena are essentially quantitative and not qualitative.* Such differences could be brought about in one of many ways:

1. New mechanisms are created, or
2. The basic underlying mechanisms are altered, *but* ||
    (*a*) Certain facilitating processes are brought into existence,
    (*b*) Normally interfering or masking processes are inhibited,
    (*c*) Normally present inhibitions are removed.

As we have seen, the third alternative can account for most if not all observed differences. It was said earlier that there are no a priori reasons to expect that the phenomena evoked in hypnosis should be physiologically or even psychologically different in any fundamental way from those seen under otherwise similar conditions in the waking state. It appears now that we can state with some reason that one possible interpretation of hypnotic phenomena is based on the postulate that hypnosis does not alter the basic psychophysiological processes which underlie similar functions in the waking and the hypnotic state, nor does it create new mechanisms. In other words, psychophysiological phenomena are *invariant* ¶ in respect to hypnosis.

In view of all this, and of the various considerations taken up in the text, the basic problem at present in understanding hypnotically induced phenomena seems to reduce primarily to one of understanding the analogous waking phenomena. In any case, there is no evidence that the material surveyed in this chapter is incompatible with the

|| This alternative is rather important, for, according to it, a process or mechanism never observed before may appear to be created by hypnosis, when actually it existed all the time, but could not manifest itself sufficiently for an observer to detect it.

¶ I am inclined to believe that this is a special case of a more general principle of invariance applicable to psychological phenomena.

Summary and Conclusions 313

theory of hypnosis presented earlier, or that it cannot be accounted for fully by this theory.

In concluding this chapter and the book as a whole, a few more comments might be made about the theoretical structure outlined in these last four chapters. Much of future criticism of it can be expected to be aimed at the basic postulates underlying the theory, namely: (*a*) All suggestibility phenomena do not result from one single process, but, of the various observed phenomena, some have different origins. In particular, hypnosis is the end result of four distinct, although not unrelated, processes. (*b*) Many phenomena obtained in hypnosis are not specific to it, that is, are not intrinsically associated with this state.

In anticipation of such criticism, it may be remarked that the first postulate may be largely the result of our lack of understanding of the basic neurophysiological processes that underlie human behavior. There may come a time when all four processes around which the theory is built will become nothing more than expressions of a single, unifying neurophysiological formula, or psychological formula in the event that all the phenomena in question turn out to be outside the domain of physiology. For the time being, however, the facts appear to point toward this postulate. A unitary principle is of course an attractive notion, but by no means a necessity. On the contrary. One look at the energetics of muscular contractions, as we understand it today, should convince anyone that simplicity is not always the key to understanding. The second postulate is really more in the nature of an observation. It is not essential to the theory itself, but rather evolves out of it as a subsidiary assumption or, better still, as a guiding principle. Whatever arguments may arise in this connection are most likely to be centered around which phenomena are to be considered in the category of "nonspecific" and will probably not be much concerned with the validity of the postulate itself. We do not have to go very far to point out a number of phenomena produced in hypnosis that are also known to take place independently of it under other circumstances. This is not to say that the theory here presented is without weaknesses. On the contrary there are some. In particular, the process of dissociation of awareness which is so basic to it needs considerably more clarification. The same is true for the mechanism and the process of revivification. This last may indeed be the weakest link in the entire structure and may prove yet to be its eventual downfall. On the other hand, it may be pointed out that the theory is able to take into account other past theories without taking over their weaknesses, explains a great many observed facts, and gives a unified picture of hypnosis and suggestibility.

In addition, it predicts as well as postdicts, a requirement of all good theories.

But, regardless of the validity of the material presented in these last chapters, if we review the material that has been discussed, it appears possible to say without being dogmatic that hypnosis is a scientifically established fact. We are beginning to know quite a few things about it as well as about related phenomena. It is clear, however, that much remains to be done along experimental lines in this area. Although in many respects investigations have shown hypnosis to be far less spectacular than had previously been believed, it remains a promising field for investigation, and may eventually throw considerable light on the nature of psychophysiological processes in general.

Bibliography

1. Abramson, M., and Heron, W. T.: An objective evaluation of hypnosis in obstetrics. *Amer. J. Obstet. and Gynaec.*, 1950, *59*, 1069–1074.
2. Adler, M. H., and Secunda, L.: An indirect technique to induce hypnosis. *J. nerv. ment. Dis.*, 1947, *106*, 190–193.
3. Allport, G.: *Personality.* New York: Holt, 1937.
4. Alrutz, S.: Die Suggestive Vesikation. *J. Psychol. Neurol.*, 1914, *21*, 1–10.
5. Arcieri, L.: Differences in the degree of suggestibility between schizophrenics, psychoneurotics, and normal subjects in the reproduction of visual forms. *Psychiat. Quart.*, 1949, *23*, 41–58.
6. Arnold, M. B.: On the mechanism of suggestion and hypnosis. *J. abnorm. soc. Psychol.*, 1946, *41*, 107–128.
7. Astruck, P.: Über psychische Beeinflussung des vegetativen Nervensystems in der Hypnose. I. Hypnotische Beeinflussung der Herztätigkeit und der Atmung. *Arch. ges. Psychol.*, 1923, *95*, 266–280.
8. Aveling, F., and Hargreaves, H. L.: Suggestibility with and without prestige in children. *Brit. J. Psychol.*, 1921–1922, *12*, 53–75.
9. Baernstein, L. N.: An experimental study of the effect on waking suggestibility of small doses of scopolamine hydrobromide. Thesis submitted for M.A. degree, 1929, Univ. Wisconsin.
10. Banister, H., and Zangwill, O. L.: Experimentally induced olfactory paramnesia. *Brit. J. Psychol.*, 1941, *32*, 155–175.
11. Banister, H., and Zangwill, O. L.: Experimentally induced visual paramnesia. *Brit. J. Psychol.*, 1941, *32*, 30–51.
12. Barker, W., and Burgwin, S.: Brain wave patterns during hypnosis, hypnotic sleep, and normal sleep. *Arch. Neurol. Psychiat.*, 1949, *62*, 412–420.
13. Barker, W., and Burgwin, S.: Brain wave patterns accompanying changes in sleep and wakefulness during hypnosis. *Psychosom. Med.*, 1948, *10*, 317–326.
14. Barry, H., Jr., Mackinnon, D. W., and Murray, H. A., Jr.: Studies in personality: A. Hypnotizability as a personality trait and its typological relations. *Hum. Biol.*, 1931, *13*, 1–36.
15. Bartlett, M. R.: Suggestibility in psychopathic individuals; a study with psychoneurotics and dementia praecox subjects. *J. gen. Psychol.*, 1936, *14*, 241–247.
16. Bartlett, M. R.: The auditory threshold during reverie as related to hypnotizability. *J. gen. Psychol.*, 1937, *17*, 167–170.
17. Bartlett, M. R.: Suggestibility in dementia praecox paranoid patients. *J. gen. Psychol.*, 1944, *30*, 97–102.
18. Bartlett, M. R.: Relation of suggestibility to other personality traits. *J. gen. Psychol.*, 1936, *15*, 191–196.
19. Bass, M.: Differentiation of hypnotic trance from normal sleep. *J. exp. Psychol.*, 1931, *14*, 382–399.

20. Baudouin, C.: *Suggestion and Autosuggestion.* London: George Allen and Unwin, 1921.

21. Baumgartner, M.: The correlation of direct suggestibility with certain character traits. *J. appl. Psychol.,* 1931, *15,* 1–15.

22. Beaunis, H.: *Le Somnambulisme provoqué.* Paris: J. B. Baillière et fils, 1886.

23. Bechterew, W. V.: What is hypnosis? *J. abnorm. soc. Psychol.,* 1906, *1,* 18–25.

24. Benedek, L.: A vegetativ idegrendozer befolyasarol hypnosisban. *Gyógyászat,* 1933, *14,* 1–2.

25. Bennett, J. H.: *Text-book of Physiology,* part II. Edinburgh, 1871.

26. Bergman, M. S., Graham, H., and Leavitt, H. C.: Rorschach exploration of consecutive hypnotic chronological age level regression. *Psychosom. Med.,* 1947, *9,* 20–28.

27. Beritoff, J.: Ueber die Entstehung der tierischen Hypnose. *Z. Biol.,* 1929, *89,* 77–82.

28. Bernheim, H.: *Suggestive Therapeutics.* New York: G. P. Putnam's Sons, 1902.

29. Berreman, J. V., and Hilgard, E. R.: The effects of personal heterosuggestion and two forms of autosuggestion upon postural movement. *J. soc. Psychol.,* 1936, *7,* 289–300.

30. Bier, W.: Beitrag zur Beeinflussung des Kreislaufes durch psychische Vorgange. *Z. klin. Med.,* 1930, *113,* 762–781.

31. Binet, A.: *La Suggestibilité.* Paris: Scheicher Frères, 1900.

32. Binet, A., and Féré, C.: *Animal Magnetism.* New York: Appleton-Century, 1888.

33. Bird, C.: *Social Psychology.* New York: Appleton-Century, 1941.

34. Bitterman, M. E., and Marcuse, F. L.: Autonomic response in posthypnotic amnesia. *J. exp. Psychol.,* 1945, *35,* 248–252.

35. Blackwell, H. R.: Psychophysical thresholds. Experimental studies of methods of measurement. *Engng. Res. Bull. 36, Univ. Mich.,* 1953.

36. Blake, H., and Gerard, R. W.: Brain potentials during sleep. *Amer. J. Physiol.,* 1937, *119,* 692–703.

37. Bloch, B.: Ueber die Heilung der Warzen durch Suggestion. *Klin. Wschr.,* 1927, *6,* 2271, 2320.

38. Boas, E. P., and Landauer, W.: The effect of elevated metabolism on the hearts of the frizzle fowl. *Amer. J. med. Sci.,* 1933, *185,* 654–664.

39. Bolten, G. C.: Vom "hysterischen Oedema." *Dtsch. Z. Nervenheilk.,* 1922, *73,* 319–328.

40. Bonjour, J.: La part du psychisme dans l'accouchement, cause, fréquence nocturne et narcose subite. *Pr. méd.,* 1927, *35,* 603–604.

41. Bonjour, J.: La guérison des condylomes par la suggestion. *Schweiz. med. Wschr.,* 1927, *57,* 980–981.

42. Bonnet, V., and Saboul, R.: Contribution à l'étude de l'hypnose animale. *J. Physiol. Path. gén.,* 1935, *33,* 887–906.

43. Bovard, E. W., Jr.: Social norms and the individual. *J. abnorm. soc. Psychol.,* 1948, *43,* 62–69.

44. Bowles, N. W., Jr., and Pronko, N. H.: Reversibility of stimulus function under hypnosis. *J. Psychol.,* 1949, *27,* 41–47.

45. Bramwell, M. J.: *Hypnotism, Its History, Practice, and Theory*. Philadelphia: J. B. Lippincott, 1930.
46. Bray, D. W.: The prediction of behavior from two attitude scales. *J. abnorm. soc. Psychol.*, 1950, 45, 64–84.
47. Brazier, M. A. B., and Finesinger, J. E.: Action of barbiturates on the cerebral cortex. *Arch. Neurol. Psychiat.*, 1945, 53, 31–38.
48. Brenman, M., and Reichard, S.: Use of the Rorschach test in the prediction of hypnotizability. *Bull. Menninger Clin.*, 1943, 7, 183–187.
49. Brenman, M., Gill, M., and Hackner, F. J.: Alterations in the state of the ego in hypnosis. *Bull. Menninger Clin.*, 1947, 11, 60–66.
50. Brenman, M.: Experiments in the hypnotic production of anti-social and self-injurious behavior. *Psychiatry*, 1942, 5, 49–61.
51. Brenman, M.: Dream and Hypnosis. *Psychoanal. Quart.*, 1949, 18, 455–465.
52. Brenman, M., and Knight, R. P. Hypnotherapy for mental illness in the aged: case report of hysterical psychosis in a 71-year-old woman. *Bull. Menninger Clin.*, 1943, 7, 188–198.
53. Brickner, R. M., and Kubie, L. S.: A miniature psychotic storm produced by a superego conflict over simple post-hypnotic suggestions. *Psychoanal. Quart.*, 1936, 5, 467, 487.
54. Britt, S. H.: *Social Psychology of Modern Life*. New York: Farrar and Rinehart, 1941.
55. Brotteaux, P.: *Hypnotisme et scopochloralose*. Paris: Vigot Frères, 1936.
56. Brown, J. F.: *The Psychodynamics of Abnormal Behavior*. New York: McGraw-Hill, 1940.
57. Brown, R. R., and Vogel, V. H.: Psychophysiological reactions following painful stimuli under hypnotic analgesia contrasted with gas anesthesia and Novocain block. *J. appl. Psychol.*, 1938, 22, 408–420.
58. Brown, W.: Individual and sex differences in suggestibility. *Univ. Calif. Publ. Psychol.*, 1916, 2, 291–430.
59. Brown, W.: Sleep, hypnosis, and mediumistic trance. *Character & Pers.*, 1935, 3, 112–126.
60. Brown, W.: *Psychology and Psychotherapy*. Baltimore: Wm. Wood, 1934.
61. Bull, N., and Gidro-Frank, L.: Emotions induced and studied in hypnotic subjects, Part II. The Findings. *J. nerv. ment. Dis.*, 1950, 112, 97–120.
62. Burnett, C. T.: Splitting the mind. *Psychol. Monogr.*, 1925, 34, No. 2.
63. Carhart, R.: An experimental evaluation of suggested relaxation. *Speech Monogr.*, 1943, 23, 434–448.
64. Carrington, H.: Hypnotizing animals. *Psych. Res.*, 1931, 25, 41–44.
65. Cason, H.: Influence of imagery in a group situation. *J. abnorm. soc. Psychol.*, 1925, 20, 294–299.
66. Cason, H.: Conditioned pupillary reactions. *J. exp. Psychol.*, 1922, 5, 108–146.
67. Caster, J. E., and Baker, G. S., Jr.: Comparative suggestibility in the trance and waking state—a further study. *J. gen. Psychol.*, 1932, 7, 287–301.
68. Charcot, J. M.: Oeuvres complètes. Tome IX. *Métallo-thérapie et hypnotisme*. Paris: Bourneville et E. Brissaud, 1890.
69. Charcot, J. M.: *Lectures on Diseases of the Nervous System*. New Sydenham Society, London: 1889, III.
70. Christenson, J. A.: Dynamics in hypnotic induction. *Psychiatry*, 1949, 12, 37–54.

71. Coffin, T. E.: Some conditions of suggestion and suggestibility: a study of certain attitudinal and situational factors influencing the process of suggestion. *Psychol. Monogr.* No. 4, *53*, 1941.

72. Cohen, M. E., and Cobb, S.: The use of hypnosis in the study of acid-base balance of the blood in a patient with hysterical hyperventilation. *Res. Publ. Ass. nerv. ment. Dis.*, 1939, *19*, 318–332.

73. Cohn, R., and Katzenelbogen, S.: Changes induced by intravenous sodium amytal. *Proc. Soc. exp. Biol., N. Y.*, 1942, *49*, 560–563.

74. Cooper, L. F.: Time distortion in hypnosis. *Bull. Georgetown Univ. Med. Center.*, 1948, *1*, 214–221.

75. Cooper, L. F., and Erickson, M. H.: Time distortion in hypnosis II. *Bull. Georgetown Univ. Med. Center*, 1950, *4*, 50–68.

76. Cooper, L. F., and Rodgin, D. W.: Time distortion in hypnosis and non-motor learning. *Science*, 1952, *115*, 500–502.

77. Cooper, L. F., and Tuthill, C. E.: Time distortion in hypnosis and motor learning. *J. Psychol.*, 1952, *34*, 67–76.

78. Cooper, L. F.: Time distortion in hypnosis with a semantic interpretation of the mechanism of certain hypnotically induced phenomena. *J. Psychol.*, 1952, *34*, 257–284.

79. Coors, D.: A determination of the density of post-hypnotic amnesia for the stylus maze. Thesis submitted for B.A. degree, 1928, Univ. Wisconsin.

80. Coriat, I. H.: The nature of sleep. *J. abnorm. Psychol.*, 1912, *6*, 329–367.

81. Corn-Becker, F., Welch, L., and Fisichelli, F.: Conditioning factors underlying hypnosis. *J. abnorm. soc. Psychol.*, 1949, *44*, 212–222.

82. Counts, R. M., and Mensh, I. N.: Personality characteristics in hypnotically-induced hostility. *J. clin. Psychol.*, 1950, *6*, 325–330.

83. Crozier, W. J.: Reflex immobility and the central nervous system. *Proc. Soc. exp. Biol.*, 1923, *21*, 55–56.

84. Curtis, J. W.: A study of the relationship between hypnotic susceptibility and intelligence. *J. exp. Psychol.*, 1943, *33*, 337–339.

85. Cushing, H. M., and Rush, G. M.: An investigation of character traits in delinquent girls. *J. appl. Psychol.*, 1947, *11*, 1–7.

86. Dahm, H., and Jenness, A.: Change in auditory threshold during reverie as related to hypnotizability. *J. gen. Psychol.*, 1937, *17*, 167–170.

87. Dahm, H., and Jenness, A.: A study of direct suggestibility and social introversion as related to auditory threshold and to reaction time during reverie. *J. soc. Psychol.*, 1937, *8*, 251–267.

88. Darrow, C. W., Henry, C. E., Gill, M., Brenman, M., Converse, M.: Frontal-motor parallelism and motor-occipital in-phase activity in hypnosis, drowsiness, and sleep. *EEG. clin. Neurophysiol.*, 1950, *2*, 355.

89. Darrow, C. W., Henry, E. C., Gill, M., Brenman, M.: Inter-area electroencephalographic relationships affected by hypnosis: preliminary report. *EEG. clin. Neurophysiol.*, 1950, *2*, 231.

90. Darwin, C.: A posthumous essay on instinct. In G. J. Romanes, *Mental Evolution in Animals* (pp. 360–364). New York: Appleton, 1900.

91. Davis, L. W., and Husband, R. W.: A study of hypnotic susceptibility in relation to personality traits. *J. abnorm. soc. Psychol.*, 1931, *26*, 175–182.

92. Davis, R. C., and Kantor, J. R.: Skin resistance during hypnotic states. *J. gen. Psychol.*, 1935, *13*, 62–81.

93. Dearborn, C. V. N.: Psychophysiology of the crayfish. *Amer. J. Physiol.*, 1900, *3*, 404–443.

94. Delhougne, F., and Hansen, K.: Die Beeinflussbarkeit der Magen und Pankreas-secretion in der Hypnose. *Dtsch. Arch. klin. Med.*, 1927, *157*, 20–35.

95. Deutsch, F., and Kauf, E.: Psycho-physische Kreislaufstudien. II. Mitteilung. Über die Ursachen der Kreislaufstorangen bei den Herzneurosen. *Z. ges. exp. Med.*, 1923, *32*, 197–216.

96. Dick, A. V.: Hypnotics in psychotherapy. *Brit. med. J.*, 1940, *1*, 865.

97. Diehl, F., and Heinichen, W.: Beeinflussung allergischer Reaktionen. *Münch. med. Wschr.*, 1931, *78*, 1008–1009.

98. Dorcus, R. M.: Modification by suggestion of some vestibular visual phenomena. *Amer. J. Psychol.*, 1937, *49*, 82–87.

99. Dorcus, R. M., Brintnall, A. K., and Case, H. W.: Control experiments and their relation to theories of hypnotism. *J. gen. Psychol.*, 1941, *24*, 217–221.

100. Doswald, D. C.: Zur Frage des posthypnotischen Hautphänomene. *Monatsh. prakt. Derm.*, 1906, *43*, 634–640.

101. Doupe, J., Miller, W. R., and Keller, W. K.: Vasomotor reactions in the hypnotic state. *J. neurol. Psychiat.*, 1939, *2*, 97–106.

102. Dunbar, H. F.: *Emotions and Bodily Changes.* New York: Columbia Univ. Press, 1947.

103. Durville, H.: *Traité experimental de magnétisme.* 2 Vol. Paris: Chamuel, 1895.

104. Dynes, J. B.: Objective method for distinguishing sleep from the hypnotic trance. *Arch. Neurol. Psychiat.*, 1947, *57*, 84–93.

105. Dynes, J. B.: Hypnotic anesthesia. *J. abnorm. soc. Psychol.*, 1932, *27*, 79–88.

106. Edwards, A. S.: Hypnosis and involuntary movements. *J. gen. Psychol.*, 1951, *45*, 265–268.

107. Ehrenreich, G. A.: The influence of unconscious factors on hypnotizability. *Bull. Menninger Clin.*, 1951, *15*, 45–57.

108. Eichelberg: Durch Hypnose erzengtes "Hysterisches Fieber." *Dtsch. Z. Nervenheilk.*, 1921, *68–69*, 352–356.

109. Eiff, A. W. v.: Der Einfluss der Hypnose auf Temperaturempfindung und Wärmeregulation. *Z. ges. exp. Med.*, 1951, *117*, 261–273.

110. Eisenbud, J.: Psychology of headache. *Psychiat. Quart.*, 1937, *11*, 592–619.

111. Erickson, M. H.: An experimental investigation of the hypnotic subject's apparent ability to become unaware of stimuli. *J. gen. Psychol.*, 1944, *31*, 191–212.

112. Erickson, M. H., and Erickson, E. M.: Concerning the nature and character of post-hypnotic behavior. *J. gen. Psychol.*, 1941, *24*, 95–133.

113. Erickson, M. H.: Hypnotic investigation of psychosomatic phenomena: I. Psychosomatic interrelationships studied by experimental hypnosis. *Psychosom. Med.*, 1943, *5*, 51–58.

114. Erickson, M. H.: A study of clinical and experimental findings on hypnotic deafness. II. Experimental findings with a conditioned reflex technique. *J. gen. Psychol.*, 1938, *19*, 151–167.

115. Erickson, M. H.: The induction of color blindness by a technique of hypnotic suggestion. *J. gen. Psychol.*, 1939, *20*, 61–89.

116. Erickson, M. H., and Erickson, E. M.: The hypnotic induction of hallucinatory color vision followed by pseudo-images. *J. exp. Psychol.*, 1938, *22*, 581–588.

117. Erickson, M. H.: A study of an experimental neurosis hypnotically induced in a case of ejaculatio praecox. *N. E. J. Med.*, 1932, *206*, 777–781.

118. Erickson, M. H.: Development of apparent unconsciousness during hypnotic reliving of a traumatic experience. *Arch. Neurol. Psychiat.*, 1937, *38*, 1282–1288.

119. Erickson, M. H., and Kubie, L. S.: The successful treatment of a case of acute hysterical depression by a return under hypnosis to a critical phase of childhood. *Psychoanal. Quart.*, 1941, *10*, 592–609.

120. Erickson, M. H.: An experimental investigation of the possible anti-social uses of hypnosis. *Psychiatry*, 1939, *2*, 391–414.

121. Erickson, M. H., and Brickner, R. M.: Hypnotic investigation of psychosomatic phenomena. II. Development of aphasia-like reactions from hypnotically induced amnesias. *Psychosom. Med.*, 1943, *5*, 51–70.

122. Erickson, M. H., and Kubie, L. S.: The translation of the cryptic automatic writing of one hypnotic subject by another in a trance-like dissociated state. *Psychoanal. Quart.*, 1940, *9*, 51–63.

123. Erickson, M. H.: Experimental demonstration of the psychopathology of everyday life. *Psychoanal. Quart.*, 1939, *8*, 338–353.

124. Erickson, M. H.: The method employed to formulate a complex story for the induction of an experimental neurosis in a hypnotic subject. *J. gen. Psychol.*, 1944, *31*, 67–84.

125. Estabrook, G. H.: A standardized hypnotic technique dictated to a Victrola record. *Amer. J. Psychol.*, 1930, *42*, 115–116.

126. Estabrook, G. H.: Experimental studies in suggestion. *J. genet. Psychol.*, 1929, *36*, 120–139.

127. Estabrook, G. H.: The psychogalvanic reflex in hypnosis. *J. gen. Psychol.*, 1930, *3*, 150–157.

128. Estabrook, G. H.: *Hypnotism*. New York: Dutton, 1943.

129. Eysenck, H. J., and Furneaux, W. D.: Primary and secondary suggestibility: an experimental and statistical study. *J. exp. Psychol.*, 1945, *35*, 485–503.

130. Eysenck, H. J.: States of high suggestibility and the neuroses. *Amer. J. Psychol.*, 1944, *57*, 406–411.

131. Eysenck, H. J.: *Dimensions of Personality*. London: Kegan Paul, 1947.

132. Eysenck, H. J.: Suggestibility and hysteria. *J. Neurol. Psychiat.*, 1943, *6*, 22–31.

133. Eysenck, H. J., and Rees, W. L.: States of heightened suggestibility: Narcosis. *J. ment. Sci.*, 1945, *91*, 301–310.

134. Eysenck, H. J.: An experimental study of the improvement of mental and physical functions in the hypnotic state. *Brit. J. med. Psychol.*, 1941, *18*, 304–316.

135. Eysenck, H. J.: Suggestibility and hypnosis—an experimental analysis. *Proc. R. Soc. Med.*, 1943, *36*, 349–354.

136. Farber, L. H., and Fisher, C.: An experimental approach to dream psychology through the use of hypnosis. *Psychoanal. Quart.*, 1943, *12*, 202–215.

137. Farris, E. J., Garrison, M., Jr., and Heintz, R. K.: The influence of hypnosis on semen. *J. Urol.*, 1951, *66*, 720–721.

138. Ferenczi, S.: Introjektion und Uebertragung. *Jb. psychoanal. psychopath. Forsch.*, 1909, *1*, 422–458.

139. Fisher, V. E.: Hypnotic suggestion and conditioned reflex. *J. exp. Psychol.*, 1932, *15*, 212–217.

140. Fisher, V. E.: *An Introduction to Abnormal Psychology.* New York: Macmillan, 1929.

141. Fisher, V. E., and Marrow, J.: Experimental study of moods. *Character & Pers.*, 1934, *2*, 201–208.

142. Foley, J. P.: Tonic immobility in the rhesus monkey (Macaca mulatta) induced by manipulation, immobilization and experimental inversion of the visual field. *J. comp. Psychol.*, 1938, *26*, 515–526.

143. Ford, L. F., and Yeager, C. L.: Changes in electroencephalogram in subjects under hypnosis. *Dis. nerv. Syst.*, 1948, *9*, 190–192.

144. Franck, B. J.: L'hypnose et l'EEG. *EEG. clin. Neurophysiol.*, 1950, *2*, 107.

145. Fresacher, L.: A way into the hypnotic state. *Brit. J. med. Hypnot.*, 1951, *3*, 12–13.

146. Freud, S.: *Group Psychology and the Analysis of the Ego.* New York: Boni and Liveright, 1922.

147. Frick, H. L., Scantlebury, R. E., and Patterson, T. L.: The control of gastric hunger contractions in man by hypnotic suggestion. *Amer. J. Physiol.*, 1935, *113*, 47.

148. Friedlander, J. W., and Sarbin, R. T.: The depth of hypnosis. *J. abnorm. soc. Psychol.*, 1938, *33*, 281–294.

149. Frolov, Y. P.: *Pavlov and His School.* London: K. Paul, Trench, Trubner, 1937.

150. Fulde, E.: Über den Einfluss hypnotischer Erregungszustände auf den Gasaustausch. *Z. ges. Neurol. Psychiat.*, 1937, *159*, 761–766.

151. Fulton, J. F.: *A Textbook of Physiology.* Philadelphia: W. B. Saunders, 1949.

152. Furneaux, W. D.: The prediction of susceptibility to hypnosis. *J. Personality*, 1946, *14*, 281–294.

153. Furneaux, W. D.: Primary suggestibility and hypnotic susceptibility in a group situation. *J. gen. Psychol.*, 1952, *46*, 87–91.

154. Gault, R. H., and Goodfellow, L. D.: Sources of error in psychophysical measurements. *J. gen. Psychol.*, 1940, *23*, 197–200.

155. Gerebtzoff, M. A.: État fonctionnel de l'écorce cérébrale au cours de l'hypnose animale. *Arch. intern. Physiol.*, 1941, *51*, 365–378.

156. Gessler, H., and Hansen, K.: Über die suggestive Beeinflussbarkeit der Wärmeregulation in der hypnose. *Dtsch. Arch. klin. Med.*, 1927, *156*, 352–359.

157. Gidro-Frank, L., and Bowerbuch, M. K.: A study of the plantar response in hypnotic age regression. *J. nerv. ment. Dis.*, 1948, *107*, 443–458.

158. Gidro-Frank, L., and Bull, N.: Emotions induced and studied in hypnotic subjects. Part I. The method. *J. nerv. ment. Dis.*, 1950, *111*, 91–100.

159. Gigon, A., Aigner, E., Brauch, W.: Über den einfluss der Psyche auf Körperliche Vorgänge. Hypnose und Blutzucker. *Schweiz. med. Wschr.*, 1926, *56*, 749–750.

160. Gilbert, J. A.: Researches on the mental and physical development of school children. *Stud. Yale psychol. Lab.*, 1894, *2*, 40–100.

322 Bibliography

161. Gill, M. M.: Spontaneous regression on the induction of hypnosis. *Bull. Menninger Clin.*, 1948, *12*, 41–48.

162. Gilman, T. T., and Marcuse, F. D.: Animal hypnosis. *Psychol. Bull.*, 1949, *46*, 151–165.

163. Gilman, T. T., and Marcuse, F. D.: "Animal hypnosis": a study in the induction of tonic immobility in chickens. *J. comp. physiol. Psychol.*, 1950, *43*, 99–111.

164. Giroud, A.: La suggestibilité chez des enfants d'école de sept a douze ans. *Année Psychol.*, 1911, *18*, 362–388.

165. Glasser, F.: Psychische Beeinflussung des Blutserumkalkspiegels. *Klin. Wschr.*, 1924, *3*, 1492–1493.

166. Goldwyn, J.: Effect of hypnosis on basal metabolism. *Arch. internat. Med.*, 1930, *45*, 109–114.

167. Gorton, B. E.: The physiology of hypnosis. *Psychiat. Quart.*, 1949, *23*, 317–343, 457–485.

168. Grafe, E., and Traumann: Zur Frage des Einflusses Psychischer Depressionen und der Vorstellung Schwerer Muskelarbeit auf den Stoffwechsel. *Z. ges. Neurol. Psychiat.*, 1920, *62*, 237–252.

169. Grafe, E., and Mayer, L.: Über den Einfluss der Affekte auf den Gesamtstoffwechsel. *Z. ges. Neurol. Psychiat.*, 1923, *86*, 247–253.

170. Grassheim, K., and Wittkower, E.: Über die suggestive Beeinflussbarkeit der spezifisch dynamischen Eiweisswirkung in Hypnose. *Dtsch. med. Wschr.*, 1931, *57*, 141–143.

171. Gray, W. H.: The effect of hypnosis on learning to spell. *J. educ. Psychol.*, 1934, *25*, 471–473.

172. Grether, W. F.: A comment on "The induction of color blindness by a technique of hypnotic suggestion." *J. gen. Psychol.*, 1940, *23*, 207–210.

173. Guidi, G.: Recherches experimentales sur la suggestibilité. *Arch. Psychol.*, 1908, *8*, 49–54.

174. Guilford, J. P., and Guilford, R. B.: Personality factors, S, E, and M and their measurement. *J. Psychol.*, 1936, *2*, 102–127.

175. Hadfield, J. A.: War neurosis: a year in a neuropathic hospital. *Brit. med. J.*, 1942, *1*, 320–323.

176. Hadfield, J. A.: *The Psychology of Power.* New York: Macmillan, 1923.

177. Hadfield, J. A.: The influence of hypnotic suggestions on inflammatory conditions. *Lancet*, 1917, *2*, 678–679.

178. Hakebush, Blinkowski, and Foundillere, R.: An attempt at a study of development of personality with the aid of hypnosis. *Trud. Inst. Psikhonevr., Kiev.*, 1930, *2*, 236–272.

179. Hansen, K.: Analyse, Indikation, und Grenze der Psychotherapie beim Bronchialasthma. *Dtsch. med. Wschr.*, 1947, *55*, 1462–1464.

180. Hardy, J. D., Wolff, H. G., and Goodell, H.: Studies on pain; a new method for measuring pain threshold: observations on spatial summation of pain. *J. clin. Invest.*, 1940, *19*, 649–657.

181. Harriman, P. L.: Hypnotic induction of color vision anomalies: I. The use of the Ishihara and the Jensen tests to verify the acceptance of suggested color blindness. *J. gen. Psychol.*, 1942, *26*, 289–298.

182. Harriman, P. L.: Hypnotic induction of color vision anomalies: II. Results on two other tests of color blindness. *J. gen. Psychol.*, 1942, *27*, 81–92.

183. Harriman, P. L.: The experimental production of some phenomena related to the multiple personality. *J. abnorm. soc. Psychol.*, 1942, 37, 244–255.
184. Hart, E.: Hypnotism and humbug. *Nineteenth Century.* January, 1882. [As reported by Bramwell (45).]
185. Haupman, A.: Versuche zur rascheren Herbeiführung einer Hypnose. *Klin. Wschr.*, 1934, 13, 437–439.
186. Headlee, C. R., and Kellog, W. N.: Conditioning and retention under hypnotic doses of nembutal. *Amer. J. Psych.*, 1941, 54, 353–366.
187. Heidenhain, R.: *Hypnotism or Animal Magnetism.* London: K. Paul, Trench, and Trubner, 1906.
188. Heilig, R., and Hoff, H.: Über hypnotische Beeinflussung der Nierenfunktion. *Dtsch. med. Wschr.*, 1925, 51, 1615–1616.
189. Heilig, R., and Hoff, H.: Beiträge zur hypnotischen Beeinflussung der Magenfunktion. *Med. Klin.*, 1925, 21, 162–163.
190. Heilig, R., and Hoff, H.: Über psychogene Entstehung des Herpes labialis. *Med. Klin.*, 1928, 24, 1472.
191. Heller, F., and Schultz, J. H.: Über einen Fall hypnotisch erzeugter Blasenbildung. *Münch. med. Wschr.*, 1909, 56, 2112.
192. Heyer, G. R.: Psychische Einfüsse auf die Motilität von Magen und Darm; zugleich ein Beitrag zur Gastroptosenfrage. *Klin. Wschr.*, 1923, 2, 2274–2277.
193. Heyer, G. R., and Grote, W.: Studien zum Phosphorsäurestoffwechsel unter besonderer Berücksichtigung der psychischen Einflüsse. Erste Mitteilung; Die Phosphorsäureausscheidung bei (Hypnotisch Erzeugten) Erregungszuständen. *Schweiz. med. Wschr.*, 1923, 53, 283–287.
194. Heyer, G. R.: Psychogene Funktionsstörungen des Verdauungstraktes. In O. Schwarz, *Psychogenese und Psychotherapie Korperlicher Symptome* (pp. 229–257). Wien: Springer, 1925.
195. Heyer, G. R.: Das körperlich-seelische Zusammenwirken in den Lebensvorgängen. An Hand klinischen und experimenteller Tatsachen dargestellt. *Grenzfr. Nerv.- u. Seelenleb.*, 1925, 121, 1–65.
196. Hibler, F. N.: An experimental investigation of negative after-image of hallucinated colors in hypnosis. *J. exp. Psychol.*, 1940, 27, 45–57.
197. Himmelweit, H. T., Desai, M., and Petrie, A.: An experimental investigation of neuroticism. *J. Personality*, 1946, 15, 173–196.
198. Hinsie, L. E., and Shatzky, J. S.: *Psychiatric Dictionary.* New York: Oxford Univ. Press, 1947.
199. Hoagland, H.: Consciousness and the chemistry of time in: Problems of consciousness. *Trans.* first conference, pp. 164–200. New York, *Josiah Macy Jr. Foundation*, 1951.
200. Hoagland, H.: Quantitative aspects of tonic immobility in vertebrates. *Proc. nat. Acad. Sci., Wash.*, 1927, 13, 838–843.
201. Hoagland, H.: On the mechanism of tonic immobility in vertebrates. *J. gen. Physiol.*, 1928, 11, 715–741.
202. Hoagland, H.: The mechanism of tonic immobility. *J. gen. Psychol.*, 1928, 1, 426–447.
203. Hoff, H., and Pötzl, O.: Über die labyrinthären Beziehungen von Flugsensationen und Flugträumen. *Mschr. Psychiat. Neurol.*, 1937, 97, 193–211.

204. Hollander, B.: *Methods and Uses of Hypnosis and Self-Hypnosis*. New York: Macmillan, 1928.
205. Holmes, S. J.: Death-feigning in Ranatra. *J. comp. neurol. Psychol.*, 1906, *16*, 200–216.
206. Holmes, S. J.: The instinct of feigning death. *Pop. Sci. Mon.*, 1908, *72*, 179–185.
207. Holmes, S. J.: *Studies in Animal Behavior*. Boston: Badger, 1916.
208. Holmes, S. J.: A note on tonic immobility. *J. gen. Psychol.*, 1928, *2*, 378.
209. Horsley, J. S.: *Narco-analysis*. New York: Oxford Univ. Press, 1943.
210. Horsley, J. S.: Narcotic hypnosis. *Brit. J. med. Hypnot.*, 1951, *2*, 2–7.
211. Houssay, B. A.: *Human Physiology*. New York: McGraw-Hill, 1951.
212. Hudgins, C. V.: Conditioning and the voluntary control of the pupillary light reflex. *J. gen. Psychol.*, 1933, *8*, 3–51.
213. Hull, C. L.: *Hypnosis and Suggestibility—an Experimental Approach*. New York: D. Appleton-Century, 1933.
214. Hull, C. L., and Huse, B.: Comparative suggestibility in the trance and waking states. *Amer. J. Psychol.*, 1930, *42*, 279–286.
215. Hull, C. L., Patten, E. F., and Switzer, S. A.: Does positive response to direct suggestion as such evoke a generalized hypersuggestibility? *J. gen. Psychol.*, 1933, *8*, 52–64.
216. Hull, C. L., and Life, C.: Reference 213, p. 86.
217. Hurlock, E. B.: The suggestibility of children. *Ped. Sem. and J. genet. Psychol.*, 1930, *37*, 59–74.
218. Huse, B.: Does the hypnotic trance favor the recall of faint memories? *J. exp. Psychol.*, 1930, *13*, 519–529.
219. Huston, P. E., Shakow, D., and Erickson, M. H.: A study of hypnotically induced complexes by means of the Luria technique. *J. gen. Psychol.*, 1934, *11*, 65–97.
220. Ingwarson, C. G., and Lindberg, B. J.: Experimental studies of suggestibility in mental disturbances. *Acta. psychiat., Kbh.*, 1935, *10*, 77–85.
221. Jacobi, W.: Die Stigmatisierten. Beiträge zur Psychologie der Mystik. *Grenzfr. Nerv. -u. Seelenleb.*, 1923, *114*, 1–57.
222. Jacobson, E.: *Progressive Relaxation*. Chicago: Univ. Chicago Press, 1938.
223. Janet, P.: *Major Symptoms of Hysteria*. New York: Macmillan, 1920.
224. Jendrassik, E.: Einiges über Suggestion. *Neurol. Zbl.*, 1888, 7, 281–283.
225. Jenness, A.: Hypnotism. In J. McV. Hunt, *Personality and the Behavior Disorders* (Vol. I, pp. 466–502).
226. Jenness, A.: Facilitation of response to suggestion by response to previous suggestions of similar type. *J. exp. Psychol.*, 1933, *16*, 55–82.
227. Jenness, A., and Wible, C. L.: Respiration and heart action in sleep and hypnosis. *J. gen. Psychol.*, 1937, *16*, 197–222.
228. Jones, E.: *Papers on Psychoanalysis*. Chapter XII. London: Bailliere, Tindall, and Cox, 1913.
229. Kantor, J. R.: *A Survey of the Science of Psychology*. Bloomington: Principia, 1933.
230. Keir, G.: An experiment in mental testing under hypnosis. *J. ment. Sci.*, 1945, *91*, 346–352.
231. Kelman, H. C.: Effects of success and failure on "suggestibility" in the autokinetic situation. *J. abnorm. soc. Psychol.*, 1950, *45*, 267–285.

Bibliography 325

232. Kellogg, E. R.: Duration and effects of post-hypnotic suggestions. *J. exp. Psychol.*, 1929, *12*, 502–514.

233. Klein, D. B.: The experimental production of dreams during hypnosis. *Univ. Tex. Bull.*, 1930, *3009*, 1–71.

234. Kleitman, N.: *Sleep and Wakefulness.* Chicago: Univ. Chicago Press, 1939.

235. Kline, M. V.: Hypnotic age regression and intelligence. *J. genet. Psychol.*, 1950, 77, 129–132.

236. Kline, M. V., and Schneck, J. M.: Hypnosis in relation to the word association test. *J. gen. Psychol.*, 1951, *44*, 129–137.

237. Kline, M. V.: Hypnosis and age progression: a case report. *J. genet. Psychol.*, 1951, *78*, 195–206.

238. Kline, M. V.: A measure of mental masculinity and femininity in relation to hypnotic age progression. *J. genet. Psychol.*, 1951, *78*, 207–216.

239. Kohnstamm, O.: No title. Demonstration reported in *Dtsch. Z. Nervenheilk.*, 1912, *43*, 447–448.

240. Koster, S.: Untersuchungen über Hypnose. *Z. ges. Neurol. Psychiat.*, 1928, *109*, 49–61.

241. Krafft-Ebing, R. von: *Eine experimentelle Studie auf dem Gebiete des Hypnotismus.* Stuttgart, 1889.

242. Kreibich, C., and Sobotka, P.: Experimenteller Beitrag zur psychischen Urticaria. *Arch. Derm. u. Syph.*, 1909, *97*, 187–192.

243. Kretschmer, M., and Krüger, R.: Über die Beeinflussung des Serumkalkgehaltes in der Hypnose. *Klin. Wschr.*, 1927, *6*, 695–697.

244. Krueger, R. G.: Variation in hypersuggestibility preceding, during, and following the hypnotic trance. *J. abnorm. soc. Psychol.*, 1931, *26*, 131–140.

245. Krueger, R. G.: The influence of repetition and disuse upon rate of hypnotization. *J. exp. Psychol.*, 1931, *14*, 260–269.

246. Kubie, L. S.: Manual of emergency treatment for acute war neuroses. *War Med.*, 1943, *4* & *6*, 582–598.

247. Kubie, L. S., and Margolin, S.: The process of hypnotism and the nature of the hypnotic state. *Amer. J. Psychiat.*, 1944, *100*, 611–622.

248. Kubie, L. S.: The use of hypnagogic reverie in the recovery of repressed amnesic data. *Bull. Menninger Clin.*, 1943, *7*, 172–182.

249. Kupfer, H. I.: Psychic concomitants in wartime injuries. *Psychosom. Med.*, 1945, *7*, 15–21.

250. Landis, C.: An attempt to measure emotional traits in juvenile delinquency. In Lashley, Stone, Darrow, Landis and Heath, *The Dynamics of Behavior.* Chicago: Univ. Chicago Press, 1932.

251. Lane, B. M.: A validation of the Rorschach movement interpretation. *Amer. J. Orthopsychiatry*, 1949, *18*, 292–296.

252. Langheinrich, O.: Psychische Einflüsse auf die Secretionstägtigkeit des Magens und des Duodenums. *Münch. med. Wschr.*, 1922, *69*, 1527–1528.

253. Leavitt, H. C.: A case of hypnotically produced secondary and tertiary personalities. *Psychoanal. Rev.*, 1947, *34*, 274–295.

254. Lecomte Du Noüy, P.: *Biological Time.* New York: Macmillan, 1937.

255. LeCron, L. M., and Bordeaux, J.: *Hypnotism Today.* New York: Grune and Stratton, 1947.

256. Lee, A.: As reported by Arnold (6).

257. Leeds, M.: An hypnotic regression series. *Persona.*, 1949, *1*, 13–16.

258. Lemere, F.: Electroencephalography as a method of distinguishing true from false blindness. *J. Amer. med. Ass.*, 1942, *118*, 884–885.

259. Leuba, C.: Images as conditioned sensations. *J. exp. Psychol.*, 1940, *26*, 345–357.

260. Leuba, C.: As reported by P. L. Harriman: The experimental induction of a multiple personality. *Psychiatry*, 1942, *5*, 179–186.

261. Levin, S. L., and Egolinsky, Y. A.: The effect of cortical functions upon energy changes in basal metabolism. *Fiziol. Zh. S.S.S.R.*, 1936, *20*, 979–992.

262. Levine, K. N., Grassi, J. R., and Gerson, J. M.: Hypnotically induced mood changes in the verbal and graphic Rorschach: A case study. Part I. *Rorschach Res. Exch.*, 1943, *7*, 130–144.

263. Levine, K. N., Grassi, J. R., and Gerson, J. M.: Hypnotically induced mood changes in the verbal and graphic Rorschach: A case study. Part II. *Rorschach Res. Exch.*, 1944, *8*, 109–124.

264. Levine, M.: Electrical skin resistance during hypnosis. *Arch. Neurol. Psychiat.*, 1930, *24*, 937–942.

265. Levine, M.: Psychogalvanic reaction to painful stimuli in hypnotic and hysterical anesthesia. *Bull. Johns Hopk. Hosp.*, 1930, *46*, 331–339.

266. Lewis, J. H., and Sarbin, T. H.: Studies in psychosomatics: I. The influence of hypnotic stimulation on gastric hunger contraction. *Psychosom. Med.*, 1943, *5*, 125–131.

267. Lewis, T.: *Pain*. New York: Macmillan, 1942.

268. Liberson, W. T.: Prolonged hypnotic states with "local signs" induced in guinea pigs. *Science*, 1948, *108*, 40–41.

269. Life, C.: The effects of practice in the trance upon learning in the normal waking state. Thesis presented for B.A. degree, Univ. Wisconsin, 1929.

270. Lifschitz, S.: Title unknown. *Žurnal nevropatologii i. psichiatrii*, 1927, *20*, 317–324. Reported by Sterling and Miller (395).

271. Lindner, R. M.: *Rebel without a Cause: the Hypnoanalysis of a Criminal Psychopath*. New York: Grune and Stratton, 1944.

272. Lodge, J. H.: The illusion of warmth test for suggestibility. *Forum. Educ.*, 1926, *3*, 180–186.

273. Loomis, A. L., Harvey, E. N., and Hobart, G. A.: Brain potentials during hypnosis. *Science*, 1936, *83*, 239–241.

274. Loomis, A. L., Harvey, E. N., Hobart, G. A.: Electrical potentials of the human brain. *J. exp. Psychol.*, 1936, *19*, 249–279.

275. Loomis, A. L., Harvey, E. N., and Hobart, G. A.: Cerebral states during sleep as studied by human brain potentials. *J. exp. Psychol.*, 1937, *21*, 127–144.

276. Lorand, S.: Hypnotic suggestion: its dynamics, indications, and limitations in the therapy of neurosis. *J. nerv. ment. Dis.*, 1941, *94*, 64–75.

277. Luckhardt, A. B., and Johnston, R. L.: Studies in gastric secretion: I. The psychic secretion of gastric juice under hypnosis. *Am. J. Physiol.*, 1924, *70*, 174–182.

278. Lundholm, H.: An experimental study of functional anesthesia as induced by suggestion in hypnosis. *J. abnorm. soc. Psychol.*, 1928, *23*, 338–355.

279. Lundholm, H.: A new laboratory neurosis. *Character & Pers.*, 1940, *9*, 11–121.

280. Lundholm, H., and Lowenbach, H.: Hypnosis and the alpha activity of the electroencephalogram. *Character & Pers.*, 1942, *11*, 145–149.

281. Lundholm, H.: Laboratory neuroses. *Character & Pers.*, 1933, *2*, 127–133.

282. Luria, A. R.: *The Nature of Human Conflict*. New York: Liveright, 1932.

283. Lush, J. L.: "Nervous" goats. *J. Hered.*, 1930, *21*, 243–247.

284. Manzer, C. W.: The effect of verbal suggestion on output and variability of muscular work. *Psychol. Clin.*, 1934, *22*, 248–256.

285. Marcuse, F. L., Hill, A., and Keegan, M.: Identification of posthypnotic signals and responses. *J. exp. Psychol.*, 1945, *35*, 163–166.

286. Marcuse, F. L.: Individual differences in animal hypnosis. *Brit. J. Med. Hypn.*, 1951, *3*, 17–20.

287. Marcuse, F. L.: Interpretation in animal hypnotism. *Personality*, 1951, *1*, 240–242.

288. Marcuse, F. L., and Moore, A. V.: Tantrum behavior in the pig. *J. comp. Psychol.*, 1944, *37*, 235–241.

289. Marcus, H., and Sahlgren, E.: Untersuchungen über die Einwirkung der Hypnotischen Suggestion auf die Funktion des vegetativen Systems. I. Mitteilung. *Münch. med. Wschr.*, 1925, *72*, 381–382.

290. Marcus, H., and Sahlgren, E.: Untersuchungen über die Einwirkung der hypnotischen Suggestion auf die Funktionen des vegetativen Systems. *Acta. psychiat., Kbh.*, 1936, *11*, 119–126.

291. Marinesco, G., Sager, O., and Kreindler, A.: Étude électroencéphalographique. Le sommeil naturel et le sommeil hypnotique. *Bull. Acad. Méd.*, 1937, *117*, 273–276.

292. Marx, H.: Untersuchungen über den Wasserhaushalt. II. Mitteilung. Die Psychische Beeinflussung des Wasserhaushaltes. *Klin. Wschr.*, 1926, *5*, 92–94.

293. Max, L. W.: An experimental study of the motor theory of consciousness: IV. Action-current responses in the deaf during awakening, kinaesthetic imagery, and abstract thinking. *J. comp. Psychol.*, 1937, *24*, 301–344.

294. Mazer, M.: An experimental study of the hypnotic dream. *Psychiatry*, 1951, *14*, 265–277.

295. McDougall, W.: *Outline of Abnormal Psychology*. New York: Scribner, 1926.

296. McDowell, M.: Juvenile warts removed with the use of hypnotic suggestion. *Bull. Menninger Clin.*, 1949, *13*, 124–126.

297. McDowell, M.: An abrupt cessation of major neurotic symptoms following an hypnotically induced artificial conflict. *Bull. Menninger Clin.*, 1948, *12*, 168.

298. McGeogh, J. A.: The relationship between suggestibility and intelligence in delinquents. *Psychol. Clin.*, 1925, *16*, 133–134.

299. McGonigal, J. P.: Immobility: an inquiry into the mechanism of fear reaction. *J. abnorm. Psychol.*, 1920, *27*, 73–80.

300. Mead, S., and Roush, E. F.: A study of the effect of hypnotic suggestion on physiologic performance. *Arch. phys. Med.*, 1949, *30*, 700–705.

301. Mead, S.: Appended discussion to Mead and Roush (283), pp. 706.

302. Memmesheimer, A. M., and Eisenlohr, E.: Untersuchungen über die Suggestivbehandlung der Warzen. *Derm. Z.*, 1931, *62*, 63–68.

303. Menzies, R.: Conditioned vasomotor responses in human subjects. *J. Psychol.*, 1937, *4*, 75–120.

304. Mercer, M., and Gibson, R. W.: Rorschach content in hypnosis: chronological age regression. *J. clin. Psychol.*, 1950, *6*, 352–358.
305. *Merck Manual*, p. 1329. Rahway: Merck & Co., 1950.
306. Messer, A. L., Hinckley, E. D., and Mosier, C. I.: Suggestibility and neurotic symptoms in normal subjects. *J. gen. Psychol.*, 1938, *19*, 391–399.
307. Messerschmidt, R.: The suggestibility of boys and girls between the ages of six and sixteen years. *J. genet. Psychol.*, 1933, *43*, 422–437.
308. Messerschmidt, R.: Response of boys between the ages of five and sixteen years to Hull's postural suggestion test. *J. genet. Psychol.*, 1933, *43*, 405–421.
309. Messerschmidt, R.: A quantitative investigation of the alleged independent operation of conscious and subconscious processes. *J. abnorm. soc. Psychol.*, 1927–1928, *22*, 325–340.
310. Miller, D. R., and Hutt, M. L.: Value interiorization and personality development. *J. soc. Issues*, 1949, *5*, 2–30.
311. Miller, J. G.: Unconscious processes and perception. Chapter 9 in: R. R. Blake and Ramsey, G. V., *Perception. An Approach to Personality*. New York: The Ronald Press, 1951.
312. Minami, H., and Dallenbach, K. M.: The effect of activity upon learning and retention in the cockroach. *Amer. J. Psychol.*, 1946, *59*, 1–58.
313. Mitchell, M. B.: Retroactive inhibition and hypnosis. *J. gen. Psychol.*, 1932, *7*, 343–458.
314. Mohr, F.: *Psychophysische Behandlungsmethoden*. Leipzig: Hirzel, 1925.
315. Moll, A.: *Hypnotism*. London: Scott, 1910.
316. Moody, R. L.: Bodily changes during abreaction. *Lancet*, 1946, *251*, 934–935.
317. Moody, R. L.: Bodily changes during abreaction. *Lancet*, 1948, *254*, 964.
318. Mosier, C. I.: A factor analysis of certain neurotic symptoms. *Psychometrika*, 1937, *2*, 263–286.
319. Mowrer, O. H.: A note on the effect of repeated hypnotic stimulation. *J. abnorm. soc. Psychol.*, 1932, *27*, 60–62.
320. Naumov, F. A.: Sbornik, posv. V. M. Bekhterevu k. 40-letnyn professorskoi deyateinosti—Leningrad: Gos. Psikhonevr. Akademii i. Gos. Refleks. Instit. po Izuchneniyu Mozga, 1926, 569–588.
321. Nemtzova, O. L., and Schattenstein, D. I.: [The effect of the central nervous system upon some physiological processes during work.] *Fiziol. Zh. S.S.S.R.*, 1936, *20*, 581–593. (*Psychol. Abstr.*, 1939, 13, #4129.)
322. Nemtzova, O. L., and Schattenstein, D. I.: The influence of the central nervous system upon physiological processes during work. *Bull. Biol. Méd. exp. U.R.S.S.*, 1936, *1*, 144–145.
323. Newman, J. B.: *Fascination or the Philosophy of Learning*. New York: Fowler Well, 1854.
324. Nicholson, N. C.: Notes on muscular work during hypnosis. *Bull. Johns Hopk. Hosp.*, 1920, *31*, 89–91.
325. Nielsen, O. J., and Geert-Jörgensen, E.: Untersuchungen über die Einwirkung der hypnotischen Suggestion auf den Blutzucker bei Nichtdiabetikern. *Klin. Wschr.*, 1928, *7*, 1457–1458.
326. Nygard, J. W.: Cerebral circulation prevailing during hypnosis. *J. exp. Psychol.*, 1939, *24*, 1–20.

327. Obermeyer, M. E., and Greenson, R. R.: Treatment by suggestion of verrucae planae of the face. *Psychosom. Med.*, 1949, *11*, 163–164.

328. Orne, M. T.: The mechanism of hypnotic age regression: an experimental study. *J. abnorm. soc. Psychol.*, 1951, *46*, 213–225.

329. Otis, M. A.: Study of suggestibility of children. *Arch. Psychol.*, 1924, No. 70.

330. Parker, G. H.: The excretion of carbon dioxide by relaxed and contracted sea anemones. *J. gen. Physiol.*, 1922, *5*, 46–64.

331. Papov, E. P.: [Suggestibility and automaticism in school children.] *Propilaktecheskaya Medetsina*, 1926, *5*, 68. Reported by Coffin (71).

332. Pasquarelli, B., and Bull, N.: Experimental investigation of the body-mind continuum in affective states. *J. nerv. ment. Dis.*, 1951, *113*, 512–521.

333. Patten, E. F., Switzer, S. A., and Hull, C. L.: Habituation, retention, and perseveration characteristics of direct waking suggestion. *J. exp. Psychol.*, 1932, *15*, 539–549.

334. Patten, E. F.: The duration of post-hypnotic suggestions. *J. abnorm. soc. Psychol.*, 1930, *25*, 319–334.

335. Patten, E. F.: Does post-hypnotic amnesia apply to practice effects? *J. gen. Psychol.*, 1932, *7*, 196–201.

336. Patten, E. F.: An attempt to induce hypersuggestibility in waking suggestions by means of specific supplementary suggestions to that effect. On file at the Yale Univ. Library and the Miami Univ. Library. Also described in Hull (213).

337. Pattie, F. A.: The production of blisters by hypnotic suggestion: A review. *J. abnorm. soc. Psychol.*, 1941, *36*, 62–72.

338. Pattie, F. A.: The genuineness of unilateral deafness produced by hypnosis. *Amer. J. Psychol.*, 1950, *63*, 84–86.

339. Pattie, F. A.: The genuineness of hypnotically produced anesthesia of the skin. *Amer. J. Psychol.*, 1937, *49*, 435–443.

340. Pattie, F. A.: A report of attempts to produce uniocular blindness by hypnotic suggestion. *Brit. J. med. Psychol.*, 1935, *15*, 230–241.

341. Pavlov, I. P., and Petrova, M. K.: A contribution to the physiology of the hypnotic state of dogs. *Character & Pers.*, 1934, *2*, 189–200.

342. Pavlov, I. P.: *Conditioned Reflexes.* New York: Oxford Univ. Press, 1934.

343. Peiper, A.: Untersuchungen über den galvanischen Hautreflex (psychogalvanischen Reflex) im Kindesalter. *Jb. Kinderheilk.*, 1924, *107*, 139–150.

344. Penfield, W., and Rasmussen, T.: *The Cerebral Cortex of Man.* New York: Macmillan, 1950.

345. Petrie, A.: Repression and suggestibility as related to temperament. *J. Personality*, 1948, *16*, 445–458.

346. Piéron, H.: *Le Problème physiologique du sommeil* (pp. 230–235). Paris: Librairie de l'Académie de Médecine, 1913.

347. Platonow, K. I.: On the objective proof of the experimental personality age regression. *J. gen. Psychol.*, 1933, *9*, 190–209.

348. Platonow, K. I.: The word as a physiological and therapeutic factor. *Psikhoterapiya*, 1930, *11*, 112. Reported by Wolberg (497).

349. Podiapolskiĭ, P.: O vazomotornykh razstroĭstvakh, vizivaemikh gïpnotischeskim vnuscheniem. *Zhurn. neïropatologii i psikhiatrii imeni C. C. Korsakova*, 1909, *9*, 101–109.

350. Povorinskji, J. A., and Finne, W. N.: Der Wechsel des Zuckergehaltes des Blutes unter dem Einfluss einer Hypnotisch Suggerierten Vorstellung. *Z. ges. Neurol. Psychiat.*, 1930, *129*, 135–146.
351. Preyer, W.: *Die Entdeckung des Hypnotismus.* Berlin: Gebruder Paetel, 1881.
352. Prideaux, E.: Suggestion and suggestibility. *Brit. J. Psychol.*, 1919, *10*, 228–241.
353. Prince, M.: Experiments to determine co-conscious (subconscious) ideation. *J. abnorm. soc. Psychol.*, 1909, *3*, 37.
354. Prince, M.: *The Unconscious.* New York: Macmillan, 1916.
355. Pronko, N. H., and Hill, H.: A study of differential stimulus function in hypnosis. *J. Psychol.*, 1949, *27*, 49–53.
356. Rabaud, E.: Le phénomène de la "simulation de la mort." *C. R. Soc. Biol. Paris*, 1916, *79*, 74–77.
357. Rabaud, E.: L'immobilization reflexe et l'activité normale des arthropodes. *Bull. Biol.*, 1919, *53*, 1–149.
358. Rapaport, D.: *Diagnostic Psychological Testing.* Vol. II. Chicago: Year Book Publishers, 1946.
359. Ravitz, L. J.: Standing potential correlates of hypnosis and narcosis. *A.M.A. Arch. Neurol. Psychiat.*, 1951, *65*, 413–436.
360. Ravitz, L. J.: The use of DC measurements in psychiatry. *Neuropsychiatry*, 1951, *1*, 3–12.
361. Reisinger, L.: Hypnose des Flusskrebses. *Biol. Zbl.*, 1927, *47*, 722–726.
362. Reisinger, L.: Katalepsie der indischen Stabheuschrecke. *Biol. Zbl.*, 1928, *48*, 162–167.
363. Reymert, M. L., and Kohn, H. A.: An objective investigation of suggestibility. *Character & Pers.*, 1940, *9*, 44–48.
364. Reynolds, S. R. M.: Uterine contractility and cervical dilatation. *Proc. R. Soc. Med.*, 1951, *44*, 695–702.
365. Riegers, C.: *Der Hypnotismus.* Jena: Gustav Fischer, 1884.
366. Rijlant, P.: Étude chez la poule des activités toniques et contractiles du muscle strié pendant l'hypnose. *C. R. Soc. Biol. Paris*, 1933, *113*, 417–421.
367. Rijlant, P.: Le tonus musculaire chez un mammifère en étât de l'hypnose. *C. R. Soc. Biol. Paris*, 1933, *113*, 421–424.
368. Rivers, W. H. R.: *Instinct and the Unconscious.* Cambridge: Cambridge Univ. Press, 1922.
369. Roach, J. H. L.: An experimental study of suggestibility in extroverts and introverts. *J. appl. Psychol.*, 1941, *25*, 458–468.
370. Roach, J. H. L.: Autosuggestion in extroverts and introverts. *J. Personality*, 1947, *15*, 214–221.
371. Rode, R.: Observations sur le phénomène d'immobilization reflexe chez la chouette chevêche, Athene noctua Scop, *Bull. Soc. Zool. France*, 1930, *55*, 451–454.
372. Roffenstein, G.: Experimentelle Symbolträume. *Z. ges. Neurol. Psychiat.*, 1923, *87*, 362–371.
373. Rogerson, C. H.: Narco-analysis with nitrous oxide. *Brit. med. J.*, 1944, *2*, 811–812.
374. Rose, E. A.: *Social Psychology.* New York: Macmillan, 1908.

375. Rosen, H.: The hypnotic and hypnotherapeutic control of severe pain. *Amer. J. Psychiat.*, 1951, *107*, 917–925.

376. Rosen, H.: Radical hypnotherapy of apparent medical and surgical emergencies. *J. Personality*, 1951, *1*, 326–339.

377. Rosenthal, B. G.: Hypnotic recall of material learned under anxiety and non-anxiety producing conditions. *J. exp. Psychol.*, 1944, *34*, 369–389.

378. Roush, E. S.: Strength and endurance in the waking and hypnotic state. *J. appl. Physiol.*, 1951, *3*, 404–410.

379. Rowland, L. W.: Will hypnotized persons try to harm themselves or others? *J. abnorm. soc. Psychol.*, 1939, *34*, 114–117.

380. Rosenzweig, S., and Sarason, S.: An experimental study of the triadic hypothesis in relation to frustration, ego-defense, and hypnotic ability. *Character & Pers.*, 1942, *11*, 1–14, 150–165.

381. Rujka, T.: Beiträge zu den biologischen Grundlagen des Zusammenhanges zwischer reflektorischer immobilization und Angstzuständen. *Riv. Biol.*, 1938, *26*, 317–342.

382. Rybalkin, J.: Brûlure du second degré provoqué par suggestion. *Rev. Hypn.*, 1890, *4*, 361–362.

383. Saltzman, B. N.: The reliability of tests of waking and hypnotic suggestibility. *Psychol. Bull.*, 1936, *33*, 622–623.

384. Sarbin, T. R., and Madow, L. W.: Predicting the depth of hypnosis by means of the Rorschach test. *Amer. J. Orthopsychiatr.*, 1942, *12*, 268–271.

385. Sarbin, T. R.: Contributions to role-taking theory: I. Hypnotic behavior. *Psychol. Rev.*, 1950, *5*, 255–270.

386. Sarbin, T. R.: Rorschach patterns under hypnosis. *Amer. J. Orthopsychiat.*, 1939, *9*, 315–319.

387. Sarbin, T. R.: Mental age changes in experimental regression. *J. Personality*, 1950, *19*, 221–228.

388. Sarbin, T. R., and Farberow, N. L.: Contributions of role-taking theory: a clinical study of self and role. *J. abnorm. soc. Psychol.*, 1952, *47*, 117–125.

389. Sargant, W., and Fraser, R.: Inducing light hypnosis by hyperventilation. *Lancet*, 1938, *235*, 778.

390. Scantlebury, R. E.: The effects of psychic phenomena on the movements of the empty stomach in man. *Grad. Stud. Monogr. Sci. Wayne Univ.*, 1940, *1*, 32.

391. Scantlebury, R. I., Frick, H. L., and Patterson, T. L.: The effect of normal and hypnotically induced dreams on the gastric hunger movements of man. *J. appl. Psychol.*, 1942, *26*, 682–691.

392. Schilder, P., and Kauder, O.: Hypnosis. *Nerv. and ment. Dis. Monogr. Ser.*, 1927, No. 46. [New edition in press, International Universities Publishers]

393. Schindler, R.: *Nervensystem und spontane Blutsungen, mit besonderer Berücksichtigung der hysterischen Ecchymosen und der Systematik der hämorrhagischen Diathesen.* Berlin: S. Karger, 1927.

394. Schneck, J. M., and Bergman, M.: Auditory acuity for pure tones in the waking and hypnotic states. *J. Speech Dis.*, 1949, *14*, 33–36.

395. Schneck, J. M.: Modified technique for the induction of hypnosis. *J. nerv. ment. Dis.*, 1947, *106*, 77–79.

396. Schneck, J. M.: A military offense induced by hypnosis. *J. nerv. ment. Dis.*, 1947, *106*, 186–189.

397. Schneck, J. M.: Psychosomatic reactions to the induction of hypnosis. *Dis. nerv. Syst.*, 1950, *11*, 118–121.
398. Schneck, J. M.: A note on spontaneous hallucinations during hypnosis. *Psychiat. Quart.*, 1950, *24*, 1–3.
399. Schneck, J. M.: Spontaneous homonymous hemianopsia in hypnotic imagery. *Brit. J. med. Hypnot.*, 1951, *2*, 2–3.
400. Schneck, J. M.: The elucidation of spontaneous sensory and motor phenomena during hypnoanalysis. *Psychoanal. Rev.*, 1952, *39*, 79–89.
401. Schneck, J. M.: Unconscious relationship between hypnosis and death. *Psychoanal. Rev.*, 1951, *38*, 271–275.
402. Schneck, J. M.: Hypnoanalytic elucidation of the hypnosis-death concept. *Psychiat. Quart. Suppl.*, 1950, #2, 1–4.
403. Schrotter, K.: Experimentelle Traume. *Zbl. Psychoan.*, 1912, *2*, 638–646.
404. Schultz, J. H.: *Das Autogene Training.* Stuttgart: George Thieme Verlag, 1950.
405. Scott, H. D.: Hypnosis and the conditioned reflex. *J. gen. Psychol.*, 1930, *4*, 113–130.
406. Sears, R. R.: Experimental study of hypnotic anesthesia. *J. exp. Psychol.*, 1932, *15*, 1–22.
407. Seashore, E. F.: Measurements of illusions and hallucinations in normal life. *Stud. Yale Psychol. Lab.*, 1895, *2*, 1–67.
408. Seeligmuller, A.: Hyperventilation und Schlaf. Kurze Mitteilung zur Technik der Hypnose. *Ther. d. Gegenw.*, 1934, *75*, 286–287.
409. Settlage, P.: The effect of sodium amytal on the formation and elicitation of conditioned reflexes. *J. comp. Psychol.*, 1936, *22*, 339–343.
410. Sherif, M.: A study of some social factors in perception. *Arch. Psychol.*, N. Y., 1935, #187.
411. Sherman, I. C.: The suggestibility of normal and mentally defective children. *Comp. Psychol. Monogr.*, 1925, *2*, No. 9.
412. Sidis, B.: *The Psychology of Suggestion.* New York: Appleton-Century, 1910.
413. Sidis, B.: An experimental study of sleep. *J. abnorm. Psychol.*, 1908, *3*, 1–32.
414. Siebert, K.: Die Gestaltbildung im Traum. *Arch. ges. Psychol.*, 1934, *9*, 357–372.
415. Sirna, A. J.: An electroencephalographic study of the hypnotic dream. *J. Psychol.*, 1945, *20*, 109–113.
416. Small, M. H.: Suggestibility of school children. *Ped. Sem.*, 1896, *13*, 176–220.
417. Smirnoff, D.: Zur Frage der durch hypnotische Suggestion hervorgerufenen vasomotorischen Storungen. *Z. Psychother. med. Psychol.*, 1912, *4*, 171–175.
418. Speyer, N., and Stokvis, B.: The psycho-analytical factor in hypnosis. *Brit. J. med. Psychol.*, 1938, *17*, 217–222.
419. Spiegel, H., Shor, J., and Fishman, S.: An hypnotic ablation technique for the study of personality development. *Psychosom. Med.*, 1945, *7*, 273–278.
420. Stalnaker, J. M., and Riddles, E. E.: The effect of hypnosis on long delayed recall. *J. gen. Psychol.*, 1932, *6*, 429–440.
421. Stalnaker, J. M., and Richardson, M. W.: Time estimation in the hypnotic trance. *J. gen. Psychol.*, 1930, *4*, 362–366.

422. Starkey, F. R.: Ether hypnosis in psychotherapy. *Med. Rec.*, 1917, *91*, 631.

423. Stein, T.: Über die hypnotische Beeinflussung des Blutzuckers, des Natriumund Chlorgehaltes des Blutes. *Inaug. Diss. Basel*, 1929.

424. Steiniger, F.: Die Biologie der sogennante "tierischen Hypnose." *Ergebn. Biol.*, 1936, *13*, 348–451.

425. Steiniger, F.: Der Einfluss der Zahmheit auf die sogennante "Tierische Hypnose" bei Vögeln. *Z. Tierpsychol.*, 1941, *4*, 260–271.

426. Steiniger, F.: Eine Erwiderung auf des Buch von Franz Volgyesi, Menschen-und Tierhypnose. *Z. Tierpsychol.*, 1941, *4*, 272–280.

427. Steisel, I. M.: The Rorschach test and suggestibility. *J. abnorm. soc. Psychol.*, 1952, *47*, 608–614.

428. Sterling, K., and Miller, J. G.: The effect of hypnosis upon visual and auditory acuity. *Amer. J. Psychol.*, 1940, *53*, 269–276.

429. Sterling, K., and Miller, J. G.: Conditioning under anesthesia. *Amer. J. Psychol.*, 1941, *54*, 92–101.

430. Stockert, F. G.: Die Physiologie der Hypnose. *Nervenarzt*, 1936, *3*, 462–467.

431. Strickler, C. B.: A quantitative study of post-hypnotic amnesia. *J. abnorm. soc. Psychol.*, 1950, *45*, 160–162.

432. Stroder, J.: Ueber der Einfluss der "tierischen Hypnose" auf den Ablauf der Narkose am Kaltblüter. *Schmerz*, 1938, *11*, 82–84.

433. Stungo, E.: Evipan hypnosis in psychiatric outpatients. *Lancet*, 1941, *240*, 507–509.

434. Sulzberger, M. B., and Wolf, J.: The treatment of warts by suggestion. *Med. Rec. New York*, 1934, *140*, 552–556.

435. Sutherland, G. F., and Curtis, Q. F.: Myotonia congenita in the goat. *Proc. Soc. exp. Biol.*, New York, 1938, *38*, 460.

436. Swank, R. L., and Foley, J. M.: Respiratory, electroencephalographic, and blood exchange in progressive barbiturate narcosis in dogs. *J. Pharmacol.*, 1948, *92*, 391–396.

437. Talbert, G. A., Ready, F. L., and Kuhlman, F. W.: Plethysmographic and pneumographic observations made in hypnosis. *Am. J. Physiol.*, 1924, *68*, 113.

438. Talbot, J. H., Cobb, S., Coombs, F. S., Cohen, M. E., and Consolazio, W. V.: Acid base balance of the blood of a patient with hysterical hyperventilation. *Arch. Neurol. Psychiat.*, 1938, *39*, 973–987.

439. Ten Cate, J.: Sur la production de ce que l'on appelle l'étât d'hypnose animale chez la raie. *Arch. néerl. Physiol.*, 1928, *12*, 188–190.

440. Ten Cate, J.: Nouvelles observations sur l'hypnose dite animale. Étât d'hypnose chez octopus vulgaris. *Arch. néerl. Physiol.*, 1928, *13*, 402–406.

441. Tonkikh, A. V.: The role of the autonomic nervous system in the phenomenon of the so-called "animal hypnosis." *Fiziol. Zh. S.S.S.R.*, 1938, *24*, 367–371.

442. Travis, L. E.: Suggestibility and negativism as measured by auditory threshold during reverie. *J. abnorm. soc. Psychol.*, 1924, *18*, 350–368.

443. Travis, L. E.: A test for distinguishing between schizophrenoses and psychoneuroses. *J. abnorm. soc. Psychol.*, 1929, *19*, 283–298.

444. True, R. M.: Experimental control in hypnotic age regression states. *Science*, 1949, *110*, 583–584.

445. True, R. M., and Stephenson, C. W.: Controlled experiments correlating electroencephalogram, pulse, and plantar reflexes with hypnotic age regression and induced emotional states. *Personality*, 1951, *1*, 252-263.

446. Valance, J. R.: Suggestibility of smokers and non-smokers. *Psychol. Rec.*, 1940, *4*, 138-144.

447. Vandell, R. A., Davis, R. A., and Clugston, H. A.: The function of mental practice in the acquisition of motor skills. *J. gen. Psychol.*, 1943, *29*, 243-250.

448. Van Pelt, S. J.: Hypnotism and its importance in medicine. *Brit. J. med. Hypnot.*, 1949, *1*, 19-34.

449. Verger, M. P., and Lafon, M. J.: La cataplexie. *Encéphale*, 1939, *34*, 121-148.

450. Verworn, M.: Die sogennante Hypnose der Tiere. *J. Physiol.*, 1899, *23*, 53-54.

451. Vogel, V. H.: Suggestibility in narcotic addicts. *Publ. Hlth. Rep. Suppl.*, 1937, No. 132.

452. Volgyesi, F.: *Menschen- und Tierhypnose*. Leipzig: Fussli, 1938.

453. Walden, E. C.: A plethysmographic study of the vascular condition during hypnotic sleep. *N. E. J. Med.*, 1932, *206*, 777-781.

454. Warnke, G.: Zur Akinese bei jungen Möwen und Störchen. *Zool. Anz.*, 1937, *118*, 17.

455. Warren, H. C.: *Dictionary of Psychology*. New York: Houghton Mifflin, 1934.

456. Watkins, A. L.: Appended discussion to Mead and Roush (283).

457. Watkins, J. G.: Anti-social compulsions induced under hypnotic trance. *J. abnorm. soc. Psychol.*, 1947, *42*, 256-259.

458. Watkins, J. G.: A case of hypnotic trance induced in a resistant subject in spite of active opposition. *Brit. J. med. Hypnot.*, 1951, *2*, 26-31.

459. Webb, W. B.: Some comments on Marion Bartlett's "Suggestibility in dementia praecox patients." *J. gen. Psychol.*, 1946, *34*, 97-100.

460. Weber, E.: *Der Einfluss psychischer Vorgänge auf den Körper*. Berlin: Julius Springer, 1920.

461. Wegrocki, H. J.: The effect of prestige suggestibility on emotional attitudes. *J. soc. Psychol.*, 1934, *5*, 384-394.

462. Weitzenhoffer, A. M.: A note on the persistence of hypnotic suggestion. *J. abnorm. soc. Psychol.*, 1950, *45*, 160-162.

463. Weitzenhoffer, A. M.: The production of anti-social acts under hypnosis. *J. abnorm. soc. Psychol.*, 1949, *44*, 420-422.

464. Weitzenhoffer, A. M.: The discriminatory recognition of visual patterns under hypnosis. *J. abnorm. soc. Psychol.*, 1951, *46*, 388-397.

465. Weitzenhoffer, A. M.: The transcendence of normal voluntary capacities in hypnosis: an evaluation. *Personality: Symposia on Topical Issues*, 1951, *1*, 272-282.

466. Welch, L.: The space and time of induced hypnotic dreams. *J. Psychol.*, 1936, *1*, 171-178.

467. Welch, L.: A behavioristic explanation of the mechanism of suggestion and hypnosis. *J. abnorm. soc. Psychol.*, 1947, *42*, 359-364.

468. Wells, W. R.: Hypnotizability vs. suggestibility. *J. abnorm. soc. Psychol.*, 1931, *25*, 436-449.

469. Wells, W. R.: Expectancy versus performance in hypnosis. *J. gen. Psychol.*, 1947, *35*, 99–119.

470. Wells, W. R.: The extent and duration of post-hypnotic amnesia. *J. Psychol.*, 1940, *2*, 137–151.

471. Wells, W. R.: Ability to resist artificially induced dissociation. *J. abnorm. soc. Psychol.*, 1940, *35*, 261–273.

472. Wells, W. R.: Experiments in the hypnotic production of crimes. *J. Psychol.*, 1941, *11*, 63–102.

473. Wells, W. R.: Experiments in waking hypnosis for instructional purposes. *J. abnorm. soc. Psychol.*, 1924, *18*, 389–404.

474. Wells, W. R.: A basic deception in exhibitions of hypnosis. *J. abnorm. soc. Psychol.*, 1946, *41*, 145–153.

475. West, L. J., Niell, K. C., and Hardy, J. D.: Effects of hypnotic suggestions on pain perception and galvanic skin response. *AMA Arch. Neurol. Psychiat.*, 1952, *68*, 549–560.

476. Wetterstrand, A. S.: Die Suggestive Vesikation. *J. Psychol. Neurol.*, 1915, *21*, 1–10.

477. White, M. M.: The physical and mental traits of individuals susceptible to hypnosis. *J. abnorm. soc. Psychol.*, 1930, *25*, 293–298.

478. White, M. M.: Blood pressure and palmar galvanic changes in normal and hypnotic states. *Psychol. Bull.*, 1940, *37*, 577.

479. White, R. W.: Two types of hypnotic trance and their personality correlates. *J. Psychol.*, 1937, *3*, 279–289.

480. White, R. W.: An analysis of motivation in hypnosis. *J. gen. Psychol.*, 1941, *24*, 145–162.

481. White, R. W.: Prediction of hypnotic susceptibility from a knowledge of subject's attitude. *J. Psychol.*, 1937, *3*, 265–277.

482. White, R. W., Fox, G. F., and Harris, W. W.: Hypnotic hypermnesia for recently learned material. *J. abnorm. soc. Psychol.*, 1940, *35*, 88–103.

483. White, R. W.: A preface to the theory of hypnotism. *J. abnorm. soc. Psychol.*, 1941, *36*, 477–505.

484. Whitehorn, J. C., Lundholm, H., Fox, E. L., and Benedict, F. G.: Metabolic rate in "hypnotic sleep." *N. E. J. Med.*, 1932, *206*, 777-781.

485. Whitehorn, J. C., Lundholm, H., and Gardner, G. E.: Metabolic rate in emotional moods induced by suggestion in hypnosis. *Am. J. Psychiat.*, 1929–1930, *9*, 661–666.

486. Whitehorn, J. C.: Physiological changes in emotional states. In: The interrelationship of mind and body. Vol. XIX. *Res. Publ. Ass. Res. nerv. ment. Dis.* Baltimore: Williams and Wilkins, 1939.

487. Williams, G. W.: A study of the responses of three psychotic groups to a test of suggestibility. *J. gen. Psychol.*, 1932, *7*, 302–310.

488. Williams, G. W.: Suggestibility in the normal and the hypnotic states. *Arch. Psychol.*, 1930, *122*, 83.

489. Williams, G. W.: The effect of hypnosis on muscular fatigue. *J. abnorm. soc. Psychol.*, 1929, *24*, 318–329.

490. Williams, G. W.: A comparative study of voluntary and hypnotic catalepsy. *Amer. J. Psychol.*, 1930, *42*, 83–95.

491. Wilson, C. P., Cormen, H. H., and Cole, A. A.: A preliminary study of the hypnotizability of psychotic patients. *Psychiat. Quart.*, 1949, *23*, 657–666.

492. Wilson, J.: *Trials of Animal Magnetism on the Brute Creation*. London: Sherwood, Gilbert and Piper, 1839.

493. Wilson, S. A. K.: Cataplexy. *J. Neurol. Psychopath.*, 1933, *14*, 45–51.

494. Wilson, S. R.: The physiological basis of hypnosis and suggestions. *Proc. R. Soc. Med.*, Sect. Anesth., 1926–27, *20*, 15–21.

495. Wittkower, E.: Über Affektiv–Somatische Veränderungen. II. Mitteilung: Die Affektleukozytose. *Klin. Wschr.*, 1929, *8*, 1082.

496. Wittkower, E., and Petow, H.: Beitrage zur Klinik des Asthma Bronchiale und Verwandter Zustande. V. zur Psychogenese des Asthma Bronchiale. *Z. klin. Med.*, 1931–1932, *119*, 293–306.

497. Wolberg, L. R.: *Medical Hypnosis*. Vol. I. New York: Grune and Stratton, 1948.

498. Wolberg, L. R.: *Hypnoanalysis*. New York: Grune and Stratton, 1945.

499. Wolff, H. G., and Goodell, H.: The relation of attitude and suggestion to the perception and reaction to pain. *Res. nerv. ment. Dis. Proc.*, 1943, *23*, 434.

500. Wolff, H. G., and Gantt, W. H. Caffeine sodiumbenzoate, sodium isoamylethyl barbiturate, sodium bromide and chloral hydrate. Effects on the highest integrative functions. *Arch. Neurol. Psychiat.*, 1935, *33*, 1030–1057.

501. Woodworth, R. S.: *Experimental Psychology*, p. 45. New York: Henry Holt Co., 1938.

502. Yerkes, R. M.: The instincts, habits and reactions of the frog. *Psychol. Rev.*, 1903, *1*, 579–597.

503. Young, P. C.: Is rapport an essential characteristic of hypnosis? *J. abnorm. soc. Psychol.*, 1927, *22*, 130–139.

504. Young, P. C.: An experimental study of mental and physical functions in the normal and hypnotic state. *Amer. J. Psychol.*, 1925, *36*, 214–232.

505. Young, P. C.: An experimental study of mental and physical functions in the normal and hypnotic state. *Amer. J. Psychol.*, 1926, *37*, 245–256.

506. Young, P. C.: Hypnotic regression—fact or artifact? *J. abnorm. soc. Psychol.*, 1940, *35*, 273–278.

507. Young, P. C.: Experimental hypnotism: A review. *Psychol. Bull.*, 1941, *38*, 92–104.

508. Zeller, M.: Influence of hypnosis on passive transfer and skin tests. *Ann. Allergy*, 1944, *2*, 515–516.

Appendix

Note 1

In reference to the effects of suggestions on heat regulation (page 132), vasomotor effects (page 134), and temperature perception (page 158), a study reported by Eiff (109) should be mentioned. This investigator has made a rather careful study of this question. He reports having been able to alter the temperature regulation of subjects placed naked in a cold room (0°C and 10°C) by giving them suggestions of warmth. He measured their body and skin temperature, as well as their oxygen consumption, and reports definite differences in the proper directions between these measures obtained with and without suggestions. Unfortunately, probably because of the small number of subjects used (five for each temperature), these differences were not of too high a degree of statistical significance. On the basis of his data, Eiff concludes that one can remove extensively the influence of chemical heat regulation by hypnosis. On the other hand, although physical heat regulation, through vasomotor effects, can also be influenced, its action cannot be removed to the same degree. Finally, oxygen consumption is altered entirely through reflex muscle tonus action. On the basis of the subjective reports of the subjects, there was a definite alteration of their perception of cold.

Note 2

To the discussion of spontaneous waking from hypnosis on page 198 might be added the following report of Dorcus, Brintnall, and Case (99) made in another connection. They tested two groups of subjects as follows. One, consisting of 20 individuals apparently in a deep trance, was asked to lie on cots and to relax. At this time, someone (an assistant) came into the room and told the experimenter in a loud voice and in the presence of the subjects that he was wanted on the phone about an appointment in town. Whereupon the assistant and the experimenter left, the latter stating that he had forgotten about it and that he would be gone for he rest of the day. For the second group of subjects the procedures were the same except that the 25 subjects used were not hypnotized. Both groups were watched unknown to them.

The investigators report that all of the subjects in the experimental group sat up and left the room within 10 to 51 minutes after the experimenter had left the room, this presumably being the duration of the trance before spontaneous waking. The control group showed a similar range of time for spontaneous pseudorecovery. There were, however, some differences between the two groups. Whereas 21 of the 25 control subjects "recovered" in less than 41 minutes and only 2 took 51 minutes or more; only 12 out of 20 experimental subjects recovered in less than 41 minutes, and 7 took 51 minutes or more. The difference of the means appears to have been statistically significant (not reported by the authors).

Obviously, this study does not answer all the questions we might ask in this connection. Certainly the conditions involved here represent only one of the many possible situations; hence the above figures are certainly not representative. In particular, it is entirely possible that the conversation between the experimenter and the assistant, and even their departure, may have acted as bona fide suggestions on the subjects. Also it is possible that subjects in either group may have dozed off, thus invalidating the results. Finally, the number of subjects used is much smaller than desirable. In spite of this, within the limitations of the study, it may be said that the above data tend to show that hypnotized subjects do recover spontaneously from hypnosis, but that the latter state does also have an inhibiting effect of some sort in this respect.

Note 3

It may be of some interest to mention, in regard to the discussion of visual alterations on pages 153–157, some earlier investigations of visual hallucinations performed by Binet and Féré (32) and Bernheim (28).

These investigators report various color disk experiments made with suggested colors. The first two investigators found that the suggested colors obeyed the laws of color mixture. Bernheim, on the other hand, found the contrary to be generally true. Furthermore, he reports that when one half of a disk was suggested to be of one color, and the other half of another color, and the disk oriented in various ways unknown to the subject, the subject located the hallucinated colors on the halves strictly by chance. Bernheim concludes that suggested colors do not act optically like real colors.

Another series of experiments made by Binet and Féré consisted of using lenses, mirrors, and prisms to view the hallucinated objects.

They report that the hallucinated objects behaved like real objects in respect to these instruments. They also found that the reaction time for hallucinated objects is much longer than for real objects. On the other hand, Bernheim, using prisms, found that this was not true in most cases, and that, in the few cases when the subjects reported an alteration of the image, their descriptions show that this effect is imaginary.

Binet and Féré offer no explanation for their results with hallucinated colors. In regard to the effects of optical instruments they consider three possibilities: (a) the effect has been suggested to the subject, the latter being aware of the properties of the optical instruments used; (b) the subject receives cues from real objects within the field of the instruments; (c) the hallucinated object is associated with external and material marks of various sorts (fine structure of ground) that are affected by the optical instruments. This, in turn, affects the hallucinations accordingly. The two investigators believed that their procedures had eliminated the first two alternatives and that the third was probably the correct solution. Bernheim appears to be of essentially the same opinion. I have also reported (464) evidence supporting the third alternative. In general, however, one can assume that all three alternatives account for the character of hallucinations as observed in practice.

Note 4

Since writing the main text, I have come to feel that some of Braid's work bears more than a passing mention as it appears to offer a possible link between "animal hypnosis" and human hypnosis. Also it appears to throw further light upon the latter. I must, however, emphasize that the following considerations are merely tentative ones at present.

Braid eventually came to the conclusion that the essential factor in the production of his form of hypnosis, which we shall call the *Braid effect,* was the concentration of attention (monoideism). Later, particularly under the influence of Bernheim, this was denied, and suggestion was made the main factor in the production of this effect. Bramwell (45) in summing up things in this regard states that (a) fixation of attention usually precedes and facilitates the production of hypnosis, but that (b) attention in hypnosis can easily be made very mobile. There is now little question that, if focusing of attention is a prerequisite for hypnotic phenomena, the existing facts indicate it is only so for the initiation of hypnosis itself. In other respects hypnosis is apparently not a state of concentrated attention. Two basic questions thus arise: (1) Can hypnosis be induced by concentrated attention alone? (2) Is concentrated attention essential for all trance inductions?

Many hypnotists since the time of Bernheim have insisted that concentration of attention alone did not produce hypnosis. As we shall see in a moment, the solution of the argument may revolve about just what we mean by "hypnosis" here. However, examination of Braid's own reports * and those of others as well seems to indicate that concentrated attention alone (as well as suggestions and imagination) can and does bring about the Braid effect. Now, this phenomenon, according to Braid's descriptions, shows an initial phase during which suggestions can be given and are carried out and a later phase during which this is not possible. Braid speaks of it as a state of stupor (or torpor). It appears also from the early reports that, if suggestions of one kind or another are given at the proper time, the Braid effect becomes limited and the phase of torpor is not reached. Whether there is hypersuggestibility is not clear. We will come back to it. These are, I think, very important points for an understanding of the possible place the Braid effect holds in hypnotism. For, as can easily be seen upon examining the modern standard method of trance induction, the procedure very nicely takes these facts into consideration—suggestions are given from the very beginning of fixation of attention so that as soon as the first phase of the Braid effect is reached the latter automatically becomes limited. It is clear that for this very reason the Braid effect would be masked. At the same time the subject's receptiveness to suggestions is made use of as soon as it appears in an automatic manner.

I said previously that this effect may be the one link between "animal hypnosis" and human hypnosis. Volgyesi (452) reports that animals have been "hypnotized" by having them fixate a bright object exactly according to Braid's method. There are no reasons for doubting this. Clearly, however, there is a difference between these cases and cases of human hypnosis as we know them, for no suggestions were used with the animals so that the Braid effect must have gone to completion in these instances. Thus, it still cannot be said that "animal hypnosis" is the same as human hypnosis. Furthermore, there is no evidence for believing that the other methods of "hypnotizing" animals described in the literature lead to the same condition. The fact remains that

---

* J. Braid, *Neurypnology*. London: George Redway, 1899.

until comparable methods are used with animals and humans, it will not be possible to say that "animal hypnosis" and human hypnosis are anything more than related. And even this appears to have some basis only in some instances.

As stated earlier, the evidence from old reports supports the reality of the Braid effect as an independent phenomenon. We have already indicated how it would enter into modern methods of induction. There is no doubt, however, but that a definite study of the question, aimed particularly at ascertaining the reality of the Braid effect, is much needed. However, presuming this reality, two questions are now in order: Is hypersuggestibility associated with the effect, and how does the latter fit into the present theory? To answer the second question first, I think we may say that the Braid effect and the narrowing of consciousness involved in the dissociation of awareness described earlier are very closely related, if not identical. Now, as we saw, individuals who are thus dissociated are particularly receptive to suggestions, although in a different sense from that involved in abstract conditioning or ideomotor action. Nevertheless, to be consistent, we must speak of hypersuggestibility here too.† This kind, I propose to call *dissociative hypersuggestibility.* In contrast, that arising from abstract conditioning can be designated as *conditional hypersuggestibility* (not to be confused with conditional suggestibility), and that arising from ideomotor action may be called *ideomotor hypersuggestibility,* or, as earlier, we may refer to it as primary suggestibility. Thus, we say that modern hypnosis, that is, hypnosis brought about by the standard method, consists of a combination of all three hypersuggestibilities, whereas, Braid's hypnosis was probably primarily dissociative hypersuggestibility; and some forms of "animal hypnosis," although probably capable of exhibiting dissociative hypersuggestibility in early phases, are the last stage of the Braid effect—or what may be referred to as *terminal dissociation.*

As for the peculiar effects, such as contractures, increased pulse and respiration, congestion, and even convulsions, recorded by Braid as characteristically accompanying the induction of hypnosis, it is my belief these may be considered as side effects incidental to the experiments but not essentially characteristic of the Braid effect (except under certain conditions). Braid himself seems to have been of this opinion. In any event there are no difficulties in accounting for these effects and their absence in modern trance induction.

† Since the definition of suggestibility does not distinguish between the origins of the latter.

Author Index

343

Subject Index

Pleasure goals, hypnosis and, 87, 230, 233, 253
see also Needs
Positive hallucinations, definition of, 288
engrams and, 290
imaging and, 290f
mechanism of action of suggested, 292f
nature of, 289ff, 292f
neural equivalence and, 289f
recall and, 290
Positive heteroaction, 43
Positive homoaction, 43
Posthypnotic alterations of functions, *see* Posthypnotic amnesia, Phenomena, *and* Suggested alterations
Posthypnotic amnesia, autosuggestions and, 107
awareness and, 303
cardiac function and, 131
character of, 106f
classification of, 172
compulsive inhibition and, 107, 173, 303
conditioned reflexes and, 174f
criterion of hypnosis and, 106f
definition of, 4, 101
duration of, 107, 175
effect of material to be recalled on, 106f
factors affecting, 106f, 172, 175
for nonverbal material (stylus maze), 173f
for verbal material, 172f
learning and, 172–174
practice effect in, 174
lie detector and, 175
magnitude of, 172f
methods of studying, 172
natural forgetting and, 173
nature of, 303
paramnesias and, 176
reality of, 106f
respiratory changes and, 131
spontaneous, 106f, 120, 172, 175f
variability of amount of, 106f

Posthypnotic phenomena, characteristics of, 101–104
definition of, 4, 101
nature of, 303, 311f
punctuality and, 159
spontaneous, 101f
state of subject exhibiting, 104
suggested, 101
Posthypnotic signal, induction of hypnosis by, 51, 70, 72, 200
latency of response to, 51, 72
Posthypnotic suggestions, awareness of, 102
conditioned reflex and, 174f
definition of, 4, 27, 101
duration of effects of, 102, 175
effectiveness of, intervening hypnotization and, 103
repeated elicitation of response and, 103
mechanism of action of, 303, 311f
persistence of, factors influencing, 103
nature of, 103f
spontaneous trance and, 104ff
Posthypnotic trance (spontaneous), as revivification, 105
character of, 104ff
duration of, 104f
nature of, 105
Postural reflexes in hypnosis, sleep, and waking, 92
Postural sway test of suggestibility, described, 11
hypnotic susceptibility and, 63, 65
nature of response to, 66
primary suggestibility and, 30
Potential performance, 214
Practice effect, posthypnotic amnesia and, 174
suggestibility and, 43, 48ff
Precedence, laws of, 201f, 304
Prediction of hypnotic susceptibility, 65ff, 243, 281
Prepotency of suggestions, imagining and, 201f
Press and release test of suggestibility, 14

Suggested alterations, of functions,
   motor, 120–138, 286–295
   uterine, 130, 136
   vasomotor, 133f, 337
   voluntary, 120–130, 286–295
   see also specific functions and re-
    sponses
  of gastrointestinal activity, 132, 135,
   179
  of gustation, 158
  of heart rate, 124, 131, 174, 178, 182,
   190
  of heat regulation, 132, 134, 337
  of hunger, 132
  of kinesthesia, 158
  of memory, see Memory
  of menstruation, 136
  of metabolism, 124, 132, 178, 337
  of motor control, 128
  of muscular fatigue, 122, 125–128
  of muscular strength, 121ff
  of muscular tonus, 337
  of olfaction, 158, 176
  of oxygen consumption, 124, 132, 337
  of perception, 146–164, 253f
   space, 162
   time, 159–162
  of personality, 180–194, 303–311
  of personality structure, 180, 183,
   185, 306, 309
  of pulse rate, 124, 131, 174, 178, 182,
   190
  of reflexes, brain stem, 137, 155
   conditioned, 130, 147, 174
   psychogalvanic skin, 133f, 149–
    153, 174
   spinal, 137
   vestibular, 137, 158
  of respiration, 124, 131, 174f, 178
  of Rorschach responses, 179f, 183ff,
   187
  of salivation, 136, 158
  of secretions, 135f
  of semen production, 136f
  of sensation, 146–164, 286–295
  of senses, pain, 149–153
   temperature, 158, 337
   touch and pressure, 148ff
  of skin temperature, 134, 337

Suggested alterations, of tissue exchanges, 134ff
  of tissues, 134ff, 139–145, 295–298
  of vision, 153–157, 176, 338–339
  of work capacity, 124f
  organic, 139–145, 295–298
Suggested effects, reality of, see Reality
   and specific effects
Suggested phenomena, 7–11, 16–19,
   117ff, 275–314
  see also Suggested alterations and
   specific phenomena
Suggested sleep, 95, 98, 253
Suggestibility, abnormal personality and,
   32–38, 78
  active, 31, 63f, 72, 81
  addiction and, drug, 88
   heroine, 88
   morphine, 88
   opium, 88
  age and, 76, 282
  alcohol and, 52
  as habituation, 48–50, 249
  attitudes and, 66, 84, 86, 282f, 286
  auditory threshold and, 33
  autokinetic streaming and, 83
  Card 12M of TAT and, 66, 84f
  character of, 32
  classification of, 29–32, 265f
  conditional, 29
  conditioning and, 228f, 234f, 239ff
   abstract, 44, 229, 249ff, 263
  continuum of, 62, 73f, 238, 281
  course of,
   during hypnosis, 46
   during trance induction, 46, 257
   following waking, 46, 241f
  daydream state and, 54
  definition of, 3, 28
  dehypnotization and, 46
  direct, 29
  distribution of, U and J, 24, 30, 260f,
   265
  see also Distribution
  drugs and, 52ff, 88, 97, 284ff
  see also specific drugs
  dynamic factors and, 86
  eroticism and, 87, 284
  expectancy and, 84, 86, 283

Suggestibility, factor analysis and, 30f
  factors affecting, 76–90
    see also Effectiveness of suggestions
    and specific factors
  feeblemindedness, 37, 78
  frustration and, types of reaction to,
    67, 86
  generalization of, 243ff, 249, 256f
  habituation and, 48–50, 249
  heightened, 39–42
    measurement of, 42
    see also Hypersuggestibility
  hyperventilation and, 54
  hypnotic, 45ff, 58–75, 237–259
    effect of waking (pretrance) sug-
      gestions on, 46
  ideomotor action and, 247f, 261, 263
  imagining and, 27, 201, 248
  immediate, 29
  indirect, 29
  individual, 29
  instincts and, 85, 230, 233
  intelligence and, 67, 78–80, 260f
  interpersonal relations and, 87f
  measurement of, 11–15, 42
    see also Hypnotic susceptibility,
    Hypnotizability, Trance Depth
  mediate, 29
  motivation and, 85f, 284
  nature of, 237–259
  needs and, 85, 283f
  negative, 32(fn)
  neuromotor enhancement and, 248
  neuroticism and, 32–35, 38, 280
  nonprestige, 24, 29f
  of adults, 76, 282
  of children, 76, 282
  of college students, 38
  of delinquents, 32
  of hysterics, 36, 38
  of men, 77, 282
  of neurotics, 32–36, 38, 280
  of normal and abnormal individuals,
    32–38
  of psychotics, 36–38, 78, 280
  of women, 77, 282
  passive, 31, 63f, 72, 81
  personal, 29
  personality traits and, 66f, 72, 81

Sugggestibility, pleasure goals and, 87,
    230, 233, 253
  see also Needs
  practice effect and, 43, 48ff
  prestige, 29f, 265
  pretrance period and, 239, 256
  primary, 30f, 260f
  psychiatric diagnosis versus personal-
    ity inventory scores and, 35
  psychosis and, 36ff, 78, 280
  reality of, 28
  relaxation and, 53f, 249
  repetition and, 43, 51, 248
  repression and, 67, 86
  role taking and, 85, 230, 233
  Rorschach responses and, 67, 81–84
  scales of, 10, 58ff
    limitations of, 61
    see also Scales
  secondary, 30f, 260–265
  sex and, 77, 87f, 282f
  smoking and, 88
  specific, 29
  submission-dominance relationship
    and, 87
  suggesting hypersuggestibility, effects
    on, 50f
  suggestions and, length (repetition)
    of, 43, 51, 248
    structure of, 274
  summary of properties of, 238, 260
  tertiary, 30f, 260–265
  tests of, 11–15
    card 12M of TAT as, 66, 84f
    see also Tests *and specific tests*
  theories of hypnosis and, 230, 232
  training (conditioning) of subject
    and, 64, 72, 275
  trance depth and, 133, 142, 148, 152f,
    186, 188f, 202, 219, 281
  transference and, 87f
  triadic hypothesis and, 67, 86f
  unconscious factors and, 86
  unitary aspect of, 29f
  universality of, 32–38, 280
  vividness of imagery and, 248
  waking, 28–44, 50ff, 76–90
    see also Waking suggestions

4359

14527